Geomarketing

Geomarketing

Methods and Strategies in Spatial Marketing

Edited by
Gérard Cliquet

First published in France in 2002 by Hermes Science/Lavoisier entitled “Le géomarketing : méthodes et stratégies du marketing spatial”
First published in Great Britain and the United States in 2006 by ISTE Ltd
Translated by Eugene Hughes

ISTE Ltd
6 Fitzroy Square
London W1T 5DX
UK

ISTE USA
4308 Patrice Road
Newport Beach, CA 92663
USA

www.iste.co.uk

Library of Congress Cataloging-in-Publication Data

Cliquet, Gérard.
[Géomarketing. English]
Geomarketing : methods and strategies in special marketing / Gerard Cliquet.-- 1st ed.
p. cm.
ISBN-13: 978-1-905209-07-1
1. Target marketing. 2. Consumer behavior. I. Title.
HF5415.127.C5513 2006
658.8'04--dc22

005035291

British Library Cataloguing-in-Publication Data
A CIP record for this book is available from the British Library
ISBN 10: 1-905209-07-X
ISBN 13: 978-1-905209-07-1

Table of Contents

Chapter 1

Spatial Marketing

Introduction

According to many philosophers [BEN 01] following Foucault [FOU 94], space characterizes our era. This would seem quite paradoxical when compared to Moscovici's [MOS 83, p. 262] remark which asserts, throughout the 20th century, nothing less than "the disappearance of geography", a logical continuation from the author of the "temporalization of space." Yet, if this temporalization of space can lead to inevitable selections, not to say exclusions, the "spatialization of time", on the other hand, opens up more generous perspectives [BEN 01] and leads to a different philosophical understanding of history.

What is good for history is also good for other social science disciplines. Marketing, in its allacticological[1] understanding [CLI 99] or its dimension of exchange, commercial or not, is not an exception. The importance of the dimension of space increases inversely with market expansion. It should be noted in passing that considering the arrival of the internet as a new form of the disappearance of the geography of markets would no doubt be committing a serious error. Consumers remain very precisely localized in geographic space, which explains that the difficulties met by certain internet distribution companies in delivering to their clients [CLI 01], and the companies themselves, although present on the web, still originate from very precise geographic zones from which they cannot easily escape [VOL 00].

---

1. Adjective taken from the Greek word *αλλακτικωσ*, which signifies things concerning exchange.

Chapter written by Gérard CLIQUET.

We have denounced the lack of interest amongst researchers in spatial analysis in marketing [GRE 83]. Marketing researchers have instead turned more towards behavioral science. However, spatial aspects have returned to the forefront with the enlargement of the horizon of firms, particularly in the retailing industry, on the one hand and with the development of geomarketing techniques on the other. The geography of markets constitutes an ensemble of important elements in the realm of marketing for at least four reasons [JON 99]:

– demand varies according to available space and can be measured just as easily in terms of revenue, number of households, budgetary structures of spending, and lifestyles;

– supply also varies according to available space in that prices, services, the products and available stores vary with location;

– supply and demand are generally separate, which justifies the role of the retailer, whose job is to overcome this separation by studying the spatial behavior of both consumers and shopping centers, as well as the logistic chain of supplies at regional, national and international levels;

– the majority of economic activities use space and space has a cost. In order to control it better, this space must be decomposed into units of analysis: this division can rest just as easily on politico-administrative considerations as on census units or even zip/postal codes.

The title of this book makes reference, as indicated by the overall theme of the area of study to which it belongs (*Information Géographique et Aménagement du Territoire*[2]), to geographic information. Defining geographic information is not so simple when it deals with "a very widespread type of information" or in other words, "objects or physical phenomena, or living beings or societies, from the moment that they are linked to a territory" [DEN 96]. Yet if geographic information is at the heart of the approach followed in this book, it will not be possible to ignore the other real and potential benefits of geography to marketing, from both the conceptual and methodological points of view.

The introduction of geography into marketing cannot be limited to a simple division of space and to the utilization of geographic software destined to process large quantities of localized data. There have been publications since the 1970s that have shown the importance of mapping in marketing decisions [BEL 78]. It is true that these studies have considerably improved our knowledge of market spheres, but they do not constitute in any way a foundation for marketing strategy. That is why this book, after describing what is happening in marketing thanks to the introduction of geographic information, will set out to open up the research perspectives, not as far as geomarketing is concerned, which represents above all a collection of

2. Geographical Information and Territory Planning.

techniques, but with the admittedly ambitious objective of developing true spatial marketing.

We will therefore begin by examining the links between marketing and geography by showing, on the one hand, the importance of space in decisions made by companies today and, on the other hand, that beyond geomarketing, it is actually a true spatial marketing that organizations need. We will then tackle the applications of geography, starting with the most classic, retail location, followed by the current and future utilization possibilities at the very heart of the other elements of the marketing mix.

1.1. Marketing and geography

Some authors define geomarketing as a "*specific application of the spatial economy*" [LAT 01, p. 37]. This affirmation, coming from a consultant, is close to the wish expressed by Grether [GRE 83]. The fact remains that studies in geomarketing confine themselves to the description of coding techniques and geographical division, together with some associated statistical functions. If the applications are mentioned, they are generally not well developed, except in rare cases [BEN 98]. However, the spatial aspects and the geographic information that characterizes them make it possible to go further than these technical aspects and provide elements indispensable to the definition of strategies, both in retail companies and in industrial and service companies. This leads towards true spatial marketing. Before getting to the details of this domain, however, both the restraints and the stakes of its implementation should be mentioned.

1.1.1. *Space and decisions in organizations*

Space is a theme that is rarely dealt with in research in management sciences, except for the work on retail location (with industrial location often being left to economists and operations researchers) and on international management and marketing, which is more commonly qualified today as intercultural. The dissociation sometimes made between "the work space" of the firm and "the international space" [JOF 85] no longer has much weight and often the two merge, regardless of the size of the company. It is precisely because of this confusion that the spatial aspects of organizational decisions currently take on a vital significance.

Here we will refer only to decisions concerning the marketing of organizations, and more specifically to the marketing of companies. An admittedly traditional distinction must be made here between industrial companies and retail and service companies. This distinction loses its pertinence concerning certain aspects when large distributors are pushed towards investing in increasingly more sophisticated equipment and when industrial companies are obliged to propose increasingly numerous services to their clients. The distinction justifies itself, however, when limited to marketing decisions. In fact, for the industrial company, generally, the choice of a location for an establishment is more a decision concerned with the restrictions of production than one concerned with market restrictions: relocations to certain countries because lower salaries can be paid there should be classified in this category. On the other hand, outlet location decisions for a retail company are about marketing. The reason for this is simple: the retail outlet is the product of the retail company [DIC 92]. Another reason must also be brought to the fore: the networking of retail and service activities. Today, this phenomenon is taking on major importance [BRA 98]. It began during the middle of the 19th century (in about 1860) in France with Félix Potin [CAM 97], followed by the development of department stores, discount stores in the USA with Woolworths and then self-service supermarkets with Piggly Wiggly, again in the USA, at the beginning of the 20th century [CLI 92]. However, it is the second half of the 20th century that has been marked by the boom of store chain networks and this has happened in every sector of the retail and service industries.

Territorial conquest has become the primary issue for all companies and especially retail companies. Territorial coverage, both from region to region and on an international level, is at least as important as sales in determining the strength of a store chain network. Of course, the American company Wal-Mart is the world's largest retailer in terms of turnover, far outdistancing the French Carrefour. Yet with over 3,000 stores and its presence in less than a dozen countries, Wal-Mart does not equal Carrefour in coverage, whose 9,600 retail outlets are scattered over 27 different countries. Less than 5% of Wal-Mart's sales came from outside the USA in 1997, compared to Carrefour which, after the merger with Promodès, saw its international sales above 20% [LHE 01], even though Wal-Mart plans to open 500 new stores in the coming years. Internal development has become too slow a process for success to be achieved in such a quest. Acquisitions aimed at expanding territorial coverage are ever-increasing, whether to improve a company's presence or in order to decrease costs. This is exactly how groups like Carrefour, again after its merger with Promodès, continue to grow. Alliances amongst airline companies, such as Skyteam, which includes Air France, Delta Airlines, Korean Air, AeroMexico, Czech Airlines, and most recently Alitalia, also reflect this idea. This presence, with a worldwide aim, is evident in industry with agreements between European, American and Japanese car manufacturers in order to obtain a foothold in all markets. By covering the world with its products or its stores, a company guarantees itself purchasing power, protection against local recessions, access to the international media and a better logistical efficiency.

This conquest of space is not only planet-wide. It also occurs at the national and local levels. This is not about leaving "holes" in the mesh of territories: sometimes it is better to be completely absent rather than to be present in an insufficient manner. The notion of critical size must not be considered in a global manner, but by family of products by family of products, store type by store type, territory by territory [FIL

98]. At the national level, insufficient coverage can lead to great difficulties in terms of access to the national media, this time for reasons of decline in audience and in terms of logistical costs [CLI 98a]. The Auchan store chain was thus very poorly established until 1996 before the buy-back of the Docks de France group and its Mammouth hypermarkets, this despite having a respectable number of stores. The Raffarin law forced the Auchan group to react very quickly by taking over another network [CLI 00], in order to cover French territory better and thus to gain access to television by sponsoring broadcasts in non-commercial spots since French law prohibits large distributors from advertising on television in order to protect the PQR (*presse quotidienne régionale*[3]). The problem is different in terms of logistics. A spatial incoherence with "holes in the coverage" is to be avoided, because this would involve higher transport costs and frequent stock shortages [RUL 00]. Finally, it cannot be forgotten that proper territorial coverage for the distributor ensures the manufacturer a good distribution of products under the same trade-name: this is unquestionably an element of the distributor's service.

At a strictly local level, or at the store outlet level, the preoccupations of the distributors and the producers come together: coordinating prices (or not) throughout the products/stores, proper targeting of clientele in terms of communication, proposing a supply adapted to the local geography of the consumers. This will be seen in the last part of this book.

1.1.2. *From geomarketing to spatial marketing*

When faced with the strategic and operational considerations mentioned in the preceding section, what can geomarketing do? Defined as a collection of techniques enabling the manipulation of geo-coded data, it can help in analysis more than in the conception of strategies and even less in decision-making. In order to do this, the contribution of geographic information has to be pushed to the fore in the different domains of marketing that are likely to be affected by this type of localized data. Furthermore, beyond geographic information, it is the geographers' methods of understanding space that interest the marketer. The approach of this book will therefore be directed more towards the way or ways in which to integrate geography, with its information, its concepts and its methods, into the traditions of marketing research as well as in its strategic and operational aspects, rather than simply towards geographic information. This is an ambitious objective, which will certainly not be met in all its dimensions. We will therefore be concentrating more on following trails than giving lessons in a domain that is yet to be fully developed.

The introduction of space into marketing decisions concerns at least three large domains of marketing:

---

3. Daily regional press.

– consumer behavior,

– retail location,

– marketing management.

These three important domains structure this book, which is composed of three parts:

Part I: *Consumer Behavior and Geographic Information*

Part II: *Retail Location and Geographic Information*

Part III: *Marketing Management and Geographic Information*

The consumer behavior mentioned here deals more precisely with spatial behavior and will be the subject of Chapter 2. The consumer behavior domain is especially highly regarded amongst marketing researchers and, without great fear of error, one can say that close to 50% of all marketing research deals with this domain: the percentage was 25% in the *Recherche et Applications en Marketing*[4] (RAM) review before 1992 [DUB 92] and made up 41% of PhD dissertations in France [LAU 92]. This phenomenon also exists in the USA, which is the leading nation in the amount of marketing research carried out, a trend that shows no signs of abating. On the other hand, it is surprising to learn that, among the numerous research studies on consumer behavior, only a small number, to say the least, deal with spatial behavior and particularly spatial behavior in France. Bringing together marketing and geography should truly put spatial behavior on the agenda of the laboratories affected! What is known of this domain essentially comes from geography [GOL 97] and from economics [EYM 95].

Marketing researchers have only been interested in work modeling the spatial behavior of the consumer [ACH 82, CLI 95, HUF 64, NAK 74, REI 31]. The development of gravitational and spatial interaction models, along with models in the realm of geography proper, have resulted in numerous publications in the USA, although very few in France and even this source seems to have dried up. In Chapter 2, we will attempt to present an explanation in terms of consumer spatial behavior. In fact, the ever-increasing mobility of consumers [DES 01] throws doubt on the polar character of the commercial attraction of certain retail outlets. Spatial modeling founded on the geo-coding of places of residence is therefore no longer as pertinent.

The study of the values and lifestyles of consumers is another aspect of consumer behavior research that has taken on considerable importance since the 1980s. Numerous specialized companies have embarked upon such studies, both in the USA and in Europe. In France, the CCA (*Centre de Communication Avancé du*

4. Research and Applications in Marketing.

groupe Havas[5]), the Confremca and Risc are the most well-known. The enlargement of the markets and especially the opening up of the EU with its common currency will bring particular importance to geographic information as it relates to consumer values. Chapter 3 shows the importance of this information and how it must be measured. The Rokeach [ROK 79] and Kahle [KAH 86] scales are presented. The author also mentions how to process geographical information according to consumer values in intercultural marketing problems. The concepts of values, styles and culture are compared, as well as the quantitative and qualitative methods associated with them, such as means–ends chains [AUR 92] and the APT (association pattern technique) [HOF 99]. These elements have arrived just in time to allow the present author to show that spatial marketing is not solely limited to computerized bases as data sources, while field studies have not yet been buried like prehistoric objects. If geomarketing normally nourishes itself with databases, spatial marketing should attempt to make the behavior results of these databases and the attitudinal results of surveys coincide.

Chapter 4 reveals the importance of geomarketing in the study of consumer behavior and in particular the importance of the analysis of the flow of clientele, thus showing that this collection of techniques is not simply static and that some information on the flows can be extracted from the databases. A concrete example is developed and allows the development of the connection between consumer spatial behavior analysis in its dynamic dimension and location problems. This chapter provides a perfect transition between Part I, on consumer behavior, and Part II, on retail outlet location applications [DOU 02]. In summary, this first part devoted to consumer behavior and geographic information is composed of three chapters: Chapter 2 *Consumer Spatial Behavior*, Chapter 3 *Consumer Values, Lifestyles and Geographic Information* and Chapter 4 *Geomarketing and Consumer Behavior*.

1.2. Spatial marketing applications

New consumer behavior, particularly greater consumer mobility, coupled with the successive openings of borders, leading to what some call globalization, has required organizations and especially companies to better integrate geographic information in order to situate the consumer properly in his or her dimensions, both topographical and cultural. Two principal applications can immediately be recognized. One deals more with retail companies and has been a subject of research for more than 60 years: retail location. The other concerns marketing management or, in other words, the fundamental elements of the marketing mix (product, price, place and promotion), but excluding place, which we will discuss under the heading "retail location".

5. The Havas Group Advanced Center of Communication.

1.2.1. *Retail location*

Retail location, which will serve as the central theme for the second part of this book, constitutes an extremely old category of marketing decisions. It is part of the very general approach to location of economic activities, as Von Thünen [THÜ 95] had already tried to describe it. When seen from the commercial business angle, it assumes very precise characteristics. If great economists [EAT 82, HOT 29] have looked into this question in order to understand where retail locations should be placed and why, others have often regretted the negligence suffered by the spatial variable in economic theories simply because the distance variable is not taken into account [ISA 52], because there is a lack of economic explanation of the presence of economic activities in centers [TIN 64], or because of the aspatial aspect of the neoclassical model [EAT 78]. A large number of publications have since appeared to fill this gap. Marketing researchers, better known for empirical considerations, have hardly been more attentive and it is often geographers dabbling in marketing who have attempted to develop methods for facilitating retail outlet establishment. Part II of this book will develop all of the spatial aspects linked to store chain location on the one hand and the management of store chain networks on the other. The title of this second Part is *Retail Location and Geographic Information* and includes four chapters: Chapter 5 *Geographic information in retail location studies: a managerial perspective*, Chapter 6 *Retail Location Models*, Chapter 7 *GIS and Retail Location Models* and Chapter 8 *Spatial Strategies in Retail and Service Activities*.

This decision is crucial in retail. The Americans have a retailing adage that shows just how much the success of a business depends on its geographic location. As Jones [JON 90] reiterates, three essential points govern the success of a point of sale, whether a store or a hotel: "Location, location and location." Retail location is a domain where geographic information has penetrated for quite some time, and whose specialists have often been geographers by trade, whether it be Reilly and his law of retail gravitation [REI 31], Huff and his probabilistic gravitation model [HUF 64], or even Applebaum and his concentric circles separating shopping center trade areas into primary, secondary, tertiary or marginal zones [APP 66].

Location studies are often completed without the necessary precautions and are often too succinct to produce analyzed data that is useful in decision-making. Too many conflicts still exist between retailers, whether between the franchiser and his franchisees, between a retailer's association and its members, or even between cooperative and cooperative member. Despite ever more sophisticated models being created for decades, intuition continues to play, as in any decision, a very important role. Attempts have been made to take intuition into account and Chapter 5, which deals with location studies, presents a method that associates intuitive aspects with the implementation of a methodological approach founded on cognitive maps [CLA 01].

Chapter 6 develops location models, most of which are mentioned above. Starting from gravitational and determinist, these models have become probabilistic, and then gradually left the orbit of gravitation to come closer to spatial interaction [CLI 88]. But the absence of real studies dealing with passing attraction (see Chapters 2 and 7), which respond more to the increase in consumer mobility, hinders the improvement of this type of approach, which has however seen great success in the USA and has now begun to entice many European distribution companies, especially thanks to the cartographic benefits of geomarketing software and geographic information systems (GIS).

A GIS can be defined in two ways [DEN 96]. In 1998, the Federal Inter-agency Committee for Coordination of Digital Cartography, or FICCDC, stated that a GIS is a "*computer system of materials, software and processes conceived to allow the collection, management, manipulation, analysis, modeling and display of spatial data in order to resolve complex management and development problems.*" In France, the National Geographic Information Council (CNIG[6]) proposed the following definition: "*Collection of data located in space, structured in a way that is able to conveniently extract syntheses useful in decision making*" [DID 90]. It is not surprising that the French definition is more general, both in the form of the GIS and in its aims, while the American definition insists more on the computer aspects and the different operations that a GIS should be capable of accomplishing. It can be added that the American definition is more precise concerning the objectives and allows a better comprehension of the advantage of a connection between geographers and marketers, at both research and applications levels, in the sense that territorial planning and development relate back more to geographers' dilemmas, with management referring back to the works of marketers. A large part of Chapter 7 deals with an application realized in the UK concerning the automobile market and shows how to use a GIS in researching a marketing network. The authors are researchers and practitioners. Certain researchers, including one of the above authors, have learned to be wary of the limits of GIS, particularly in retail location operations [BEN 97]. The integration of spatial interaction models provides, in his opinion, a quality superior to the results of traditional GIS.

The reticulation of the retail trade is an essential phenomenon of the economy of the end of the 20th century. Chapter 8 discusses the different spatial strategies of retail outlet establishments [CLI 02] on the one hand, and a method for measuring territorial coverage [CLI 98a], based on the notion of relative entropy already used in geography to measure the phenomenon of rural depopulation, on the other. During an acquisition, one can thus evaluate the gain in spatial value brought by the buyout of a certain store chain network compared to others [CLI 98b].

Thus, Part II of this book essentially deals with place problems and more specifically with retailing, one of the four elements of the marketing mix along with

---

6. *Conseil national de l'information géographique.*

product, price and communication, also known as the 4 Ps (Product, Price, Place, Promotion) [BOR 64, MCC 60]. The other three elements of the marketing mix are tackled in Part III and will be described in the following section.

1.2.2. *Marketing management*

A very widespread idea is that geographic information only provides benefits in market studies and, as has just been seen, in retail outlet location studies. Thus, the Chamber of Commerce and Industry of Nice (France) uses computerized cartography to evaluate in real time shopping centers, trade areas and sales of businesses located by GPS (Global Positioning System) [DUR 01]. Marketing, in its managerial aspects, can therefore also wittingly utilize geographic information. This will be the object of Part III of this book entitled *Marketing Management and Geographic Information.* Four chapters make up this section: Chapter 9 *Price and Geographic Information*, Chapter 10 *Advertising Policy and Geographic Information*, Chapter 11 *Direct Marketing and Geographic Information* and Chapter 12 *Products and Geographic Information: Geo-Merchandizing.*

With marketing management, we are right in the middle of the marketing action: setting prices, communicating with customers, choosing products adapted to them. Three of the principal elements of what can be called the marketing mix are thus found here [KOT 00]. The following paragraphs succinctly present what will be further developed concerning price, communication and products, from the knowledge and applications in the chapters of Part III. It is very evident that the key point of rapid and intelligent utilization of geographic data in terms of marketing management thus becomes the database, where all the elements likely to help the decision-maker in his understanding of the localized markets that he confronts are assembled [BER 96]. The utilization of GIS software is, of course, essential, but the quality of the results will depend most of all on the geographic data that feeds them.

Chapter 9 develops the relationship between price and geographic information. This connection does not seem natural *a priori*. However, it exists even if the works in this domain remain restricted to the international level. It must also be admitted that price is far from being the major preoccupation of marketing researchers, despite very interesting and different studies on their conception of the traditional approach of economists [DES 97]. The authors of this chapter describe the geography of costs, from demand to competition, before tackling geographic price policy in international trade. The problems of transfer pricing and gray markets are discussed in depth. Let us imagine a company that manufactures products in both France and Germany. In Germany, a powerful competitor is the national market leader, while in France our company is the sales leader. The price strategies are normally different in the two countries, with prices being higher in France than in Germany. What do the French distributors do? They will get their supplies in

Germany, causing problems for the group's French factories. This is exactly the misfortune experienced by the multinational company 3M at the beginning of the 1990s, and to this type of misadventure the name gray or parallel markets is given. What will become of these dilemmas following the opening of borders and the globalization of the marketing of companies? This is a fundamental question for the economic world. In fact, price is the only variable of the marketing mix that brings in money, with all of the others bringing a cost, which is at times rather high.

Chapters 10 and 11 deal with communication, with Chapter 10 taking a closer look at advertising while Chapter 11 concentrates on direct marketing and special offers. Once again, it may seem strange to link advertising policies to geography. However, this connection is fundamental as media are increasingly destined to reach a target audience in specific regions. Whether through outdoor advertising, the cinema or the press, specialized companies and agencies have developed very sophisticated geomarketing systems that marketing researchers seem to have failed to integrate, or have simply ignored. Published work in this domain is extremely rare [BEN 98]. This is why the author of this chapter has opted for a very interesting description of the geomarketing practices associated with advertising practices. That this work could serve as a starting point for other research in this field would be a heartening perspective. Both radio and television are discussed but more as part of a vision of development potential. In its corner, direct marketing is perfectly tailored for geomarketing and its techniques [DES 01]. Once the analysis is accomplished, one of the essential dilemmas resides in the choice of direct marketing techniques adapted to the territories studied. Moreover, an important question arises in the analysis of these territories, which geomarketing is capable of answering: in how sophisticated a way can the analysis of territories be carried out? Legal considerations, linked to the French Act *Computer uses and individual freedom* of January 6, 1978, are not necessarily absent from this debate.

Geo-merchandizing is a very practical neologism for distinguishing the clear, but difficult to realize, link outside of databases currently available, between the product line of an industrial or retail company and customers, whether local or just passing through, of a point of sale. In fact, studies in this field remain inadequate, despite their rapid development. The stakes are extremely high [GRE 99]. Driven by the near oligopoly of today's markets, large retail and distribution companies are orienting themselves more and more towards differentiation strategies. Yet, this differentiation is communicated only if it is felt by the consumer in what is offered in the aisles of a store. This is exactly the dilemma of attracting the consumer by an assortment of items adapted to the needs of either the local or the passing clientele. On the basis of this statement, the range on which evaluation is based is the entire sales space of the store involved and negotiations between manufacturers and retailers change what is thought to be important. Online internet business must not be forgotten either, because the merchandizing of products presented in electronic catalogues is a primary element in the attraction of internet users [VOL 00]. The premises of geo-merchandizing are thus described in Chapter 12 and open up towards perspectives involving consumer behavior, strategic marketing and marketing management, which mean that this final chapter can definitely be described as last but not least.

1.3. Conclusion

This chapter has shown, on the one hand, the importance of space in marketing decisions and, on the other hand, the stakes of geomarketing and, beyond that, the contribution that marketing can expect from geography, as long as it does not wait too long.

Geographic data, as well as a certain number of concepts and methods used in geography for years would, and already do, allow the resolution of problems posed by the increasing spatial dispersion of markets from companies and even amongst the companies themselves.

Of course, the most common of geographical techniques remains connected to retail location decisions and marketing researchers have significantly contributed to the advance of knowledge in this domain. However, there has been a definite delay in the implementation of these techniques, especially in continental Europe, and especially in the business world. Nevertheless, the contributions of geomarketing techniques and the software devoted to them have at least made decision-makers cognizant of the vast realm of possibilities at their disposal.

Other applications are, however, already underway with some, including advertising and direct marketing applications, being the product of companies themselves. Price remains a delicate subject and its spatializing will probably have to wait, except on the international level where the opening of borders is more likely to smooth tariff policies. Finally, one can sense the dawning of a geo-merchandizing that is likely to revolutionize both the range and nature of the negotiations between manufacturer and retailer. The reader may be surprised at not finding a chapter on using geomarketing in managing the sales force. A certain number of companies have launched themselves into this adventure, as reported in certain professional reviews [PAC 97], but researchers have carried out few observations of this development, making it a rather rich field for research and applications.

1.4. References

[ACH 82], Achabal D., Gorr W. L., Mahajan Vijay , MULTILOC: A Multiple Store Location Decision Model, *Journal of Retailing*, 58, 5-25, 1982.

[APP 66], Applebaum W., Methods for Determining Store Trade Areas, Market Penetration and Potential Sales, *Journal of Marketing Research*, 3, 2, 127-41, 1966.

[AUR 92], Aurifeille J.M., Valette-Florence P., A 'chain-constrained' clustering approach in means-end analysis: an empirical illustration, Marketing for Europe-Marketing for the Future, *Proceedings of the EMAC Annual Conference*, Aarhus, 49-64, 1992.

[BEL 78], Bell R. R., Zabriskie N. B., Assisting Marketing Decisions by Computer Mapping: A Branch Banking Application, *Journal of Marketing Research*, 15, 1, 122-28, 1978.

[BEN 01], Benoist J., Merlini F., *Historicité et spatialité: Le problème de l'espace dans la pensée contemporaine*, Librairie Philosophique J. Vrin, Paris, 2001.

[BEN 97], Benoit, D., Clarke G. P., Assessing GIS for Retail Location Planning, *Journal of Retail and Consumer Services,* 4(4), 239-258, 1997.

[BEN 98], Benoit J.-M., Benoit P., Pucci D., *La France redécoupée: enquête sur la quadrature de l'hexagone*, Belin, Paris, 1998.

[BER 96], Bernard C., La géographie du lieu de vente, *Points de Vente*, 626, 20-21, 1996.

[BOR 64], Borden N. H., The Concept of Marketing Mix, *Journal of Advertising Research*, 4, 2, 2-7, 1964.

[BRA 98], Bradach J. L., *Franchise Organizations*, Harvard Business School Press, Boston, Mass., 1998.

[CAM 97], Camborde P., L'installation de Félix Potin à Paris, in *La révolution commerciale en France: du Bon Marché à l'hypermarché*, J. Marseille ed., Mémoire d'entreprises, Le Monde ed., Paris, 1997.

[CLA 01], Clarke I. and Mackaness W., Management Intuition: An Interpretative Account of Structure and Content of Decision Schemas Using Cognitive Maps. *Journal of Management Studies,* 38(2), 147-72, 2001.

[CLI 88], Cliquet G., Les modèles gravitaires et leur évolution, *Recherche et Applications en Marketing*, 3, 3, 39-52, 1988.

[CLI 92], Cliquet G., *Management stratégique des points de vente*, Sirey, Paris, 1992.

[CLI 95], Cliquet G., Implementing a Subjective MCI Model: An Application to the Furniture Market, *European Journal of Operational Research*, 84, 279-91, 1995.

[CLI 98a], Cliquet G., Integration and Territory Coverage of the Hypermarket Industry in France: A Relative Entropy Measure, *International Review of Retail, Distribution and Consumer Research*, 8, 2, 205-224, 1998.

[CLI 98b], Cliquet G., Valeur spatiale des réseaux et stratégies d'acquisition des firmes de distribution, in *Valeur, marché et organisation*, *Actes des XIVèmes Journées Nationales des IAE*, volume 1, Nantes, J.-P. Brechet ed., Presses Académiques de l'Ouest, 1998.

[CLI 99], Cliquet G., Grégory P., Marketing, in *Encyclopédie de la gestion et du management*, R. Le Duff ed., Dalloz, Paris, 1999.

[CLI 00], Cliquet G., Des Garets V., Réglementation des implantations commerciales et stratégies des distributeurs, *15èmes Journées des IAE*, Biarritz, 6-8 September, 2000.

[CLI 01], Cliquet G., Rôle des NTIC dans l'évolution des canaux de distribution, *Proche Orient, Etudes en Management*, 13, 71-93, 2001.

[CLI 02], Cliquet G., Fady A., Basset G., *Le management de la distribution*, Dunod, Paris, 2002.

[DEN 96], Denègre J., Salgé F., *Les systèmes d'information géographique, Coll. Que-sais-je?* no. 3122, PUF, Paris, 1996.

[DES 01], Desse R.-P., *Le nouveau commerce urbain – dynamiques spatiales et stratégies des acteurs*, Presses Universitaires de Rennes, 2001.

[DES 97], Desmet P., Zollinger M., *Le prix: de l'analyse conceptuelle aux méthodes de fixation*, Economica, Paris, 1997.

[DIC 92], Dicke T. S., *Franchising in America: The Development of a Business Method 1840-1980*, The University of North Carolina Press, Chapel Hill, 1992.

[DID 90], Didier M., *Utilité et valeur de l'information géographique*, Economica, Paris, 1990.

[DOU 02], Douard J.P., Géomarketing et localisation des entreprises commerciales, in *Stratégies de localisation des entreprises commerciale et industrielles: de nouvelles perspectives*, G. Cliquet and J.-M. Josselin eds, De Boeck Université, Bruxelles, 2002.

[DUB 92], Dubois P.-L., Garmon R.-Y., Derbaix C., La recherche en marketing dans les communautés francophones, *Recherche et Applications en Marketing*, 7, 1, 19-42, 1992.

[DUR 01], Durnerin J., Géomarketing: localiser les commerces au GPS, *Points de Vente*, 835, 80-81, 2001.

[EAT 78], Eaton B. C., Lipsey R. G., Freedom of Entry and the Existence of Pure Profit, *The Economic Journal*, 88, 455-469, 1978.

[EAT 82], Eaton B. C., Lipsey R. G., An Economic Theory of Central Places, *The Economic Journal*, 92, 56-72, 1982.

[EYM 95], Eymann A., *Consumers' spatial choice behavior*, Physica-verlag, Berlin, 1995.

[FIL 98], Filser M., Taille critique et stratégie du distributeur: analyse théorique et implications managériales, *Décisions Marketing*, 15, 7-16, 1998.

[FOU 94], Foucault M., Des espaces autres, repris in *Dits et écrits*, Defert D. and Ewald F. eds, Gallimard, Vol. IV, 752-762, 1994.

[GOL 97], Golledge R. G., Stimson R. J., *Spatial behavior: a geographic perspective*, The Guilford Press, NY, 1997.

[GRE 83], Grether E. T., Regional-Spatial Analysis in Marketing, *Journal of Marketing*, 47, 4, 36-43, 1983.

[GRE 99], Grewal D., Levy M., Mehrotra A., Sharma A., Planning Merchandizing Decisions to Account for Regional and Product Assortment Differences, *Journal of Retailing*, 75, 3, 405-424, 1999.

[HOF 99], Ter Hofstede F., Steenkamp J.-B., Wedel M., International market segmentation based on consumer-product relations, *Journal of Marketing Research*, 36, 1-17, 1999.

[HOT 29], Hotelling H., Stability in Competition, *The Economic Journal*, 39, 41-57, 1929.

[HUF 64], Huff D.L., Defining and Estimating a Trade Area, *Journal of Marketing*, 28, 34-38, 1964.

[ISA 52], Isard W., A General Location Principle of an Optimum Space-Economy, *Econometrica*, July, 406-30, 1952.

[JOF 85], Joffre P., Koenig G., *Stratégie d'entreprise: anti-manuel*, Economica, Paris, 1985.

[JON 90], Jones K. Simmons J., *The retail environment*, London: Routledge, 1990.

[JON 99], Jones K., Pearce M., The Geography of Markets: Spatial Analysis for Retailers, *Ivey Business Journal*, 63, 3, 66-70, 1999.

[KAH 86], Kahle L., The Nine Nations of North America and the Value basis of Geographic Segmentation, *Journal of Marketing*, 50, 37-47, 1986.

[KOT 00], Kotler P., Dubois B., *Marketing management*, Publi-Union, Paris, 2000.

[LAT 01], Latour P., Le Floc'h J., *Géomarketing: principes, méthodes et applications*, Editions d'Organisation, Paris, 2001.

[LAU 92], Laurent G., Grégory P., Les thèses de marketing depuis 1986, *Recherche et Applications en Marketing*, 7, 1, 43-63, 1992.

[LHE 01], Lhermie C., *Carrefour ou l'invention de l'hypermarché*, Vuibert, Paris, 2001.

[McC 60], McCarthy J., *Basic marketing: a managerial approach*, Richard D. Irwin, Homewood, Ill., 1960.

[MOS 83], Moscovici S., L'espace, le temps et le social, in *L'espace et le temps aujourd'hui*, Du Seuil ed., coll. Points, Inédits Sciences, 261-72, 1983.

[NAK 74], Nakanishi M., Cooper L. G., Parameter Estimate for Multiplicative Interactive Choice Model: Least Squares Approach, *Journal of Marketing Research*, 11, 303-311, 1974.

[PAC 97], Pack T., Mapping a Path to Success, *Database*, 20, 4, 31-35.

[REI 31], Reilly W., *The Law of Retail Gravitation*, W. J. Reilly ed., 285 Madison Ave., NY, 1931.

[RUL 00], Rulence D., Les stratégies spatiales des firmes de distribution: mesures et comparaisons, in *Etudes et recherches sur la distribution*, P. Volle éd., Vuibert, Paris.

[ROK 79], Rokeach M., *Understanding human values*, Free Press, NY, 1979.

[THÜ 95], Thünen (von) J. H., *Der isolierte Staat in Beziehung auf Landwirtschaft und Nationalökonomie*, Berlin, Hempel and Parey, 1895.

[TIN 64], Tinbergen J., Sur un modèle de la dispersion géographique de l'activité économique, *Revue d'économie politique*, 30-44, 1964.

[VOL 00], Volle P., Du marketing des points de vente à celui des sites marchands: spécificités, opportunités et questions de recherche, *Revue Française du Marketing*, 177-178, 83-101, 2000.

PART I

Consumer Behavior and Geographic Information

Chapter 2

Consumer Spatial Behavior

Introduction

The usage of geomarketing software tends to simplify or even mask the complexity of consumer behavior. The availability of databases, which are often succinct, only containing socio-demographic data and addresses, does not suffice in understanding this complexity. It therefore seems necessary to develop a true approach to spatial marketing in order to improve decision-making, whether in retail location (see Part II of this book) or in the management of the marketing mix elements: price, advertising, direct marketing, merchandizing (see Part III).

A spatial marketing approach must begin with the understanding of the spatial behavior of consumers. Several approaches have been proposed to comprehending the movements of individuals linked to the process of store choice. Economic approaches are based on the neoclassical model and consumer theory, mainly applied to tourist trips [EYM 95, EYM 97]. In marketing, the approaches are much more varied and can just as easily be founded upon the work of geographers, who have been abundantly inspired by analogies with physics (gravitational models, entropy models), as upon observations and considerations of a psycho-sociological nature, without forgetting the economic approach of utility maximization. For example, *a priori* simple (not to say simplistic) marketing approaches have aimed at dividing the marketing territory of a point of sale (its trade area) into primary, secondary and service or marginal zones [APP 66], with an attempt at modeling [MAI 67], or segmenting it in terms of time of access [BRU 68]. These methods are

---

Chapter written by Delphine DION and Gérard CLIQUET.

still current in the work of many professionals and particularly in numerous marketing studies produced prior to the establishment of a new point of sale. Other more complex and more promising marketing approaches look to model consumer spatial behavior. Throughout the course of research, models describing the spatial behavior of consumers have been greatly enriched by the introduction of new variables and new estimation algorithms. These developments have considerably improved the understanding of consumer spatial behavior. While some of these models have produced encouraging results, the applications are limited to a few activity sectors and to specific spatial configurations [CLI 97]. Most important of all, these models are based on a static geography. They are comparable to the capture of a "stock" of clientele residing in a determined geographic zone and do not allow integration of the parameters linked to the new mobility of consumers. Recently, semiotics was called in as a reinforcement to help comprehension of tourist behavior [GRA 01].

Consumer mobility has greatly increased in the past few years. Individuals move about more often, more rapidly, and along increasingly complex paths. This new-found consumer mobility calls for the creation of new establishment strategies. In fact, mobility has become an essential variable in adjusting a commercial territory [MAR 96]. In order to keep up with the intensification and increasingly complex nature of consumer movement, it is important to follow consumers in their trips in order to capture the flow of clientele passing through retail space.

We will successively examine spatial behavior studies and modeling attempts. After having presented the principal elements of consumer spatial behavior and the traditional models of the store choice process founded on the capture of "stocks" of clientele, we will attempt to lay down the basis of a more dynamic geomarketing approach founded on the flow of clientele.

2.1. Observation of spatial behavior

Paradoxically, the study of consumer spatial behavior has been the object of a relatively small number of publications in scientific marketing reviews. The principal works have concentrated more on modeling than on behavior and what was bound to happen has happened. Many of these behavior models that are used for retail location no longer correspond to the new trends in consumer store choice. It is therefore important to revisit a certain number of the fundamental elements before developing the new facets of consumer mobility.

2.1.1. *The principal concepts linked to consumer spatial behavior*

Consumer spatial behavior is important to retail marketing [JAL 94] in so far as it allows a better understanding of store attraction. This attraction can be explained by at least three important factors, which can be described as structural: the classification of goods and services, the principle of least effort and distance [CLI 92]. Special offers are also factors of attraction and can change the itinerary of a consumer, but, apart from the diversion of a customer from one store to another, the holy grail of every store manager, this phenomenon of attraction generally remains temporary [CLI 92, CLI 02a].

The classification of goods and services, more generally of products, refers back to the theory of central places [CHR 33, LOS 54]. In fact, it is a very ancient question (in marketing!) and, from as early as 1923 in the first issue of the *Harvard Business Review*, Copeland [COP 23] produced a typology that is still used today, even after numerous debates [HOL 63, LUC 59, TOR 82]. Three categories of goods are designated:

- convenience goods: frequently bought, without any particular effort;
- shopping goods: requiring a search for information;
- specialty goods: for which brand name is decisive.

This classification has the merit of showing how different consumer trips can be allocated according to product category. Insofar as the first and third categories imply either little effort or an affirmed choice of brand, and result in a behavior that can correspond to the gravitational model (see section 2.2), the second category carries with it a search for information and *a fortiori* a much more erratic spatial behavior on the part of the consumer (at least from the retailer's point of view). However, the increasing mobility of the consumer is increasingly obliging retailers to revisit the traditional gravitational model in the first case also (see section 2.4).

The principle of least effort, developed over many years in psychology [ZIP 49] and also established in animal ethology [TSA 32], is directly related to the research on the minimization of the distance or the time of a trip. Distance has been extensively studied and remains paradoxically the variable that is often the most difficult to understand. Section 2.1.2 attempts to define the evolution of distance in both economic and socio-psychological terms. This principle of least effort can also result in a reactive trade name loyalty. Marketing specialists know, however, that loyalty is not eternal and conflicts with the behavior of searching for variety [AUR 91, KEM 00, LAN 90, SIR 00]. The increase of differentiation strategies of large distributors [CLI 02a, MOA 01] can only lead to a worsening of the phenomenon of the search for variety, no longer concerning only brands, but also trade names.

Other concepts also affect the study of consumer spatial behavior. Just as there exists a trade area designating the territory from which a point of sale's customers come [APP 61], one can also define a consumer travel zone within a range of activities. This range varies according to the category of products. It can take on a linear nature when applied to convenience goods, while it is considered to be a threshold [MAL 83] beyond which the consumer refuses to search for information when applied to shopping goods. A linear function is seen again with specialty goods as long as they are in stock [CAM 00].

2.1.2. *From the study of trip time to the study of mobility*

At one time, the study of consumer spatial behavior could be summed up as the analysis of the distances traveled between home and the point of sale. The strict definition of the law of gravitation and its application to retail [REI 31] imposed this restriction, for gravitation is defined by distance and mass. However, the extraordinary development of modern business formulas in the 1960s rapidly imposed a new view of this distance. In fact, to quote Braudel, the French historian [BRA 86], "the true measure of distance" is "the speed of human movement." In other words, the time spent getting from point A to point B is more important than the distance between the two. Studies therefore endeavored to understand these trip times better in a very broad way by tracing isochrones [CHA 38], and then by applying them to marketing dilemmas [BRU 68]. Thus one can easily obtain maps broken down according to this "distance in time" between home and store for all the principal residential areas surrounding a store [CLI 02a].

Distance in time is itself often deceptive as an explicatory factor for spatial behavior. In fact, consumers do not all have the same perception of time [BER 88, BER 89]. These differences of perception come from various causes: the trip can be made at different times of the day or of the week and lead to a totally distinct appreciation between one individual and another, even if they are neighbors. Furthermore, there exists a perceptual bias that differentiates us from our contemporaries and imposes upon us an evaluation of time, as well as other things that are unique to our personality: our culture, our mood, etc. The introduction of this perception allows an improvement in the model results (see Chapter 6) [CLI 90].

Is not the best way to confront these difficulties simply to eliminate the use of distance? The development of new information technology in the 1970s fostered the idea that, in a more or less distant future, we would no longer need to move about as much as we do today. The telephone, the fax and even the internet and mobile phones were supposed to lead to our being able, for example, to work and do our shopping exclusively from home. Reality is very different. These new technologies create more trips than they replace: information technology and communications users are those who travel the most. For example, cyber-buyers spend as much time on the road as before to make their purchases [ALL 01].

Mobility has greatly increased in the past few years [MOA 01]. The French cover an average of 14,300 kilometers (km) per year (compared to about 9,000 km at the beginning of the 1980s), which is slightly higher than the European average, but half that of the USA. Most of these trips are made within an 80 km radius of home. The French cover an average of 23 km per weekday (excluding long-distance trips) or about a third more than 25 years ago [ORF 99], even if the durations of the trips remain fairly stable due in large part to progress in transportation, both individual or collective, as well as the number of trips.

Until now, trips between home and the workplace represented the majority of overall trips. A reduction of the percentage of this type of trip has been observed due to the mobility linked to purchases and to leisure [MAR 99]. In fact, from 1982 to 1994, the number of trips per person per day for business reasons has fallen 20%, while those for leisure have increased 33%; shopping represents 20% of trips during the week and 2% at the weekend [DES 01].

"The tyranny of distance" [LEO 00] is being reduced as it is no longer the only variable to dominate consumer spatial behavior. Mobility is more complex and trips are less and less related to time. The spatial norm of trips is no longer considered as radial, but as presenting loops. Peregrination has become the dominant way things operate; travel for warehousing is a part of a more complex chaining. This peregrination is the result of a cross between the utilization strategies of urban space by households, on the one hand, and an offer of services and trade increasingly fragmented throughout the collective urban region on the other. Depending on the place of work and the mode of transportation, and also on more individual variables (age, household make-up, etc.), the intensity of peregrinations can vary [DES 01]. Figure 2.1 presents the variables that influence peregrinations linked to purchases.

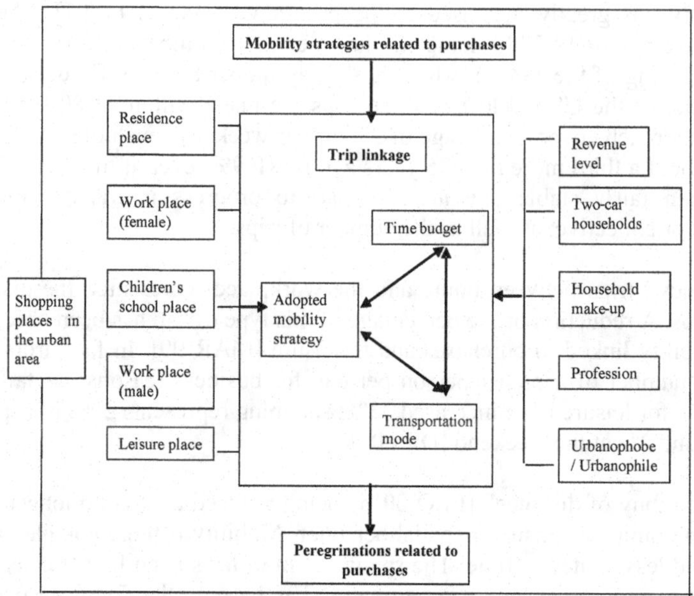

Figure 2.1: *Mobility behavior systems related to the frequenting of shopping places [DES 01]*

One can distinguish between an *insular* mobility, characterized by a trip and a routine schedule, and an *archipelago* or *network* mobility, characterized by trips less concentrated in space and time [ALL 01]. The time devoted to transportation has remained relatively stable. The French devote about 55 minutes per day to travel. They travel longer distances but without devoting more time to this travel. They simply travel faster: speed of travel increased 34% between 1982 and 1994 [DES 01]. Trips are no longer concentrated at certain times during the day or week. These trips tend to spread out in time to such an extent that speaking of rush or peak hours and off-peak hours has lost much of its pertinence.

The automobile is the predominant form of transportation. The French increasingly use their cars for transport (82% of all trips less than 80 km compared to 74% in 1982). The number of automobile trips has increased 33% in 15 years [MAR 96]. This progression can be explained by the increase in parking lots and the development of suburban living. However, the efforts of certain municipalities, such as Nantes and Strasbourg, to improve public transportation to combat congested town centers and air pollution have met with notable success. Only the hyper-center of the city can organize itself around public transportation using clean transportation methods such as tramways. Inside this space, foot traffic multiplies. As for the periphery and the suburbs, "fordian" (= related to the fordian economy) transport, or the same for everyone at the same time, is no longer conceivable [ASC 00].

Most studies dealing with consumer travel emphasize the very low rate of public transportation usage for purchases. For example, in 1995, 60% of the inhabitants of the metropolis Grenoble said that they went to downtown-area businesses by car, 33% by tramway and 7% by bus. Regardless of the type of purchase, the utilization of the automobile is enormous, particularly for outlying towns not connected to the tramway. However, differences can be noted depending on the types of purchases. Home equipment and grocery purchases are usually made by car, while clothes shopping trips or leisure trips are more likely to be made by public transport [DES 01]. The means of transport used by consumers also depends on the clientele. People of reduced motorization (young people, the elderly and families who do not own cars) are the principal users of public transportation.

Furthermore, the strong development of multi-modal transport, or alternating use of different modes of transportation depending on the destination or motive for the trip, can be seen. The profile of travelers has evolved. Executives and employees have traditionally traveled the longest distances, but working-class travel has greatly increased and is approaching that of executives and employees. Moreover, the proportion of women with driving licenses and the development of multi-car households have particularly increased the mobility of women, who continue to play an essential role in household purchases [MOA 01].

Given the expansion of trips in space and in time, as well as the multiplication of individual transport, it seems that we are witnessing a *fordian* model (according to which everyone takes the same trip at the same time) giving way to a *postfordian* model, where each individual moves about at his or her own rhythm, no longer at specific times, but responding to opportunities of the moment [MOA 01]. In other words, consumers do not necessarily do their shopping near to their home or to their workplace, nor during a particular time-slot. Store choice is made more according to opportunity: people shop in a large retail store because it is on their way, and because they have the time to stop there at that precise moment [DES 01].

The intensification and increasingly complex nature of mobility has resulted from a combination of social, economic and cultural transformations. This new mobility is due first of all to the development of high-speed transport (RER – regional express networks, TGV – high-speed trains, air transport and motorways). Thus, distant cities are now more easily accessible than cities that are actually closer as the crow flies. The accelerated diffusion of the automobile and the increase of two-car households must be added to the factors linked to means of transport that have favored consumer mobility. In 1998, 30% of French households had at least two cars compared to only 18% in 1981 [DES 01]. It can be noted that the fact that families have two or more cars should be considered both a cause and a consequence of mobility.

The intensification and increasingly complex nature of mobility is also due to social transformations, including the arrival of women in the job market and new forms of organizing work (35-hour week, cyber-jobs, arranged schedules, continuous working day, etc.).

New spatial behaviors are also explained by the development of "suburbanization" (the expansion of cities beyond their traditional borders with the formation of suburbs that are more or less distant and separate).

Furthermore, it is important to note an evolution in mentalities. Transportation is no longer perceived as negatively as it was in the past. It is considered to be the mark of a greater autonomy and individual liberty. It represents the values of today's society [ORF 01]. Transportation is no longer simply a way of getting to an activity, or a place or a function, but has also become a time and an activity that has its own qualities [ASC 00].

Before dealing with the problems linked to these new means of transportation, it is important to truly understand the traditional approaches that led to the modeling of consumer behavior. These models were conceived to give better understanding of some of the descriptions above and were founded both on the analogy with the law of gravitation and on the modeling of the attraction linked to the measure of relative utility.

2.2. Gravitational modeling or the management of "stocks" of clients

The simplest idea, which is still retained at least in part today, concerns the modeling of consumer spatial behavior through analogy with Newton's phenomenon of universal attraction: it is, in chronological order, the retail law of gravitation [REI 31], followed by other modeling attempts (see Chapter 6 for more details on these models, which are also used for retail outlet location). This, in fact, amounts to a capture of a "stock" of customers and constitutes the most traditional approach. It consists of attracting a stock of customers living in a given geographic zone. Two concepts are generally distinguished: the deterministic concept and the probabilistic concept. The deterministic models are constructed from analysis of trips made by consumers. These models suppose that consumers are attracted to a store according to a determined utility function and that they exclusively frequent the store to which they are most attracted. The probabilistic models are built from the past behavior of individuals or from experimental procedures. They postulate that consumers are attracted to a store according to a function that specifies the probability that a consumer frequents this store.

2.2.1. *The deterministic concept*

The simplest store choice model is founded on the hypothesis of the closest center. This premise, at the core of the retail law of gravitation [REI 31] (see Chapter 6) and taken up again in the theory of central places [CHR 33, LOS 54], stipulates that the consumer frequents the closest town (or point of sale) that provides the sought-after goods and services. The spatial behavior is explicitly described as a form of optimization, with the consumer looking to minimize the distance covered.

Numerous studies have been aimed at testing the validity of this premise of the closest center in different situations (intra- and interurban trips). This approach has not received a great deal of empirical support except where the number of stores is limited, the region is sparsely populated and transport is limited (notably in rural regions or in developing countries) [HUB 78]. The results of these studies indicate that distance is obviously an important factor in explaining consumer travel. However, the weakness of the predictions obtained with the model forces one to think that this notion should be introduced in a more realistic manner. The principal limitation of this premise rests in its rudimentary character since spatial behavior is explained exclusively by spatial proximity. These assessments have led to the introduction of the notion of spatial indifference.

Coming from the expression "just noticeable distance" used in psychology, the principle of spatial indifference postulates that the consumer does not necessarily choose the closest store, but that a zone of spatial indifference exists in which the marginal cost required to reach another store is minimal [NYS 67]. Thus, a visit to a more distant store does not contradict the principle of central places insofar as the difference in distance is not perceived by the individual.

From a conceptual point of view, spatial indifference offers a more satisfying and realistic framework of analysis for studying consumer travel. The major reason for the notion of spatial indifference was to introduce the idea according to which trips made by individuals do not depend on the absolute distance but on the relative distance between other alternatives [CRA 84]. However, the difficulties of operationalization have limited its utilization. Moreover, the principle of spatial indifference remains in the framework of the optimization of behaviors and of the minimization of distances covered [HUB 78]. Finally, even if distance is considerably important in consumer store choice, the idea about which consumers frequent the closest store seems too simplistic. Other variables need to be taken into account in order to understand consumer travel.

Ghosh [GHO 86] integrated the notion of multiple purpose trips into the theory of central places. In fact, in order to reduce the time and the cost of transport, consumers may not frequent the closest store, but more distant shopping centers where they will buy several different things in one place with one trip. This type of trip represents between 30% and 50% of trips made by consumers [OKE 81]. Christaller [CHR 35] and Lösch [LOS 54] had previously mentioned the possible impact of these behaviors, but without introducing them into their models. More recently, several authors have introduced this notion, albeit in a very restrictive manner [EAT 82, KOH 84]. They suppose that the proportion and the frequency of multiple purpose trips are independent of the topography of places. Ghosh has proposed a more complete approach in which multiple purpose trips are at the heart of the consumer decision-making process. He postulates that individuals choose their place of purchase in such a way as to minimize the total cost of shopping. While Christaller supposes that consumers always frequent the closest store and buy only one product (or a similar set of products on each trip), the Ghosh model supposes that consumers abandon the closest store so that they are able to group together several types of purchases. The analysis of joint measures was recently used in an attempt to understand multiple shopping purpose trips [DEL 98].

In order to determine the optimal number of multiple shopping purpose trips, it is necessary to take the stocking of products into consideration. On the one hand, this type of travel leads to a multiplication of the costs of the stocking of products. On the other hand, more frequent and non-grouped purchases limit stocking costs and increase transport costs. As a result, consumers make adjustments between stocking costs and transport costs in order to determine the optimal number of trips. Insofar as transport costs vary according to the location of individuals in relation to possible shopping areas, frequency of trips depends on the location of the individuals and their trips. Furthermore, the frequency of multiple purpose trips depends on the degree of compatibility of the purchases. Therefore, Ghosh proposes a model that determines consumer travel in both spatial and temporal terms based on travel costs, product prices and stocking costs. These three types of costs allow the frequency and nature of trips to be determined. This model has been the object of numerous empirical validations and several extensions. For example, Keane [KEA 89] proposed an extension of this model by differentiating two types of goods: lower order goods and higher order goods. Claycombe [CLA 91] further developed the notion of transport costs.

Consumer spatial behavior models developed from the central places theory have evolved significantly. From the idea according to which the consumer looks to minimize his or her efforts and therefore frequents the closest store, we have moved to more sophisticated models where consumer travel is determined according to an optimization of spatial and temporal factors. In these models, one supposes that consumers are attracted to a store according to a determined utility function and that they exclusively frequent the store to which they are most attracted. Other models, known as probabilistic models, assert that consumers are attracted to a store according to a function that specifies the probability that a consumer frequents this store [WON 99].

2.2.2. *The probabilistic concept*

In order to model more precisely the spatial behavior of consumers, it is important to define a utility function based on spatial and not on non-spatial elements. These models, called *spatial choice models*, are as follows:

$$U_{ij} = A_j^{\alpha} D_{ij}^{-\beta} \qquad [2.1]$$

where:

– U_{ij} represents the utility of a store j for a consumer i,

– A_j is a measure of attractiveness of a store j,

– D_{ij} measures the distance separating store j from consumer i,

– α and β are the parameters that reflect the sensitivity of the consumer to the attractiveness of the store and to the distance respectively.

While the models coming from the theory of central places are deterministic and are specified at a global level, spatial choice models are probabilistic and are defined at the individual level from preferences shown by individuals. Consumer spatial behavior is henceforth considered in terms of preferences for locations and not strictly in terms of allocation [GOL 97].

The first spatial choice model based on preferences shown by consumers was developed by Huff [HUF 64]. Then, numerous extensions known as Multiplicative Competitive Interaction models or MCI models (see Chapter 6) followed.

Using the works of Reilly [REI 31], Huff defined store attractiveness by its floor area. The size of the store is considered the best store attractiveness indicator. In fact, when faced with larger stores offering a wider and larger assortment of goods, the consumer is more likely to find the sought-after products and is therefore willing to travel longer distances to shop there. This echoes a principle of the central places theory. The consumer therefore balances the advantages linked to the size of the store and the disadvantages generated by the distance to be covered. Distance is measured by the time spent reaching the destination, the distance and the transport costs. Thus, the utility of a store for a consumer depends on the size of the store (S) and on the distance between home and store (D). When a consumer is susceptible to frequenting several stores, the probability of frequenting a particular store is equal to the relationship between the utility taken from this store and the sum of the utilities of the other stores considered by the consumer, or:

$$P_{ij} = U_{ij} \Big/ \sum_{k=1}^{n} U_{ik} \qquad [2.2]$$

where:

– P_{ij} represents the probability that a consumer i frequents store j,
– n is the number of stores considered by the consumer.

By integrating equation [2.1] into equation [2.2], the following equation is obtained, known more commonly as the Huff model:

$$P_{ij} = S_j^{\alpha} D_{ij}^{-\beta} \Big/ \sum_{k=1}^{n} S_{kj}^{\alpha} D_{kj}^{-\beta} \quad [2.3]$$

where S_j represents the size of the store in square meters.

The Huff model has been the object of numerous empirical studies. The procedure used for testing it consists most often of dividing a geographic space into several zones according to characteristics of the inhabitants and to their mode of transportation. In each of these zones, people are randomly selected and questioned in order to identify the stores frequented (number and frequency of visits to each store). Information concerning the size of the store and the distance are obtained through observation or through the bias of secondary sources. From these data, it is possible to estimate consumer sensibility according to two attributes considered, the size of the store and distance. Thus, preferences for choice possibilities are obtained from past consumer behaviors or their preferences shown for each of the alternatives [CRA 84].

Most models are based on the Huff formula. However, the usefulness of a store for a consumer depends on a multitude of factors: environmental, situational and individual variables [GRA 84]. Yet the Huff model includes only two variables: distance and the attractiveness of the store. Even if these variables are considered the most determinant in certain cases (supermarkets, convenience stores, etc.), the question of possibly introducing supplementary variables can be raised. The nonlinear formulation of the model causes the parameters to be estimated only by usual econometric techniques [HUF 75]. In order to avoid this difficulty, Nakanishi and Cooper [NAK 74] used the least squares approach to estimate the parameters of the model and thus were able to introduce supplementary variables. This extension is known as the MCI model.

Nakanishi and Cooper proposed a more complete model, which integrates other parameters than attraction and store size. The MCI model supposes that the choice of a consumer between m choice possibilities is the following:

$$P_i = \left(\prod_{k=1}^{q} A_{ik}^{\beta k} \right) \Big/ \left(\sum_{i=1}^{m} \prod_{k=1}^{q} A_{ik}^{\beta k} \right) \quad [2.4]$$

where:

– P_i represents the probability that a consumer chooses store i, with $i = (1, 2, \ldots, m)$,
– A_{ik} is the attribute k of the alternative i, with $k = (1, 2, \ldots, q)$,
– β_k measures the sensibility for attribute k.

Shopping centers	Supermarkets	Bank branches	Furniture stores
– Number of cars owned by the household – Home-store trip time – Total time of transit – Trip cost by $1000 revenue section – Total number of stores – Presence of general merchandise and clothes – Other shopping goods – Stores for low-revenue people – Planned shopping center	– Store image (product quality, price, personnel welcome, etc.) – Store display (sales surface, check-out number, etc.) – Appearance (external and internal) – Accessibility (location at an intersection) – Services (credit cards, check acceptance, meat department, delicatessen department) – Employee make-up (black/white)	– Location – Drive-in ATM (Automatic Teller Machine) – Pedestrian ATM – Novelty – Bank trade name	– Product quality – Average price level – Promotional offers – Service offers – Store accessibility – Merchandise immediate availability – Assortment width – Store reputation – Internal decoration – Credit facilities – Salesmen skills – Distance beyond a certain threshold

Table 2.1: *Variables used in MCI models (from [CLI 97])*

Numerous variables have been introduced (see Table 2.1). For example, Lakshmanen and Hansen [LAK 65] used a more complete measure of store attractiveness based on parking facilities, store ambiance and functionality. Stanley and Sewal [STA 76] introduced the image of the store. They showed that stores with a better image attracted consumers from greater distances than similarly sized stores less favorably perceived by consumers. Jain and Mahajan [JAI 79] proposed a model integrating store image, price and product level, customer services, the number of check-out lanes, the type of employees, the possible means of payment, etc. Gautschi [GAU 81] introduced four characteristics of the mode of transport: performance, comfort, cost and security. However, it seems that distance or drive-time remains the essential factor in explaining store choice [BLA 85, STA 76, UNC 96].

The Huff model and the MCI model are in fact disaggregated models, meaning that their results are theoretically destined for one consumer. In fact, for evident reasons of efficiency for store managers (see Chapter 6), most of the research studies and other work are carried out at the aggregate level, for the entire population of a market area.

Other models are called disaggregated discrete choice models, also known as random use models. The MultiNominal Logit (MNL) model, the nested MNL model, the dogit model, the generalized extreme worth model and the multinomial probit model are all examples of this type [GOL 97b]. The best known model, the

MNL, simply results in discrete store choice among a collection of choice possibilities. The rule is the maximization of usefulness, and one finds in fact a structure close to that of the MCI model [COO 88]. The MNL model was used to show the stability of supermarket choice behavior both in time (period of four years) and in space with data collected in Canada, the USA and Norway [SEV 01].

Both these models, MCI and MNL, have a major defect, which was pointed out in the study cited previously: Independence of Irrelevant Alternatives (IIA). This means that the arrival of a new choice possibility (a new store) will compete in an equal manner with existing stores. In other words, it will "cannibalize" other stores already in place in an exactly proportional way regardless of their attributes, which is far from being realistic [GOL 69]. This difficulty can be overcome by using the transformation of zeta squared [CLI 95, COO 83] (see section 2.3 and Chapter 6).

2.3. The subjective approach and choice models

One can obviously consider gravitation models and their generalization in the form of market share models as choice models. However, they fail to integrate any of the fundamental variables of human choice that are perceptions. In a path-analytical exploration of retail patronage influences, Monroe and Guiltinan [MON 75] showed the importance of perceptions in the overlapping choices of product and store, of the brand and the trade name. More formalized models have attempted to introduce these perceptions as well and others have taken consumer cognitive limitations into account.

2.3.1. *The subjective approach and attraction models*

Fressin [FRE 75] attempted to introduce a variable of a psychological nature taken from behaviorist theory and linked to store image. Founded on learning models dealing with store choice and based on two linear operators (a purchase operator and a rejection operator) [AAK 71], the Fressin model essentially retains two variables: on the one hand, the distance or access time of a store, which constitutes an obstacle to consumer travel, and, on the other, the usefulness of the store, which represents the measure of attraction for the consumer. This is not a gravitation model since only distance is present (and not mass) and its structure is nothing like that of a gravitation model. Furthermore, the model takes total cost (purchase + transport) into account. The complex nature of the model's formulation has kept it from being re-worked in subsequent studies. However, the basic idea according to which distribution companies should substitute the image of their stores for that of the products they sell quite simply constituted, beginning in 1975, the foundation of trade-name marketing [CLI 02a].

In more recent years, behaviorist research has turned more towards consumer spatial perceptions. The perceived distance and time to destination have been revealed to be as important as the objective distance and the objective duration of the trip [MCK 75]. When the cognitive map[1] of a consumer is incomplete, fragmented or deformed or when it displays any sort of spatial or temporal bias, individuals do not behave in a rational manner (in an economic sense) in their spatial choices and do not optimize their trips [GOL 69]. Thus, if objective distance is replaced by perceived distance, spatial choice models are of a higher quality [CAD 81]. However, these notions are difficult to incorporate into aggregate models [GOL 97]. Moreover, it is necessary to gain a better understanding of the way in which consumers deal with spatial information and establish spatial and temporal estimations. For example, spatial perceptions depend on the number of obstacles met (intersections, turns), the diversity of the landscape, the context, individual preferences, etc. [MCK 75, RAG 96]. Finally, the possible existence of the effects of interaction on these models should not be forgotten. In other words, several variables taken independently may individually have little influence, while their interaction can lead to a high degree of synergy in terms of spatial behavior. It is therefore necessary to construct a structural equation model in order to capture these interactions more effectively [CAD 95].

The idea of a globally subjective approach, or one in which all variables are measured as perceptions, will be taken up again later and integrated into an MCI model (see Chapter 6). The primordial problem is of a methodological order. In fact, MCI models require data measured on scales of proportion. Yet perceptions are generally measured on ordinal scales and are therefore non-metric. The use of equal-appearing interval scales with semantic supports [PRA 76] followed by a transformation of these data by zeta squared [COO 83] has allowed the introduction of perceptions into an MCI, as in the case of the furniture market [CLI 90]. However, the model developed in this fashion will be implemented in a quasi-disaggregated way, or the calibration of the model will be done by unit of geographic division (see Chapter 6): this model is not totally disaggregated at the consumer level, neither is it a total aggregate model at the complete market level [GON 00]. Two rules have governed this choice: on the one hand, respecting the stationarity restrictions in the implementation of the MCI [GHO 84] and, on the other hand, a better apprehension of the behavior using an administrative division and an adapted typology showing the influence of certain socio-demographic variables in the spatial behavior of furniture consumers in the zone studied. The subjective MCI was used in the framework of food stores in Salamanque, Spain in order to put forward the segmentation variables [GON 00].

MCI models, like gravitation models, are built from a collection of premises concerning the economic and spatial rationality of consumers [GOL 97]. For example, it is supposed that individuals have a set of coherent and fixed preferences,

1. The cognitive map concept dates back to the beginning of the century [GUL 08] and deals with the way in which individuals inwardly imagine the environment.

which are transitive[2] and that consumers are capable of making optimal choices. In fact, it is supposed that consumers evaluate each store in terms of the usefulness of each of the choice possibilities (stores) and then select the store that maximizes the usefulness.

During the 1960s and 1970s, these premises were challenged by a collection of theoretical and empirical analyses showing the limits of the abilities of information processing and the difficulty of realizing optimal choices [SIM 57, TVE 74]. Thus, the spatial choice process is undermined when choice possibilities are numerous. In fact, with the limited abilities of processing information, a procedure simplifying the choice process is necessary. Even if it were possible for an individual to take all of the choice possibilities into consideration, temporal pressures and other distractions are likely to encourage the consumer to short-circuit the decision-making process [FOT 85]. This difficulty led to the development of a new type of model based on the integration of information theory: hierarchical models.

2.3.2. *The information processing approach*

More recently, hierarchical models have appeared that enable the limitations of individuals in processing information and their difficulties in establishing optimal choices to be taken into account. In the integration of information theory, also called the theory of functional measure, individual choice is considered to be a process and not a purpose; the choice is an objective to reach and the individual researches and analyzes a set of data in order to make a decision. The idea of a learning process, or of consumer search behavior [MIL 93], is thus very close to this theory and studies, for the most part at the conceptual stage, have led to the establishment of a connection between consumer behavior models and cognitive process decision and choice models, which are well known to specialists in cognitive sciences and artificial intelligence [GOL 97]. The objective of the functional measurement approach is to model the process by which individuals or groups process information and establish their choices when faced with numerous possibilities. This leads to the supposition that choice results from a hierarchical or sequential decision process in which the consumer starts by selecting several possibilities from choices that present similar characteristics, and then makes his choice from within this group [REC 81]. Thus, by avoiding evaluating all of the possibilities, the choice process is greatly simplified.

To illustrate this decision process, one can consider the clothing store choice made by a consumer residing in a large city. The consumer most probably has neither the time nor the ability to evaluate every store in the city. He or she therefore selects a group of stores (from a certain neighborhood for example) and then makes his or her choice from this selection [FOT 88].

---

2. If an alternative *a* is preferred to an alternative *b* and if *b* is preferred to *c*, *a* is thus preferred to *c*.

In these models, individuals are assumed to be able to discern the essential attributes (called *functional*) of all possible choices, realize arbitrages between the attributes linked to different possibilities, numerically evaluate each of these possibilities and classify them by order of preference [GOL 97]. Thus, it is possible to give a weighting coefficient to each of the possibilities and to establish choices based on a simple algebraic reasoning: additive process, if the attributes are independent of one another, or multiplicative process, if the attributes interact with each other. A trade-off function can be used. Despite its complexity and the operationalization difficulties, the theory of the integration of information [LOU 74] has been the object of many studies.

The probabilistic models founded on revealed preferences (gravitation models, MCI models and hierarchical models) have considerably improved the comprehension of consumer spatial behavior. They possess a very high quality predictive power. Nevertheless, several limitations and utilization conditions should be mentioned. In order to use spatial choice models correctly, it is important to know their limitations and to respect certain conditions during the specification procedure (see Chapter 6). Furthermore, these models are based on a static geography. They aim to capture "stocks" of customers. Yet, increasing consumer mobility forces retailers to follow consumers in their travels and to enact actions to catch the flow of customers.

2.4. The management of the flow of customers: new research perspectives

In contrast to models founded on the attraction of a stock of customers residing in a determined geographic zone, the capture of the flow of customers deals with capturing the flow of customers moving about a trade area.

Strategies for capturing customer flow were developed to deal with the intensification and increasingly complex nature of consumer trips. This new consumer mobility is due to a set of social-economic and cultural transformations and calls for the implementation of new location strategies.

2.4.1. *Consumer mobility and non-gravitational attraction*

The increasing mobility of consumers calls for the development of a new conception of spatial marketing in retail and a new store location logic. Given the increasingly complex nature of consumer mobility, the peripheral commercial offer can no longer be organized in a homogeneous way, based on hypermarkets, by tracing simple isochrones of a quarter or a half an hour. Retailers see themselves obligated to follow the flow of clientele and to adjust their offer in relation to daily, weekly and seasonal transhumances. A geographic space should not only be defined according to the individuals who reside or work there, but also by thinking of those who pass through it.

Service and retail trade activities	Pure stock of clientele = gravitational attraction	Mixed clientele = (mixed attraction)	Pure passing clientele = non-gravitational attraction
Car spare parts		x x	
Bank branches		x x x	x
Temporary staff	x	x	
Travel agency	x	x x x	
Real estate agency		x	
Furniture		x	
Pet store		x	
Gunsmith		x x	
Bus stop		x x x	
Sports items		x	
Insurance	x		
Hi-Fi/TV		x	
Driving school	x		
Bar café		x x x	
Jewellery		x x x	
Butcher		x	
Bakery		x x	
Do-it-yourself		x	
Post Office		x x x	x
Office computers		x	
Dentist		x	
Phone box		x	
Surgery		x	
Gifts		x x x	x
Shopping center		x x x	
Leisure center		x x x	
Delicatessen		x	
Shoes		x x	
Movie theater		x x	
Hairdresser	x	x	
Auto dealer		x x	
Confectionery		x x x	
Shoemender	x		
Nightclub		x x x	
Record dealer		x x x	
Vending machine	x	x x x	x
Hardware shop		x	
School	x	x	
Household electrical	x		
Grocer		x x x	
Tricks and jokes		x x x	

Florist		x	x	x	
Cheese dairy	x				
Fruits and vegetables			x		
Gadgets		x	x	x	
Garage		x	x	x	(x)
Department store		x	x	x	(x) Paris
Hospital		x	x		
Hotel		x	x		x
Hypermarket			x		
Garden center			x		
Toy store		x	x	x	
Launderette	x		x		
Bookstore		x	x	x	
High school	x	x	x		
Variety store		x	x	x	
Fine leather goods shop		x	x	x	
Musical instruments			x		
Stationery			x		
Perfume shop		x	x	x	
Cake shop		x	x	x	
Fishing and hunting		x	x	x	
Pharmacy		x	x	x	
Fishmonger	x				
Restaurant		x	x	x	x
Fast food		x	x	x	x
Gas station		x	x	x	x
Convenience store		x	x	x	
Supermarket			x		
Tobacco/newspapers		x	x	x	x
Dry cleaners	x		x		
University		x	x	x	
Clothes		x	x	x	
Wine and spirit		x	x	x	(x) ***duty free***
Total: 74 activities					

Table 2.2: *Classification of 74 French retail trades according to their type of attraction (from [CLI 97])*

NOTE: the crosses in the third column of Table 2.2 show that some retail trade types are:

– equally gravitational and non gravitational (cross in the middle of the column),

– predominantly gravitational but non-exclusive (cross on the left-hand side),

– predominantly non-gravitational but non-exclusive (cross on the right-hand side).

This is not to say, however, that gravitational attraction is in the process of disappearing. Far from being exclusive, these two approaches, attraction of a stock and capture of a flow of customers, are complementary and are often carried out in a more or less intuitive manner. Cliquet [CLI 97] proposes a classification of retail businesses according to types of commercial attraction (see Tables 2.2 and 2.3).

Table 2.2 shows, based on 74 retail and service activity sectors, that purely polar attractions are rare, with none being purely non-gravitational. Most are at times purely or predominantly polar, at times predominantly non-gravitational, at times both at the same time. Each of the activities analyzed has its own scenarios in relation to attraction for they are subject to a specific consumer spatial behavior. Many of these activities manage both a gravitational type clientele living in the immediate environs of the store and a so-called passing clientele. The proportion between the two can vary according to the time of day, the day of the week and the season (holidays for example, with ever-changing patterns following the implementation of the reduction of the working week).

Due to the rise in consumer mobility, the tendency has been towards an increasing non-gravitational attraction. Yet, hitherto, among tourist activities characteristic of flow activities, researchers have primarily attempted to model gravitational attraction. The utilization of gravitation models has often been advised in order to forecast the flow of tourists [SHE 85], but, for quite some time, people have spoken out against the use of models that do not correspond to the phenomenon studied or which may lead to bad predictions. This is the case for the use of gravitation models in situations where sites are close to one another [BUC 71b]. Arc tangent functions have been proposed in order to better understand the degree of overlapping of trade areas, or in other words the problems of escape from one zone into another [BUC 71a]. What is true between two adjacent zones is even more the case with flows.

Retail trade category	"Stocks" of clientele or gravitation	"Flow" of clientele	Location model type
Supermarkets			
– community	Yes	No	Huff
– tourist area	Yes	Yes	Huff + ?
Shopping centers			
– community	Yes	No	Reilly's law
– regional	Yes	Yes	Reilly's law + ?
Furniture stores			
– low level reputation	No	No	Subjective MCI
– high level reputation	Yes	No	Subjective MCI
Convenience stores			
– unique	Yes	No	MCI
– multiple	Yes	No	Multiloc = location-allocation + MCI

Table 2.3: *Classification of retail trades according to attraction type and models usually employed in each case (from [CLI 97])*

2.4.2. *For a modeling of non-gravitational attraction and new location strategies*

To our knowledge, modeling of this nature has yet to be realized, this despite numerous authors having highlighted the issues linked to the new mobility of consumers [DES 01, CLI 97, MAR 96, MOA 01]. Table 2.3 takes the principal applications of gravitation models, whether objective or subjective. Compared to the list of activities in Table 2.2, the models presented in store chain marketing essentially cover four store categories: supermarkets, shopping centers, furniture stores and convenience stores.

The models used have become classics, sometimes for decades (and the professional world continues to use them): the law of retail gravitation [REI 31], the Huff model, gravitational and probabilistic [HUF 64], the generalization of this model called the MCI model [NAK 74], the Multiloc model for multiple location [ACH 82] and the subjective MCI model [CLI 90] (see Chapter 6 for the technical details of this model). However, these models seek only to model consumer behavior in relation to a store in the framework of a gravitational attraction phenomenon. So, what about non-gravitational attraction (symbolized by the question marks in Table 2.3)?

Non-gravitational attraction, in fact, has only been the subject of studies in geography and tourism economics [EYM 95]. For retail applications, it would be necessary to develop modeling connected to the flow of clientele [CLI 02b]. What is at stake is important if the incessant increase in consumer mobility is considered. If the decision dilemma is clear and directly concerns store location strategies and the management of the marketing of stores, the research dilemma is much more complex to define. Despite few attempts [LOU 78, MCF 79] to point out this problem, nothing really attractive has been published concerning non-gravitational attraction. Looking at analogies with certain phenomena in physics, particularly in hydrology, that deal with flows would surely help. Other problems are connected to the capture of clientele: number of parking lots, number of check-out aisles, which imply decisions and an extremely sophisticated management of queues [CLI 97].

Store location strategies are in the process of evolving and bringing themselves closer to consumer spatial behavior. Networks like Zara (Spanish clothing stores) or H&M (Swedish clothing stores) go as far as locating three or four stores on the same street. They hope thus to "capture" the regular customer when they pass the second, third or even fourth store! Entire chains have located themselves in heavy traffic areas such as railway stations (Relay H, a bookstore–newsagent subsidiary of Hachette). Even certain shopping centers, like the Mall of America in Minneapolis, Minnesota (USA), integrate this new concept of consumption. The Mall of America, conceived by the Triple Five company and opened in August 1992, had a provisional trade area of 1200 km^2 [CLI 92]! Some consumers, coming from Chicago for example, spent several days at this immense mall (the largest in the world, along with the mall in Edmonton, Canada). Foreign tourists, Japanese in particular, are now part of the passing clientele of this mall and tour operators offer Japanese travelers trip packages to the USA that include a stay at the Mall of America. Auchan located its newest hypermarket, Val d'Europe, near Disneyland Paris. This therefore signifies that small stores are not the only ones that undergo this phenomenon.

2.5. Conclusion

Store choice models (determinist and probabilistic approaches) have hitherto been based on a static and simplistic view of consumer spatial behavior. These models favor the minimization of distance in the form of accessibility and cost. Determining a trade area in relation to a stock of clientele residing therein is of utmost importance. Naturally, this dilemma exists and always will!

However, the new mobility of consumers requires a more dynamic approach. In fact, today it is less the store that has a trade area than the individual who has a supply zone [MAR 99]. It is necessary to develop new consumer spatial behavior models based on a wider study of spatial behaviors, integrating the intensification and increasingly complex nature of consumer mobility.

Gravitational (we avoid saying determinist) attraction sees itself strongly challenged by the growing freedom of the consumer in relation to transportation and information. Technology, both in means of transportation and in the media, allows consumers to manage their time in a different manner. Retail activities are not exempt from this rule. Advancements in individual and public transport and e-commerce [VOL 00] are going to force the retail world to rethink its attraction strategies with the requirement to follow the consumer in his or her peregrinations or to dramatize its offer.

2.6. References

[AAK 71], Aaker D., Jones M., Modeling Store Choice Behavior, *Journal of Marketing Research*, 8, 38-42, 1971.

[ACH 82], Achabal D., Gorr W. L., Mahajan Vijay , MULTILOC: A Multiple Store Location Decision Model, *Journal of Retailing*, 58, 5-25, 1982.

[ALL 01], Allemand S., Les enjeux des mobilités quotidiennes, *Sciences Humaines*, June, 46-62, 2001.

[ANS 77], Ansah J. A., Determination Choice Set Definition in travel Behavior Modeling, *Transportation Research*, 11, 127-140, 1977.

[APP 61], Applebaum W., Cohen S., The Dynamics of Store Trading Areas and Market Equilibrium, *Annals of the Association of The American Geographers*, 51, 1, 73-101, 1961.

[APP 66], Applebaum W., Methods for Determining Store Trade Areas and Market Equilibrium, *Journal of Marketing Research*, 3, 2, 127-141, 1966.

[ASC 00], Ascher F., *Ces événements nous dépassent, feignons d'en être les organisateurs*, Editions de l'Aube, 2000.

[AUR 91], Aurier P., Recherche de variété: un concept majeur de la théorie en marketing, *Recherche et Applications en Marketing*, 6, 1, 85-106, 1991.

[BER 88], Bergadaà M., Le temps et le comportement de l'individu (première partie), *Recherche et Applications en Marketing*, 3, 4, 57-72, 1988.

[BER 89], Bergadaà M., Le temps et le comportement de l'individu (deuxième partie), *Recherche et Applications en Marketing*, 4, 1, 57-72, 1989.

[BLA 85], Black W., Ostlund L., Westbrook R., Spatial demand models in an intrabrand context, *Journal of Marketing*, 49, 106-113, 1985.

[BRA 86], Braudel F., *L'identité de la France*, Espace et Histoire, Arthaud, Paris, 1986.

[BRU 68], Brunner J. A., The Influence of Driving Time upon Shopping Center Preference, *Journal of Marketing*, 32, 2, 57-61, 1968.

[BUC 71a], Bucklin L. P., Trade Area Boundaries: Some Issues in Theory and Methodology, *Journal of Marketing Research*, 8, 1, 30-37, 1971.

[BUC 71b], Bucklin L. P., Retail Gravity Models and Consumer Choice: A Theoretical and Empirical Critique, *Economic Geography*, 47, 4, 489-97, 1971.

[CAD 81], Cadwallader M.T., Towards a Cognitive Gravity Model: The Case of Consumer Spatial Behavior, *Regional Studies*, 15, 275-284, 1981.

[CAD 95], Cadwallader M.T., Interaction Effects in Models of Consumer Spatial Behaviour, *Applied Geography*, 15, 2, 135-145, 1995.

[CAM 00], Campo K., Gijsbrechts E., Nisol P., Towards Understanding Consumer Response to Stock-Outs, *Journal of Retailing*, 76, 2, 219-42, 2000.

[CHA 38], Chabot G., La détermination des courbes isochrones – géographie urbaine, *Congrès International de Géographie*, Amsterdam, 1938.

[CHR 33], Christaller W., *Die Zentralen Orte in Suddeutchland,* Iena (translation Baskin C. W., as *Central places in southern Germany*, Englewood Cliffs, NJ: Prentice Hall, 1966), 1933.

[CLA 91], Claycombe R., Spatial Retail Markets, *International Journal of Industrial Organization*, 9, 303-313, 1991.

[CLI 02a], Cliquet G., Fady A., Basset G., *Le management de la distribution*, Dunod, Paris, 2002.

[CLI 02b], Cliquet G., La localisation commerciale, in *Stratégies de localisation des entreprises commerciales et industrielles: de nouvelles perspectives*, Cliquet G., Josselin J.-M. ed., De Boeck Université, Bruxelles, 2002.

[CLI 90], Cliquet G., La mise en œuvre du modèle interactif de concurrence spatiale (MICS) subjectif, *Recherche et Applications en Marketing*, 5, 1, 3-18, 1990.

[CLI 92], Cliquet G., *Management stratégique des points de vente*, Dalloz-Sirey, Paris, 1992.

[CLI 95], Cliquet G., Implementing a Subjective MCI Model: An Application to the Furniture Market, *European Journal of Operational Research*, 84, 279-91, 1995.

[CLI 97], Cliquet G., Attraction commerciale, fondement de la modélisation en matière de localisation différentielle, *Revue Belge de Géographie*, 21, 57-69, 1997.

[COO 83], Cooper L. G., Nakanishi M., Standardizing Variables in Multiplicative Choice Models, *Journal of Consumer Research*, 10, 96-108, 1983.

[COO 88], Cooper L. G., Nakanishi M., *Market-Share Analysis: Evaluating Competitive Marketing Effectiveness*, Kluwer Academic Publisher, ISQM, Boston, Mass., 1988.

[COP 23], Copeland M., Relation of Consumers' Buying Habits to Marketing Methods, *Harvard Business Review*, 1, 1923.

[CRA 84], Craig C. S., Ghosh A., McLafferty S., Model of Retail Location Process: A Review, *Journal of Retailing*, 60, 1, 5-36, 1984.

[DEL 98], Dellaert B.G.C., Arentze T.A., Bierlaire M., Borgers A.W.J., Timmermans H.J.P., Investigating Consumer's Tendency to Combine Multiple Shopping Purposes and Destinations, *Journal of Marketing Research*, 35, 2, 177-88, 1998.

[DES 01], Desse R-P., *Le nouveau commerce urbain – dynamiques spatiales et stratégies des acteurs*, Presses Universitaires de Rennes, 2001.

[EAT 82], Eaton B., Lipsey R., An Economic Theory of Central Places, *The Economic Journal*, 92, 56-72, 1982.

[EYM 95], Eymann A., *Consumers' spatial choice behavior*, Physica-verlag, Berlin, 1995.

[EYM 97], Eymann A., Ronning G., Micro-economic Models of Tourists' Destination Choice, *Regional Science and Urban Economics*, 27, 735-61, 1997.

[FOT 85], Fotheringham A. S., Spatial Competition and Agglomeration in Urban Modelling, *Environment and Planning A*, 17, 213-30, 1985.

[FOT 88], Fotheringham A. S., Consumer Store Choice and Choice Set Definition, *Marketing Science*, 7, 3, 99-310, 1988.

[FRE 75], Fressin J-J., Le comportement du consommateur-client de la grande entreprise de distribution et le choix du lieu d'achat, *Revue Française du Marketing*, 58, 27-61, 1975.

[GAU 81], Gautschi D. A., Specification of Patronage Models of Retail Center Choice, *Journal of Marketing Research*, 18, 162-174, 1981.

[GHO 84], Ghosh A., Parameter of Nonstationarity in Retail Choice Models, *Journal of Business Research*, 12, 425-436, 1984.

[GHO 86], Ghosh A., The Value of a Mall and Other Insights from a Revised Central Place Model, *Journal of Retailing*, 62, 1, 79-95, 1986.

[GOL 69], Golledge R. G., Briggs R., Demko D., The configurations of distances in Intra-Urban Space, *Proceedings of the Association of American Geographers*, 1, 60-65, 1969.

[GOL 97] Golledge R. G., Stimson R. J., *Spatial behavior: A Geographic Perspective*, The Guilford Press, NY, 1997.

[GON 00], Gonzàles-Benito Ó., Greatorex M., Muñoz-Gallego, Assessment of Potential Retail Segmentation Variables: An Approach Based on a Subjective MCI Resource Allocation Model, *Journal of Retailing and Consumer Services*, 7, 3, 171-79, 2000.

[GRA 01], Graillot L., La sémiotique comme analyse des comportements touristiques, *Revue Française du Marketing*, 181, 7-27, 2001.

[GRA 84], Granbois D., Predicting Temporal and Spatial Patterns of Aggregate Consumer Demand, *Advances in Consumer Research*, 11, 396-399, 1984.

[GUA 81], Gautsch D.A., Specification of Patronage Models for Retail Center Choice, *Journal of Marketing Research*, 18, 162-174, 1981.

[GUL 08], Gulliver F.P., Orientation of Maps, *Journal of Geography*, 7, 55-58, 1908.

[HOL 63], Holton, R. H., What is Really Meant by Specialty Goods?, *Journal of Marketing*, 28, 1963.

[HUB 78], Hubbard R., A Review of Selected Factors Conditioning Consumer Travel Behavior, *Journal of Consumer Research*, 5, 1-21, 1978.

[HUF 64], Huff D.L., Defining and Estimating a Trade Area, *Journal of Marketing*, 28, 34-38, 1964.

[HUF 75], Huff D.L., Batsell R., Conceptual and Operational Problems with Market Share Models of Consumer Spatial Behavior, *Advances in Consumer Research*, 2, 165-172, 1975.

[JAI 79], Jain A. K., Mahajan V., Evaluating the Competitive Environment in Retailing Using Multiplicative Competitive Interactive Models, in *Research in Marketing*, J. Sheth ed., Greenwich, Conn.: JAJ Press, 217-235, 1979.

[JAL 94], Jallais J., Orsoni J., Fady A., *Marketing du commerce de détail*, Vuibert, Paris, 1994.

[KEA 89], Keane M, Function and Competition among Urban Centers, *Journal of Regional Science*, 29, 2, 265-276, 1989.

[KEM 00], Kemperman A.D.A.M., Borgers A.W.J., Oppewal H., Timmermens H.J.P., Consumer Choice of Theme Parks: A Conjoint Model of Seasonality Effects and Variety Seeking Behavior, *Leisure Science*, 22, 1, 1-18, 2000.

[KOH 84], Kohsaka H., An Optimization of the Central Place System in Terms of Multipurpose Shopping Trips, *Geographical Analysis*, 6, 250-29, 1984.

[LAK 65], Lakshmanan T.R., Hansen W., A Retail Market Potential Model, *Journal of American Institute Planners,* 3, 134-143, 1965.

[LAN 90], Lancaster K, The Economics of Product Variety: A Survey, *Marketing Science*, 9, 3, 189-206, 1990.

[LEO 00], Léo P-Y., Philippe J., Centres-villes et périphéries commerciales: le point de vue des consommateurs, *Cahiers de Géographie du Québec*, 44, 123, 363-97, 2000.

[LOS 54], Lösch A., *The Economics of Location*, Yale University Press, New Haven, Conn., 1954.

[LOU 74], Louviere J., Predicting the Response to Real Stimulus Objects from an Abstract Evaluation of their Attributes: the Use of Trout Streams, *Journal of Applied Psychology*, 59, 572-577, 1974.

[LOU 78], Louviere J., Levin I., Functional Measurement Analysis of Spatial and Travel Behavior, *Advances in Consumer Research*, 5, 435-439, 1978.

[LUC 59], Luck D. J., The Nature of Specialty Goods, *Journal of Marketing*, 24, 1959.

[MAI 67], Maillet G., L'attraction des grandes surfaces de vente: étude d'un modèle, *Revue de Statistique Appliquée*, 15, 3, 5-29, 1967.

[MAL 83], Malhotra N. K., A Threshold Model of Store Choice, *Journal of Retailing*, 59, 2, 3-21, 1983.

[MAR 96], Mazloff B., Bellanger F., *Les nouveaux territoires du marketing*, Ed. Liaisons, Paris, 1996.

[MAR 99], Marzloff B., Le Carpentier Th., Parcours et escales: une approche cinétique du consommateur et des lieux, *2ème Colloque Etienne Thil,* Université de La Rochelle, 338-344, 1999.

[MCF 79], McFadden D., Quantitative Methods for Analyzing Travel Behavior of Individuals: Some Recent Developments, in *Behavioral Travel Modelling*, D. A. Hensher and P. R. Stopher eds., Croom Helm, London, 1979.

[MCK 75], McKay D. B., Olshavsky R., Cognitive Maps of Retail Location: An Investigation of Some Basic Issues, *Journal of Consumer Research*, 2, 197-205, 1975.

[MIL 93], Miller H. J., Consumer Search and Retail Analysis, *Journal of Retailing*, 69, 2, 160-92, 1993.

[MOA 01], Moati P., *L'avenir de la grande distribution*, Odile Jacob ed., Paris, 2001.

[MON 75], Monroe K. B., Guiltinan J. P., A Path-Analytic Exploration of Retail Patronage Influences, *Journal of Consumer Research*, 2, 19-28, 1975.

[NAK 74], Nakanishi M., Cooper L. G., Parameter Estimate for Multiplicative Interactive Choice Model: Least Squares Approach, *Journal of Marketing Research*, 11, 303-311, 1974.

[NYS 67], Nystuen J. D, A Theory and Simulation of Intraurban Travel, in *Quantitative geography, Part I: Economic and cultural topics*, W.L. Garrison & D.F. Marble eds., Northwestern University Press, Evanston, Ill., 54-83, 1967.

[OKE 81], O'Kelly M., A Model of Demand for Retail Facilities Incorporating Multistop, Multipurpose Trips, *Geographical Analysis*, 13, 134-148, 1981.

[ORF 01], Orfeuil J.-P., L'évolution de la mobilité quotidienne, *Inrets Synthèse*, 37, 2001.

[PRA 76], Pras B., Echelles d'intervalles à supports sémantiques, *Revue Française du Marketing*, 61, 87-95, 1976.

[RAG 96], Raghubir P., Krishna A., As the Crow Flies: Bias In Consumers' Map-Based Distance Judgments, *Journal of Consumer Research*, 23, 26-39, 1996.

[REC 81], Recker W. W., Schuler H.J., Destination Choice and Processing Spatial Information: Some Empirical Tests with Alternatives Constructs, *Economic Geography*, 57, 373-383, 1981.

[REI 31], Reilly W. J., *The Law of Retail Gravitation*, Knickerbrocker Press, NY, 1931.

[SEV 01], Severin V., Louviere J. J., Finn A., The Stability of Retail Shopping Choices over Time and Across Countries, *Journal of Retailing*, 77, 185-202, 2001.

[SHE 85], Sheldon P. J., Var T., Tourism Forecasting: A Review of Empirical Research, *Journal of Forecasting*, 4, 183-95, 1985.

[SIM 57], Simon H. A., *Models of Man*, John Wiley,NY, 1957.

[SIR 00], Siriex L., L'influence de la recherche de variété sur la fidélité au magasin, in *Etudes et recherches sur la distribution*, P. Volle éd., Economica, Paris, 2000.

[STA 76], Stanley T., Sewal M., Image Inputs to a Probabilistic Model: Predicting Retail Potential, *Journal of marketing*, 40, 48-53, 1976.

[TOR 82], Tordjman A., *Stratégies de concurrence dans le commerce: Les services au consommateur*, Editions d'Organisation, Paris, 1982.

[TSA 32], Tsai L. S., *The Laws of Minimum Effort and Maximum Satisfaction in Animal Behavior*, Monograph of the National Institute of Psychology (Peiping, China), n°1, 1932.

[TVE 74], Tverky A., Kahneman D., Judgment under uncertainty: Heuristics and Biases, *Sciences*, 18, 1124-1131, 1974.

[UNC 96], Uncles M., Classifying Shoppers by Their Shopping Trip Behavior: A Polyethetic-Divisive Method, *Marketing Intelligence and Planning*, 14, 1, 1996.

[VOL 00], Volle P. (2000) Du marketing des points de vente à celui des sites marchands: spécificités, opportunités et questions de recherche, *Revue Française de Marketing*, 177/178, 83-101, 2000.

[WON 99], Wong S., Yang H., Determining Market Areas Captured by Competitive Facilities: A Continuous Equilibrium Modeling Approach, *Journal of Regional Science*, 3, 1, 51-72, 1999.

[ZIP 49], Zipf G. K., *Human Behavior and the Principle of Least Effort*, Addison-Wesley Press Inc., Cambridge, 1949.

Chapter 3

Consumer Values, Lifestyles and Geographic Information

Introduction

For the launch of a new product in Europe, a company hesitates between using visual advertising that differs from one country to another and using the same advertisements and simply translating them. For example, Polaroid, for the launch of an identical camera, presented in the commercial characters, slogans, a context and a tone specific to Germany and Spain, while Lufthansa addressed itself to European businessmen in England and Spain in the same manner, apart from the necessary translation [DUB 94, pp. 174-75]. In the first case, the cultures and values distinct from one country to another were taken into account, while in the second case, the similar lifestyles of a group of individuals, independent of their nationality, were taken into account.

Thus, culture, social and individual values and lifestyles are major marketing concerns for companies in their product marketing strategies. This importance is addressed in a study comparing the French and the Germans [MEN 91]. Table 3.1 shows the cultural nuances and their marketing implications for two dimensions (family and security) taken from the group of dealt with by the author (security, relation to nature, national identity, family, religion, definition of time, hierarchical distance). Thus, since Germans rate risks and protection as important, the advertising must faithfully represent the eventual dangers and new products are adopted only if they have proved themselves.

Chapter written by Valérie CHARRIERE.

Security	
France (Fr)	**(a)** Importance of the objective given to the government, transfer of the responsibility to the government **(b)** Regulation not always respected and can be infringed **(c)** Looking for security, despite a weaker anxiety than in Germany **(d)** Low level of planning except in the long run
Germany (Ger)	**(a)** Cooperation and mutual responsibility (government, companies, individuals) **(b)** Severe norms, warning, punishment, respect of the rules **(c)** Fear of risks, protection **(d)** Strong planning in the long run
Marketing implications	
Advertising	More information in Ger on risks related to the product and on protection (c, d)
Product/ Service	* Higher importance in Ger for product and service conformity, reliability (warranty, maintenance) (b, c), for harmfulness of food products (conservation, sterilization) (c) * In Ger, purchasing goods is considered an investment (durability, resale value) (d) *Higher reluctance in Ger vis-à-vis new not well-tried products (c) * Higher interest in Ger for foresight products (insurance, maintenance) (d, c)
Distribution, sales, negotiation	* Stricter regulation concerning the use of consumer's files and some marketing techniques (direct marketing) in Ger (b, c, a) * Bigger need to trust the retailer and his services (information, advice, after-sale service) (c)
Price, means of payment	* Higher reluctance vis-à-vis credit in Ger (c) * Lack of trust in Ger of all automatic means of payment (c) * Systems and credit cards favored by the government in Fr (a)
	Family
France	**(a)** Wider circle of family **(b)** Importance of public institutions in education: career and motherhood are not contradictory for women and this phenomenon is well accepted by society **(c)** Society based on more "female" values, valorization can be given by a job, but also by the search for happiness and security
Germany	**(a)** Restricted family **(b)** Dominant role of the mother in education; difficulty for women to combine professional and family life, plus guilty conscience **(c)** Society based on more "male" values (ambition, success), hence a feminist movement more developed
Marketing implications	
Advertising	Commercials in Ger show either an image of a woman succeeding in her professional life or an image of a perfect housewife, whereas in Fr they show more often a woman succeeding in her professional and family life (b, c)
Product/ Service	Items in Fr are assimilated into attractive or luxury products, dedicated to women, whereas merchandise in Ger is assimilated into heavy industry and is more famous for its reliability and robustness (d) The packaging corresponds more to a family size in Fr
Distribution, sales,	Shopping as a family is part of social life in Fr (c) Promotions in Fr more often concern quantities of products (a)

Table 3.1: *Cultural nuances and their marketing implications [MEN 91]*

The goal of this chapter is not a review of the literature, in the sense that the presentation of publications is not meant to be exhaustive, but thematic. The measurement instruments implemented in marketing, in the framework of commercial or academic research, will be discussed in order to foster understanding of the cultural phenomena of consumption from diverse geographic points of view. Because there is a vast field of study covered by these diverse themes, neither the convergence of publications in these diverse disciplines nor the statistical techniques used in this type of study will be fully described.

3.1. Values and related concepts

The influence of culture on consumer behavior has long been recognized, as shown not only in the numerous research articles on the subject, but also by the commercial successes experienced in France by the studies produced by marketing companies such as CCA, COFREMCA and RISC.

3.1.1. *Values and culture*

Two individuals from different cultures are characterized by the way and what they eat, the way they dress, in what type of housing they live, the way they speak, how they express their feelings, etc. Behaviors "are in fact nothing more than the concrete manifestation of a group of norms, or prescriptions governing life in society, which themselves come from a system of values expressing, in the form of ideals (individual liberty and equality for example), the purpose of a culture and its desired means of functioning" [DUB 94]. In Figure 3.1, which illustrates the phenomenon, the notions of social values, personal values and lifestyles appear. Social values are characterized as being shared by a group at a given moment, while individual values, as their names imply, are specific to an individual, even if they are influenced by social values.

3.1.2. *Values and lifestyles*

The concept of lifestyle is rather complex owing to its multidisciplinary aspect (psychology, sociology), and to the diversity of methodological approaches adopted by researchers and by research companies. The importance of business applications of the concept of lifestyle is another specificity that can explain the virulence of the debates which have surrounded this concept [FIL 94].

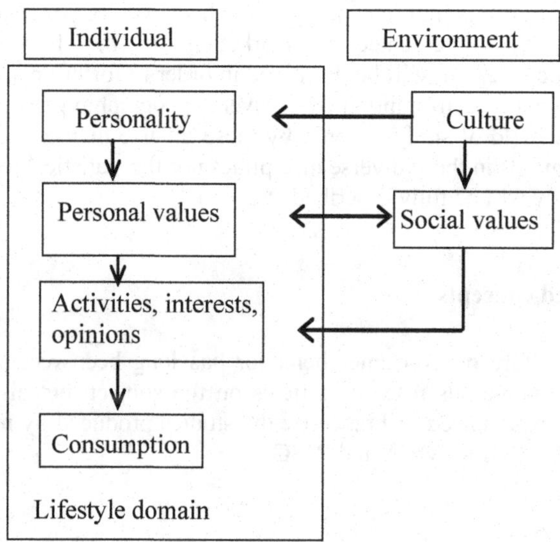

Figure 3.1: *Values, culture and consumption [FIL 94]*

The international literature reveals six lifestyle analysis trends:

1) *personality traits* are studied. However, the inadequacy of personality tests in understanding consumption behaviors has led practitioners no longer to use this type of measure;

2) *personal values* also interest researchers, being at a stable and enduring level of a behavior. The latter thus allow the foundation of long-term marketing decisions;

3) attitudes and activities, now centered on a class of products, now in a more general framework founded on the collection of the *activities, interests and opinions* (AIO) are analyzed. Less stable than the preceding approach, this method is however closer to the act of buying than that of studying values, and therefore more concrete for the manager of a company;

4) a more specifically French trend, developed by companies like the CCA, the COFREMCA and RISC, examines *social values*, and more specifically lifestyles in general, all while integrating AIO-type questions;

5) a basic premise of the lifestyle of a consumer is that it is reflected by the *goods and services bought and used.* This approach consists in examining *a posteriori* the purchases made and consumptions carried out, based on survey or panel data, either on a large group of products or on a specific type of product, like

the liquor market for example. This approach, based on the fact that it is directly connected to the universe of products, is very operational and finds an immediate application in the segmentation of markets, but is not very stable in time. Furthermore, the profiles generated are often limited to only one universe and can therefore not be generalized [DUB 94];

6) among the products that can be studied, the *choice of housing* as a reasoned *act of consumption* is interesting, conditioned by social and financial constraints, and leading to specific usage and purchasing behaviors, thus culminating in geosocial segmentations.

This chapter deal solely with personal or social values and, just like academic or professional research on this subject, is based on three main themes:

– development of a sufficiently exhaustive and universal scale;

– analysis of the connections between these concepts and consumption behaviors;

– study of the issue from a geographic angle (according to countries or regions).

If the academic studies can be adequately categorized according to the three themes thus defined, the research work carried out by marketing companies cannot be developed with the same approach. Because of confidentiality issues, the questionnaires enabling the understanding of the notion of value are not made public and only rather cursory results are presented. Finally, we will tackle the case of geosocial segmentations, where geographic information is integrated at the onset of the development of the measuring instrument.

3.2. Values in marketing

Philosophy, anthropology, sociology, psychology and psycho-sociology have all contributed to defining the notion of values. Around 20 or so measurement instruments have been proposed in order to understand this concept. Two scales, one developed by Rokeach [ROK 73], and the other by Kahle [KHA 86], have frequently been used in marketing. While the first identifies 36 individual and societal values, the second counts only nine, which are essentially oriented towards the person. However, the approaches are on the whole the same, notably for data collection. Because of the cost of international studies and generally for budgetary reasons, a measurement tool is preferred if it is concise. Because of this, in the remainder of this chapter, the work of Kahle will be favored.

More recently, Schwartz and Bilsky [SCH 93] constructed, with an innovative methodology, a nomenclature of values even more complete in order to work within the framework of cross-cultural analyses. Compared to the two inventories previously cited, this list was, from the very beginning, conceived to be used internationally, with a different methodology. Because of its original and high-performing character, it will be described here.

3.2.1. *Value measure instruments*

In constructing his scale, Kahle [KHA 86] selected the following values: sense of belonging; fun and enjoyment in life; warm relationships with others; self-fulfillment; being well respected; excitement; sense of accomplishment; security and self-respect.

In practice, individuals are asked to rank the values according to their importance as life principles, leaving them free to decide for themselves which is most important for them. Another method consists of recording the importance accorded by individuals in the form of Likert scales, considered to facilitate the task of the respondent and allow easier statistical processing: analysis of variance, factor analysis, typology, regression [VAL 94]. As an example (see Table 3.2), a sample of French students noted, on the one hand, each value according to the importance that it takes on in their life on a Likert scale of one to nine (with *one* representing *extremely important* and *nine not important at all*) and, on the other hand, indicated which of the proposed values was the most important for them [VAL 91a].

The lack of exhaustiveness is the principal limitation of this approach. If the 36 values identified by Rokeach barely represent a third of the values spontaneously mentioned by individuals [JON 78], the Kahle inventory supports this critique even more strongly. Thus, Schwartz and Bilsky [SCH 93], in the framework of international studies, combine and extend these two scales to form the list presented in Table 3.3.

These values are structured in domains of motivation resulting in goals that are aimed at. At the beginning of their research, the authors counted seven domains. Since then the number has been raised by studying more countries:

– power: social status and prestige, control or dominance over people and resources;

– achievement: personal success through demonstrating competence according to social standards;

– hedonism: pleasure and sensuous gratification for oneself;

– stimulation: excitement, novelty, and challenge in life;

– self-direction: independent thought and action – choosing, creating, exploring;

– universalism: understanding, appreciation, tolerance and protection for the welfare of all people and for nature;

– benevolence: preservation and enhancement of the welfare of people with whom one is in frequent personal contact;

– tradition: respect, commitment and acceptance of the customs and ideas that traditional culture or religion provide to the self;

– conformity: restraint of actions, inclinations, and impulses likely to upset or harm others and violate social expectations or norms;

– security: safety, harmony and stability of society, of relationships, and of self.

	Means scores	Frequency of value most important (%)
Sense of belonging	5.58	1.0
Fun and enjoyment in life	2.16	19.2
Warm relationships with others	2.27	12.1
Self-fulfillment	2.05	41.4
Being well respected	3.27	3.0
Excitement	4.90	0.0
Sense of accomplishment	2.82	15.2
Security	4.58	3.0
Self-respect	3.21	5.1

Table 3.2: *Khale's list for Germany [VAL 91a]*

In theory, the simultaneous search for several variables can be incompatible if they coincide with conceptually opposed domains. Thus, the search for values corresponding to benevolence and achievement is contradictory. Preoccupying oneself with others would interfere, in the author's opinion, with the obtaining of personal success.

Equality	Inner harmony	Social power
Pleasure	Freedom	A spiritual life
Sense of belonging	Social order	An exciting life
Meaning of life	Politeness	Wealth
National security	Reciprocation of favors	Self-respect
A world at peace	Respect of tradition	Creativity
Mature love	Self-discipline	Detachment
Family security	Social recognition	Unity with nature
Successful	A varied life	Wisdom
Authority	True friendship	A world of beauty
Social justice	Independent	Moderate
Loyal	Amibitious	Broadminded
Humble	Protecting the environment	Daring
Protecting	Honoring parents and elders	Influential
Choosing own goals	Healthy	Capable
Intelligent	Accepting my portion in life	Honest
Enjoying life	Preserving my public image	Helpful
Responsible	Curious	Devout
Forgiving	Clean	

Table 3.3: *Schwartz's list [SCH 87]*

Figure 3.2 is the representation of the structural links between the motivation domains, obtained by projecting in a two-dimensional spatial representation of the inter-correlation among all the values. These correlations are measured on a Likert scale, for it is not possible for an individual to rank 50 items in order of importance. The opposition between benevolence and achievement is verified in Figure 3.2.

Although these tools, developed by different researchers [KHA 83, ROK 73, SCH 90] can be criticized, they have been widely used to explain consumption behaviors.

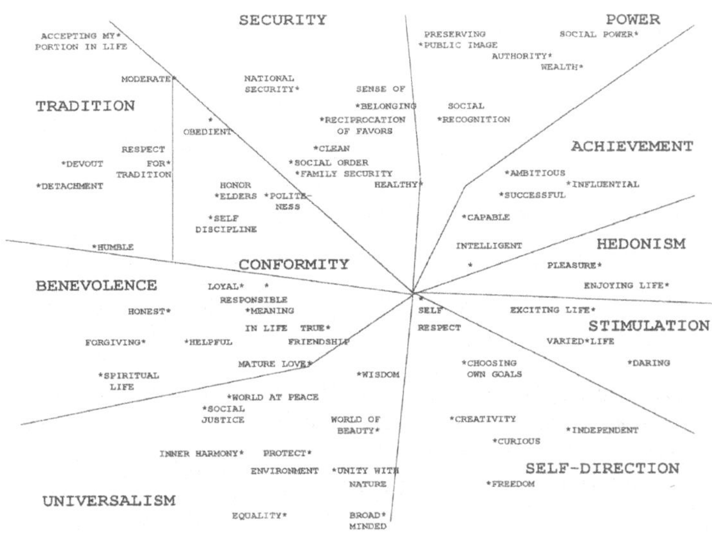

Figure 3.2: *Value structure [SCH 87]*

3.2.2. *Applications to consumer behaviors*

In addition to measurement instruments, several other approaches have been used to show the links between values and behaviors.

Quantitative approach

Based on surveys of rather large sample groups, researchers have measured the adherence to the values, then their attitudes or directly their consumption *vis-à-vis* a product. Kamakura [KAM 93] highlighted the importance for the manager of analyzing the predictive powers of systems of complete values, rather than those of values taken specifically one by one. The projects generally consist in constructing factors that regroup the values via multivariate methods of first (ACP or ACM) or second generation (model of structural equations), then testing the influence of one or several values (via factors) on consumption behaviors by linear regression, discrete choice models (logit type) or PLS models.

Thus, numerous marketing publications have highlighted the connections between values, identified by the measure instruments of Rokeach or Kahle, and the behaviors *vis-à-vis* products, distribution, communication and price. Studies have concerned products with high or low involvement, such as cars, travel, cigarettes, deodorants, table oils, media, etc. Certain authors [ROE 89] have shown the influence of the values on mediatory variables, such as involvement or innovation, in order to characterize diverse types of innovative behavior, for example *vis-à-vis* perfumes.

The Schwartz inventory has allowed the prediction of consumption behaviors, notably *vis-à-vis* the media [ODI 96]. Thus, more than 2,000 people evaluated the list of values based on a Likert scale, and then answered the following questions:

– Do you regularly read a daily newspaper? 0 = no, 1 = yes;

– What television channel do you most often watch? 0 = TF1, 1 = France 2;

– How many hours of television do you watch each day? 1 = less than an hour, ..., 6 = more than 5 hours.

The first two questions are nominal, while the last is considered continuous. First, a confirmatory factor analysis based on values was realized on each of the motivational domains identified by Schwartz. Then logistic regressions (for the two questions on attitudes) and a linear regression (for consumption) were carried out with the factor scores calculated in the first stage as independent variables. By way of illustration, Table 3.4 shows the coefficients (and their associated student t values) of some domains of motivation (among the 11) in the statistical processing mentioned above. Finally, the rates of ranking, χ^2 for the logistic regressions, the R^2 and the Fisher test for the linear regression are obtained while taking the entirety of the domains of motivation into account.

As can be seen from this study, the explicative powers are rather weak, whether on the basis of the R^2 or even the rates of ranking, which are slightly better than those obtained simply by chance. Researchers have therefore attempted to develop other, more efficient qualitative approaches, such as means–ends chains.

	Logistic regression		Linear regression
	Reading daily	TV	Spent time
Conformity	Non-significant (Ns)	Ns	Ns
Achievement	–0.279 (2.846**)	–0.457(–3.447**)	Ns
Security	Ns	–0.384(–2.810**)	Ns
Tradition	Ns	Ns	0.1237(2.93**)
Rates of ranking	58.24	60.49	
** significance level 95%	$\chi^2(11) = 73.694$**	$\chi^2(11) = 80.992$**	$R^2 = 0.081$ F10,1758 = 15.581**

Table 3.4: *Some regression results [ODI 96]*

Qualitative analysis

In fact, products are rarely associated with values. The values are more often connected to the attributes of a product, which themselves are linked to the consequences. These consequences are, however, directly related to values. A qualitative approach, called means–ends chains, tries to explain the connections between the products purchased and the values of the consumer. Through individual interviews, researchers retrace the progression that exists between the attributes (abstract or concrete) of a product, the functional or psycho-sociological consequences that it satisfies and the values: attributes – consequences – values. Figure 3.3 shows the hierarchical map of values for coffee, with the attributes in bold, the consequences in ordinary type, and the values in italics [GUT 86].

Energising → to stimulate → to feel better → to do more, to turn towards → achievement → *self esteem*

Figure 3.3: *Means–end chain analysis of coffee purchases [GUT 86]*

The connections can be much more complicated and be applied to products with more implications. Thus, Figure 3.4 gives an example for the purchase of perfume by German consumers.

Limited by the qualitative character of this approach, Valette-Florence [VAL 91] and Aurifeille [AUR 92a, AUR 92b] proposed a more quantitative method combining the theory of graphs (for the automated construction of hierarchical maps) and multiple correspondence analysis, resulting in a mapping representation of different component elements of chaining. Based on the spatial coordinates, a constrained typology of consumers is realized. This approach has been used for the purchase of perfume in Europe [VAL 91]. Figure 3.5 shows the multiple correspondence analyses with the attributes, the consequences and the values as active variables, while the countries and the four specific types of consumers (A, B, C, D) are illustrative.

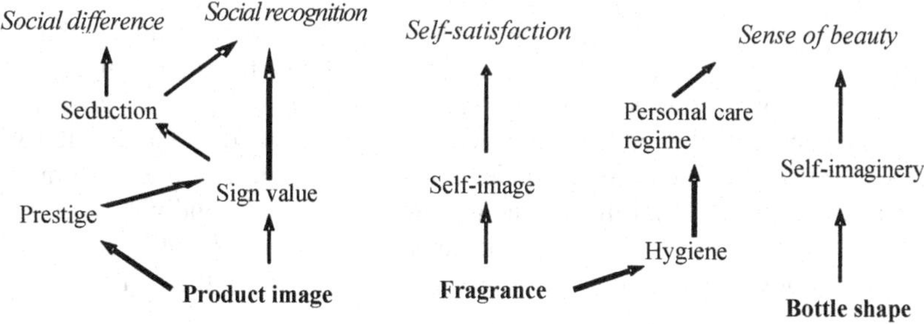

Figure 3.4: *Means–end chain analysis of perfume purchases [VAL 91b]. The arrows size shows the frequency of the means–end chain: the heavier the arrow, more the link is often evoked by the population*

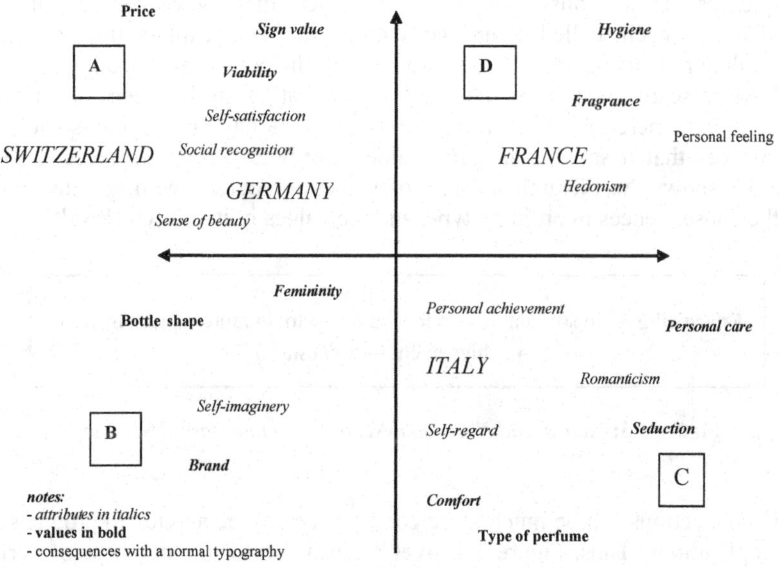

Figure 3.5: *Consumption of perfume in four European countries [VAL 94]*
A,..., D are four specific types of consumer

Another method, the APT (association pattern technique), consists of questioning consumers about the connection existing between attributes and benefits looked for, and then asking them to evaluate the connections between benefits and values. Through successive modeling, the two responses can be merged. Table 3.5 presents an extract of the chaining between the attributes of a yoghurt (high or low price, low-fat product, mild yoghurt, organically produced yoghurt, individual packaging, biobifidus yoghurt, with fruit) and Kale's values. A first grid, with the attributes in rows and the benefits in columns (convenient to use, choice for each member of the family, good for digestion, etc.) is submitted to the interviewee. The interviewee indicates for each column, whether the benefit is perceived to be associated with each product attribute. Then the respondent fills a second grid in the same manner with the benefits in rows and the values in columns. Thus the individual indicates for each column whether the value is perceived as associated with each benefit. Finally, the responses to these two questions are merged with methods [HOF 99].

Benefits→	Good quality	Good taste	Good if you are on a diet	Convenient to use
Attributes				
High-priced yoghurt				
Low-fat yoghurt				
Low-price yoghurt				
Mild yoghurt				
Values→	Excitement	Security	Self-respect	Sense of belonging
Benefits				
Good quality				
Good taste				
Good if you are on a diet				
Convenient to use				

Table 3.5: *Extract of association pattern technique on yoghurt [HOF 99]*

These means–ends chains, which seem *a priori* more complicated to implement, have predictive powers on consumption behaviors that are twice as good as those estimated via classical approaches centered solely on the values explained above [AUR 92b].

These analyses, quantitative or qualitative, have also been carried out in international and regional contexts. The research has consisted of examining the external validity of the studies realized within the national framework and either developing a sound basis for statistical processing of international studies or establishing new approaches.

3.3. Geographic analysis of values

Values have also been examined from a geographic angle. The goal of research is to demonstrate cultural differences in diverse geographic areas. In addition to the measurement instruments, the statistical methods and the geographical divisions change according to the perspective of the research.

3.3.1. *From an international point of view*

Researchers study the mean scores of values, the instability of the linkage values or the predictive powers of values concerning consumption in an international context.

High or low mean scores

The inventories produced by Rokeach and Kahle have helped to develop understanding of the cultural specificities of several countries: Australia, New Guinea, Israel, Thailand, Mexico, the United States, Vietnam, India, Great Britain, Bangladesh, Hong Kong, Japan, Malaysia, New Zealand, Taiwan, France and Germany. More descriptive than explicatory, these works show the high or low mean score of one or several values for a particular country. Table 3.6 gives the results of a study carried out in France and Germany dealing with students and their parents [VAL 91a]. The subjects were asked to evaluate the values identified by Kahle, on a Likert scale (1 = completely agree, 9 = completely disagree).

	Mean scores				Observed significance level (Test F Manova)	
	France		Germany		Country	Generation
	Students	Parents	Students	Parents		
Sense of belonging	5.58	5.38	2.49	2.35	0.00	0.26
Fun and enjoyment in life	2.16	3.61	3.56	5.70	0.00	0.00
Warm relationships with others	2.27	2.15	2.55	3.56	0.00	0.00
Self-fulfillment	2.05	2.53	2.51	3.18	0.00	0.00
Being well respected	3.27	3.56	3.21	3.57	0.84	0.09
Excitement	4.90	6.23	4.23	7.00	0.95	0.00
Sense of accomplishment	2.82	2.89	3.12	3.08	0.16	0.89
Security	4.58	3.55	3.76	2.71	0.00	0.00
Self-respect	3.21	2.76	2.08	2.26	0.00	0.38

Table 3.6: *Values of two generations in different countries [VAL 91a]*

First, the mean scores of the French and the German subjects were compared, and then those of the students and their parents. Based on Table 3.6, significant differences (with the exception of accomplishment) can be seen both between the cultures (notably concerning the sense of belonging, warm relationships) and between generations (concerning the need for excitement).

Other authors work with factors based on regrouping several variables. Kamakura [KAM 93] studied the distribution of certain factors in three countries (the United Kingdom, Italy, Germany) and their regions, dealing with 1.573 people. Each individual was asked to rank the items in the Rokeach list in order of importance. Based on a cluster wise rank-logit model, the author obtained five segments of the population attracted respectively towards values representing maturity, security, amusement, autonomy and conformity.

Segments	United Kingdom (%)	Italy (%)	Germany (%)	Total (%)
Maturity	7.6	2.6	30.3	14.4
Security	5.9	1.1	47.3	19.8
Enjoyment	53.8	8.8	7.5	20.8
Autonomy	15.8	40.8	7.6	21.4
Conformity	16.9	46.9	7.3	23.6
	100	100	100	100

Table 3.7: *Values in four European countries [KAM 93]*

Instability of linkages between values

In practice, researchers wonder, when they work with factors based on the regrouping of several variables, if there are similar structures in the factors for each country, if the number of selected factors is the same, if the factorial rotations are carried out with the same angles, etc. [GRU 93]. From a conceptual point of view, Schwartz [SCH 93] wonders about the stability of the connections between values. In Germany, Israel, Australia, the United States, Hong Kong, Spain and Finland, the compatibilities and incompatibilities of the domains were not found to be stable from one country to the next. The existence of conflict between success and harmonious social relations is not universal and nor even is the belief that friction should exist between the search for one's own pleasure and comfort and devotion to others. For example, the domains of enjoyment, achievement and autonomy contribute to individual interests, while prosocial, restrictive conformity and security are collective interests, and the values linked to maturity bring together the two types of interest. Based on this finding, in the two-dimensional geometric representation, via projections, the three individualistic domains should be contiguous, while the three other collectives should also be adjacent, although in another part of the graph, with maturity at the border between these two regions. Figure 3.6 shows the structural links between motivation domains relating to values taken from smallest spaces analysis (SSA) in two countries. In Finland, maturity is situated between autonomy and achievement, not at the boundary between the collective and the individual.

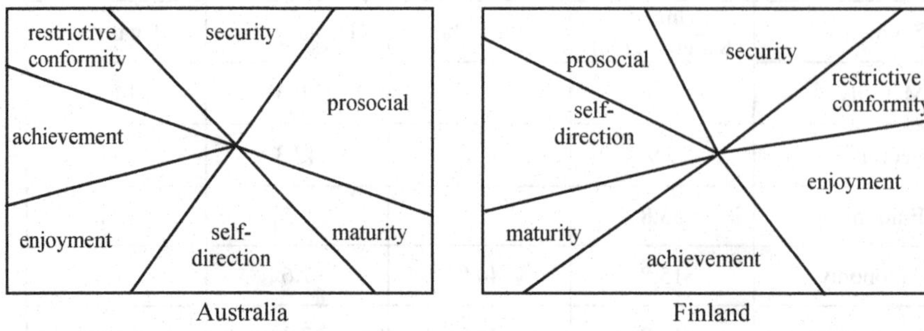

Figure 3.6: *Projections of interests served and motivational domains facets of values from smallest space analysis in two countries [SCHW 93]*

Furthermore, Schwartz remarks that values do not belong to the same domain from one country to the next. For example, being logical appears in the domain of achievement in Spain and in Finland, while for other nations logic is synonymous with the ability to make a decision for oneself, and therefore with independence. For a certain number of values, Table 3.8 shows the difference between the expected and the observed locations in certain countries.

Value	**Predicted location**	**Observed location**
A sense of accomplishment	ACH or SD	MAT (Spain), ENJ (Finland)
Freedom	SD or SEC	ACH (Hong Kong), MAT (Spain)
Mature love	MAT	SEC (Hong Kong)
National security	SEC	RS (Australia, Spain)
Self-respect	MAT or SD	ACH (Australia)
True friendship	PS or SEC	MAT (Israel)
Capable	ACH	PS (Germany)
Cheerful	ENJ	MAT (Finland)
Clean	RS	PS (Hong Kong)
Courageous	MAT	SD (Finland)
Honest	PS	SEC (Australia)
Logical	SD	ACH (Spain, Finland)
Loving	PS	SD (Germany)
Responsible	SEC or RS	PS (Finland)
Self-controlled	RS	SEC (United States), ENJ (Finland)
PS = prosocial, RS = restrictive conformity, ENJ = enjoyment, ACH = achievement, MAT = maturity, SD = self-direction, SEC = security		

Table 3.8: *Predicted and observed locations of values in motivational domains [SCH 93]*

The approach proposed by Schwartz [SCH 93] is the only academic research that, from its conception, is directed towards the international scene and towards cross-cultural applications [VAL 94].

Instability of the connections between value chains and consumption behaviors

One type of study consists of verifying the homological validity of research carried out in a national framework. If the results of a study in a particular country have shown the explicative power of a value or of a group of values concerning consumption behaviors (via regressions or PLS models), the same methodology is then applied in another country in order to verify the conclusions.

Other analyses proceed differently. The examination of the connections between consumption values and behaviors can be carried out simultaneously in several different countries. General conclusions are drawn, and then the researcher examines the cultural nuances of the results. The example of the chain relating to perfume purchases can be used as an example (see Figure 3.5). More recently, for a lower-involvement product, Valette-Florence [VAL 99] studied fish consumption preferences in France and Denmark[1]. During individual interviews (85 in Denmark and 96 in France), people were asked to rank four types of fish (fresh salt-water fish, fresh fresh-water fish, frozen fillet, frozen breaded), to choose the attributes they deemed most important, and then compare consequences and values. After a non-linear generalized canonical analysis of the data, seven chains explaining the choice or rejection of a certain type of fish had appeared. A brief summary of this can be seen in Table 3.9. The distribution changes from one country to the other. Thus the first group represents 26.5% of the overall sample, and concerns 31.3% of the French interviewees, but only 21.2% of the Danes.

Using the APT [HOF 99], a study concerning the linkages between the desired attributes or rejection of a yoghurt and the Kahle value survey identified four segments of consumption (S1, S2, S3, S4) with, for some of these, marked national specificities. Table 3.10 gives the distribution in different European countries.

1. Denmark is the world's third largest fish exporter, with lower per capita fish consumption than France.

Chain	Attributes	Consequences	Values	% respondents	% in France	% in Denmark
1. Variety seeking	Can be prepared in many different ways	Exciting to prepare	Happiness and well-being	26.5	31.3	21.2
2. Dislike	Poor taste and texture	Do not like eating it	Happiness and well-being	3.3	6.3	
3. Lack of experience	Am not used to the product	Difficult to make a delicious dish from it	Good health and a long life	23.2	43.8	
4. Freshness/ nature	Is fresh	Enjoy family meal	Inner harmony	1.1	2.1	
5. Lack of convenience	To be bought at the fishmonger's/ it contains bones	Is time-consuming	Family's quality of life	13.8	5.2	23.5
6. Taste	Good and nourishing	Wholesomeness and physical well-being/ sense of good mood	Happiness and well-being	30.4	10.4	52.6
7. Price	Is expensive	Tight budget/ avoid waste	Good conscience	1.7	1.0	2.4

Table 3.9: *Means–ends solutions for fish consumption [VAL 94]*

Country	**S1**	**S2**	**S3**	**S4**	Country	**S1**	**S2**	**S3**	**S4**
Belgium	12.2	17.5	8.5	61.8	Netherlands	31.5	14.3	17.9	36.3
Denmark	47.6	2.6	27	22.8	Portugal	35.2	27.8	4.9	32.1
France	2.4	21.8	3.3	72.4	Spain	25.1	8.5	3.8	62.6
Germany	3.2	45.1	26.3	25.4	Ireland	40.6	12.1	17.9	29.5
Great Britain	41.2	7	26	25.9	Italy	5.9	10.2	5.1	78.8
Greece	28.2	13.4	6.5	52	Total	17.4	20.9	15.8	46

Table 3.10: *Means–ends chains for yoghurt in different countries [HOF 99]*

3.3.2. *A regional point of view*

Regional academic studies are much less numerous than analyses realized in one or several countries. However, the issues are the same, mean score values and the instability of consumption value–behavior connections; only the geographic divisions change.

High or low mean scores

Marketing studies began by researching administrative or physical divisions before looking at other types of spaces identified by the economic or social geography, such as cities, rural areas and regions in recession. The distribution of values in North America was thus studied according to three divisions [KHA 86]. More than 2,000 people from all over North America indicated that one of the items presented in the study was the most important (Table 3.11). For two of the three geographic segmentations, significant links (tested via Chi-squared) between values and regions appeared. Thus, in the Midwest, "security", for example, is chosen more often, while in the West, "self-respect" is favored. On the other hand, in the Midwest "amusement" is the value more frequently selected, while in the West it is "to be respected".

Values in %	East	Midwest	South	West	*N*
Self-respect	19.7	19.1	23.4	21.6	471
Security	18.9	21.6	22.0	18.4	461
Warm relationship with others	16.0	17.8	14.5	17.1	362
Scenes of accomplishment	13.2	12.5	9.2	11.4	254
Self-fulfillment	9.5	9.0	8.1	13.5	214
Being well-respected	8	9.1	11.6	3.6	196
Sense of belonging	8.4	7.3	8.0	8.3	177
Fun–enjoyment–excitement	6.3	3.3	3.4	6.2	100
Total	100	100	100	100	
N	476	634	740	385	2,235
$\chi^2(21) = 50.50$, $p = 0.0003$					

Table 3.11: *Distribution of values across regions of the United States [KHA 86]*

The stability of values, also based on administrative divisions, was studied in East and West Germany [JOS 97]. The interviewees were first asked to indicate the importance that they accorded a certain number of values before the fall of the Berlin Wall, in 1985, in 1989 and at the time of the study. The research showed that a certain number of these values ("a passionate life", "a search for harmony", "family", "individual responsibility", "sense of accomplishment", "self-discipline", "honesty", "security") appear more stable in the East than in the West. After studying values present in three nations, Kamakura [KAM 93] examined regions in each country more precisely. He showed that the regions behave like the country of which they are a part. Thus, the regions of Great Britain are attracted by the "amusement" segment, German regions by "maturity" and "security"; and the Italian provinces by "autonomy" and "compliance." However, differences within certain countries could be observed. "Cleanliness", "obedience" and "politeness" are less important in the capital than in the rest of Great Britain. On the other hand, Londoners accord more importance to pleasure, to a comfortable life and to ambition. The people interviewed in Tuscany are more inclined to compliance than the rest of the country, while the people interviewed in Lombardy are oriented more towards independence. By using a division borrowed from economic geography, the cultural differences between rural and urban people in Germany were analyzed based on the values proposed by Kahle, and evaluated on a Likert scale [SCH 91]. Testing the equality of the means between these two populations indicated only one significant difference, in the importance accorded to "security". With the same methodology, values such as "security", "family" and "personal development" have higher or lower mean scores in French rural areas, working-class neighborhoods, and French recession regions, this time based on elements of social geography [CHA 98].

Instability of links between values

Charrière [CHA 98] shows that, while values may have neither high nor low mean scores, they can simply have connotations that are different from one region to another but of equivalent importance. If friendship is an important notion for everyone, what this means varies from one social class to another. Thus, in the working-class and therefore in working-class neighborhoods, friendship manifests itself in a non-market economy where material mutual aid is important: one helps a friend move or repaints his apartment for free, or one graciously distributes part of one's garden's produce. In wealthier classes, and therefore in more affluent neighborhoods, a friend is someone to whom one can tell all, someone who understands you, someone with whom one can talk about anything, with whom one shares an intellectual complicity.

Values	Regional connotations	Rural area	Urban area	Working-class neighborhoods	Area in recession
Sense of belonging	Local belonging	X			X
	Familial belonging	X		X	
	Social class belonging		X		
Friendship	Free material mutual aid			X	
	Egalitarian world				X
	Intellectual support		X		
Self-respect	Respect of rules and good manners	X		X	
	Self-regulation		X		
	Research of the social status				X
"X" means that, in this area, there is a regional connotation for this specific value					

Table 3.12: *Value connotations in different areas [CHA 98]*

The Rokeach [ROK 73], Kahle [KHA 86] and Schwartz [SCH 93] inventories have been examined by Charrière [CHA 98] in terms of different types of geographic spaces: cities, rural areas, working-class neighborhoods, and regions in recession. After carrying out surveys, with a sample of 800 people, and integrating the classical instruments measured on Likert scales, the author tested for the existence of connotations, via logit regressions. Table 3.12 gives three values among those studied, in which the reality of these regional evocations has been statistically demonstrated.

A "sense of belonging" can be local, cantonal or national, global or social depending on whether one lives in a rural town or in the Parisian region, whether one comes from a working-class background or from a more affluent milieu [BRE 00]. Because of this, the predictive powers of values on consumption behaviors vary from one region to another. For example, the more an individual places importance on the "sense of belonging" in a region where this value has the connotation "sense of regional belonging", the more this individual will tend to read the regional press. On the other hand, the sense of belonging, treated globally and at a national level, has a very weak predictive power on the reading of the regional press [CHA 98]. It should therefore be noted that most research deals with cultural phenomena based on differences between countries, contrasting the national cultures (the values of the French compared to those of the Spanish). However, different regional behaviors exist inside particular countries, while homogeneous behaviors can cross over borders. Todd [TOD 90] reminds us that family structures greatly condition economic attitudes and behaviors and describes four family types (see Figure 3.7).

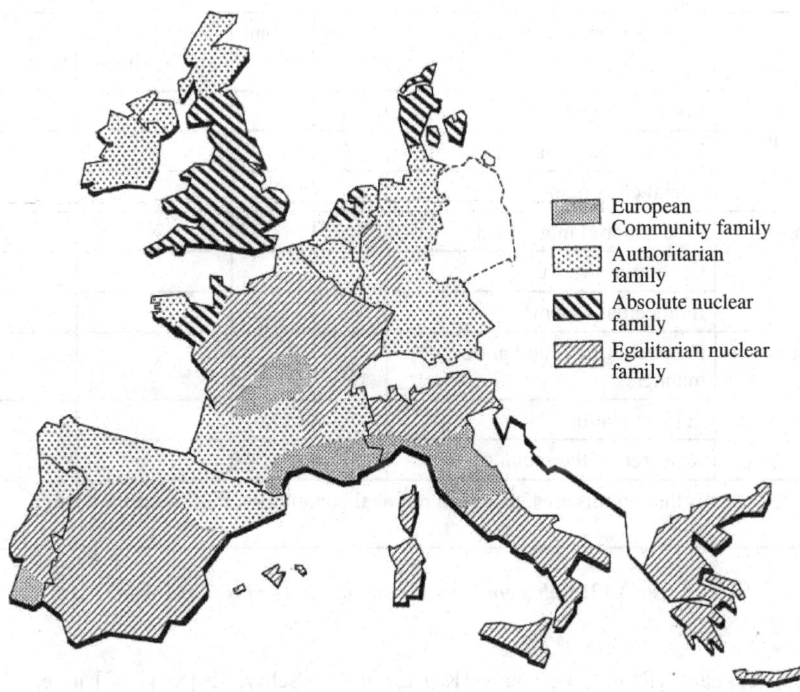

Figure 3.7: *Different types of families in Europe [TOD 90]: Type 1 European Community family; Type 2 Authoritarian family; Type 3 Absolute nuclear family; Type 4 Egalitarian nuclear family*

Although interesting, this analysis has had no application in marketing. Dubois [DUB 94] speaks of quasi-virgin territory in the subject of European studies on consumer values. For him, "this research should be carried out […] on bases other than national territories. It could, for example, take on identifying the existing sub-cultures at the heart of a country as well as the existing similarities between the cultures coming from different countries." However, certain research companies have realized other cultural and national divisions. Pinet[2] [PIN 90] thinks that the Europe of consumers should be a map of Europe defined based on proximities in their consumptions, insisting on the fact that the French population in regions bordering Germany displays a behavior much closer to that of Germans on the west of the Rhine than to that of Bretons.

2 CEO of the SECODIP company.

3.4. Values and lifestyles examined by research companies

Marketing companies have developed a certain number of tools that highlight the links between consumer behavior and values, socio-cultural trends, or lifestyles (with as many names as there are companies). Amongst the most well known, the American approaches of Yankelovitch [YAN 71] and Mitchell [MIT 81] work from a list of questions and then carry out factor analyses leading to typologies. This American work influenced the French approaches (by CCA, RISC, COFREMCA, etc.) at the beginnings. Since then, however, these French studies have been more widespread and will therefore be favored throughout the rest of this discussion. It will not be possible to present them in detail, for reasons of confidentiality. Nevertheless, in general, brief conclusions about completed studies can be obtained without exact knowledge of the constitution of the samples, the questions asked or the statistical processing. Furthermore, certain companies have not published results for the past 15 or 20 years. Finally, most of the studies can be identified in the cross-cultural framework, while all remain within national borders. A choice should therefore take place in the presentation of these different companies and this has been guided by the following criteria: the accessibility of results, the date of publication of results, and the innovative character of the approach. Because of this, only the CCA and RISC approaches will be examined. It is possible to refer to publications concerning them in 1994. On the other hand, the approach taken by the CCA, which has been greatly commercialized, was marked by its originality in taking regions into account. Despite the relatively classic nature of their approaches, the studies carried out by RISC continue to be sold to manufacturers and also deserve mention. Naturally, this presentation of values and lifestyles is succinct; ideally, the concept of lifestyles should be developed further in order to give a better analysis of the problem. Finally, the geographic segmentations developed by research companies that connect housing zones with lifestyles and values will be considered. Here again, a choice must take place among the set of available commercial provisions on the market. The same criteria have been retained: availability of results and recent original publications on the approaches taken. On the basis of these criteria, the Experian Company will be given most attention.

3.4.1. *The Eurosociostyles of the CCA*

The CCA chose an ambitious analysis, which consisted of creating a typology taking into account the 15 European countries and their regions via studies based on activities, interests, opinions and values. After having carried out multidimensional analyses based on the responses, 16 groups, called Eurosociostyles, were constructed based on factorial coordinates. Figure 3.8 gives the position, in the first factorial plane, of the 16 types, with a brief description. This company revealed links that exist between these different groups of individuals and their consumption behaviors. In 1991, during a European study on the health strategies of 14,000 people, it emerged that:

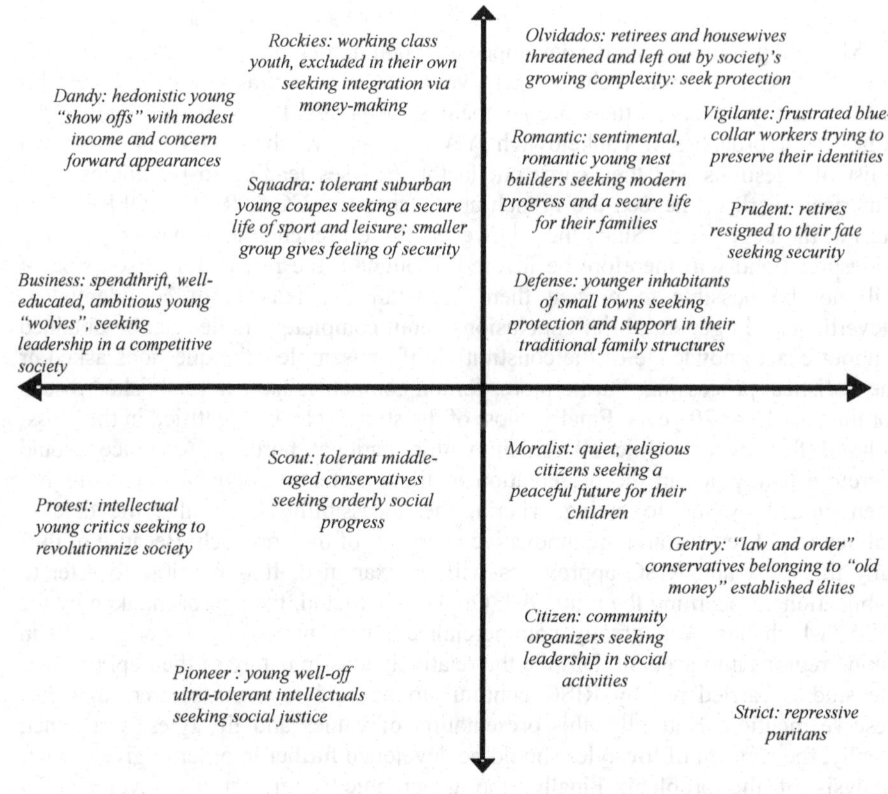

Figure 3.8: *Eurosociostyles [CCA 90]*

– the *Dandy, Rocky, Business* and *Protest* styles are more concerned with fitness than health and prefer self-medication; the pharmacist is the favored interlocutor;

– the *Romantic* and *Squadra* are very attached to their health, take the advice of the medical profession and are very open to all sorts of treatment;

– the *Olvidados, Vigilante, Prudent* and *Defense* have confidence in the medical profession and rely on traditional treatments;

– the *Moralist, Gentry* and *Strict* are over-informed and simply apply medical prescriptions and resort at times to herbal medicines;

– the *Scout, Pioneer* and *Citizen* are very motivated by fitness, open to innovation and all types of medicines and are large consumers of herbal medicines.

This typology has also been used to explain lower-involvement consumption behaviors [CAT 94]. Table 3.13 shows different consumption indexes for 17 Eurosociostyles (the Rocky type was divided into Rocky Opportunist and Rocky

Ego), with indexes over 100 in bold type. These Eurosociostyles were grouped into six broad mentalities (see Table 3.14). The CCA also analyzed the lifestyles and mentalities at the regional level. The distribution of the six mentalities changes from one country to the next and from one region to the other. Table 3.15 gives the distributions in the different provinces of Germany and Belgium.

	Coca-Cola	Textile buyers by mail-order	Public of weekly news TV program
Rocky Opportuniste Rocky Ego	**122** **112**	75 98	88 88
Dandy	**156**	83	55
Business	**144**	83	71
Squadra	**106**	**129**	80
Protest	**112**	67	**110**
Scout	**125**	96	105
Pioneer	**123**	60	**110**
Olvidados	64	**171**	87
Romantic	98	**175**	75
Vigilante	74	**120**	97
Prudent	57	**139**	75
Defense	86	84	91
Moralist	60	**114**	**150**
Gentry/Strict	60	82	**145**
Citizen	79	68	**146**

Table 3.13: *Consumption by Eurosociostyles [CAT 94]*

For each country and for each family, the difference between the national and regional percentage was calculated, thus allowing comparable groups of regions in terms of values to be shown. Regions more conservative than the national average emerged, while others more liberal than the average crossed borders. Altogether, seven groups of regions were revealed (see Figure 3.9). This gives the CCA approach its originality, for it is no longer bound to the national framework. Region type number 1 is rather traditional and deals with rural regions or places that have suffered rural depopulation and/or economic crises: Midlands (GB), Abruzzi (IT), Sur (SP), Connaught Ulster (IRE). Unfortunately, these studies have never been commercialized because of a lack of manufacturer interest. The CCA has since stopped its analyses dealing with Eurosociostyles. For Ladet [LAD 94], "although marketing practices require increasingly localized information, strategic reflection has become worldwide, including for the small business (…). Although most think of supply and production in a global manner, few groups possess a centralized global management of consumer studies, which severely limits the real impact of such an information system, so necessary however in appreciating the weight of intercultural influences on the one hand, and the degree of convergence of the motivations and the cultures of consumption on the other." In fact, most international companies have commercial divisions structured by country, with national sales objectives to meet, and not by trans-border regions. On the same token, distributors are still organized by country. However, it is through these economic players in the market that requests for studies can change. A retail chain in Belgium might want to attract French customers with certain products reputed to be less expensive (CD or DVD) in Belgium. With the common currency of the Euro, price comparison from one country to the next should lead distributors to request studies that go beyond national frameworks.

Eurosociostyles	Mentality	% in Europe	% in France
Dandy, Rockies, Business	Ambitious (M1)	25	29
Squadra, Romantic	Dreamer (M2)	15	9
Olvidados, Vigilante, Prudent, Defense	Withdrawn (M3)	23.2	25
Protest, Pionnier	Contestor (M4)	8.4	8
Scout, Citizen	Militant (M5)	10.8	18
Moralist, Gentry, Strict	Notable (M6)	17.6	25

Table 3.14: *Six mentalities in Europe and in France*

	M1	M2	M3	M4	M5	M6		M1	M2	M3	M4	M5	M6
Belgium	32.1	8.2	23.8	8.3	9.3	18.2	Germany	22.5	17.6	24.8	9.9	6.9	18.2
West–Oost Vlandereen	30.8	10.4	23.5	7.7	5.9	22.3	RH–PF/Saarland/Hessen	18.4	21.2	28.5	9	6.7	16.3
Antwerpen–Limburg–Vlaams Brabant	35.4	9	23.3	7	7.4	17.9	Nordrhein–Westfallen	23.3	18.6	22.2	10.8	7.3	17.5
Brussel	27.8	3.5	23.1	14.9	12.6	18.2	Nord	23	16.4	25.9	8.9	6.6	19.1
Henegouwen–Walls Brabant	27.4	8.1	23.2	8	14.6	18.8	Baden–Wurtenberg	21.1	15.4	24.7	12.3	7.1	19.5
Luik–Namen–Luxembourg	34.3	6.3	27.2	8.7	11.7	11.8	Bayern	25.3	17.3	22.9	8.3	6.6	19.5
							Berlin	24.4	9.9	31.1	11.1	8.4	15.1

Table 3.15: *Distributions of mentalities for the different provinces in Germany and Belgium [CCA, internal communication]. All figures are percentages*

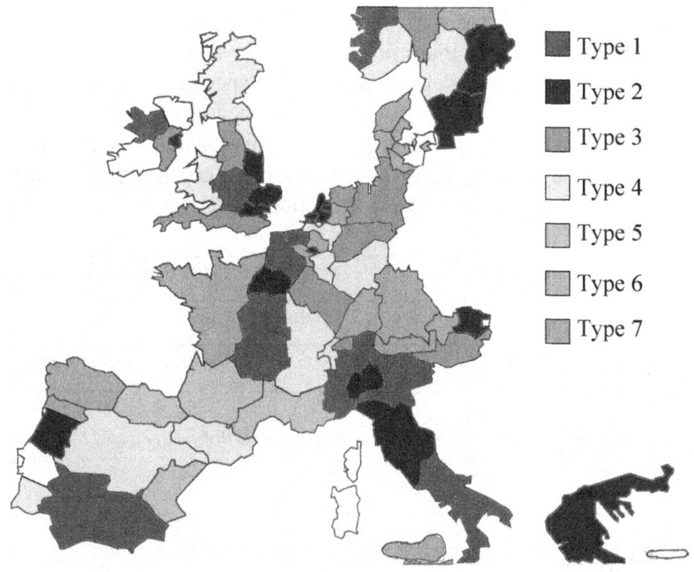

Figure 3.9: *Geographical distribution of different regional types in Europe [CCA, internal communication]*

3.4.2. *The RISC approach*

The RISC and CCA approaches are essentially the same: administering rather long questionnaires covering a broad range of subjects followed by multidimensional data analysis. However, the RISC company prefers staying at the factorial axes level and refuses to resort to typologies said to be too "reductionist." Based on 110 questions tested at the European level (12 countries), the company counts nine "great socio-dynamic forces" [LAD 94]. After a factor analysis on values, the scatter plot of the interviewees' projections presents itself in the form of a diamond. The upper part (A) symbolizes the driving force of change and concerns 26% of Europeans, generally well educated and well paid, attracted by trans-nationality, ethics and hedonism. The lower part (C) represents 34% of Europeans, who resist change and are rather immobile with local horizons. Finally, 41% of Europeans, integrating change, situate themselves in the intermediary zone of transition between the two other segments (B).

This division of the population into three groups is applied to the universe of consumption. Thus, Ladet [LAD 94] gives an example of their approach for the purchase of Yves Saint Laurent products: 11% of the French population bought one or more products of the brand studied during the last two years. Within segments A, B and C the percentage of purchase is 14%, 10% and 5% respectively. Furthermore, the company distinguishes between those for whom the brand is a dream and those for whom the brand is not a dream amongst those who buy or do not buy, leading to four distinct targets: Addicted, Platonic brand lover, Blasé, and Indifferent. Table 3.16 reproduces these different segmentations and specifies the strategic branding issues that have to be carried out (in italics) according to the targets. The segmentation of values is shown along on top of this partition of consumers. Table 3.17 shows this double distribution in three European countries. As shown by this example, the work of RISC it is divided into national frameworks.

	Purchased	**Not Purchased**
Dream	Addicted: *Reward loyalty*	Platonics: *Facilitate access to the dream*
No Dream	Blasé: *Stimulate desire*	Indifferents: *Create desire*

Table 3.16: *Segmentation and strategic branding issues [LAD 94]*

		France		**Italy**		**Germany**	
		Purchased	**Not Purchased**	**Purchased**	**Not Purchased**	**Purchased**	**Not Purchased**
Dream	A	7	23	4	10	2	9
	B	5	26	3	8	2	6
	C	3	24	1	9	1	6
		Addict=5	*Platon=25*	*Addict=2*	*Platon=9*	*Addict=1*	*Platon=7*
No dream	A	7	50	5	54	4	46
	B	5	49	4	35	2	45
	C	2	47	2	43	1	37
		Blase=5	*Indiffer=49*	*Blase=4*	*Indiffer=50*	*Blase=2*	*Indiffer=42*
Addict= Addicted; Platon = Platonic brand lover; Indiffer = Indifferent to the brand							

Table 3.17: *Breakdown of groups by country [LAD 94]. All figures are percentages*

These socio-cultural systems (of the CCA, RISC and COFREMCA) have been criticized by researchers for the changing number of socio-cultural trends from one company to the next and from one year to the next within the same measurement instrument. Another critique deals with the explicatory powers of the different tools in predicting the consumption behaviors that are weaker than those of the values. Moreover, these companies' results are more descriptive than explicatory. However, these studies have been used frequently by companies: Carrefour, La Poste, Shell, Pernod, Kronenbourg, le Crédit Agricole, les Galeries Lafayette [DUB 94]. In France, certain products have been launched with success thanks to life-style studies, for example "Magie-Noire" from Lancôme, while others have met with failure as in the case of the "Vivre" review of the Hachette group.

Rather than working on values to predict consumption behaviors, a manufacturer can work on the basis of geosocial segmentations. By combining socio-economic and demographic information with geographic variables (nature of housing, location) and consumption data (normally taken from panels), groups of individuals or homogenous households can be pinpointed by their mode of consumption, their buying power and their housing location [VAL 94].

3.4.3. *Geosocial segmentations*

Based on the hypothesis that the choice of housing is a reasoned act of consumption, linked to the network of households, and a function of financial and social constraints, but also conditioned by values and lifestyles, a certain number of companies have established geographic segmentations. The most well known are Claritas INC with its Prizm tool in the USA, Compusearch with Psyte in Canada, and Experian with Mosäic in Europe. Although these companies often use the same methodology, Experian will be favored here because of its truly international approach. In France, based on the census (source INSEE), the communal inventory, the general agricultural census and indexes of communal wealth from the *Direction générale des impôts* (Tax Administration), Experian combine data concerning individual revenue, age distribution, and type of housing, thanks to a multiple correspondences analysis, and build a typology of homogeneous geographic groups. There are 28 such groups, called "îlotypes", which can be subdivided into 52 or regrouped into nine groups, depending on what is needed.

Charrière [CHA 98] shows the importance of specific values to certain French îlotypes such as regions in recession, rural communities and working-class neighborhoods, based on both Kahle and Rokeach measurement instruments.

Experian carried out the same type of work in the USA and obtained 12 groups that can be subdivided into 62 more specific divisions. From one country to the next, the variables available to Experian are not the same. The "*informatique et liberté*" ("Computer and freedom") law in France keeps companies from obtaining information on ethnic or racial backgrounds, which is not the case in the USA. Thus, Prizm includes among others the specific types with the following explanations [WEI 00]:

– "American Dreams": *Established urban immigrant families,*

– "Mid-City Mix": *African American singles and families,*

– "Latino America": *Hispanic middle-class families.*

Thus, from one country to the next the numbers of classes and subdivisions are not the same. For a manufacturer wishing to commercialize a product in several countries at the same time, using several national segmentations at the same time becomes complicated.

Based on the most refined version of each national geosegmentation, Experian has constructed a typology, in 14 groups, called Global Mosaic, dependent on age distribution, family status, degree of urbanization and revenues in the îlotypes. This typology, the description of which is found in Table 3.18, is applied in the USA, Canada, Belgium, Great Britain, Northern Ireland, France, Spain, Denmark, Norway, Sweden, Finland, Germany, the Netherlands, South Africa, Australia, New Zealand and Peru. A business manager can therefore tackle several countries by international segmentation and, locally, work with the national îlotypes by studying the distributions of these in different regions.

Old Wealth: Affluent metro sophisticates who prefer premium products and conservative ideas
Career Focused Materalists: Upscale suburban families who are heavy users of credit, early adopters of technology, and prime followers of leisure pursuits
Educated Cosmopolitans: Young urban professionals who enjoy nightlife, diverse cultures and alternatives lifestyles
Midscale Metro Office Workers: Middle-class suburban commuters who lives in mortgaged houses, are futures-oriented in their purchases, and seek value for their money
Farming Town Communities: Remote towns of midscale families whose ideas and lifestyles are influenced by local networks of friends, shopkeepers and social groups
Greys, Blue Sea and Mountain: Scenic areas with a service economy catering to vacationing tourists and well-off retirees
Inner City Melting Pot: A downscale mix of urban neighborhoods with a high concentration of immigrants and foreign-born singles and families
Agrarian Heartlands: Remote agricultural areas where families tend to be traditional, self-reliant, and dependent on the land
Blue Collar Self-Sufficiency: Working-class families in booming areas who have parlayed manual skills into middle-class, materialistic lifestyles
Lower Income Elderly: Downscale retirees living in low-density, sometimes government-owned housing, with few children, low mobility rates and relatively little consumer spending
Hardened Dependency: Inner-city areas with a high rate of unemployed residents, welfare recipients, elderly poor, and single-parent families struggling at basic levels of survival
De-industrial Legacy: Very poor industrial areas where craft workers retain old-fashioned tastes in food, clothing and furnishings
Shack and Shanty: Impoverished villages concentrated in Third World countries that are home to indigenous people in poorly built housing who retain rural, traditional lifestyles
Non-Family Residences: Institutions such as college dormitories, military barracks, prisons, etc.

Table 3.18: *Description of 14 global mosaic types [WEI 00]*

These approaches offer the advantage of being based on more objective criteria than values, and of being directly measurable, which makes them directly usable for mailings or for billboard advertising.

3.5. Conclusion

Table 3.19 summarizes the different issues studied in marketing concerning values and geographic information. This table lacks two dimensions, a third linked to the statistical processing used and a fourth specifying the academic and professional character of the issues.

	Issue		
	National	International	Regional
Quantitative approach about values	1.The development of a sufficiently exhaustive and universal scale	1. Analysis of mean scores level for one value or a group of values in different countries. 2. Instability of connections between values	1. Identification of a regional geographical division (physical, economical, social) for a national analysis 2. Identification of a geographical division crossing national borders 3. Analysis of mean score level for one value or a group of values according to areas (physical, economical, social) 4. Instability of connections between values according to areas. 5. Identification of the regional connotations of values
Quantitative approach about the linkages between values and behaviours	Predictive validity of values on consumers' behaviours	External validity of national results: checking predictive validities for consumers' behaviours in different countries	1. Instability of value–consumer behaviour links dependence on areas 2. Local and national predictive validity of connotations
Qualitative approach about the linkages between values and behaviors	Identification of means–end chain	External validity of national results	
Geo-segmentations	National Ilotypes	Distribution of ilotype in a specific area	Development of international ilotypes based on each national geo-segmentation

Table 3.19: *Different issues concerning values and geographic information*

3.6. References

[AUR 92a], Aurifeille J. M., Valette-Florence P., A 'chain-constrained' clustering approach in means–end analysis: an empirical illustration, *Marketing for Europe-Marketing for the Future*, *Proceedings of the EMAC Annual Conference*, Aarhus, 49-64, 1992.

[AUR 92b], Aurifeille J. M., Valette-Florence P., An empirical investigation of the predictive validity of micro versus macro approaches in consumer value research, *Marketing for Europe-Marketing for the Future*, *Proceedings of the EMAC Annual Conference*, Aarhus, 65-81 1992.

[BRE 00], Bréchon P., Galland O., Herpin N., Lambert Y., Lemel Y., Millan Game H., Schweisguth E., Tchernia J.-F., *Les valeurs des Français*, edited by Armand Colin, collection U, série sociologie, Paris, 2000.

[CAT 94], Cathelat B., Le socio-styles-système: une intelligence systémique du citoyen-consommateur-audience pour s'adapter et anticiper, *Décisions Marketing*, 2, 63-71, 1994.

[CCA 90], Internal memo, "Eurosociostyles in European areas".

[CHA 98], Charrière V., L'influence des espaces géographiques sur les valeurs et sur le comportement du consommateur, PhD thesis, Paris IX – Dauphine University, 1998.

[DUB 94], Dubois B., *Comprendre le consommateur*, Dalloz, Paris.

[FIL 94], Filser M., *Le comportement du consommateur*, col Précis de gestion, Dalloz, Paris, 1994.

[GRU 93], Grunert K., Grunert S., Kristensen K., Une méthode d'estimation de la validité interculturelle des instruments de mesure: le cas de la mesure des valeurs du consommateur par la liste des valeurs L.O.V., *Recherche et applications en marketing*, 8 , 4, 5-28, 1993.

[GUT 86], Gutman J., Analyzing Consumer Orientations Toward Beverages Through Means–end Chain Analysis, *Psychology and Marketing*, 3, 28-42, 1986.

[HOF 99], Hofstede F., Steenkamp J.-B., Wede, M., International Market Segmentation based on Consumer-product Relations, *Journal of Marketing Research*, Vol XXXVI, 1-17, 1999.

[JON 78], Jones A., Sensenig J., Ashmore R., Systems of Values and their Multidimensional Representations, *Multivariate behavioural research*, 13, 255-270, 1978.

[JOS 97], Joseph S., Le contexte politico-économique et son influence sur la stabilité des valeurs politico-économiques et individuelles: le cas de l'Allemagne réunifiée, *Actes du 13ème congrès international de l'Association française du marketing*, Toulouse, 36-69, 1997.

[KHA 86], Kahle L., The Nine Nations of North America and the Value Basis of Geographic Segmentation, *Journal of Marketing*, 50, 37-47, 1986.

[KAM 93], Kamakura W., Novak T., Steenkampf J.-B., Verhallen T., Identification de segments de valeurs pan-européen par un modèle logit sur les rangs avec regroupements successifs, *Recherche et applications en marketing*, 8, 4, 29-56, 1993.

[LAD 94], Ladet M., RISC: une analyse systémique du changement social pour l'international, *Décisions Marketing*, 2, 73-80, 1994.

[MEN 91], Mendel D., Comparaison des cultures allemande et française et implications marketing, *Recherche et Applications Marketing*, 6, 3, 31-76, 1991.

[MIT 81], Mitchell A., *Changing Values and Lifestyles*, SRI International, 1981.

[ODI 96], Odin Y., Vinais J.-Y., Valette-Florence P., Analyse confirmatoire des domaines motivationnels de Schwartz: une application au domaine des media, *Actes de l'association française du marketing*, Poitiers, 12, 125-141, 1996.

[PIN 90], Pinet B., Quels sont les consommateurs européens?, *Revue française du Marketing*, cahier 130, 1990/5, 1990.

[ROE 89], Roehrich G., Valette-Florence P., Combined incidence of personal values, involvement and innovativeness on innovative consumer behaviour: is marketing keeping up with the Consumer?, *ESOMAR Seminar* Vienna, 261-279, 1989.

[ROK 73], Rokeach M., *The nature of human values*, Free-Press, 1973.

[SCH 87], Schwartz S.H., Bilsky W., Toward a Universal Psychological Structure of Human Values, *Journal Of Personality and Social Psychology*, 53, 550-562, 1987.

[SCH 90], Schoppoven I., Toward a Theory of the Universal Content and Structure of Values: Extensions and Cross Cultural Replications, *Journal of Personality and Psychology*, 58, 5, 878-891, 1990.

[SCH 91], Schoppoven I., Values and Consumption Patterns: A Comparison between Rural and Urban Consumers in Western Germany, *European Journal of Marketing*, 25, 12, 20-35, 1991.

[SCH 92], Schwartz S.H., Universalis in the Content and Structure of Values: Theorical Advance and Empirical Tests in 20 Minutes, *Advances in Experimental Social Psychology*, 25, Academic Press, 1-65, 1992.

[SCH 93], Schwartz S.H., Bilsky W., Vers une théorie de l'universalité du contenu et de la structure des valeurs: Extensions et reproductions interculturelles, *Recherche et Applications en Marketing*, 8, 4, 78-106, 1993.

[TOD 90], Todd E., *Invention de l'Europe*, Editions Seuil, Paris, 1990.

[VAL 91a], Valette-Florence P., Grunert S., Grunet K., Beatty S., Une comparaison franco-allemande de l'adhésion aux valeurs personnelles, *Recherche et Applications en Marketing*, 6, 3, 5-20, 1991.

[VAL 91b], Valette-Florence P., Rappachi B., A cross-cultural means–end chain analysis of perfume purchases, *Proceedings of the Third Symposium on Cross-Cultural Consumer and Business Studies*, 161-173, 1991.

[VAL 94], Valette-Florence P., *Les styles de vie: bilan critique et perspectives. Du mythe à la réalité*, coll Connaître et pratiquer la gestion, Nathan, Paris, 1994.

[VAL 99], Valette-Florence P., Sirieix L., Grunert K., Nielsen N., A Comparison of Fish Consumption in Denmark and France: A Multidimensional Perspective, *Journal of Euromarketing*, 8, 1-2, 15-27, 1999.

[WEI 00], Weiss M., *The Clustered World: How we Live, What we Buy, and What it all Means about Who we Are*, Little, Brown, 2000.

[YAN 71], Yankelovitch D., What Life Style Means to Market Planners, *Marketing Communications*, 6, 38-45, 1971.

Chapter 4

Geomarketing and Consumer Behavior

Introduction

If knowledge of the consumer is fundamental to the implementation of a marketing approach, geomarketing adds to this knowledge about where consumers are situated geographically. Initially, geomarketing was limited to cartographic representations and appeared in population typologies. Today, strengthened by behavioral databases, these applications have multiplied in number. The considerable possibilities offered by geomarketing have led to the emergence of relational marketing, a source of innovative strategies for companies. A decade ago, geomarketing essentially consisted of representing, in the form of maps, various types of information, sometimes coming from multidimensional analyses in the form of typologies or segmentations. These analyses dealt with existing data, principally taken in France from the INSEE (*Institut National pour la Statistique et les Etudes Economiques*, the National Institute for Statistics and Economic Studies) for population census, from the Taxes Authorities (*Direction Générale des Impôts*) for revenues and the IGN (*Institut Géographique National*, the National Geographic Institute) for highway infrastructure and equipment.

The need for a more precise comprehension and knowledge of markets, which manifests itself through increasingly more precise segmentations, constitutes one of the pillars of the development of geomarketing. This segmentation of markets is based on an increasing fragmentation of the population, observed over the past few years, and the necessity of defining a differentiation strategy for companies in an increasingly competitive context.

Chapter written by Jean-Pierre DOUARD.

From 1945 to 1960, the segmentation of consumers was founded on simple approaches linked to a relatively frozen pyramidal society. The period from 1960 to 1980 was greatly marked by the appearance of a mass society, which market studies described with precision. In the light of these mass markets, an inverse reaction developed in the 1980s, which gave rise to a post-industrial matrix society composed of micro-markets where the consumer is no longer a passive spectator, but seeks individualized consumption and manifests the desire to become active. This is the emergence of the consumer–entrepreneur. This new consumer is mobile and varies his or her behavior from day to day, depending upon his or her mood. He or she escapes the classic model, founded on analyses by socio-professional categories and on age groups, becomes "fickle" and chameleon (see Chapter 2). Consumer mobility is redrawing a new geography of marketing territories.

The entirety of information that will henceforth be available about the consumer, in addition to the traditional information (age, sex, socio-professional category, etc.) should be crossed with data on consumption and purchase behaviors, leisure activities and the labor pools that are linked to them. Consequently, geomarketing becomes a fundamental tool of the mix through the understanding of and knowledge about consumers that it makes possible [BOY 00].

This chapter is made up of two parts: the first part deals with the foundations of geomarketing from classical methods and evolutions in consumer behavior, leading to the analysis of the flows of clientele linked to purchase behaviors of households as a territory analysis tool. The second part deals with an application that is based on a certain number of indicators and uses an analysis model of the flows that are based on the development of databases of studies concerning consumers' behaviors managed by the chambers of commerce and industry. A calculation of potential for the establishment of a specialized superstore will be used as a short illustration.

4.1. The foundations of geomarketing

This section will deal first with the weight of the geographic variable in the analysis of consumers, by showing both the limitations of classic methods and the necessity of integrating this dimension, taking into account recent evolutions in consumer behavior. The importance of the notion of the flow of purchase in the determination of a potential business on a territory and the necessity of developing adapted databases will then be justified. The main current uses of geomarketing will also be mentioned briefly.

4.1.1. *The weight of the geographic variable in consumer behavior analysis*

A retail store involves a triple choice: a trade area, a site, and an adapted supply (see section 4.2). Different methods exist to measure the economic potential of a territory, such as demographic analysis, which highlights the demographic structure of an area, analysis by resources, which depends on the revenues of the population, and analysis by expenses, which are based on the breakdown of the average expenses of households. These methods have different weaknesses, which are linked principally to research in modeling, to the rationality of the location decision, and to the behaviors of more *mobile* consumers.

Demographic phenomena are too often considered as presenting permanence and continuity that they do not always possess. The age of the data also constitutes a weakness of this type of approach.

Reports concerning the number of businesses per 1,000 inhabitants or retail area for 1,000 inhabitants, calculated either globally, or by separating the sales of hypermarkets and supermarkets from the rest of the trade, often provide a general picture of the situation by separating out food stuffs, personal apparel, home equipment and culture/leisure. The disadvantage of this method lies in the fact that it does not go down to the level of retail activity, but remains at the large-category level when calculating the number of square meters and the number of stores within an activity. Furthermore, the notion of market saturation, defined [APP 60, GHO 87] by a sufficient number of stores to respond to the needs of the population, should take into account the external attraction of the area considered, which can be extremely important.

In addition, calculating sales by square meter, when it integrates hypermarkets and supermarkets, is not a very strong indicator, for it does not identify the distinction between foodstuffs and non-foodstuffs for these forms of sales [DUC 91]. Finally, the "theoretical" market seems linked to residents of the area, as trips with work, health, leisure, etc. motives have become quasi-daily in the urban population. The organization of space consequently makes the definition of theoretical markets difficult.

The economic potential of the trade area and the potential sales of a store are, of course, major elements in the location decision, but most often integrate strategic options into them [JAL 94]. Territorial coverage is determined according to the position of competitors, by looking for potential areas, or by going to territories already commercially equipped. The chosen option is thus not to allow competitors to take root solidly in an area. The current multiplication of specialized superstore location projects similar to those already existing in a trade area leads to an escalation of location that does not always take into account real potentials (it is not uncommon, in the home-improvement sector, to see a company establish itself in a shopping center where a competitor already exists).

The approach to a trade area of a store is made more complex today by new behaviors amongst more mobile and less loyal consumers (see Chapter 2). The theoretical models (see Chapter 6) founded on "rational" travel modulated by distance (central places theory [CHR 33], law of retail gravitation [CON 48, REI 31]) or past consumer behaviors [HUF 64] appear insufficient to grasp this new reality. Determining the potential of a trade area henceforth supposes more qualitative analyses based on the flow of purchase linked to the behaviors of households inside a given territory.

The traditional ways of interpreting consumers' behaviors no longer meet the challenge of understanding purchase behaviors. Lifestyles, mobility and geography have become dimensions of marketing that cannot be ignored in defining a commercial territory [MAR 96]. Current purchase behaviors more closely match the *archipelago* model [VEL 94, VIA 94], in which the consumer moves about between different sub-zones constituted by professional activities, schools attended, hobbies, the organization of purchases, the break-up of the family, etc., linked together on the basis of multiple interest and disregarding the rest of the territory. Distance no longer assumes its role as regulator and organizer of space and travel. Mobility, dominated in the past by travel to and from work, is now developing in the leisure, shopping and education domains, to name but a few. The distances traveled are 10 times those of 30 years ago, with a particular increase in the periphery of cities. The flows linked to this mobility [CHE 98, CLI 97] create spaces distanced from the concentric model centered on the home and which evokes an archipelago of regularly frequented places at varying distances from one another. These flows are at the heart of the definition of trade areas and understanding them becomes fundamental in store location decisions. Fuzzily delineated areas thus appear which require an adaptation of the methods of analysis. The increased mobility of consumers (see Chapter 2), linked in part to automobiles, generates life spaces in new geographic forms. The traditional territory, concentric around the home, gives way to archipelagos of zones of interest, more or less spread out around where the modern consumer goes in relation to his occupation, ignoring intermediate zones. The act of travel becomes more important than where one lives. This mobility draws a new geography that becomes vital to understand, both for companies and advertisers.

At the same time, the development of behavioral databases, offering multiple data on consumer behavior, allows, thanks to geomarketing, new clientele approaches to be realized. This phenomenon is both facilitated by the development of more complete and more user-friendly cartography software programs and made possible by the development of information technology turned based on Geographic Information System (GIS). More and more sectors are integrating geomarketing tools into their research department. Companies possessing store networks are particularly aware of these techniques, which combine marketing and geography. Banks, insurance companies, the press and large retail companies are sectors where the development of the tools is currently exponential. The vocation of geomarketing is to develop the information capital of companies. Thus, the objectives of geomarketing can be summed up in four fundamental points:

– to manage multiple information;

– to master marketing territories;

– to adapt to customers;

– to predict evolutions.

Among the most frequent applications in geomarketing, one finds:

– adapting the retail supply of a store (optimizing performances);

– working on micro-markets;

– (re)structuring a network;

– determining a new location site;

– fixing objectives in relation to potential;

– targeting the best customers using an adapted advertising campaign (see Chapter 10);

– optimizing investments in direct marketing (see Chapter 11);

– supporting sales;

– analyzing the competition.

Geomarketing allows a targeting of prospects with strong potential in a given trade area. Starting from the principle that the location of residence is in part responsible for purchase behavior, the archetypical profile of the best customers, for example, can be drawn by superimposing the sales by area and data on the inhabitants residing in these zones. This profile can allow a targeting of similar non-customer populations and react in relation to the hypothesis that people living in the same neighborhood or within the same territory possess relatively similar socioeconomic and cultural characteristics. It will also be possible to adapt the offer to the profile of its clientele by taking into account the evolution of its trade area (see Chapter 12).

Geomarketing also allows, for example, the determination of new location sites for distributors by identifying, over a vast territory, geographic zones corresponding, in their structure, to the profile of zones where stores realizing the best sales are located. The goal here is not to know why a store functions better than another, but to identify the characteristics of location areas of stores realizing a sizable score and to look for similar areas in which to place new stores (see Chapters 5–7). Superstores use the characteristics of populations in their trade area (socio-demographic data, housing type, etc.) in order to fix the sales objectives by department, in relation to the potentialities of different types of assortments and to better reach their customers by knowing the purchase flows that characterize their territory (see an example of flow mapping in Figure 4.1).

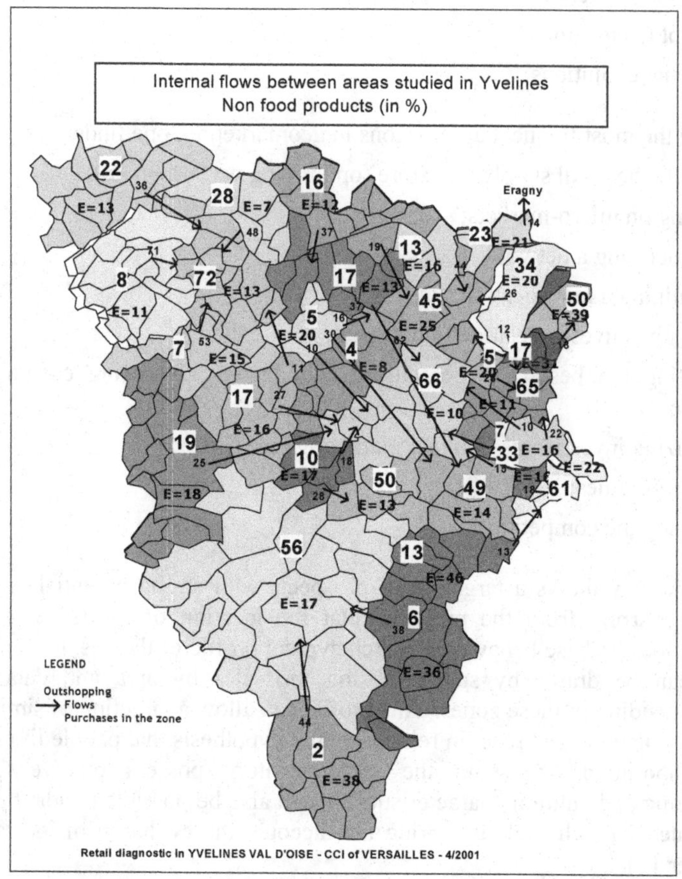

Figure 4.1: *Example of a map representing flows related to household buying behaviors for an enlarged territory divided into sub-areas*

Finally, geomarketing can serve as a tool in mapping the position of competitors and in allowing a company to keep up with competitive innovations. In a more strategic domain, geomarketing allows companies to verify the efficacy of the networking of a territory by avoiding the cannibalization of different stores or the "holes" within a geographic area. This will allow a relocation of certain stores likely to improve the performance of the retail system. Likewise, a rationalization of the network will be possible by highlighting the trade areas with great potential in relation to the given sector and where the competition is not too strong. Real network audits become standard, including the analysis of the potential sales of a territory by superimposing several maps (state of the competition, population density, socioeconomic characteristics, housing type, equipment, etc.) on the one hand, and the definition of the type of store to be established (nature of the offer, positioning, etc.) on the other [DOU 97]. Finally, geomarketing can supply information on micro-markets defined street by street, in terms of customer location.

The different aspects mentioned above should not overshadow the fact that confining marketing to its geographic dimensions is not satisfactory. To understand the consumer as a very mobile individual is to define him or her as a unique target, which changes the manner in which he or she should be approached. Geomarketing thus leads to relational marketing, which establishes new types of dialogues between companies and their customers.

4.1.2. *The flows linked to household purchase behaviors: an analytical tool of enlarged territories*

The existence of numerous shopping centers must henceforth be taken into account in the logic of flows of consumption. The notion of trade area is evolving, moving from stores to shopping centers, now covering a much larger area that can be understood as a territory connected by a competitive offer and used by the same consumers. This extension of trade areas leads to distortions in consumer purchase behavior and the hierarchical system of shopping centers induced in part by the flows and is explained by these flows. The analysis of a territory should therefore allow:

– a study of the retail environment (strengths/weaknesses);

– the observation of the consumption behaviors and habits of households (attraction and outshopping (or the part of residing consumer purchase making out of an area)) in relation to these different shopping centers.

The expansion of trade areas leads to modifications in the purchase behaviors of consumers. For example, a consumer will be much more attracted to a trade area that has two hypermarkets and numerous specialized superstores than by an area composed of a few stores, even if the latter is closer or more easily accessible.

The current confrontation between downtown and suburban retail activities constitutes an example of the weight of shopping centers in the retail network of a territory. The areas of influence of the different shopping centers of a territory overlap and the hierarchical system of the centers is explained by the flows linked to consumer purchase behaviors. The flows linked to trips of diverse origins are at the heart of the definition of the trade area, and the comprehension of these flows becomes decisive in determining the marketing potential of an eventual location area.

The analysis of the marketing potential of a territory for a given activity depends on the evaluation of the outshopping behaviors of households residing in the territory, and of the attraction of households living elsewhere towards this territory as well as the structure of this commercial outshopping and of this attraction. Outshopping, which measures the loss of purchasing potential on the part of the residents of a territory, constitutes an overall performance indicator of the supply. The nature of the outshopping outside the area is estimated in relation to a diffuse outshopping criterion, oriented towards several commercial sites or centers; or outshopping concentrated on a site or a city. It is also estimated in terms of distance to a distant outshopping zone within an area not adjoining the area studied, or a close outshopping zone peripheral to the area studied. The flow of attraction indicates the sales of external origin, coming, in other words, from residents of other areas under the influence of the area studied. The same criteria used for outshopping can be used for attraction, by distinguishing diffuse and concentrated, distant and close attractions. The value of the information concerning the flows of attraction and outshopping resides in the fact that these flows describe a reality [MAR 96]. They are calculated based on studies of a sample of households on the most recent purchases made for a series of products. This approach appears preferable to that of frequentation studies, which suppose a regularity of behavior. The information obtained is recent, pertinent, in the sense that it truly explains purchase behaviors, viable and valid if the information is obtained through well-developed surveys based on the territorial sampling strategies that are currently used by several Chambers of Commerce and Industry in France and by private marketing companies (Calyx, Consodata, among others).

The reality of the purchase behaviors expressed in these studies constitutes a necessary source for evaluating the marketing potentials of a territory.

4.1.3. *Geomarketing in marketing strategy*

Marketing will need to consider space more and more in the marketing offer and this should be at two levels:

– for products and services possessing a strong territorial dimension, such as retail stores, billboards, automatic teller machines, etc;

– when one or more components of the offer is linked to the territory (adaptation of the offer, price management, specific communications, etc.).

In fact, geomarketing has progressively become a new element of the marketing mix, by allowing the improvement of knowledge and understanding of the markets. Geographic space, like sociological, economic or demographic space, today strengthens consumer analysis: geography constitutes a unifying dimension of different data. Both the management and organization of information becomes a major stake. GIS (see Chapter 7) provides a way to represent the different data in a cartographic and implementation databases. Geomarketing processes the location analysis on consumption activity together with data from companies (marketing department, merchandizing, accounting, etc.) or external data (census). The variables taken into account are of various categories, for example:

– objective internal company variables: customer addresses, sales, products consumed, etc;

– objective variables characterizing the consumer: age, socio-professional category, etc;

– subjective variables such as loyal customer, "good" credit, etc;

– location variables available at regular intervals of time or whose values are collected by survey: residence, workplace, etc;

– variables concerning space itself: organization, logistics.

These different data, which make possible a better understanding of the customer and therefore better performing relational marketing (CRM: customer relationship management) [LEF 00], make necessary the creation of adapted computer systems. These systems are in line with the notion of data mining [LAT 01]. The customer/prospects databases suppose a data warehouse, which represents an important investment. The available tools can be divided into four categories:

– data mining or extraction of data with display of data, updated with relationships between variables, construction of models;

– decision analysis tool for evaluating alternative solutions;

– statistical tools for predicting and modeling;

– GIS.

A consumer's address makes it possible to give to this consumer a set of external information, which qualifies him or her in a more precise manner, by supplying information on the geographic area of residence (today Iris 2000 of the INSEE, which covers areas of 2,000 inhabitants, or ZAD defined by ADDE, which divides the territory into units of 5,000 people). The constitution of databases integrating different levels of information is described by Figure 4.2. The consequences for companies appear at two levels: to improve the knowledge of their territories and to develop differentiated approaches in space. Space is not a neutral support and therefore requires a better knowledge of the territories. It plays a role in the behaviors of consumers and becomes a constituent of complex behaviors linked to the augmentation of travel.

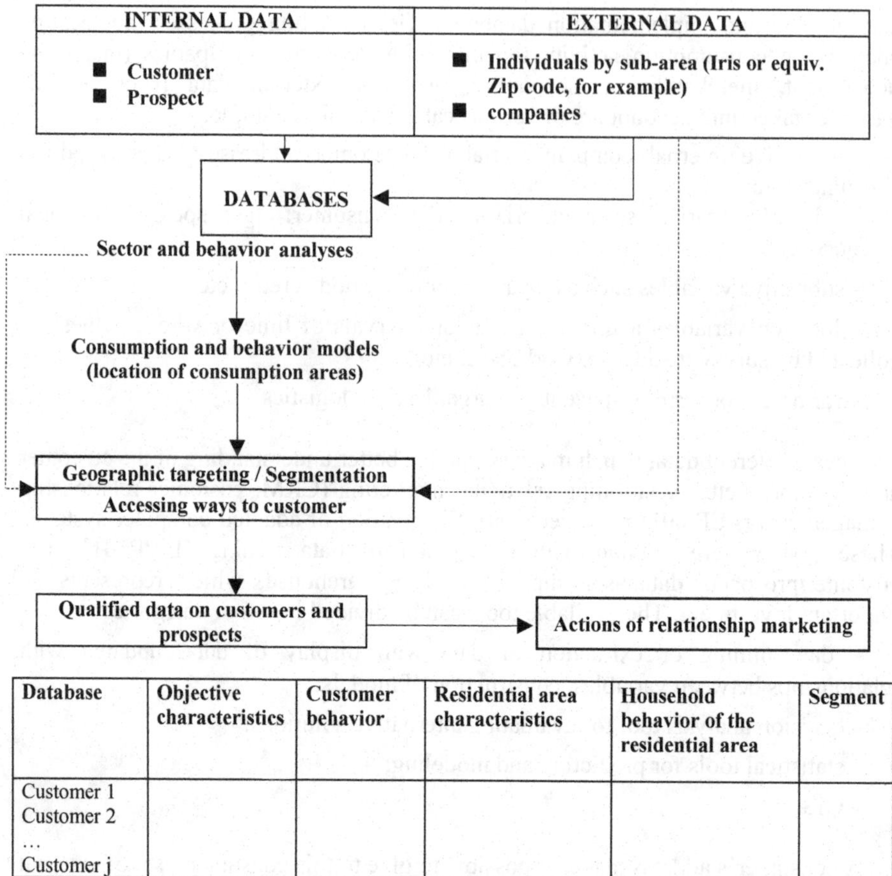

Database	Objective characteristics	Customer behavior	Residential area characteristics	Household behavior of the residential area	Segment
Customer 1 Customer 2 … Customer j					

Figure 4.2: *Management information system*

Geomarketing today suggests the development of new behavior comprehension models. Models developed on the basis of behavioral data, which involve the interaction of numerous variables, augment the intelligibility of these more complex and more varied behaviors and suggest new enriched approaches to analyzing the consumer.

Operational geomarketing, seen as a means of observation and action directed at certain targets, today easily implements these attempts at modeling of new purchase behaviors. Geomarketing provides the keys for decoding the meaning the territory carries. From now on, in the marketing mix, companies should progressively integrate this, often still small, geographic component. A better understanding of the connections between consumers and space provides the possibility of innovative marketing approaches, modified locally and thus providing a competitive advantage.

The knowledge of the dynamics of consumer behaviors in a territory that is possible today needs to be developed by marketing, which can exploit the potential contained in the data currently available with a geographic "root". Regardless of the level of computerization and therefore of available data in each company, the company does at least have data concerning its sales per product and per customer, and therefore per marketing channel and geographic region. From the market and competition point of view, the company, depending on its activity, may also have panel data at its disposal, frequentation studies, image studies, etc. Today, the time-based aspect of these studies and of their paper-based nature makes it difficult to compare these sources of information in order to develop a global management vision. Instead, a point of view is developed on the basis of a particular promotion or mailing, rather than determination of the relative impact on sales of price, the use of a particular medium, the marketing activity and the image of rival products (among other factors) (see Part III). Geomarketing allows global analysis of quantifiable parameters that condition the marketing performance of the company. Once data collection processes are determined, the database should be populated in order to implement analysis software.

The second benefit of geomarketing is the reactivity that these instruments, once integrated into the decision processes, provide to the company. For example, a competitor has just adjusted its prices; the company can simulate the impact of his or her sales and rapidly take appropriate measures founded on the comprehension of the actual importance of competitive price compared to all the other factors. Geomarketing has the particular characteristics of the principal decision-making tools and provides a supplementary dimension linked to the geography of the point of sale; in other words the geographic characteristics surrounding the points of sale, as well as the proximity of consumers and the other factors influencing the frequentation of the location. Behaving in space, in a territory, means making use of it. The study of the behaviors of people in a particular territory is the subject of different sciences (sociology, ethnology, etc.); the relatively recent marketing component still remains to be developed. Marketing can orient itself more towards taking advantage of the specific characteristics of a territory. It can also aim to meet the needs of consumers in relation to their trips. Consumers consume according to the territory they occupy (rural, urban, neighborhood, street, etc.) both because individuals living in the same place have the propensity to conduct themselves in the same manner and because this territory has specificity (a level of equipment, accessibility, etc.). The observation of links between the consumer and the territory constitutes a new field of exploration for companies; to understand the mechanism which, based on a territory, engenders given flows, which themselves transform this territory, involves resorting to new techniques that are based in part on cartography software, databases and the content of maps but also on new consumer comprehension models that have yet to be developed.

4.2. An application: the development of behavioral databases for a territory

In this section, a behavioral database, as implemented by different chambers of commerce and industry (CCI), will first be presented in terms of the approach and content. Then, an approach will be founded on analysis by the flows of consumption in order to determine the potential of commercial development at the sub-area level. This will be illustrated succinctly with an example.

4.2.1. *The development of behavioral databases: an example developed by the chambers of commerce and industry*

For too long, market potential studies have been based on calculations of surface areas or of ratios per inhabitant. Recently, the idea emerged that, in addition to the observation of the retail infrastructure, it is necessary to integrate a spatial dimension and to position the business in its competitive territory. Consequently, a territorial analysis should be able to deal with the principal domains [DOU 99]:

– the situation of the retail environment (inventory, strengths, weaknesses, imbalances);

– household consumption habits (the phenomena of attraction and outshopping);

– the hierarchy of shopping centers and their diversity.

The marketing offer is analyzed through an inventory of businesses, and the demand through the flows linked to purchase behaviors. Carried out through the surveying of retail stores and consumers, the studies should allow the creation of databases from which the following can be extracted:

– the elements that make possible a clear definition of the development perimeter of a marketing policy due to a knowledge of store chain establishment and of the attraction of shopping centers [GHO 87];

– the understood state of retail saturation derived from comparing the retail entities using the market shares of different forms of businesses and of shopping centers;

– the potentialities of development, which rely, in part, on knowledge of outshopping and attraction;

– the quality of the retail network within the study's perimeter, analyzed according to the spatial retail distribution of shopping centers, their varying level of specialization and the retail market shares.

The mastery of databases, developed through the surveys mentioned, gives a new approach to a territory. In fact, very often in marketing, market studies are taken at a particular time and cover a well-defined zone. Studies that are distant in time are rarely comparable. In addition, the defined zone to be studied corresponds poorly *a priori*, in certain cases, to the understood perimeter of a development project. Purchase behaviors are spread over increasingly larger territories (the archipelago economy), so that the area to consider for a given city is often quite large and at times goes beyond the borders of the department/county. This territory should be broken down into sub-divisions that are defined in terms of consumption habits. In each sub-division, the economic information about supply and demand (the customer flows) is determined. Figure 4.3 below shows the architecture of the methods used.

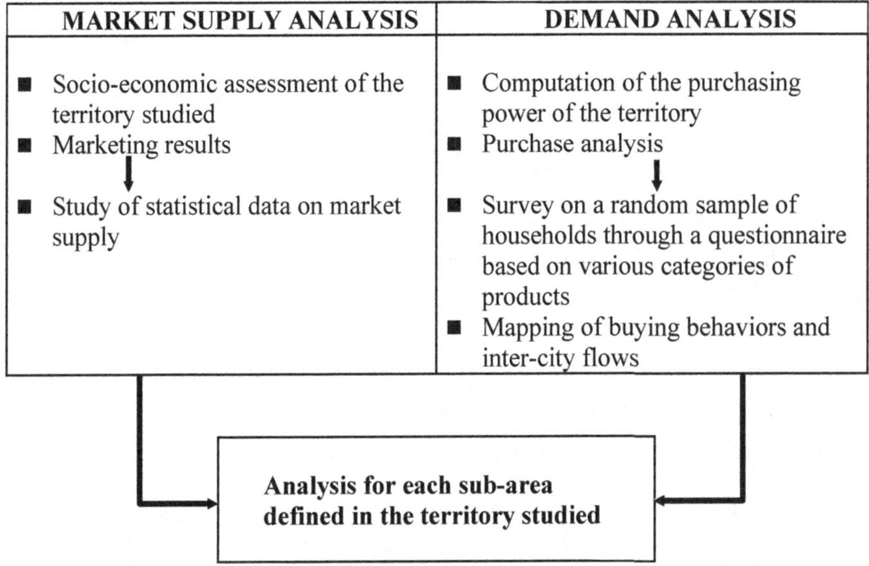

Figure 4.3: *Constitution of the behavioral databases used by Chambers of Commerce and Industry in France*

The data produced are numerous, which requires an even more sophisticated division of the territory. The use of an information management tool becomes necessary. A computer system capable of aggregating these different sub-areas should be constructed so that trade/trade areas can be studied effectively. The possibilities of aggregation, which are now infinite because they are not limited by the perimeter of study, allow the construction of scenarios and the analysis of development projects. Different computerized systems that make possible analysis of the market supply and of the demand for a given territory exist today in the chambers of Commerce and Industry. These systems group all the data concerning retail equipment into two categories, supply and demand; they allow the zone studied to be reconstituted by the aggregation of sub-territories and they contain data linked to consumer purchase behaviors. This now becomes about commercial development decision-making tools. The data generally integrated into the geomarketing information system concerning supply are as follows:

– stores of more than 300 m² per activity (areas and ratios per 1,000 inhabitants);

– a typology of businesses by activity for traditional businesses (number of businesses, ratios per 1,000 inhabitants, calculation of sales floor area);

– number of retail businesses by geographic grouping;

– number of retail activities within each group;

– distribution of retail activities between the different groups;

– management information on the businesses in each geographic group

The data concerning demand are as follows:

– purchasing power for different categories of products (ratios per person, accumulation by category of products);

– purchasing power per area group;

– distribution of purchasing power per retail type (traditional store, hypermarket, supermarket, etc.);

– retail types frequented by households per area group and per activity;

– retail attraction of each area group on these households, per product;

– outshopping of each area group, per product;

– main shopping places per area group, per product.

With the data used being refocused (through surveys) and founded on the actual facts (acts of purchase), they can adapt themselves more easily to different economic, political and financial actors. Decision-makers are called to work from common bases, which can favor more concerted decisions and therefore decisions that are more rational in relation to development.

The notion of adapted information systems supposes here the integration of "good" decision variables and this from a threefold perspective:

– that of the actual character of the managed data (with an acceptable time range);

– that of the pertinence of the territorial divisions used (freed from simple administrative limits);

– that of their capacity to allow an interpretation of the trade situations (in a non-competitive objective framework).

The guiding lines for the composition of territories and the developments therein are founded on the reality of consumer buying behaviors interpreted in relation to the strengths and weaknesses of the current market supply.

4.2.2. *Analysis by flow to measure the potentials of territory development*

In this approach, a "territory" is a collection of geographic sub-areas for which the set of data concerning household purchase behaviors is available for each area and is comparable through an appropriate information system. The possibilities of aggregation allow the analysis of development projects at several territorial levels [DOU 00]. The territory studied will, normally, be composed of several demand groups, which will be aggregated in relation to the studied project. The different indicators to be used are as follows [DOU 02]:

– the potential of consumer purchasing power in the area;

– the rate of internal attraction per sub-area;

– outshopping;

– the flow of customers.

The potential of consumer purchasing power in the area corresponds to the total purchases that can be realized by the inhabitants of the area. In general, 25 to 30 families of products are included, which corresponds to a choice between the products taken into account by the IDC (index of consumer spending) and the elements supplied for the budget of the households included in INSEE [CLI 92].

The rate of internal attraction per sub-area, which represents the share of consumer spending for an area actually spent in that area, is calculated by product and by category of products (food products, apparel, home products, culture and leisure products).

Outshopping defines itself as the part of the purchasing power not realized in its area of origin. This is characterized by three elements: diffuse or concentrated outshopping (at "dominant" sites or several locations), strongly or weakly cumulative outshopping (understood by comparison with the rate of global outshopping for different products in a given territory), and distant or close outshopping.

The flows of customers, characterized by the area from which they leave and the area in which they arrive, are measured in part by consumer spending. These flows are known per sub-area and per product.

The proposed geomarketing approach based on these data relies on two levels of analysis: static, by geographic sub-area, and dynamic, through the study of the structure of outshopping and attraction.

The first level is carried out in terms of sub-areas and is generally composed of three stages:

– taking into account the weak points of the current supply: here this deals with determining which are the products whose internal attraction rate is lower than the overall internal attraction rate for all products in the area. This latter rate can, in fact, serve as a reference for the purchase behavior of the inhabitants of the area. Weak internal attraction rates can be modified by giving them the reference value (the overall internal attraction rate). It is therefore possible to determine the supplementary sales generated by the corresponding sales surface area;

– measurement of the incidences of overall attraction rate variation: this calculation corresponds normalizing the internal attraction rates of all the products relative to a fixed rate. Thus, if the overall internal attraction rate is fixed at 50%, the rate of each product will be modified and also placed at 50%. This enables measurement of the consequences of a more radical change in behavior in the area studied, as could be possible with the creation of a new shopping center;

– measurement of the incidences of internal attraction rate per product: this calculation is carried out with the same goal as the preceding ones, which is to measure the impact of an internal attraction rate variation on the sales surface area for a given activity in the area studied.

The second level of analysis consists of determining the structure of outshopping by taking into account the points of sale where inhabitants usually shop. These points of sale have previously been studied, since the internal attraction rate is calculated in relation to purchases that a resident makes in his or her own area. What is of interest here is the resident's consumption in other areas. It is also possible to study "internal" expenses in a more sophisticated way by examining the exact locations of purchases, such as in terms of trade names for example. Outshopping analysis is principally carried out according to two evaluation criteria: the concentrated or diffuse nature of the outshopping and its cumulative or non-cumulative character. The near or distant character can also be considered if need be.

The outshopping will be considered to be *strongly cumulative* if the overall outshopping rate towards one site is pronounced. Inversely, if this outshopping rate is weak, the outshopping will be qualified as weakly cumulative. This indicates that several places of outshopping coexist without any one being dominant. The study of this rate makes possible analysis of the attraction of one area or another and the determination, for example, whether an area attracts a large share of the spending of other areas. If this is the case for several neighboring areas, it is possible to look for phenomena explaining such behavior. It often appears that this attraction is due to a well-developed and therefore attractive shopping center. It is interesting to know the main points of sales in order to compare the distance with the area of origin, the existing marketing supply, etc. and this is the case even if the outshopping is weakly cumulative, in order to determine which portion of this outshopping could be taken back by the establishment of a larger store.

In the case of concentration, the rate does not concern the whole array of products, but one product at a time. The outshopping will be considered concentrated if it takes place for one product and for one given area mainly towards a common site. Inversely, if a common site does not capture a large part of the outshopping for this product in this area, the outshopping will be qualified as diffuse. It is therefore useful, in determining this characteristic of outshopping, to calculate the proportion of each site in the total outshopping for each product. This calculation is made with the help of a matrix showing recapture of outshopping (i.e. bringing purchases back to the area). Based on these analyses, it is possible to identify, for a given product, its position in the matrix of Table 4.1, which presents different degrees of outshopping recapture. This recapture matrix for outshopping brings together the two previously cited characteristics: the cumulative or non-cumulative character of the outshopping of an area and the concentrated or diffuse character of the outshopping for a product. As the latter characteristic is product specific, the analysis carried out in the matrix only deals with one product at a time. The results obtained correspond to three possible levels of product outshopping recapture, when the surface area of a store can be expanded [DOU 01]. These three levels are: + for weak recapture possibilities, ++ for slightly more promising possibilities and finally, +++ for *a priori* very strong recapture possibilities. This last level corresponds to the combination of weakly cumulative outshopping for the area studied and concentrated product outshopping. This may signify, for example, that the residents of an area are not attracted to any particular site but spend wherever they can. The establishment of a store in their area would surely convince them to make their purchases in this area; this is the slightly cumulative character of outshopping.

	Outshopping for a product	
Outshopping for the area	**Concentrated**	**Diffused**
Strongly cumulative	++	+
Weakly cumulative	+++	+

Table 4.1: *Matrix of outshopping recapture, from + to +++ depending on the importance of the outshopping recovery potential in the case of increased supply*

This can also indicate that the outshopping for a product is concentrated at one site, meaning that the market supply of this product is limited. The opening of a new store could therefore be largely justified.

This approach also takes into account the performance of the entire retail supply for all products.

4.2.3. *An illustration: the establishment of a specialized sports superstore at Vendôme (Loir-et-Cher)*

Figure 4.4 shows the current division of the department of Loir-et-Cher (south east from Paris), as carried out by the Chamber of Commerce and Industry. This division was made by looking for maximum homogeneity in the areas affected. For each area, the CCI has information on the retail supply and the demand of households. This deals with a project concerning the location of a sports superstore at Vendôme for a nationally known trade name. What potential currently exists for such a project?

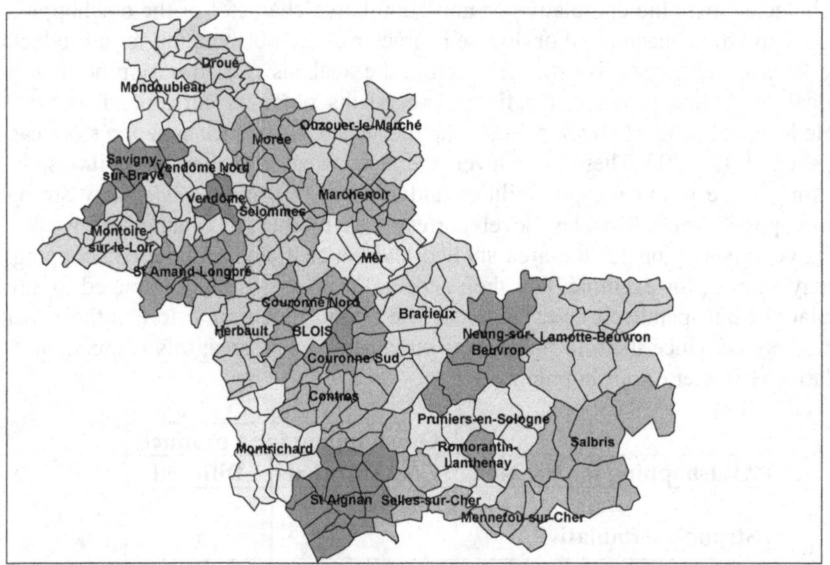

Figure 4.4: *Geographic division of Loir-et-Cher*

Statistics on the retail sector, taken from the database of the Chamber of Commerce and Industry of Loir-et-Cher, will be used and will relate to the following:

– a store of more than 300 m² for sports activities and other activities;

– details of overall spending for Vendôme;

– the retail performance for 25 families of products for Vendôme and other sub-areas;

– details of purchasing patterns for sports equipment and apparel for Vendôme, in other words the flows of attraction;

– wheresports equipment and apparel are currently purchased, in other words the outshopping for Vendôme and the other sub-areas;

– spending on sports products in millions of Euros for each of the sub-areas in the attraction area of Vendôme.

From these data, it is possible to define Vendôme's area of attraction in the sports sector, as shown in Figure 4.5, by distinguishing the territories under the influence of Vendôme at two levels: influence from 30% to 61% and from 14% to 29%.

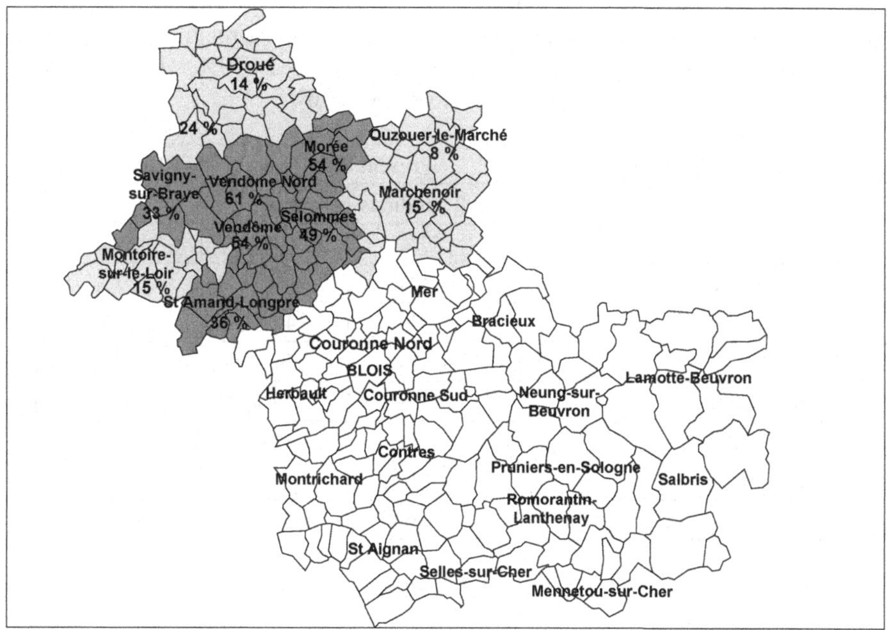

Figure 4.5: *The attraction of Vendôme for sports retail activities*

The share of Vendôme's residents' expenditure in Vendôme itself, for all products, is 77% (endogenous attraction). In the sports sector, this rate is only 54%. The retail supply for sports is therefore under-represented compared to the average. For the sports sector, outshopping is fairly high (46%) and is essentially done outside the area. The purchasing places identified are Tours-Chambry (30%), mail order purchases (8%), and Paris and the Parisian region (8%). In addition, analysis of the commercial supply indicates that there is only one sports store larger than 300 m² at Vendôme (Rédouin Sport – 360 m²).

Based on these items of information, a first series of recapture hypotheses in the event of the establishment of a new specialized sports superstore can be formulated. The following is a simplified illustration:

– reinforcement of attraction in the current trade area: the rates of recapture are predicted on the basis of a hypothesis of alignment with the average for all products and are brought up to the level of expenditure for each sub-area (see Table 4.2). This potential corresponds to about €750,000;

– with the outshopping mostly centered on Tours (and being moderately cumulative), the possibility of outshopping recapture is envisioned if there is a supply increase in the sports sector. If the store proves to be relatively attractive, a hypothesis of an increase in outshopping recapture of at least 30%, which represents around €225,000 of potential sales, is possible [DOU 96];

Sub-areas	Present Situation		Recovery
	All products	Sports	
Vendôme	77%	54%	23%
Nord Vendôme	71%	61%	10%
Selommes	58%	49%	9%
Morée	53%	54%	–
St Amand Longpré	48%	36%	12%
Savigny-en-Braye	23%	33%	5%
Droué	20%	14%	6%
Montoire-sur-le-Loir	16%	15%	3%

Table 4.2: *Reinforcement of the trade area attraction*

– the envisioned store also takes back a share the business of existing stores, hypermarkets and specialized superstores. The current sales of these stores are around €1 million. A hypothesis is possible of 15% recapture, which corresponds to approximately €240,000 of potential sales. The overall realistic potential of Vendôme is therefore €1.225 million, which, for average sales of €3,300 per square meter, the norm in the sports domain, is equivalent to a potential store of approximately 400 m². The different hypotheses and their outcomes can be "adjusted" by researching how the potential "varies" and what the thresholds are.

Following this calculation of retail development potential, there is still the issue of choosing the site for the store. This means moving from a "macro" territorial vision that integrates household buying behaviors, to a more sophisticated vision that takes into account other parameters. This will be the subject of the second part of this book.

4.3. Conclusion

In the commercial domain, the geographic weighting is directly linked to consumer purchase behaviors, which generate complex purchase flows in a territory. Theoretical models founded on rational consumer travel have been shown to have limitations in the current environment. Geomarketing, by generating behavioral databases and by developing multiple data, allows a better mastery of retail territories and better adaptation to customer needs. Consequently, geomarketing is integrated into the strategic approach by allowing the development of models that are differentiated in space. Geomarketing allows the decoding of the meaning found for each territory.

New analysis models need to be constructed on the basis of these behavioral databases, similar to that briefly described above for the evaluation of the commercial potential of a territory. Current research is oriented to the evaluation of the need for commercial stores in a sub-territory in relation to the behaviors of its inhabitants and to the existing supply, and to the impact of a new retail location on the existing retail supply. Behavioral databases coupled with territorial information encourage new marketing approaches; knowledge about territories and about the dynamic of consumption behaviors that are linked to them still has to be developed by the marketing world and the new data exploited so that customers can be known and understand better. The observation of links between the consumer and the territory thus constitute a new field of exploration for companies and research.

4.4. References

[ALA 00], Alard P., Dininger D., Stratégie de relation client: une nouvelle approche, *Banque Stratégie*, 169, 2000.

[APP 60], Applebaum W., Cohen S.R., Evaluating Store Sites and Determining Store Rents, *Economic Geography*, 36, 1-15, 1960.

[BAN 97], Le géomarketing appliqué au Crédit Lyonnais, *Banque*, 580, 1997.

[BOY 00], Boyer L., Burgaud D., *Le marketing avancé. Du one to one au e-business,* Editions d'Organisation, Paris, 2000.

[CAI 94], Caillosse J., Intercommunalités, invariances et mutations du modèle communal français, *Presses Universitaires de Rennes,* 25, 1994.

[CHE 92], Chetochine G., *Marketing stratégique de la distribution*, Editions Liaisons, Paris, 1992.

[CHE 98], Chetochine G., *Quelle distribution pour 2020?*, Editions Liaisons, Paris, 1998.

[CHR 33], Christaller W., *Die Zentral Orte in Süd Deutschland*, Iena, translated into English under the title (1966): *Central Places in Southern Germany*, Prentice Hall Inc., Englewood Cliffs, New Jersey, 1933.

[CLA 96], Clarke I., Horita M., Mackaness W., Capturing intuition in retail site assessment: towars the integration of hard and soft modelling approaches, Working Paper, University of Durham, 1996.

[CLI 92], Cliquet G., *Le Management stratégique des points de vente*, Sirey, Paris, 1992.

[CLI 97], Cliquet G., *L'attraction commerciale: fondements de la localisation différentielle, Revue belge de Géographie*, 121, 57, 1997.

[CON 48], Converse P. D., New Laws on Retail Gravitation, *Journal of Marketing*, 14, 4, 339-84, 1948.

[DES 01], Desse R.P., *Le nouveau commerce urbain*, Presses Universitaires de Rennes, 2001.

[DHA 97], Dham V., Localisez vos clients avec le géomarketing, *L'Essentiel du Management*, 1997.

[DIM 98], Dimensions Villes, *Les Dossiers de l'ADEUS*, 19, 2, 1998.

[DOU 96], Douard J.P., Servas J.P., Politique d'urbanisation commerciale: l'apport d'un système d'information dans le choix des politiques de développement commercial, *Les Cahiers de Recherche ICN, ERESTRATE, 96/09*, Nancy II University, 1996.

[DOU 98], Douard J.P., La zone de chalandise, *Les Cahiers de la Fonction Commerciale*, 5, Editions ERAG, 1998.

[DOU 98], Douard J.P., Les maires, acteurs de développement commercial: la nécessité d'outils d'information adaptés, *2ème Rencontres Ville Management Maires, Entrepreneurs, Emplois*, Bayonne, Dalloz, 1998.

[DOU 99], Douard J.P., Déterminer le potentiel d'une zone de chalandise: vers une approche par les flux, *Les Cahiers de la Fonction Commerciale*, 6, Editions ERAG, 1999.

[DOU 99], Douard J.P., La cartographie: un outil fédérateur des données, *Les Cahiers de la Fonction Commerciale*, 10, Editions ERAG, 1999.

[DOU 99], Douard J.P., Le développement de bases de données par les CCI: nouvel outil du commerce, *2ème Colloque Etienne Thil, Le Commerce: mémoire et enjeux à la veille du nouveau millénaire*, La Rochelle, 1999.

[DOU 00], Douard J.P., Heitz M., Methods of analysing commercial potential in an area and a geomarketing information system, *5ème Conférence franco-allemande AFM sur le commerce et la distribution en Europe*, Saint-Malo, 2000.

[DOU 01], Douard J.P., Heitz M., Déterminer les potentiels en matière de développement commercial pour un territoire: proposition d'une méthode basée sur les flux d'achat, *4e Colloque Etienne Thil*, La Rochelle, 2001.

[DOU 02], Douard J.P., Géomarketing et localisation des entreprises commerciales, in *Stratégies de localisation des entreprises commerciale et industrielles: de nouvelles perspectives*, De Boeck University, 2002.

[DUC 91], Ducrocq C., *Concurrence et stratégies dans la distribution*, Collection Entreprise Vuibert, Paris, 1991.

[GHO 87], Ghosh A., Mc Lafferty S., *Location Strategy for Retail and Service Firms*, Lexington Books, Mass., 1987.

[GHO 90], Ghosh A., *Retail Management*, The Dryden Press, Chicago, 1990.

[HUF 64], Huff D. L., Defining and Estimating a Trading Area, *Journal of Marketing* , 28, 3, p. 34-38, 1964.

[JAL 94], Jallais J., Orsoni J., Fady A., *Le marketing dans le commerce de détail,* Vuibert, Paris, 1994.

[LAT 01], Latour P., Le Floc'h J., *Géomarketing: principes, méthodes et applications*, Editions d'Organisation, Paris, 2001.

[LEF 00], Lefébure G., Venturi R., *La gestion de la relation client,* Editions d'Organisation, Paris, 2000.

[LES 97], Localisez vos clients avec le géomarketing, *L'essentiel du Management*, 1997.

[MAR 96], Marzloff B., Bellanger F., *Les Nouveaux Territoires du Marketing, Enquête sur le géomarketing et le marketing relationnel*, Editions Liaisons, Paris, 1996.

[REI 31], Reilly W. J., *The Law of Retail Gravitation*, William J. Reilly ed., 285 Madison Ave., NY, 1931.

[VEL 94], Veltz P., (1994), *Des Territoires pour apprendre et innover*, Editions de l'Aube, Paris, 1994.

[VIA 94], Viard J., *La Société d'Archipel*, Editions de l'Aube, Paris, 1994.

PART II

Retail Location and Geographic Information

Chapter 5

Geographical Information in Retail Store Location: A Managerial Perspective

Introduction

Store location has been a consistent component of the retailing literature, stemming for example from early texts that stressed the role of geography in retailing and marketing [DAV 76, DAW 79], through compilations of papers from those working on a variety of aspects of consumer store choice, store assessment and site research [DAV 84, WRI 88], to more recent attempts to define and isolate the strategic aspects of location that can be managed by retail organizations [BEN 93, BEN 95, CLA 94, CLA 97].

Set against this background, the purpose of the current chapter is to outline the key features of the existing literature on retail store location and provide a critique of it, with a view to helping to stimulate the beginnings of a new research agenda. From the outset, it is important to distinguish this chapter from those that it precedes. Chapter 6, for example, provides an overview of store location models that have been used by retail organizations; Chapter 7 emphasizes geographic systems and information; and Chapter 8 focuses on the spatial strategies used in retail development. The current chapter provides a critical context for each of these topics. It does this in the first section by summarizing the heritage of location research with reference to the geographical and marketing traditions from which it has developed. It especially highlights the significance of the "positivistic" and "empirically-directed" nature of most retail location research to date that describes and analyses the changing spatial structure of retailing [CLA 96b]. The discussion serves to

---

Chapter written by Ian CLARKE.

underline the gap in understanding regarding how strategic decisions by retailers are played out in time and space and, in particular, the way in which location decisions is made. Consequently, this theme is discussed in greater depth in section 5.2, which refers to recent location research that directly addresses this issue. In turn, however, this overview demonstrates another important theme, the central role of geography in retail competition and the importance of regulatory systems as a vehicle for controlling (and in some cases enhancing) the economic power of retail firms, which is addressed in section 5.3. The discussion naturally highlights the dual influence of retailers' corporate strategies and consumer culture on the form of retail development, and points towards an increasing need for store location researchers to explore the politics of location and consumer choice by bringing together discussions on the "new retail geography" [WRI 98b] and the geography of consumption practices [GRE 95, JAC 95a].

5.1. The location research tradition

A useful starting point for discussion is the sketch provided by Clarke and others [CLA 97] of how retail location research has developed historically. They conclude that retail location is an area that can scarcely claim to have been neglected over the past two decades. The reasons they give for this are the practical significance of location analysis to retailers' development; and the fact that geographers themselves have been at the forefront of inter-disciplinary retail studies within university business schools. They were critical of the existing corpus of research because of its increasing inadequacy in addressing the strategic dimensions of location. As they go on to elaborate:

> When Jones and Simmons (1990) commented on the growing convergence between "academic" and "practitioner" approaches to retail location, they were referring primarily to techniques of locational analysis, and not to conceptual links between geography and management/marketing. Indeed, for some time it seemed that, from different starting points, the two disciplines were like ships sailing almost parallel courses to the same destination each unaware of the other. Yet both potentially have much to gain from a closer fusion of approaches, frameworks and techniques since the former provides an understanding of the critical importance of space and how it is structured, and the latter of how decisions that have significant spatial imprints are reached. [CLA 97, p. 60]

5.1.1. *The contribution of geographers*

It is perhaps not surprising then that most of the research into retail location has come from geographers working in the retail field, covering three themes. First, there has been a substantial amount of work carried out on the spatial patterns of retailing, in terms of the macro-scale distribution of shops, shopping centers and retailers, and patterns of shoppers' behavior; at the micro-scale it has involved examination of the internal arrangements of shops and centers and the relationships to shoppers' movements. Brown's 1992 synthesis is typical of much of this type of work within the neo-classical, behavioral and structuralist paradigms [BRO 92]. The second geographic theme is the development of data and techniques for locational analysis and evaluation derived from the work of Nelson, Applebaum and, more recently, the rule-based approaches of property managers and surveyors [APP 66, NEL 58, WIG 86]. The principal achievements over the last two decades have been the building of sophisticated geo-demographic classifications; the growth and refinement of spatial interaction modeling; and the development of geographic information systems (GIS). The integration of these three achievements into spatial decision support systems (SDSS) represents the subsequent and on-going next phase of this development. The third and final theme concerns a focus on land-use planning and public policy issues surrounding retail location, where we see the influence of early theories (like Christaller's Central Place Theory or CPT) on planning philosophy and practice, which have been significant: see [DVA 84].

In simple terms, geography's contribution to our understanding of the importance of location in retailing stems from the strong geographical interrelationships between retail outlets and where customers live; consumers' choices of stores and the influence of the attributes of those stores; and the spatial distribution of retail outlets within urban areas [GUY 99]. Guy's recent review shows how geographical research has focused on the forecasting of store or center sales and the analysis of impacts of major new shopping developments. Largely as a result of this emphasis, however, he argues that:

> A major deficiency in much of the retail locational literature is perhaps its detachment from mainstream economic and social theory. Both 'central place' methods and spatial interaction modeling have been criticized many times for their simplistic assumptions and their lack of a sound theoretical basis. The subject has also in recent years failed to follow mainstream geography into more subjective and experiential areas of investigation. [GUY 99, p. 458]

Guy argues that the remedy for this imbalance is for geographers interested in store location to concentrate in the future on the implications of retailer strategy for the process of store location and network structure; to develop the focus on consumers who have been disadvantaged and marginalized by retail change; and by studies of the cultural interpretations of retail spaces and consumption. In effect, there is, therefore, an emergent recognition that a more substantive conceptualization of location dynamics needs to take into account the newer retail geographies based on culture, consumption and capital and the importance of wider theoretical frameworks concerned with underlying capitalist social relations and shifts in national and international political economies in understanding them [CLA 99, WRI 98]. I will return to this important fusion of geographic research interests later in the chapter.

5.1.2. *The contribution of marketing*

In contrast with the theoretical consideration and ramifications given to location within geography, within the marketing tradition, the emphasis has tended to be either strategic or operational. In this context, the importance of location is underplayed as a result of the tendency to take a rather formulaic approach to delivering marketing objectives through what is simplistically termed the retail "marketing mix" [McD 93]. The primary focus of writing here has been on the concept of "place" in the role of marketing management, rather than location as such, with the emphasis very much on the use of alternative channels of distribution to get goods from the producer to the end-user. Retailing is, essentially, treated in an aspatial fashion, with the overt importance of location being stressed as simply a matter of choosing (strategically, of course) the *type* of outlets that are used rather than their location relative to the market. Consequently, issues such as store environment and image are held to be of paramount importance, whereas the features of the site and the trade area around it are less so. Thus, whilst harsh, it is still fair to say that the emphasis on "place" in marketing literature has tended to under-represent work that has been carried out in other disciplines, where the absolute dimensions and attributes of place as locality (whether aesthetic, spiritual, natural, artificial or historical) rather then the relative aspects of location such as the spatial relationships of outlets to their customers and competitors [CLA 97, CLA 95] have been more emphasized.

As Clarke *et al* (1997) go on to point out in their review of this area, this clear division of approaches to location by geographers and marketers began to be recognized in the 1980s as a result of the emergence of management and marketing programs specialized in retailing. The focus of more recent research into retail location reflects the pragmatic preoccupation of retailers at that time on growth through the expansion of store networks, particularly in terms of technical and policy issues. This emphasis is perhaps not surprising, given the expansionary preoccupations of retailers – who were interested in using location techniques to manage investment risk – in the 1980s and 1990s and is reflected in some of the main academic retailing texts of that period [DAV 84, KNE 85, McG 90, WRI 88]. This emphasis is also found in the more strategic considerations of the role of location in retail planning, where attention is given to optimizing the portfolio or network of stores. Ghosh and McLafferty's contribution to this theme (the roots of which lie firmly in the geographic tradition) is most significant, where the preoccupation is with the analytical tools and technologies underlying spatial decision support that was increasingly being enabled by the growing analytical power of geographic information systems [GHO 82, GHO 87]. The second area in which geography has contributed to location strategy is provided by a number of studies of the spatial spread of individual companies, which have served to illustrate how retail organizations use space both defensively and aggressively, for example [LAU 86, LAU 88]. Such location strategy options open to retail firms have been summarized extensively elsewhere [CLA 93, JON 90]. It can be seen, therefore, that retail marketing research has tended to borrow from the geographic contributions to retail location, rather than contribute to an understanding of the spatial dimensions and challenges facing retail firms. The absence of a wider strategic perspective of location in retailing is notable [DAV 89], with only one or two exceptions, such as the location component of the retail 'policy decision tree' [KNE 85] and the location dimensions of the corporate environment [JON 90]. This under-representation of location aspects of strategy has been accentuated by the increasing levels of retail competition, market saturation and pressures and opportunities for retailers to internationalize their activities, which has led to the need to conceptualize the complex decision-making processes involved in retail planning.

The preceding synopsis of store location research traditions outlined more fully by Clarke *et al* [CLA 97] serves as a back-cloth for the contributions in this book on store location models (Chapter 6), geographic systems and information (Chapter 7); and the spatial strategies used in retail development (Chapter 8). More importantly, it provides a basis for responding to the criticism of the store location research literature levied by Guy (cited above) that it has over-emphasized location analysis and impact assessment techniques at the expense of new research areas. In the discussion that follows, therefore, I attempt to develop these new areas for store location research by focusing on two distinct themes and interpreting the relationship between them: the importance of the organizational decision-making processes underlying retailers' site investments and network restructuring; and the ramifications of such decisions for retail competition, the growth of retail power, and the changing geography of consumption.

5.2. Location and decision-making

The gap in understanding of organizational decision-making underlying location restructuring was most notably addressed in a paper by Bennison and others, which attempted to interpret how retailers managed their locations with reference to the rapid growth and restructuring occurring in UK retailing in the 1980s and 1990s [BEN 95]. The empirical evidence they collated, coupled with a review of the location literature, identified a variety of features inherent in location decision-making: the tendency to reduce investment risk and obtain local distribution and marketing economies by "contagious" store development; the inherent understanding of many retailers for the position of new locations within the urban hierarchy; the defensive and aggressive use of space in location decisions; the tendency in some circumstances to avoid competitors or to collude to control competition; the importance of the spatial dimensions of corporate acquisitions; and the implicit link between the consumer segments and the location of marketplace structures.

5.2.1. *Retailers and space awareness*

Underlying these features, however, the paper identified an implicit focus on technical and policy issues relating to the evaluation of individual sites [e.g. BOW 84, SIM 85], which contrasted with the more complex processes being used by retailers in the real world to develop and restructure their store networks. In short, what Bennison *et al.* concluded was that there was a need for a "broader framework for analysis based on an explicitly strategic perspective which puts location (place) *primus inter pares* [first among equals] in the retail marketing mix" [BEN 95, p. 18]. In a later paper, the same authors went on to develop a framework that contextualized space within retail marketing activity by conceptualizing location decisions at the heart of retailers' strategic thinking [CLA 97]. They coined the term "monadic" decision to reflect the fact that retailers invest and divest in individual outlets on a store-by-store basis, as a vital conceptual link to reflect how retailers' strategic decisions are operationalized. The framework emphasized the importance of the retailer having a clear idea of the customer location drivers or motivations underlying store success, rather than just the product conception, framed as a *location position.* Realizing this location position is the second component of retail strategy, in terms of having a clear idea of the size of outlet, the type of site it will occupy, and the extent of its geographic spread, with the management of the network being achieved through a series of decisions relating to individual ("monadic") decisions based on roll-out of new outlets, or the relocation, refitting, or rationalization of existing stores. Essentially, this means that each retailer should have a clear understanding of the likely spatial extent of the market for each outlet, which clearly varies with the attraction of the store itself, and the hierarchical type of location within which it is based (the "pull" of a major regional city will be substantially greater and geographically wider than that of a small market town, for example). The methodical way in which many retailers now "fit" particular store formats to appropriate locations in this way can be illustrated with examples such as the B&Q "Warehouse" concept and Tesco "Extra" hypermarket formats positioned in prominent accessible and free-standing locations within major cities. At the other extreme, many of the major food retailers have complemented their out-of-town provision with stores in major city center locations to cater for the needs of walk-in office and residential shoppers, using formats such as J. Sainsbury's "Central" and Tesco's "Metro" formats. Many retailers like these have adopted multi-format strategies to enable them to continue their expansion, with a consequence that their market shares have been able to continue expanding despite the threat of saturation, even without overseas growth.

Clearly, retailers have not always used geographic space as strategically and subtly as the above examples suggest. Over a decade and a half ago, for example, a survey of the extent of location planning in UK retailers by Simkin and others found retailers' awareness and application of geographic principles to be limited and largely the preserve of the leading grocery retailers [SIM 85a]. Since then, however, the growth in cheaper, more accessible geographic data and geographical information systems (as discussed in Chapter 7) has enabled many retailers to realize the strategic benefits of investment in them as a vehicle for integrating all parts of the retail marketing "mix" and as a means of interrogating data to aid decision-making [CLA 95]. More recently, a significant survey by Hernandez has explored the role of geographical information systems within retail location decision-making [HER 98, HER 99a] in several UK retail sectors. Whilst the use of geographic information and systems was shown to have increased substantially since the work of Simkin in the mid-1980s, the study for the first time drew explicit attention to the importance of organizational culture and the nature of decision-making in the successful adoption and application of GIS and location planning systems. The issues and challenges facing store location analysts have also been further illustrated and amplified by a comparative study of the adoption of GIS by retail organizations in the Netherlands, the UK and Canada [HER 99b]. Such research has drawn attention to the fact that relatively little is known about the *organizational context* of store location, and in particular, how retailers themselves conceive and understand geographic dimensions of store performance. Thus, this recent work has drawn attention to the need to explore how retail executives develop spatial awareness, and how they reach investment decisions in what is now almost always a *group* situation rather than decisions simply being made by an individual entrepreneur.

Retail decision-makers have long been known to take a nonchalant approach to the evaluation of new sites for store development [BRO 91, HER 98] and this cavalier approach still occurs despite the substantial technical advances made in location modeling and information systems [DAV 96]. Indeed, retail decision-makers continue to pride themselves in their "gut feel", "finger-in-the-air", "intuitive" or "qualitative" approaches [BOW 84, BRE 88, CLA 99a, CLA 99b, HER 99, ROG 87], frequently making location investment decisions on a combination of hunch, experience, and few rudimentary calculations [GUT 80].

5.2.2. *Individual and collective decision-making*

This understanding of retail location decision-making as a phenomenon relating to individual managers is, however, out of step with the general management literature, which emphasizes that strategic investment decisions (like new stores), are of such significance that in most organizations these are decisions that are made by groups of managers, rather than individuals acting alone. In fact, most strategic decisions involve substantial financial investment and typically relate to changes in the structure and location of the activities of organizations to improve effectiveness [HIC 86, MAR 88]. In this respect, longitudinal research [BUT 93] has demonstrated that decision effectiveness is the outcome of (1) the interaction between the shape and definition of the problem as seen by participants; (2) how individuals build and develop support for strategic solutions within the group; and (3) the influence particular people have on the nature and timing of the decision process itself. What we can glean from this is that, whilst retail location decisions may be arrived at *within* a group, an understanding of the cognitive abilities of individuals is still essential to our understanding of the effectiveness of store location decisions. Indeed, in environments dealing with large, unstructured decisions of this type [MIN 76], how *individuals* judge a particular situation or problem directly affects the effectiveness of the *group* decision in terms of the attainment of objectives and learning arising from a particular situation, as does the type of conflict present [BUT 93, DEA 96, HIC 86, MAR 88]. Thus, the collective cognition of top management is central to the success of the group in comprehending uncertainty inherent in a decision [BAN 93, KOR 95, LUC 94]. Understanding the conceptual models used by individuals is, therefore, vital both to the researcher attempting to understand the decision process and to the manager trying to evaluate the quality of ideas generated within the group [EDE 92, MAS 96].

Recently the relationship between the intuition of individual retail managers and decision-making groups is one that has begun to be highlighted and explored [CLA 01]. Clarke & Mackaness's exploratory investigation developed propositions about the structure and content of management intuition from the literature, using qualitative in-depth case studies to construct cognitive maps of their decision schemas. It illustrated that "retailer intuition" seems to come more into play as a means of "going beyond" the rational data and information, by using experiences to "cut through" to the essence of a situation, helping to make sense of it, and as a test of its validity. It also highlighted the need for future research on store location to compare the amount of "factual" content within individual managers' "spatial knowledge", since this appears to vary between managers and may reflect their intuitive tendencies. These differences may be because of the demands of their positions, or as a result of the depth of their previous experiences. The same research also suggested it would be useful to conduct longitudinal research with individual managers, getting them to repeat the mapping process at certain times in order to examine if and how their insight changes under different environmental conditions [REG 96]. Of course, a further explanation for the differences between the maps of executives exhibited in this paper might be their contrasting cognitive styles [ALL 96, McD 95, PAY 88]. This is clearly another area that deserves exploration through qualitative case studies to explore how the demographic, personality and psychological characteristics of individual retail managers affect the structure and content of their cognitive maps [LAN 75, McD 95, NAH 93]. Clarke and Mackaness also concluded that the cognitive maps of chief executives and more senior managers display a tendency to be simpler than those of their functional counterparts, and with a comparable level of coherence. Importantly, rather than displaying additional depth to their explanations, the study showed that more intuitive managers might seek to focus on the key elements of a decision, with the implication being that they might be *less* complex than those of functional managers. Finally, the same paper emphasized the questioning outlook of more senior retail managers – for instance, chief executives 'seeing' things in situations that their functional counterparts do not – and suggested that such insight might be reflected in the composition of the constructs in their cognitive maps. It could also be that it is the *connections* that more experienced executives make between different constructs, rather than the constructs themselves, which enable them to 'see' things that others do not, which is the basis for their intuitive insight. The study raised two additional propositions: that chief executives may have a preference for less complex decision schemas because they have less time to devote to detail and are able to compare and rationalize their understanding with those of other functional managers; and how these individual schemas are brought to bear in live group decision-making contexts [LAN 92, WEI 93]. How, for example, do individual schemas exert influence on the group? How does the group "make sense" of a situation using these cognitive starting points? Are individual schemas adjusted as a result of such interactions? Such questions are currently being raised in on-going research into retail store location decision-making, which is exploring how the cognitive maps of individual managers can be combined [CLA 00b] in order that this same qualitative information can be used within the decision process to complement more normative methods of site assessment (see Chapter 6) [CLA 00a]. Subsequent stages of this research will be examining how these decision schemas and outlooks are used to influence and affect decisions in a group context and, indeed, whether this process leads to more or less effective decisions as a result. Clearly, this research will require a methodological approach that involves more ethnographic "in-the-boardroom" observation, as a way of exploring not only how managers begin to make sense of their own intuitive judgement, but also in fact to ascertain whether the decisions they reach make intuitive sense.

5.3. Location, retailers and consumers

The preceding discussion on retail decision-making and retailers' strategic use of space may appear to be relatively unconnected with considerations of consumption – indeed, this was a point made earlier in the chapter with reference to the undue emphasis given to site location analysis compared to the strategies of retailers and the changing cultures of consumers [CLA 99, GUY 99]. Moreover, the conceptual split is also reflected in the retail literature in the debate between what has been termed the 'new retail geography' [WRI 98a] and changing patterns of consumption [MIL 95]. This relative separation of debates is surprising, given that, on the one hand, research into the quality of retail floor-space in terms of its age and attractiveness through investment in new outlets has been shown to be central to retailers being able to maintain their local competitiveness (LAN 198). On the other hand, we know that, from the consumer perspective, their perceptions of outlets, store choices and purchasing patterns change as a result of developments in the number, size and attraction of outlets available to them locally. The literature has tended to play down the substantial change in the marketing activities *within* the stores that has, to a large extent, been at the forefront of fuelling new patterns of consumption. Given that the stores themselves create "a space where everyday life meets the machinations of capitalism" [CLA 96b], it is encouraging that some social scientists working in the retail arena are beginning to stress the crucial links between the processes of store development and marketing by retailers, changes in consumption practices by consumers, new corporate geographies and store formats offering "different kinds of shopping experience ... [that] ... demand different kinds of shopping knowledge" [MIL 98a, p. 9]

5.3.1. *The retailer–consumer relationship*

In this light, a distinct but often undervalued contribution to store location research is the "situated" view of consumption stressed in the social science literature [FIN 96, GLE 98, GLE 96, JAC 95c, PRE 96]. Hitherto, however, the connection between the changing form of the retail system and changes in consumption has tended to be implicit rather than explicit. Whilst historical work reflects the reflexive relationship between retailer and consumer, as a space that is both conceived and contested by retailers and consumers (e.g. [ALE 99, SDPA 93]), the emphasis of some researchers is on the store as an "active context rather than a passive backdrop" to retail change [GLE 96]. Although such a grounded approach to understanding consumption embedded in changing urban lifestyles has been recently reinforced [GLE 98, MIL 98b], up to this point the intersection between retailers and consumers has tended only to be treated in a reductionist way in the literature of retail geography and consumption arenas [CLA 96a]. As has been pointed out elsewhere, what is now required is empirical research that isolates the two-way influence between retail provision and changing patterns of consumption, sensitive to situational interactions by using methodologies that enable the subtleties of social and cultural influences on consumption to emerge [CLA 00]. Some recent work serves to illustrate the way forward in this respect, coupling the sensitivity of the ethnographic approach to consumer moods, motivations and situations with the political economy approach to understanding the strategic priorities of retailers [MIL 98, PRE 96]. However, there is substantial commercial market research in this vein, and with few exceptions [GRE 95], academic work is extremely limited and empirically unanchored in terms of its corporate context.

If the ethnographic and political economy approaches are to be integrated, retail location research will need to be sensitive to the inequalities and politics of consumption, particularly in terms of how spatial relations between stores and consumers are developed and worked out in real terms [LAS 94, SAU 85, URR 85]. As Miles has noted, urban consumption can exclude as much as it provides, with many theorists taking it for granted that the resources for consumption are universally available [MIL 98]. As I have outlined at length elsewhere (CLA 00), what this means is that store location researchers must be as open not only to the effects of new stores on the existing retail system, but also to the various ways in which the behavior of some groups of consumers may undermine and exclude other groups. For instance, because of the differential levels of accessibility of stores by particular social groups, the impact of a new store may lead to the closure of small local outlets, on which less mobile groups may have been dependent. Certain consumer groups have more power to decide where to choose to shop, as illustrated in studies in Swansea and Cardiff [BRO 93, GUY 96], where less mobile groups were unable to take advantage of the larger product ranges of new shopping facilities and, therefore, became marginalized in urban life by a re-territorialization of urban space around new sites of consumption. Most existing accounts of consumption, however, actually say very little about what people do when they go shopping [JAC 95], despite some earlier studies that used micro-diaries to help explain patterns of store choice [WRI 80]. Recent ethnographic style research around two north London shopping centers has illustrated just how useful inter-disciplinary approaches can be in exploring the "performance" of consumption under the constraints of the existing retail system and on-going changes made to it by retailers [MIL 98c]. The potential contribution of this approach is that it serves to expose the simplistic notion of rational consumer "choice", replacing it with a fuller understanding of how consumer action and constrained embodiment affect the ability of consumers to consume within their everyday lives.

5.3.2. *Consumer choices and retail investments*

The challenge for store location researchers in understanding the retailer–consumer relationship more fully, however, is to be able to simultaneously articulate just how consumption choices are affected by retailers' strategic decisions over their investments in, and divestments from, their operating locations, as well as by the constraints and potentials brought about by their own lifestyles. I have argued at much greater length elsewhere that a reconceptualization of retail competition as a reflection of the actions embedded within a network of power relationships between retailers, and between retailers and manufacturers within the channel of distribution, is crucial to developing this fuller and richer account of consumption [CLA 00]. This is because decisions about store locations by retailers are the effective means by which power is exercised by "reconstructing the spaces and reorganizing the timings" of society [FOU 77]. New retail formats effectively re-mould consumer behavior and patterns of consumption by shaping the product choices that are available to them in particular locations at a given point in time [WRI 98]. In this broader process of redefining and legitimating rights to consume through store development [MAR 95], much is clearly dependent on what, politically, constitutes "acceptable" levels of competition at the national level and, at the local level, by persuading town planners that their own form of retail innovation is "what the customer wants" (see for example [PAL 99]). In this sense, the creation of demand is central to retailing, not exogenous from it, with retailers' power deriving from being able to offer a differentiated service, which can in turn act as a barrier to entry to smaller and weaker operators.

More fundamentally, however, retail competition at the local level is bound up with the inherent nature of the relationship with the consumer. A recent review on retail competition [LON 97] underlined the reasons for this being the small average purchase size of consumers relative to the retailer; the consumers' relative immobility, and the generally uniform nature of consumers, which makes a detailed comparison of prices and products in different outlets difficult. As a result of this power asymmetry within the marketing channel, enhanced retail buying power may or may not be passed on to consumers, since as has been put forward elsewhere, competition as far as the consumer is concerned is essentially a *local* phenomenon in which competitiveness is influenced by the intersection between the amount and quality of retail provision and the size of the local market [CLA 00]. This is because "perfect" competition is only possible when new entrants can capture a perceptible share of their competitors' local geographic market [STE 91]. What this argument belies is our poor understanding of the effects of changes in the structure of local retail systems and how these are utilized by different groups of consumers. There is an obvious need to look at how consumers' spending patterns change over time as a result of retail change, in terms of what consumers purchase, how much they spend, and where they buy it – but to do so informed by an understanding of how the retailer sees the strategic role of the new store (political economy approach) and the embeddedness of consumption within household dynamics (ethnographic approach).

5.4. Conclusion

This chapter began with the critique from a number of authors that the literature on retail store location research has been too preoccupied with the two themes of sales forecasting and retail impact assessment, arguably driven by the twin demands of retail organizations and planners. The review illustrated how these foci have developed historically, with the result that certain critical aspects of the underlying dynamic of retail store locations have tended to be underplayed in research priorities. The discussion in the chapter, therefore, has focused on how strategic decisions are made and played out by retail firms in time and space, and the importance in this process of geography to retail competition and consumer choice.

The chapter has, therefore, underlined three imperatives for store location research. The first imperative, I believe, has to center on the process of articulating the inter-relationships between retailers' strategic decisions about location and consumers' responses to the changing retail landscape. The argument I have put forward is that store location research will benefit substantially from a reintegration of location theory with mainstream debates in economic and social theory, in order to develop a fuller conceptualization of the dynamics of retail location. The primary challenge, then, is the need to integrate debates concerning changing retail corporate geographies, with the spatially localized nature of consumption [CLA 00]. In practical terms, the chapter has emphasized that this will mean empirical research that explores store location subjectively and experientially – both in relation to how *retail executives* make decisions about where to locate, and how *consumers'* lives are affected by their own experiences of shopping in different stores and locations.

This inter-relationship between retailers' strategic decisions about locations and consumer choices about where to shop seem, on the surface, to be only superficially related. However, as Dawson has forcefully pointed out in a recent prospective review of the challenges facing retail managers and researchers [DAW 00], retailing, compared to manufacturing, is much more closely connected to consumer culture, which means that consumer culture itself is central to whether or not retail brand-names are recognized and accepted by consumers in new locations – either in new localities or in new national markets. A combined reconceptualization of the political-economy approach – which emphasizes the *strategic* imperatives of the retail landscape – and the highly contextualized approach to consumption favored by other social scientists, coupled with grounded empirical work – is central to exploring how this relationship between retailers and consumers plays out in real terms, a point very recently made by Miller [MIL 01].

I have argued also that there is a secondary imperative in developing the store location research agenda, which is the need to explore in much greater depth how retail decision-makers themselves develop their own spatial awareness that underlines their investment decisions in new and existing stores. Research could be usefully informed by both marketers and geographers working in this area being willing to draw off the extensive literature on individual and group decisions that is available in the general management literature. A recent example of the contribution that can be made by such a genuinely inter-disciplinary approach to research is provided by the recent exploratory work referred to in this chapter, which is exploring the form and role of "management intuition" in retailers' decision-making [CLA 01]. Such an approach would enable store location academics in the future to play a much more central role in helping to improve management *practice*, rather than just inform decisions *per se* by helping retailers to make better and more effective location decisions, based on richer appraisals of risk and uncertainty inherent in both the decision-making process and the environment in which they operate. This is the same conclusion that has also been reached in a more general context by others (e.g. [DAW 00]).

A final imperative for store location researchers emerging from this review and discussion centers on the value of employing deeper ethnographic-style approaches to consumption. If it proves possible for researchers to undertake this difficult balance of providing strategic insight to retail decisions *and* a sensitive approach to the grounded aspects of consumer choice, embedded within household dynamics, and an understanding of the inherently *local* nature of retail competition and consumer choice, then it academics should be able to make more insightful contributions to public debates surrounding the implications of retailers' strategies for the effects on the social inclusion and exclusion of different consumer groups.

5.5. References

[ALE 99], Alexander A. and Shaw G., Guest Editorial: Contesting Retail Space. Competition in the Retail Trades, 1879-1960, *The International Review of Retail, Distribution and Consumer Research*, 9(3), 223-224, 1999.

[ALL 96], Allison C. and Hayes J., The Cognitive Style Index: A Measure Of Intuition-Analysis For Organizational Research, *Journal of Management Studies*, 33(1), 119-135, 1996.

[APP 66], Applebaum W., Methods for Determining Store Trade Areas, Market Penetration, and Potential Sales, *Journal of Marketing Research*, 3(2), 127-141, 1966.

[BAN 93], Bantel K. A., Strategic Clarity in Banking: Role of Top Management Team Demography, *Psychological Reports*, 73(3), 1187-1201, 1993.

[BEN 93], Bennison D., Clarke I. and Pal J., *The Locational Imperative: Store Networks and Corporate Strategies in the 1990s,* Paper presented at the ESRC Seminar: Research Themes in retailing, Manchester Business School, 1993.

[BEN 95], Bennison D., Clarke I. and Pal J., Locational Decision Making in Retailing: An Exploratory Framework for Analysis, *The International Review of Retail, Distribution and Consumer Research, 5*(1), 1-20, 1995.

[BOW 84], Bowlby S., Breheny M. J. and Foot D., Store Location: Problems and Methods 1: Is Locating a Viable Store Becoming More Difficult?, *Retail & Distribution Management*, 12(5), 31-33, 1984.

[BRE 88], Breheny M. J., Practical methods of retail location analysis, in N. Wrigley (Ed.), *Store Choice, Store Location and Market Analysis*, London: Wiley, 1988, pp. 39-86.

[BRO 91], Brown S., Retail Location: The Post Hierarchical Challenge, *The International Review of Retail, Distribution and Consumer Research,* 1(3), 367-81, 1991.

[BRO 92], Brown S., *Retail Location: A Micro-scale Perspective*. Aldershot: Avebury, 1992.

[BRO 93], Bromley R. D. F. and Thomas C. J., The Retail Revolution, the Carless Shopper and Disadvantage, *Transactions, Institute of British Geographers, New Series,* 18, 222-36, 1993.

[BUT 93], Butler R., Davies L., Pike R. and Sharp J., *Strategic Investment Decisions: Theory, Practice and Process,* London: Routledge, 1993.

[CLA 00], Clarke I., Retail Power, Competition And Local Consumer Choice In The UK Grocery Sector, *European Journal of Marketing*, 34(8), 975-1002, 2000.

[CLA 00], Clarke I., Horita M. and Mackaness W., The Spatial Knowledge of Retail Decision-Makers: Capturing and Interpreting Group Insight Using a Composite Cognitive Map. *The International Review of Retail, Distribution & Consumer Research*, 10(3), 265-85, 2000.

[CLA 00a], Clarke I., Horita M. and Mackaness W., *"Making Sense" of Retail Decision-makers Spatial Knowledge: Towards an Analogue-based Decision Support System using Clustering Analysis.* Paper presented at the 7th European Institute of Retailing & Services

Science Conference, *Recent Advances in Retailing & Services Science*, Sintra, Portugal, 2000.

[CLA 01], Clarke I. and Mackaness W., Management "Intuition": An Interpretative Account of Structure and Content of Decision Schemas using Cognitive Maps, *Journal of Management Studies,* 38(2), 147-72, 2001.

[CLA 93], Clarke I., *Managing Location,* Papers and Proceedings of the Applied Geography Conferences, 16, 123-129, Toronto, 1993.

[CLA 94], Clarke I., Editorial: Retail location - A strategic perspective on planning and management. *International Journal of Retail and Distribution Management*, 22(6), 4-5, 1994.

[CLA 95], Clarke I. and Rowley J., A Case for Spatial Decision Support Systems in Retail Location Planning, *The International Journal of Retail and Distribution Management,* 23(3), 4-10, 1995.

[CLA 95], Clarke I. and Schmidt R., Beyond the Servicescape: The Experience of Place, *Journal of Retailing and Consumer Services*, 2(3), 49-62, 1995.

[CLA 96a], Clarke D., The Limits to Retail Capital, in N. Wrigley & M. Lowe (Eds.), *Retailing, Consumption and Capital: Towards the New Retail Geography*, London: Routledge, 1996, (pp. 284-301).

[CLA 97], Clarke I., Bennison D. and Pal J., Towards a Contemporary Perspective of Retail Location. *The International Journal of Retail and Distribution Management*, 25(2), 59-69, 1997.

[CLA 99], Clarke G., Geodemographics, marketing and retail location, in M. Pacione (Ed.), *Applied Geography: Principles and Practice*, London: Routledge, 1999, pp. 577-92.

[CLA 99a], Clarke I., Horita M. and Mackaness W., *Capturing Intuition in Retail Site Assessment: Towards the Integration of "Hard" and "Soft" Modelling Approaches*, paper presented at the Localisation des Enterprises Commerciales, Industrielles et des Services Publics dans L'espace Europeen: Theories et Pratiques, Rennes, Brittany, 1999.

[CLA 99b], Clarke I., Mackaness W. and Horita M., *Integrating "Hard" and "Soft" Approaches to Modelling Intuition in Retail Site Assessment*, paper presented at the Human-Computer Interaction – INTERACT'99, Edinburgh, 1999.

[DAV 76], Davies R. L., *Marketing Geography, with Special Reference to Retailing*, London: Methuen, 1976.

[DAV 84], Davies R., *Retailing and Commercial Planning*, London: Croom Helm, 1984.

[DAV 84], Davies R. and Rogers D. (Eds.), *Store Location and Store Assessment Research.* Chichester: Wiley, 1984.

[DAV 89], Davies G. and Brookes J., *Positioning Strategy in Retailing*. London: Paul Chapman, 1989.

[DAW 00], Dawson J., Retailing at Century End: Some Challenges for Management and Research, *The International Review of Retail, Distribution and Consumer Research,* 10(2), 119-48, 2000.

[DAW 79], Dawson J. A., *The Marketing Environment*, London: Croom Helm Ltd, 1979.

[DEA 96], Dean J. W. and Sharfman M. P., Does Decision-process Matter? – A Study of Strategic Decision-making Effectiveness, *Academy of Management Journal,* 39(2), 368-396, 1996.

[EDE 92], Eden C., Strategy Development as a Social Process, *Journal of Management Studies,* 29(6), 799 - 811, 1992.

[FIN 96], Fine B., Heasman M. and Wright J., *Consumption in the Age of Affluence: The world of food*, London: Routledge, 1996

[FOU 77], Foucault M. *Discipline and Punish: The Birth of the Prison*, London: Allen Lane, 1977.

[GHO 82], Ghosh A. and McLafferty S. L., Locating Stores in Uncertain Environments: A Scenario Planning Approach, *Journal of Retailing*, 58(4), 5-23, 1982.

[GHO 87], Ghosh A. and McLafferty S. L., *Location Strategies for Retail and Service Firms*, Lexington, Massachusetts: Lexington Books, 1987.

[GLE 96], Glennie P. D. and Thrift N. J., Consumers, Identities, and Consumption Spaces in Early-modern England, *Environment and Planning A*, 28, 25-45, 1996.

[GLE 98], Glennie P., Consumption, Consumerism and Urban Form: Historical Perspectives, *Urban Studies*, 35(5-6), 927-951, 1998.

[GRE 95], Gregson N., And Now It's all Consumption?, *Progress in Human Geography*, 19(1), 135-141, 1995.

[GUY 96], Guy C., Corporate Strategies in Food Retailing and their Local Impacts: A Case Study of Cardiff, *Environment and Planning A*, 28, 1575-1602, 1996.

[GUY 99], Guy C., Retail Location Analysis, in M. Pacione (Ed.), *Applied Geography: Principles and Practice*, London: Routledge, 1999, pp. 450-62.

[HER 99], Hernandez T., Scholten H. J., Bennison D., Biasiotto M., Cornelius S. and van der Beek M., *Explaining Retail GIS: The Adoption, Use and Development of GIS by Retail Organisation in the Netherlands, the UK and Canada*, (Vol. 258). Utrecht, 1999.

[HER 99a], Hernandez J. A., *The role of geographical information systems within retail location decision making,* unpublished PhD in Philosophy, Manchester Metropolitan University, Manchester, 1998.

[HER 99b], Hernandez T. and Bennison D., *The Art and Science of Retail Location Decisions*, paper presented at the The 10th International Conference on Research in the Distributive Trades, University of Stirling, 1999.

[HIC 86], Hickson D., Butler R., Cray D., Mallory G. and Wilson D. *Top Decisions: Strategic Decision Making in Organizations*, Oxford: Basil Blackwell, 1986.

[JAC 95a], Jackson P., Guest Editorial: Changing Geographies of Consumption, *Environment and Planning A*, 27, 1875-6, 1995.

[JAC 95b], Jackson P. and Holbrook B., Multiple Meanings: Shopping and the Cultural Politics of Identity, *Environment and Planning A*, 27, 1913-1930, 1995.

[JAC 95c], Jackson P. and Thrift N., Geographies of consumption, in D. Miller (Ed.), *Acknowledging Consumption: A Review of New Studies*, London: Routledge, 1995, pp. 204-237.

[JON 90], Jones K. and Simmons J., *The Retail Environment*, London: Routledge, 1990.

[KNE 85], Knee D. and Walters D., *Strategy in Retailing: Theory and Application*, Oxford: Philip Alan, 1985.

[KOR 95], Korsgaard M. A., Schweiger D. M. and Sapienza H. J., Building Commitment, Attachment and Trust in Strategic Decision Making Teams: The Role of Procedural Justice, *Academy of Management Journal*, 38(1), 60-84, 1995.

[LAN 75], Langer E. J., The Illusion of Control, *Journal of Personality and Social Psychology*, 32(2), 311-38, 1975.

[LAN 92], Langfield-Smith K., Exploring the Need for a Shared Cognitive Map, *Journal of Management Studies,* 29/3 (Special Issue: On the Nature of Cognitive Maps), 349-361, 1992.

[LAN 98], Langston P., Clarke G. P. and Clarke D. B., Retail Saturation: The Debate in the Mid-1990s, *Environment and Planning A*, 30, 49-66, 1998.

[LAS 94], Lash S. and Urry J., *Economies of Signs & Space*, London: Sage Publications Ltd., 1994.

[LAU 86], Laulajainen R. and Gadde L., Locational Avoidance: A Case Study of Three Swedish Retail Chains, *Regional Studies*, 20(2), 131-40, 1986.

[LAU 88], Laulajainen R., Chain Store Expansion in National Space, *Geografiska Annaler*, 70 B(2), 293-299, 1988.

[LON 97], London Economics, *Competition in Retailing* (Research Paper 13), London: Office of Fair Trading, 1997.

[LUC 94], Luce R. D. and Winterfeldt D. V., What Common Ground Exists for Descriptive, Prescriptive and Normative Utility Theories? *Management Science*, 40(2), 263-279, 1994.

[MAR 88], Marsh P., Barwise P., Thomas K. and Wesley R., *Managing Strategic Investment Decisions in Large Diversified Companies*, London: Centre for Business Strategy, London Business School, 1988.

[MAR 95], Marsden T. and Wrigley N., Regulation, Retailing, and Consumption. *Environment and Planning A*, 27, 1899-1912, 1995.

[MAS 96], Massey A. and Wallace W., Understanding and Facilitating Group Problem Structuring and Formulation: Mental Representations, Interaction and Representation Aids, *Decision Support Systems*, 17, 253-274, 1996.

[McD 95], McDougall Y. B., Decision-making Under Risk: Risk Preference, Monetary Goals and Information Search, *Personality and Individual Differences*, 18(6), 771-82, 1995.

[McG 90], McGoldrick P. J., *Retail Marketing*, London: McGraw-Hill, 1990.

[MIL 01], Miller D., *The Dialectics of Shopping*, Chicago: University of Chicago Press, 2001.

[MIL 95], Miller D. (Ed.), *Acknowledging Consumption: A Review of New Studies*, London: Routledge, 1995.

[MIL 98], Miles S., The Consuming Paradox: A New Research Agenda for Urban Consumption, *Urban Studies*, 35(5-6), 1001-8, 1998.

[MIL 98], Miller D., *A Theory of Shopping*, Cambridge: Polity Press, 1998.

[MIL 98], Miller D., Jackson P., Thrift N., Holbrook B. and Rowlands M. (Eds.), *Shopping, Place and Identity*, London: Routledge, 1998.

[MIN 76], Mintzberg H., Raisinghani D. and Theoret A., The Structure of Unstructured Decision Processes, *Administrative Science Quarterly*, 21(2), 246-75, 1976.

[NAH 93], Nahavandi A. and Melekzadeh A. R., Leader Style in Strategy and Organizational Performance: An Integrative Framework, *Journal of Management Studies*, 30(3), 405-425, 1993.

[NEL 58], Nelson R. L., *The Selection of Retail Locations*, New York: Dodge, 1958.

[PAL 99], Pal J., *The Power to Influence: The role of UK central government land use planning policies in influencing retailers' location strategies*, unpublished Masters by research, The Manchester Metropolitan University, Manchester, 1999.

[PAY 88], Payne J. W., Bettman J. R. and Johnson E. J., Adaptive Strategy Selection in Decision Making, *Journal of Experimental Psychology: Learning, Memory and Cognition*, 3, 534-52, 1988.

[PRE 96], Pred A., Interfusions: Consumption, Identity and the Practices and Power Relations of Everyday Life, *Environment and Planning A*, 28, 11-24, 1996.

[ROG 87], Rogers D., Shop location analysis in E. McFayden (Ed.), *The Changing Face of British Retailing*, London: Newman Books, 1987.

[SAU 85], Saunders P., Space, the city and urban sociology in D. Gregory & J. Urry (Eds.), *Social Relations and Spatial Structures*, London: MacMillan, 1985, pp. 67-89.

[SIM 85a], Simkin L. P. *et al*, How Retailers Put Location Techniques into Operation, *Retail and Distribution Management, May/June*, 21-6, 1985.

[SPA 93], Sparks L., The rise and fall of mass marketing? Food retailing in Great Britain since 1960, in R. S. Tedlow & G. Jones (Eds.), *The Rise and Fall of Mass Marketing*, London: Routledge, 1993, pp. 58-92.

[STE 91], Steiner R. L., Intrabrand Competition – Stepchild of Antitrust, *The Antitrust Law Bulletin*, 36 (Spring), 155-200, 1991.

[URR 85], Urry J., Social relations, space and time, in D. Gregory & J. Urry (Eds.), *Social Relations and Spatial Structures*, London: MacMillan, 1985, pp. 20-48.

[WEI 93], Weick K. E. and Roberts K. H., Collective Mind in Organizations – Heedful Interrelating On Flight Decks, *Administrative Science Quarterly*, 38(3), 357-381, 1993.

[WIG 86], Wiggins K. P., *Principles of Valuation*, Reading: University of Reading, College of Estate Management, 1986.

[WRI 80], Wrigley N., An approach to the modelling of shop-choice patterns: An exploratory analysis of purchasing patterns in a British city, in D. T. Herbert & R. J. Johnston (Eds.), *Geography and the Urban Environment: Progress in Research and Applications*, Chichester: John Wiley, 1980 Vol. III, pp. 45-85.

[WRI 88], Wrigley N. (Ed.), *Store Choice, Store Location and Market Analysis,* Chichester: Wiley, 1988.

[WRI 98a], Wrigley N., How British retailers have shaped food choice, in A. Murcott (Ed.), *The Social Science of Food Choice*, London: Longman, 1998, pp. 112-128.

[WRI 98b], Wrigley N. and Lowe M. (Eds.), *Retailing, Consumption and Capital: Towards the New Retail Geography*, Harlow: Longman, 1998.

Chapter 6

Retail Location Models

Introduction

Understanding the location of economic activities is a research topic that has concerned researchers for quite some time [THÜ 95]. Very quickly, however, the most important part of this work came to concern industrial activity. It was not until the 20th century that the first specific studies on what was called retail location, in other words store site location, were undertaken. The initial models relied on the analogy with Newton's theory of universal attraction: the law of retail gravitation [REI 31]. With the evolution of urbanization, of the spatial behavior of consumers, whose mobility is increasing, and of marketing differentiation practices implemented by retail companies, the models have evolved considerably [HUF 64, NAK 74], even if none of the most well-known models have been totally rejected. It is rather curious to note that for several years certain retail location models have been based on models originally designed for industrial location [ACH 82].

For the past 15 or so years, numerous authors have proposed state-of-the-art location models, in articles [CLI 88, CRA 84, SIM 85], in books dealing with store location [BER 88, BRO 92, CLI 92a, DAV 84, GHO 87a, HAY 84, PON 88, WRI 88], or in more general works on management or retail marketing [DAV 88, JAL 94, GHO 90]. Works dealing with market share models [COO 88, HER 95, LIL 92] give interesting syntheses, because gravitation and market share models have mutually enriched one another to the point that it is currently possible to distinguish between the two only by using particular variables or indicators. However, most of these works, not to say all of them, only deal with modeling intended to facilitate the location of stores. We aim to show here that these gravitation models have evolved

Chapter written by Gérard CLIQUET.

to the point when they are no longer as static as certain authors would have wished [LAU 87].

Most retail location models are founded on the study of retail attraction. This is a phenomenon that all store managers should understand and numerous modeling attempts have been made over the past 70 years to try to understand it better. The analogy with universal attraction at first appeared obvious before its limitations were discovered and the field of application of so-called "gravitation" models was broadened. These models were used in order to facilitate the decision-making process in store location. This fundamental decision has polarized the attention of researchers and retailers for quite some time, even if current demand has been favored over potential demand [STE 88]. Yet a bad choice in this domain can be very expensive, which shows the need for modeling, or rationality, which increases in proportion to the rise in the cost of errors [LEB 74]. But the implementation of these models is costly; using them once (to locate a store) constitutes a large investment with doubtful profitability compared to empirical methods, which often give good results but without predictive power. One can be tempted to adapt this modeling in order to improve the management of retail attraction once the store is established [CLI 95].

The retail attraction exerted by stores is a phenomenon that is based on a supply on the one hand and a behavior *vis-à-vis* this supply on the other. The supply is constituted equally by the products, in the overall sense, proposed for the store and by the principal attributes of the store. The products have been the subject of various classifications, among which Copeland's [COP 23] distinguishes between convenience goods, shopping goods and specialty goods; this classification can lead to a veritable hierarchical system of products, which is the foundation of the central places theory [CHR 33]. The behavior of the demand in relation to this supply often depends on the distance to be traveled and is therefore linked to the principle of least effort in varying degrees (depending on the product) [ZIP 49]. Consumer travel time to reach stores has been considered the most reliable measure of distance [BRU 68]. The retail attraction of the store is defined as the ability of the store to make consumers travel and is measured in terms of absolute or relative frequentation (market share). Two principal factors affect store attraction: topography (difficult to model) and competition. Store retail attraction is measured according to the range of its trade area. The analogy with universal attraction, despite seeming rather trivial today, seems natural and for this reason formed the foundation of the first models. The influence of these choice models [LUC 59] has made it possible to go from a deterministic conception to a probabilistic conception of attraction models, leading to an interactive type of modeling.

We will first deal with gravitation models used in retail location before developing spatial interaction models and multiple location models. Finally, we will examine the links between retail location models and geographic information systems through the notion of site marketing, currently considered very promising in certain professional domains.

6.1. Gravitation models

Founded on the analogy between universal gravitation with the location of cities and their reciprocal attraction, gravitation models are actually attraction models that essential rely on two variables: distance and mass. These models, initially defined as deterministic through the law of retail gravitation [REI 31], will little by little free themselves from this limitation, which poses applicability problems, especially in urban realms, and become more probabilistic. They can therefore be implemented in cities and particularly for specialized stores [HUF 62].

We will therefore first look at the law of retail gravitation, followed by the Huff model [HUF 64], which, although fairly old, are both still the subject of academic research in geography and marketing, as well as being applied in the professional realm.

6.1.1. *The law of retail gravitation: a deterministic model*

Reilly's law is one of the foundations of the theory of spatial interaction. Based on a formulation close to that of Newton in explaining universal gravitation, Reilly proposed, through analogy, a law of retail gravitation. He gives the following pronouncement of this operational conception of business: "Two cities attract retail trade from an intermediate city or town in the vicinity of a breaking-point, approximately in direct proportion to the populations of the two cities and in inverse proportion to the square of the distances from these two cities to the intermediate town." [REI 31, p. 9].

The general formulation is as follows:

$$B_a / B_b = (P_a / P_b)^N * (D_b / D_a)^n \quad [6.1]$$

where:

B_a is the activity attracted by the city a from an intermediate town;

B_b is the activity attracted by the city b from an intermediate town;

P_a is the population of a;

P_b is the population of b;

D_a is the distance from city a to the intermediate town;

D_b is the distance from city b to the intermediate town;

N is an exponent that indicates the rate at which the external business attracted by a city increases as the population of the city rises;

n is an exponent that indicates the rate at which the external business attracted by a city decreases as the population of this city decreases.

Even though an attempt of generalizing the law has been made [BAT 78], the exponents N and n have been estimated empirically [CON 49, REI 31] and their values are 1 for N and 2 for n. From this, a simpler formulation than [6.1] has been proposed:

$$B_a / B_b = (P_a / P_b) * (D_b / D_a) \qquad [6.2]$$

Concerning this, there have been many academic works [COH 60, DOU 49, FUS 88, GIR 60, GUI 71, OKE 89, STR 48] and professional studies [APP 68, ELL 54, FIN 54, McK 89]. Criticism has not been lacking, especially concerning its determinism [PIA 69]. In fact, according to this law, a consumer is condemned to making his purchases in a precise city. Furthermore, this law is not suited to describing the phenomenon of attraction in urban areas because of the overlapping of different trade areas. This is why Laulajainen [LAU 87] suggested reserving the use of the law of retail gravitation [REI 31] to small agglomerations in exploratory studies intended to estimate potential trade areas. However, its use is still also recommended for determining the limit points between cities [NOI 89] or between two shopping centers [COL 90]. Nevertheless, the determinism and the overlapping of trade areas constituted operational obstacles that had to be bypassed and research became oriented towards a probabilistic approach [HUF 64].

6.1.2. *The Huff probabilistic model*

The Huff model [HUF 64] is indeed a gravitation model, because it uses the notions of distance and mass (in this case, the sales surface area of the store). It is considered probabilistic in the sense that it supplies the probability P_{ij} that a consumer situated at point i makes his purchases in a store j:

$$P_{ij} = \frac{S_j / (T_{ij})^{\beta}}{\sum_{j=1}^{n} S_{ij} / (T_{ij})^{\beta}} \qquad [6.3]$$

where:

T_{ij} is the accessibility time (here as a measure of distance);

S_{ij} is the size of the store measured in square meters of sales surface area;

β is the empirically estimated parameter reflecting the effect of the length of trips in time on different consumer purchases (varying according to product).

The expected number of potential consumers for each store can be calculated by applying the probability to the total number of consumers in a given geographic area, generally called a *cell*. Only taking into account surface area and distance, this model should be applied to homogeneous areas *vis-à-vis* uncontrollable variables (socio-demographic criteria of potential customers), which shows the necessity of a preliminary geographic division into distinct cells of the trade area studied [HUF 63]. This division should take into account eventual natural ruptures and lines of communication on the one hand, and outshopping phenomena of the studied trade area towards other trade areas, and *vice versa*, on the other.

The Huff model is original in that it relies on two essential provisions in the understanding of the retail attraction phenomenon [JAI 79]: the law of retail gravitation [REI 31] and Luce's choice axiom [LUC 59] – in other words on the stochastic character of consumer spatial behavior in relation to store usefulness. This model, by integrating the problems of hierarchical systems, the question of product classification and the superposition of trade areas, therefore provides an answer to the limitations of the study of attraction in urban areas. Hierarchical problems are taken into account, where all the competitors of a given trade area are considered. Product classification appears through the coefficient β, which involves a different model per product. Finally, the overlapping of trade areas is represented since this model supplies an individual probability of a consumer visit and, at the aggregate level, a probable frequentation percentage for each cell of the zone studied (neighborhood, city, region, etc.). However, several difficulties limit the application of the Huff model [McK 71]:

– the use of the model is restricted by the condition of homogeneity concerning both potential consumers and stores equally;

– in all ways, the explanatory power is considerably reduced by the insufficient number of variables considered [ENG 82], even if, in certain cases, this can be proven to be sufficient [NEV 80];

– there have been several proposals for estimation procedures for the determination of coefficient β [HAI 72, HUF 66, KUE 66, PES 68, NAK 74a, NAK 82] with none being truly satisfactory.

Micro-analytical store choice models [CRA 79] have permitted a loosening of the homogeneity restriction. They introduce into the Huff model an indicator of congruence between the image of the stores and that which consumers have of themselves, or by extension of gravitation models with the help of Poisson regression destined to take into account consumer characteristics and the attributes of shopping centers that can have an influence on behavior [OKO 88]. In the Poisson regression, the variable to be explained is the number of monthly visits to the shopping centers.

In fact, the problems alluded to above can be resolved by the generalization of the Huff model and the conception of spatial interaction models (see the next section). This model has nonetheless allowed the implementation of numerous research studies [FOR 68; HAI 72]. Certain studies [STA 76, NEV 80] have even attempted to generalize the Huff model by including in it the store image. The professional world has likewise adopted it and it has often been recommended in the preliminary studies of retail location, both in France [TAI 71] and in the USA, especially at the site determination stage [BAR 88, LAU 87]. In fact, while its predictive power is of an acceptable precision in a number of cases, such as supermarkets or shopping centers [BER 88], the location of stores requires the consideration of many other variables [CRA 84]. A generalization of this model was proposed by Nakanishi and Cooper [NAK 74a], founded on the idea of spatial interaction.

Spatial interaction is actually a specific characteristic of human behavior insofar as it allows mankind, no matter what the distance, to move about to exchange information and products [HAY 84]. Spatial interaction models are multiplicative, for they are conceived based on interactions between all the elements of one pole with all the elements of another pole. They are founded on the work of regional economy specialists [CAR 56, ISA 60, OLS 65] and on Dodd's interaction hypothesis [DOD 50], Wilson's entropy model [WIL 70] and Stouffer's opportunity model [STO 60]. Wilson [WIL 71] gives it in a very general form:

$$T_{ij} = K \frac{W_i^{(1)} W_j^{(2)}}{c_{ij}^{\ n}} \qquad [6.4]$$

where:

T_i is a measure of the interaction between zones i and j;

$W_i^{(1)}$ is a measure of the mass associated with zone i;

$W_j^{(2)}$ is a measure of the mass associated with zone j;

C_{ij} is a measure of distance (or travel cost);

N is a parameter to be estimated;

K is a constant of proportionality.

Applications of this model concern both the habitat in the home–workplace relationship [WIL 69] and retail [HAY 84].

6.2. Spatial interaction models

The idea of generalizing the Huff model [HUF 64] was therefore in the air at the beginning of the 1970s. In marketing, Nakanishi and Cooper [NAK 74a] took this on, while proposing a simpler resolution method in order to estimate the coefficients from the variables. The variables are no longer limited to distance and mass, and their number can theoretically be without limit. It is possible for distance no longer to be significant in the explanation of the retail attraction studied. Attempts were made to impose a model composed of a spatial part and a non-spatial part [JAI 79], but the scientific legitimacy was questioned [CLI 88].

The implementation of this model encountered difficulties for several years. These concerned the measurement scales of the variables [GAU 81], the stationarity of the data and a suitable geographic division [CLI 90, GHO 84], and the integration of so-called subjective variables [CLI 90] that allow this model to distinguish between an objective form and a subjective form.

6.2.1. *The MCI model*

The generalization of the Huff model, mentioned in the preceding section, was the work of Nakanishi and Cooper [NAK 74] and came from a cross between spatial interaction models, close to gravitation models, on the one hand, and market share models founded on Kotler's fundamental theorem [KOT 00] on the other. The attraction of the consumer can be measured with the aid of a generally proportional relationship between market shares and marketing actions. The formalization of this theorem can be presented as follows [BEL 75]:

$$s_i = \frac{A_i}{\sum_{j=1}^{m} A_j} \qquad [6.5]$$

where:

s_i is the market share of i;

m is the number of objects (in this case, stores) exercising the attraction;

A_i is the attraction exerted by i such that:

$$A_i = \prod_{k=1}^{K} f_k(X_{ki})^{\beta_k} \qquad [6.6]$$

where:

X_{ki} is the value of the kth explanatory variable of the object studied (price, attributes, advertising, sales force for a product);

K is the number of explanatory variables;

F_k is a monotonic transformation on X_k with $f_k > 0$;

β_k is a parameter to be estimated.

The marketing effort or the attraction is therefore a function of the marketing mix. This function can assume many forms: linear, multiplicative or exponential.

Each of these forms corresponds to a different category of models [COO 88]. This naturally leads to the MNL (MultiNomial Logit) [McF 74], the MCI (Multiplicative Competitive Interaction) and the spatial MCI models [CLI 88]. In other words it takes into account the distance between home and store for the consumer formulated as follows:

$$P_{ij} = \frac{\prod_{k=1}^{q}(X_{kij}\beta_k)}{\sum_{j=1}^{m}\left[\prod_{k=1}^{q}(X_{kij}\beta_k)\right]} \qquad [6.7]$$

where:

P_{ij} is the probability that a consumer residing in i chooses the possibility or object j (here being a store);

X_{kij} is the kth variable describing the object j in situation i;

β_k is the parameter of relative sensitivity to variable k;

m is the number of stores or choice alternatives;

q is the number of variables.

The development of the MCI model was carried out in stages [BUC 67, HLA 66, KOT 71, URB 69]. The Nakanishi [NAK 72] proposal used in the context of the attraction of promotions was decisive, because with the formulation of the model being non-spatial in its application (in other words, distance is not taken into account), two categories of models can be found in the literature. On the one hand, market share models were developed [BUL 73], or more generally choice share models, for these models have also been applied in the framework of an election [NAK 74b]. On the other hand, spatial MCI models were proposed by using areas created based on a geographic division of the trade area, as in the Huff model, and represented in the model by the indicator i (i being a cell of the division). The latter category has been developed further. The gravitational aspect, symbolized by the presence of variable distance in the Reilly law and in the Huff model, is, in the case of the MCI model, represented by an indicator corresponding to the cells of the geographic division. This signifies that the location is taken into consideration without distance playing a part. The distance variable can also be integrated into the model, but without any certainty. In fact, the resolution of the MCI model finds expression in a multiple regression analysis [NAK 74a], and in this type of analysis, one can no more ensure the significance of one variable than another (see below). Yet, the number of variables that can possibly be integrated into the MCI model is theoretically very high and there is no fixed limit of this number other than comparison with the number of observations (in this case of stores), as in all regression analysis. This clearly signifies that the distance variable may or may not emerge as significant in, for example, a step by step regression [CLI 90]. In other words, the spatiality of the model is always implicit since indicator i represents the cells of geographic division, and can be explicit if the distance between the consumer's residence and the store is included. It is therefore with difficulty that one can describe the MCI model as a gravitation model, except to consider the indicator i as the symbol of the gravitational character of the MCI model [CLI 88]. It is equally important to point out that, in the case of a location study, the validity of the MCI model is only assured in the absence of non-generic attribute [GAU 81], in other words a particular relationship between the store and the residence of consumers likely to visit them, which would render travel more or less difficult. This is an idea developed by Berry and Parr [BER 88], who proposed a more general formulation of the Huff model including a more complex function of the decline in distance.

The modeling process of Nakanishi and Cooper [NAK 74a] is superior to that of Huff because it not only allows the integration of a greater number of variables, but also facilitates the resolution of the model itself and makes it more efficient in that the coefficients of regression β in equation [6.7] can be rather simply determined. Nakanishi and Cooper showed, by geometric means and through a logarithmic transformation, that the MCI model had the form of a multiple regression model whose resolution procedure, founded on the ordinary least squares (OLS) method, was subsequently simplified [NAK 82]. Other suggestions have been made concerning the evaluation of the coefficients [COO 83a]. This transformation into a regression model leads to the obligation to integrate only variables measured on a relative scale [ANS 88, GAU 81]. Yet, in marketing, it is rather rare to encounter only variables of this type. The so-called zeta squared transformation [COO 83b] gives to data measured on interval scales the properties of a relative scale. This transformation was used in an application in the furniture market in France [CLI 90].

Numerous applications of the MCI model to retail location have been published [CLI 92a, CLI 97, CLI 02, GHO 87a, HAN 79, JAI 79, JAL 81, WEI 84], even if many of them actually end up as studies of the Huff model [HUF 64] partly in a concern for simplification, but also because the field of application chosen was often supermarkets. Yet, as already stated, the Huff model often suffices when the environment is not overly complex (a small city) [CLI 92a]. The MNL model has also been used in store choice research [FOT 88].

The retail location process can therefore lead to complex calculations in modeling and it can be asked whether the game is worth the candle. In fact, such an investment is only useful if it can be used again later. This is the essence of the subjective concepts involved in the MCI model and in multiple location models.

6.2.2. *Objective and subjective MCI models*

Retailing has gradually become a veritable industry, as a result, on the one hand, of the technological means that it mobilizes and, on the other, of the increasing investment that its development necessitates [CLI 02]. In this section we will see that this phenomenon is amplified by the networking of retail activities. Yet, the mortality rate in retail has at times been relatively high in certain sectors [STA 81]. Making profitable the investment required today and reducing this mortality rate requires the implementation of increasingly sophisticated methods and techniques.

The most simple use of the MCI model consists in integrating only so-called objective variables: surface area, distance between home and store, number of salespeople and/or check-out lines, parking places, number of items available to consumers, etc. [CLI 92a]. The more complex and specialized the concept of the store to be studied, the more sophisticated is the analysis of the variables involved; otherwise the explanatory power of the regression model is likely to be insufficient. More qualitative variables, and especially more subjective variables, thus become indispensable. Store image has been introduced by taking into account the perceptions held by prospective consumers [STA 76], but not always with success [NEV 80]. Perception remains weak however, especially without the detail of this image; the range of decision is thus reduced.

In most of the published research using gravitation models, the rate of explanation of the variance in the regression rarely goes above 60%. The so-called subjective approach of the MCI model [CLI 95], founded not on objective data but on the consumer's perceptions of these data, often allows higher percentages to be obtained. Three reasons can explain this superiority:

1. The consumer's perceptions of the attributes of a store play an essential role in his or her choice [COO 83a, MON 75]. These perceptions evolve more rapidly than real characteristics. They are therefore essential to modeling.

2. If the analyst takes the necessary precautions at the measurement level, he has at his disposal a larger maneuver margin concerning the variables to be tested since many of them (quality of products or of customer service, trade name reputation, design of or interest in services offered) would be difficult to measure on classic measurement scales.

3. Ghosh [GHO 84] warned of the danger that could possibly result from the so-called *non-stationary* character of the results of these models from one cell to the next. Actually, the condition of homogeneity of cells within the geographic division, imposed in the Huff model [HUFF 64], is almost impossible to maintain. A suitable methodology consists therefore in implementing the model while respecting the situation in each cell of the division, which enables a greater sophistication in the analysis. The choice of objective data supposes a calibration of the model based on the entirety of the cells of the trade area studied. This equally reduces precision and constitutes a major inconvenience [GHO 84]. Actually, consumers are not expected to react in the same manner everywhere to the opening of a same store. Two solutions have been proposed to test the stationary character of the results: the partition of the data and the jackknife technique. The relative frequentation of stores is obtained

through a survey and measured with the help of a constant sum scale. The stationary nature of the model's results will be better if the calculation of regression coefficients is carried out in a more homogeneous environment and therefore separately in each cell. Yet, the approach of the subjective MCI model is founded on a much more localized implementation of the model [CLI 90].

The application of the subjective MCI model goes through the gathering of data from customers, which are on the one hand the perceptions of the most determinant attributes of the stores visited in a trade area (ordinal data) and on the other hand the frequentations of these same stores. But, as seen earlier, the MCI model can only accept data measured on proportional scales. How can ordinal data be integrated? A two-step procedure is proposed [CLI 90]: transformation of the ordinal data into metric data (or quasi-metric) by using an interval scale with semantic supports [PRA 76]; conferring on these data proportional properties using the zeta squared transformation [COO 83b]. The cells of the geographic division can be numerous and collecting data in each can prove to be as costly as it is detailed. The number of these cells can be reduced with the aid of a cluster analysis relating to consumer characteristics judged to be relevant in the purchase process studied: in the case of a furniture purchase [CLI 97], the age and the socio-professional category of the head of the household, his/her status (owner or renter), the number of people in the household and the number of rooms in the house. The INSEE (French National Institute of Statistics) is able to supply this type of information concerning classic divisions like cantons. Next, the coefficients of regression β are calculated for each cell representative of each group of cells revealed by the cluster analysis. Even though a sampling error appears as a result of the use of the survey, the determination coefficient is often far superior to that obtained in an objective approach, because the specification error, which measures the insufficiency of the number of variables, is considerably reduced. The formula of the subjective MCI model is very close to that of the classic MCI model [NAK 74a], but a supplementary index of coefficient β linked to the cell of the division studied provides a reminder that the model is calibrated by division cell [CLI 90]:

$$P_{ij} = \frac{\prod_{k=1}^{q} (X_{kij}{}^{\beta_{ki}})}{\sum_{j-1}^{m} \left[\prod_{k=1}^{q} (X_{kij}{}^{\beta_{ki}}) \right]} \qquad [6.8]$$

The subjective MCI model is well adapted to the furniture market [CLI 90] and, in a more general manner, to the distribution of shopping goods with a degree of involvement. The comparison between the results of the subjective MCI model and those of the objective MCI model in the furniture market (insofar as it was possible to supply equivalent objective variables, which was not always the case except sometimes with the aid of "very proxy" variables) showed a clear superiority of the subjective MCI model. The internal validity of the objective MCI model is therefore often insufficient. As for its external validity, its application is not guaranteed in all markets. In addition, the distance variable between the consumer's home and the store does not always emerge as significant, especially where the sale of furniture is concerned [CLI 92a]. In practice, one finds that there are threshold effects [MAL 83]. Beyond a certain distance, the consumer is no longer willing to travel to a store. On the other hand, within that distance, the consumer is likely to visit all or some of the stores.

The MCI model allows for simulations. If the surface area variable is retained as explicative, together with the frequentation of competing stores in the trade area (or sales if data are available), the consequences of an eventual increase in store surface area, with the other variables remaining fixed, can be simulated. The subjective MCI model enables one to simulate market behavior based on consumer expectations and beliefs [COO 83b]. However, it is true that the subjective MCI model, if it authorizes the testing of diverse consumer perceptions, does not furnish the keys of correspondence between these perceptions and the tools of retail policy that must be improved; the process of decision support will therefore be less explicit for the manager or the retailer. However, the subjective MCI model offers the advantage of varying in time without changing the attributes of the store, because the perception of the attributes and the image of stores can evolve, something that the subjective MCI model is capable of taking into account rather well as long as the databases are updated regularly by using, for example, telephone surveys.

By integrating data from joint analyses [GRE 78] measured with trade-off matrices [JOH 74] linked to promotional arguments, the subjective MCI model, calibrated in the furniture market [CLI 95], enabled the simulation of the effects of promotional campaigns proposed by competing stores in a market where these campaigns constitute a quasi-permanent tactical tool [CLI 95] and the abuse of which can lead to a rapid deterioration of the stores' image. The subjective MCI model has also served supermarkets by showing that demographic and socioeconomic variables are good indicators, simple to measure, of consumer shopping behavior [GON 00].

The MCI model has been criticized by certain researchers. The complexity of its resolution mode and the burden of the implementation of the subjective MCI model are obviously obstacles when a rapid decision process is necessary. Certain researchers have proposed a simplification in terms of estimating the model's weighting coefficients. Instead of using a regression model, Cooper and Finkbeiner [COO 83] recommended the implementation of a dual questioning method [ALP 71], or a questionnaire with double responses [JOL 79], in order to give weight to each of the model's determinant variables. This procedure is integrated in the implementation of the subjective MCI model [CLI 90]. It seems currently to be the path followed by IRI-Secodip, a French–American marketing company, in its approach to the concept of a site marketing (see section 6.4). Other researchers have attempted to introduce the intuition of the decision-maker into the commercial site choice location process (see Chapter 5). Laparra [LAP 95] compared the results of the MCI model with those of an interactive decision support system. Durvasala, Sharma and Andrews [DUR 92] developed the STORELOC model based on the judgments of the manager in charge of the location operation. More recently, the cognitive maps proposed by McKay [McK 75], fuzzy logic [ALT 94] and neural networks [FOO 95] have enabled the proposition of an approach to understanding retailers' knowledge of the territory [CLA 02].

6.3. Combined attraction models for multiple locations

The networking of retail and service activities will no doubt remain one of the defining factors of the second half of the 20th century when the management of companies [CLI 02a] is considered at the economic level. In addition to its consequences for the economic power of large retail and service firms, the development of store chain networks presently requires retail and service companies to orient themselves towards location methods that allow them to operate several locations simultaneously. For chains, therefore, store management goes through an optimized management of locations.

6.3.1. *Location-allocation models*

Competition in large retail markets has become so heightened that retail companies must envision market penetration with the help of multiple locations. This is already the case in the USA with convenience store chains and large chains like Wal-Mart [CLI 92b]. It is also developing in Europe through, for example, acquisitions and mergers in the retail sector [CLI 98]. Research projects have been carried out in order to develop so-called multiple location models, which allow the study of simultaneous establishment of several stores [ACH 82, GHO 83, GHO 84, GOO 83, GOO 87]. Applications within a franchise system were proposed in order to limit conflicts [KAU 90] or, with the FRANSYS model, to avoid cannibalization between trade areas [GHO 91] (see section 6.3.2).

The retail networking objective encouraged researchers to turn towards a research dilemma that is well known by industrial location specialists. The problem confronting researchers is the problem of the *p-median* [COO 63]. In fact, the dilemma has historically been the following: where to locate a production center in such a way as to minimize the weighted distance between this center and the sources of raw materials [WEB 09]. The answer to this problem has given birth to a class of so-called *location-allocation* models [GHO 87b]. The components of the location-allocation models are as follows:

– an objective function to be optimized according to the different possible sites;

– demand areas reduced to a central point or centroid where the demand for goods and services is concentrated;

– the possible sites with location, accessibility and infrastructure;

– the distance or time-of-access matrix;

– the rule of allocation, or the manner in which consumers choose amongst the proposed supply locations.

Originally used for industrial locations [FRA 74, TOM 84], these models were then applied to retail location [ACH 82]. They aim to maximize the net converted-to-current value of the expected revenue of the opening of *p* stores compared to that of *q* stores by a competitor chain. Location-allocation models have the advantage of being able both to integrate the central places theory [BEA 87] and to be combined with interaction models [BEA 80]. The first published model for retail activity, MULTILOC [ACH 82], will be described in section 6.3.2. The objective is to optimize the number and the location of stores on the one hand and the allocation of consumers *vis-à-vis* these stores on the other, in order to determine the supply capacity. The principal applications of these models have dealt with multiple purchases [McL 87] and convenience stores [GHO 84], since for this purchase process and this type of store distance is the first choice criterion.

However, location-allocation models and the dilemma on which they are based, that of the *p-median*, have a major disadvantage. The number of solutions to be examined very rapidly appears insurmountable and the process time can amount to centuries [ROB 02]! Heuristic propositions have been made, intended only to consider locations likely to interest the decision-maker. However, it is still necessary for him to know his needs and the sites well. These location-allocation models have been used to establish food stores [ACH 82], supermarkets [GHO 83] and a fast-food chain [MIN 87]. Despite the efforts of researchers to develop computerized procedures destined to reduce the time of calculation [GOO 83], this model remains subject to heuristics that impede real optimization processes and particularly takes up the decision-makers' precious time. Very recently, proposals have been put forward to get around these difficulties: Robert-Demontrond and Thiel [ROB 02] proposed the use of genetic algorithms, while the development of a method based on signal processing and on screening and convolution was intended to accelerate the resolution of the *p-median* [BAR 01]. The advantage of this last approach is that the zones corresponding to the residences of consumers concerned by the supply can be represented graphically and a limit placed on the number of locations to be evaluated.

There are two models that are the fundamental works in the multiple location domain: MULTILOC and FRANSYS.

6.3.2. *The MULTILOC and FRANSYS models*

MULTILOC [ACH 82] combines a location-allocation model and the MCI model. Once the MCI regression coefficients are calculated, the implementation of the location-allocation model enables one to determine the market equilibrium and thus to deduce the expected profit. Each of the possible locations is then tested in order to determine the best site according to the provisional profitability of the future stores. The MULTILOC model is especially intended for small stores like mini-markets, convenience stores, service stations and fast-food units. However, stores inside shopping centers or superstores are not included because the number of locations is limited.

The profit maximization function is as follows:

$$MaxZ = \sum_{i=1}^{m}\sum_{j=1}^{n} C_j E_i P_{ij} - \sum_{j=1}^{n}\sum_{l=1}^{L} F_{jl} x_{jl} \qquad [6.9]$$

where L is the set of designs based on the store attributes (any combination of store attributes is possible on a given site) with the following conditions:

$$\sum_{l=1}^{L} x_{jl} \leq 1 \quad j = 1,\ldots,n$$

$$\sum_{j=1}^{n}\sum_{l=1}^{L} x_{jl} = r = \text{number of proposed sites}$$

Where:

x_{jl} = 1 if a store of design 1 should be built on site j, 0 otherwise;

E_i = total expenditure per group i in the market;

F_{jl} = fixed costs of a store of design 1 on site j;

C_j = fraction which multiplies $\sum_{j=1}^{n} E_i P_{ij}$

given then profits before deduction of fixed costs of P_{ij}, the probability:

$$P_{ij} = \sum_{l=1}^{L}\left(\prod_{k=1}^{q} A_{ijkl}\beta_{kl}x_{jl}\right)\left[\sum_{j=1}^{n}\sum_{l=1}^{L}\left(\prod_{k=1}^{q} A_{ijkl}\beta_{kl}x_{jl}\right)\sum_{j=n+1}^{n+s}\prod_{k=1}^{q} A_{ijkl}\beta_{kl}\right] \qquad [6.10]$$

given that k_l is the lth value of the attribute k, j the potential sites and $n + s$ the existing locations.

The possible sites are then examined with the support of a heuristic based on the judgments of the managers concerning the quality of the sites. If the number of sites were considerable, the calculation time would be extremely long. Lagrangian heuristics have been proposed as a way of providing high-quality solutions.

Some American companies have implemented the MULTILOC model. Twenty years ago, SuperValu Stores, based in Eden Prairie (Minnesota), a suburb of Minneapolis, developed the SLASH model for the location of its chain of convenience stores. Powerful American retail groups have since developed their own models: Scrivner in Oklahoma City with its supermarkets; the Dayton-Hudson group, with its large Dayton stores, its Target discount stores and its B. Dalton bookstores. Specialized retail location companies also have their own models; these include Retail System's LOCUS, Landauer Associates in Houston (Texas), Howard Green and Associates Inc. in Bloomfield Hills (Michigan), and Nash Finch C° in Minneapolis (Minnesota) [CLI 92a]. Currently, companies like IRI-Secodip in France are developing approaches of this type in order to make them available to retail businesses. In practice, the mission is two-fold: to move quickly and not to be mistaken. The Raffarin law in France is extremely severe for new big store locations [CLI 00] and, therefore, as new store constructions become very difficult, buy-outs will multiply according to network optimization decisions that will be made by the directors of retail companies who have a need for new methods (see Chapter 8).

The FRANSYS model is an application both of the MULTILOC model and of work dealing with conflicts in franchised store networks [ZEL 80]. A specific requirement of the franchise system is concerned with location. In a company-owned system, the choice of the best site for a new store for the network operator consists in selecting the site that allows the maximization of one of the performance measures, whether it be sales or profit [GHO 91]. On the other hand, when the ownership of the stores is in the hands of the franchisees, if the goal of the franchisor is analogous to that of the company-owned operator, which is to maximize the profit, the maximization objective of the franchisor's sales may not be compatible with a franchisee's maximization objective of sales for a given store [KAU 90]. It is always in the franchisor's interest to increase the number of stores and thus his or her overall network sales, and it matters little to him or her if this sales figure comes from other franchised stores in the chain. From this, a source of conflict is born. The FRANSYS model presents three major components, which form a procedure intended to avoid the difficulties that have previously been mentioned:

1. Models are developed to estimate the impact of a new store on:

– the demand;

– the competitiveness of other network franchises;

– the allocation of demand amongst competing stores.

2. A multi-objective framework is organized in such a way that the desirability of the different potential sites can be evaluated with the impact of a new store on the set of participants in the franchise system taken into account.

3. A network optimization algorithm is conceived in order to select the optimal sites for the expansion of the franchise system.

As with the MULTILOC model, a location-allocation model and the MCI model contribute to the development of the FRANSYS model. Depending on the situation, the new implantation should distance itself from the other stores of the chain, on the one hand, in order to increase both the demand and the promotion budget of the network thanks to a sales surplus and, on the other hand, to avoid any cannibalization of sales that would run the risk of reducing the preceding advantages to zero. This FRANSYS model has been applied to fast-food chains in the USA [GHO 91].

It is clear that location models are fed by geographic data. However, the progress of GIS (Geographic Information Systems) today allows model results to be visualized with the help of maps.

6.4. Location models and geographic information

Geographic information is obviously indispensable to the implementation of location models. However, the improvements in GIS have allowed the results to be considerably refined. We will first examine how this is done and then we will see which research paths may still enhance what is now called *site marketing* [CLI 02a].

6.4.1. *Modeling and GIS: foundations of site marketing*

The modeling of retail location is probably one of the oldest marketing research traditions. Publications on the law of retail gravitation date back to the end of the 1920s, an initial version being dated 1929. Progress since has led to very sophisticated models.

Marketing companies today offer information-related products that are either based on models supported by the Huff or the MCI model, or that use weighting approaches. The use of geographic data enables the creation of cartographic representations that are particularly useful and visual for the decision-maker, the store network developer who has at his disposal technical and financial means to acquire GIS (see Chapter 1). The advantages of the GIS in location were developed by researchers long before user-friendly software programs were available to professionals [GOO 91] (see Chapter 7). Researchers have praised the integration of spatial interaction models in GIS, especially in retail location operations [BEN 97].

Specifically concerning location models, GIS bring considerable improvements. The two main improvements are: a greater sophistication in the data used and therefore in the results obtained; and a more precise demarcation of trade areas.

Concerning the improvement of the data precision, it is important to recall that very successful localized databases are available today that group precise consumer information. Several sources have been used in the creation of these databases. We will cite three: panels, loyalty cards and mega-bases [CRO 02]. Traditional panels of consumers (Secodip), or of retailers (Nielsen or Iri-Secodip), are permanent samples of several thousand consumers or several thousand stores that allow data about consumers to be collected at regular intervals [VER 01]. The implementation of data scanning both at check-out exits and in consumers' homes, thanks to the well-known small scanning systems that allow barcodes to be read and the data sent at night to a mainframe computer, has provided richer and more rapid data collection than previously. The maintenance of such panels is relatively onerous, which explains why this solution is rivaled by other collection techniques. Loyalty cards, in addition to their interest at the promotional level, give to retailers, superstores or mail-order companies the possibility of being aware, with great precision, of the actual purchase behavior of their customers. Of course, in contrast to panels made up of consumers frequenting different stores with various trade names, these internal databases only supply information about the customers of one trade name. The mega-bases (Consodata or Calyx) open quantitatively impressive horizons. One can almost talk of exhaustiveness when one knows that consumers in countries like the Netherlands or the UK have almost all been put into databases through huge survey campaigns. The principle is simple: several million copies of a rather long questionnaire of possibly 200 or more questions on the most diverse products is sent out. To ensure consumer interest, product samples are promised. A bias has been denounced in relation to the orientation of certain responses linked to the sample wished for by the consumer, who in the end acquires a certain dexterity in the utilization of these questionnaires. Test effects [EVR 97] should therefore not be neglected. Thus, this improvement in the precision of data is not exempt from defects, but the improvement is indisputable as long as several precautions are taken and the limitations of the databases used are known.

As for the demarcation of trade areas, as well as the trade areas of stores, progress has once again been particularly significant. In fact, it is indistinguishable from the previously described databases. The geographic coordinates of consumers' addresses and of stores, or a geo-coding operation, make it possible to move away from the limitations of traditional geographic units such post codes in France, or even census zones, residence blocks or zip codes in the USA [TAY 95].

The assembly of GIS-location models can be considered as the basis of what some call site marketing [CLI 02a], which has been developed in France by IRI-Secodip. This modeling actually allows diverse situations to be simulated, thus allowing the spatial distribution of clients relative to stores to be understood. The negotiation of store access with public officials and the development of strategies to win over and win back customers also contribute. One can thus not only fine tune the distribution of printed matter concerning direct marketing [DES 01], but also develop real geo-merchandizing, which is intended to better pilot the assortments in relation to customers residing in the zone studied (see Chapters 11 and 12).

It seems certain today that location models and geographic information are closely linked and a good number of research perspectives will continue for quite some time to associate the two.

6.4.2. *Research perspectives for retail location models*

Research perspectives dealing with location models are oriented towards two principal paths: the acceleration of the process of modeling results and the development of models of passing attraction.

Concerning the acceleration of the production of modeling results, it can be seen that most of the optimization software programs for retail location are rather slow and require following rather onerous heuristics. Yet, time is an essential element in the retail location decision-making process [KAU 00]. Gains in speed are an important factor. Screening and convolution techniques, taken from signal processing, enable acceleration in the production of the results of models, particularly those founded on the *p-median* for multiple locations [BAR 01]. Based on data on consumers, including at least their address, the approach consists initially in geo-coding and then representing on a map the locations of these consumers. In a second stage, screening techniques allow the highlighting of the principal geographic zones where actual or potential customers are found. Finally, in a third step, the use of the convolution product leads to the precise and rapid demarcation of the contours of these zones. This method is founded on the analogy between the sensors used in industry and those taken from human or virtual sources, such as market studies or data coming from direct observation [BAR 01]. In this case, one is definitely dealing an approach that is as promising in its scientific dimension as in its potential in professional uses. Another perspective allowing both precision and rapidity has recently been developed with the aid of a process of hierarchical analysis and of a neuro-fuzzy network [KUO 99].

Finally, with retail attraction having been essentially dealt with in its polar sense (in other words a pole – here a store – attracts peripheral elements, through the action of what is called "bodies" in the theory of gravitation), taking the increasing mobility of consumers into account is recommended (see Chapter 2). This mobility manifests itself in an increase in consumer travel, both in the number of trips and in time spent traveling. Retail location relating to the passage of consumers during their travel, whether daily in their home-to-work trips, or with a less regular frequency in business or leisure travel, or even tourist trips, thus takes its entire shape. This attraction, which is both temporary and passing [CLI 97], has attracted little attention from researchers aside from the numerous studies on tourist travel [EYM 95]. This represents an incontestably important research field for models that allow this phenomenon of passing or temporary attraction to be better understood (see Chapter 2).

6.5. Conclusion

Retail location is an old domain in marketing. It has been the object of many very rich models for numerous decades: Reilly's law, the Huff model, the MCI model, MULTILOC, FRANSYS. The use of geomarketing software and more complete databases concerning the attitudes and/or the real behaviors of consumers is leading today to a revival in interest that goes far beyond the academic community and has invaded the world of companies and organizations in general. American retailers are more aware of the use of this kind of model, even though some of them have gone back to less sophisticated methods like the analogue method [APP 68]. Many professional applications of these models are available: Locus, Model, Winsite, Mpsi system and the difficulties met by some retailers who have neglected store location studies before settling on a site show first that well-known methods should be more generally known and second that new methods have to be tested [ROG 03].

Numerous improvements have been made in order to take into account both subject consumer data and that of the decision-makers, and others that are intended to accelerate the study method in terms of location are on the way, for if "location, location, location" are the three key points of the success of a business (this is also applicable for a number of services), "timing, timing, timing" provides the basis for more rapid strategic and tactical decision-making than that of the competitors. It is in this way that geomarketing will be able to evolve towards real spatial marketing intended to facilitate the rapid implementation of marketing operations, thus reinforcing Customer Relationship Management or CRM [LEF 00].

These location models are currently rather well understood technically, but they are only applicable in classic cases of polar attraction (see Chapter 2). It is therefore now necessary to develop passing attraction models that will allow the increasing mobility of consumers to be taken into account.

6.6. References

[ACH 82], Achabal D., Gorr W. L., Mahajan V., MULTILOC: A Multiple Store Location Decision Model, *Journal of Retailing*, 58, 5-25, 1982.

[ALP 71], Alpert M., Identification of Determinant Attributes: A Comparison of Methods, *Journal of Marketing Research*, 8, 2, 184-91, 1971.

[ALT 94], Altman D., Fuzzy Set-theoretic Approaches for Handling Imprecision in Spatial-Analysis, *International Journal of Geographical Information Systems*, 8, 3, 271-89, 1994.

[APP 68], Applebaum W., *Guide to Store Location Research*, Supermarket Institute Inc., Addison-Wesley, 1968.

[BAR 01], Baray J., Cliquet G., Delineating and Analyzing Trade Areas through Filtering and Convolution, *INFORMS Conference*, Miami, 2001.

[BAR 88], Barrett C. V., Blair J. P., *How to Conduct and Analyze Real Estate Market and Feasability Studies*, 2nd ed., Van Nostrand Reinhold, 1988.

[BAT 78], Batty M., Reilly's Challenge: New Laws of Retail Gravitation which Define Systems of Central Places, *Environment and Planning A.*, 10, 185-21, 1978.

[BEA 80], Beaumont J. R., Spatial Interaction Models and the Location-allocation Problem, *Journal of Regional Science*, 20, 1, 37-50, 1980.

[BEA 87], Beaumont J. R., Spatial interaction models and central place theory, in Ghosh A., Rushton G. (eds), *Spatial Analysis and Location-Allocation Models*, Van Nostrand Reinhold, 1987.

[BEL 75], Bell D. E., Keeney R. L., Little J. D. C., A Market Share Theorem, *Journal of Marketing Research*, 12, 136-41, 1975.

[BEN 97], Benoit D., Clarke G. P., Assessing GIS for retail location planning, *Journal of Retailing and Consumer Services*, 4, 4, 239-258, 1997.

[BER 88], Berry B. J. L., Parr J. B., *Market Centers and Retail Location: Theory and Applications*, Prentice Hall, Englewood Cliffs, NJ, 1988.

[BRO 92], Brown S., *Retail Location: A Micro-Scale Perspective*, Avebury, 1992.

[BRU 68], Brunner J. A., Mason J. L., The Influence of Driving Time upon Shopping Center Preference, *Journal of Marketing*, 32, 1, 57-61, 1968.

[BUC 67], Bucklin L. P., The Concept of Mass in Intra-Urban Shopping, *Journal of Marketing*, 31, 37-42, 1967.

[BUL 73], Bultez A. A., Naert P. A., Estimating Gravitational Market Share Models, Working Paper no. 36, *European Institute for Advanced Studies in Management*, 1973.

[CAR 56], Carrothers G. A. P., An Historical Review of the Gravity and Potential Concepts of Human Interaction, *Journal of the American Institute of Planners*, 22, 94-102, 1956.

[CHR 33], Christaller W., *Die Zentral Orte in Süd Deutschland*, Iena, translated in English (1966): *Central Places in Southern Germany*, Prentice Hall Inc., Englewood Cliffs, New Jersey, 1933.

[CLA 02], Clarke I., Horita M., Mackaness W., Intuition et évaluation des sites commerciaux: appréhender la connaissance des commerçants, in *Stratégies de localisation des entreprises commerciales et industrielles: de nouvelles perspectives*, G. Cliquet, J-M. Josselin ed., De Boeck Université, Bruxelles, 2002.

[CLI 88], Cliquet G., Les modèles gravitaires et leur évolution, *Recherche et Applications en Marketing*, 3, 3, 39-52, 1988.

[CLI 90], Cliquet G., La mise en œuvre du modèle interactif de concurrence spatiale (MCI MODEL) subjectif, *Recherche et Applications en Marketing*, 5, 1, 3-18, 1990.

[CLI 92a], Cliquet G., *Management stratégique des points de vente*, Sirey, Paris, 1992.

[CLI 92b], Cliquet G., Décisions et méthodes de localisation multiple dans la distribution, in volume 2 des *Annales du Management*, R. Le Duff & J. Allouche ed., Economica, Paris, 861-77, 1992.

[CLI 95], Cliquet G., Implementing a Subjective MCI Model: An application to the Furniture Market, *European Journal of Operational Research*, 84, 2, 279-91, 1995.

[CLI 97a], Cliquet G., La localisation d'un magasin de meubles: application d'un modèle interactif de concurrence spatiale (MCI MODEL) subjectif, *Revue Belge de Géographie*, 121, 261-273

[CLI 97b], Cliquet G., L'attraction commerciale: fondement de la localisation différentielle, *Revue Belge de Géographie*, 121, 57-70, 1997.

[CLI 98], Cliquet G., Integration and Territory Coverage of the Hypermarket Industry in France: A Relative Entropy Measure, *The International Review of Retail, Distribution and Consumer research*, 8, 2, 203-24, 1998.

[CLI 00], Cliquet G., des Garets V., Réglementation des implantations commerciales et stratégies des distributeurs, *15èmes Journées des IAE*, Biarritz, 6-8 September, 2000.

[CLI 02a], Cliquet G., Fady A., Basset G., *Le management de la distribution*, Dunod, Paris, 2002.

[CLI 02b], Cliquet G., La localisation commerciale: méthodes, stratégies et perspectives, in *Stratégies de localisation des entreprises commerciales et industrielles: de nouvelles perspectives*, G. Cliquet et J-M. Josselin ed., De Boeck Université, Bruxelles, 2002.

[COH 60], Cohen S. B., Applebaum W., Evaluating Store Sites and Determining Store Rent, *Economic Geography*, 25-30, 1960.

[COL 90], Colbert F., Côté R., *Localisation commerciale*, Gaëtan Morin, Quebec, 1990.

[CON 49], Converse P. D., New Laws on Retail Gravitation, *Journal of Marketing*, 14, 4, 339-84, 1949.

[COO 63], Cooper L., Location-Allocation Problems, *Operations Research*, 11, 331-43, 1963.

[COO 83a], Cooper L. G., Finkbeiner C. T., A Complete MCI Model for Integrating Attribute and Importance Information, *Advances in Consumer Research*, 109-113, 1983.

[COO 83b], Cooper L. G., Nakanishi M., Standardizing Variables in Multiplicative Choice models, *Journal of Consumer Research*, 10, 96-108, 1983.

[COO 88], Cooper L. G., Nakanishi M., *Market Share Analysis*, Kluwer Academic Publisher, ISQM, 1988.

[COP 23], Copeland M. T., Relation of Consumer's Buying Habits to Marketing Methods, *Harvard Business Review*, 1, 1923.

[CRA 79], Crask M. R., A Simulation Model of Patronage Behavior within Shopping Centers, *Decisions Sciences*, 10, 1-15, 1979.

[CRA 84], Craig C. S., Ghosh A., McLafferty S., Model of Retail Location Process: A Review, *Journal of Retailing*, 60, 1, 5-36, 1984.

[CRO 02], Croizean J-P., Information et études dans la distribution, in *Management de la distribution*, Cliquet G., Fady A., Basset G. éd., Dunod, Paris, 2002.

[DAV 84], Davies, R.L. Rogers, D.S., *Store Location and Store Assessment Research*, Chichester: Wiley, NY, 1984.

[DAV 88], Davidson W. R., Sweeney D. J., Stampfl R. W., *Retailing Management*, 6th ed., Wiley, NY, 1988.

[DES 01], Desmet P., *Marketing direct: concepts et méthodes*, 2nd ed., Dunod, Paris, 2001.

[DOD 50], Dodd S. C., The Interactance Hypothesis: A Model Fitting Physical Masses and Human Groups, *American Sociological Review*, 15, 245-57, 1950.

[DOU 49], Douglas E., Measuring the General Retail Area: A Case Study, *Journal of Marketing*, 13, 481-97 ; 14, 46-60, 1949.

[DUR 92], Durvasula S., Sharma S., Andrews J. C., STORELOC: A Retail Store Location Model Based on Managerial Judgments, *Journal of Retailing*, 68, 4, 420-44, 1992.

[ELW 54], Ellwood L. W., Estimating Potential Volume of Proposed Shopping Centers, *The Appraisal Journal*, 22, 581-89, 1954.

[ENG 82], Engel J. F., Blackwell R. D., *Consumer Behavior*, 4th ed., The Dryden Press, Chicago, Ill., 1982.

[EVR 97], Evrard Y., Pras B., Roux E., *Market: Etudes et recherche en marketing*, 2nd ed., Nathan, Paris, 1997.

[EYM 95], Eymann A., *Consumers' Spatial Choice Behavior*, Physica-verlag, 1995.

[FIN 54], Fine L. V., Retail Trade Area Analysis: A Guide to Effective Use of Retail Trade Area Studies, *Wisconsin Commerce Paper*, 1(6), Madison (Wi): University of Wisconsin School of Commerce, 1954.

[FOO 95], Foody G. M., Land-cover Classification by an Artificial Neural-Network with Ancillary Information, *International Journal of Geographical Information Systems*, 9, 5, 527-42, 1995.

[FOR 68], Forbes J. D., Consumer patronage behavior, in R. L. King (ed), *Marketing and the New Science of Planning*, AMA, 1968.

[FOT 88], Fotheringham A. S., Market share analysis techniques: a review and illustration of current US practice, in N. Wrigley (ed), *Store Choice, Store Location and Market Analysis*. Routledge, 120-159, 1968.

[FRA 74], Francis R. L., White J. A., *Facility Layout and Location*, Prentice Hall, Englewood Cliffs, NJ, 1974.

[FUS 88], Fustier B., Les interactions spatiales, in Claude Ponsard, *Analyse économique spatiale*, PUF, Paris, 1988.

[GAU 81], Gautschi D. A., Specification of patronage models for retail center choice, *Journal of Marketing Research*, 18, 162-74, 1981.

[GHO 83], Ghosh A., Craig C. S., Formulating Retail Location Strategy in a Changing Environment, *Journal of Marketing*, 47, 3, 56-68, 1983.

[GHO 87a], Ghosh A., McLafferty S. L., *Location Strategies for Retail and Service Firms*, Lexington Books, 1987.

[GHO 87b], Ghosh A., Rushton G., *Spatial Analysis and Location-Allocation Models*, Van Nostrand Reinhold, 1987.

[GHO 90], Ghosh A., *Retail Management*, The Dryden Press, Chicago, Ill., 1990.

[GHO 91], Ghosh A., Craig C. S., FRANSYS: A Franchise Distribution System Location Model, *Journal of Retailing*, 67, 4, 466-95, 1991.

[GIR 60], Giraud L., L'attraction commerciale et la loi de Reilly. *Cahiers de l'ISEA*, 11-17, 1960.

[GON 00], Gonzalez-Benito O., Greatorex M., Munoz-Gallego P. A., Assessment of Potential Retail Segmentation Variables: An Approach Based on a Subjective MCI Resource Allocation Model, *Journal of Retailing and Consumer Services*, 7, 3, 171-79, 2000.

[GOO 83], Goodchild M. F., Noronha V. T., Location-allocation for Small Computers, *Monograph 8*, Department of Geography, The University of Iowa, Iowa City, Iowa 52242, 77 p., 1983.

[GOO 87], Goodchild M. F., Noronha V. T., Location-Allocation and Impulsive Shopping: The Case of Gasoline Retailing, in *Spatial Analysis and Location-Allocation Models*, Ghosh A. and Rushton G. eds., Van Nostrand Reinhold, NY, 1987.

[GOO 91], Goodchild M. F., Geographic Information Systems, *Journal of Retailing*, 67, 1, 3-15, 1991.

[GRE 78], Green P. E., Srinivasan V., Conjoint Analysis in Consumer Research: Issues and Outlook, *Journal of Consumer Research*, 5, 103-23, 1978.

[GUI 71], Guido P., Vérification expérimentale de la formule de Reilly en tant que loi d'attraction des supermarchés, *Revue Française de Marketing*, 39, 101-107, 1971.

[HAI 72], Haines G. H., Simon L. Jr., Alexis M., Maximum Likelihood Estimation of Central City Food Trading Areas, *Journal of Marketing Research*, 10, 154-59, 1972.

[HAN 79], Hansen M. H., Weinberg C. B., Retail Market Share in a Competitive Environment, *Journal of Retailing*, 55, 37-46, 1979.

[HAY 84], Haynes K. E., Fotheringham A. S., *Gravity and Spatial Interaction Models*, Sage Publication, Scientific Geography, vol. 2, 1984.

[HER 95], Hermet G., Jolibert A., *La Part de Marché: Concepts, déterminants, et utilisation*, Economica, Paris, 1995.

[HLA 66], Hlavac T. E. Jr., Little J. D. C., A geographic model of an urban automobile market, in D. B. Hertz, J. Meese (eds), *Proceedings of the 4th International Conference on Operational Research.* Wiley, 303-11, 1966.

[HUF 62], Huff D. L., A Probabilistic Analysis of Shopping Spatial Behavior, *Emerging Concepts in Marketing*, Decker ed., Chicago AMA, December, 443-61, 1962.

[HUF 63], Huff D. L., A Probabilistic Analysis of Shopping Center, *Land EconoMCI model*, 39, 81-90, 1963.

[HUF 64], Huff D. L., Defining and Estimating a Trading Area, *Journal of Marketing*, 28, 3, 34-38, 1964.

[HUF 66], Huff D. L., Blue L. A., *A Programmed Solution for Estimating Retail Sales Potentials*. Lawrence University of Kansas, Center of Regional Studies, 1966.

[ISA 60], Isard W., *Methods of Regional Analysis*, MIT, Wiley, 1960.

[JAI 79], Jain A. K., Mahajan V., Evaluating the Competitive Environment in Retailing Using the Multiplicative Competitive Interactive Model, *Research in Marketing*, 2, 217-35, 1979.

[JAL 94], Jallais J., Orsoni J., Fady A., *Le marketing dans le commerce de détail*, Vuibert, Paris, 1994.

[JOH 74], Johnson R. M., Trade-Off Analysis of Consumer Value, *Journal of Marketing Research*, 1, 11, 121-27, 1974.

[JOL 79], Jolibert A., Hermet G., Les critères de choix d'une banque: segmentation du marché des PMI, *Revue Française du Marketing*, 77, 2, 87-100, 1979.

[KAU 00], Kaufmann P. J., Donthu N., Brooks C. M., Multi-Unit Retail Site Selection Processes: Incorporating Opening Delays and Unidentified Competition, *Journal of Retailing*, 76, 1, 113-27, 2000.

[KAU 90], Kaufmann P. J., Rangan V., A Model for Managing Conflict during Franchise Expansion, *Journal of Retailing*, 66, 2, 155-73, 1990.

[KOT 00], Kotler P., *Marketing Management: Analysis, Planning, Implementation and Control*, 10th ed., Prentice Hall, 2000.

[KOT 71], Kotler P., *Marketing Decision Making: A Model Building Approach*, Holt, Rinehart and Winston, 1971.

[KUE 66], Kuehn A. A., McGuire T. W., Weiss D. L., Measuring the effectiveness of advertising, *Proceedings Fall Conference AMA*, 185-94, 1966.

[KUO 99], Kuo R. J., Chi S. C., Kao S. S., A Decision Support System for Locating Convenience Store through Fuzzy AHP, *Computers & Industrial Engineering*, 37, 323-26, 1999.

[LAP 95], Laparra L., L'implantation d'hypermarché: comparaison de deux méthodes d'évaluation du potentiel, *Recherche et Applications en Marketing*, 10, 1, 69-79, 1995.

[LAU 87], Laulajainen R., *Spatial strategies in retailing*, Reidel Publishing Cy, 1987.

[LEB 74], Lebraty J., Evolution de la théorie de l'entreprise, *Revue Economique*, 25, 1, 1-29, 1974.

[LEF 00], Lefébure R., Venturi G., *La gestion de la relation client*, Eyrolles, Paris, 2000.

[LIL 92], Lilien G. L., Kotler P., Moorthy K. S., *Marketing Models*, Prentice Hall, Englewood Cliffs, NJ, 1992.

[LUC 59], Luce R. D., *Individual Choice Behavior*, Wiley, NY, 1959.

[MAL 83], Malhotra N., A Threshold Model of Store Choice, *Journal of Retailing*, 59, 2, 3-21, 1983.

[McF 74], McFadden D., Conditional Logit Analysis of Qualitative Choice Behavior, in *Frontiers in Econometrics*, Zarembka P. ed., Academic Press, NY, 105-42, 1974.

[McK 71], McKay D. B. *Consumer movement and store location analysis*, unpublished. PhD Dissertation, Northwestern University, 40-43, 1971.

[McK 75], McKay D. B., Olshavsky R. W., Cognitive Maps of Retail Locations: An Investigation of some Basic Issues, *Journal of Consumer Research*, 2, 197-205, 1975.

[McK 89], McKenzie B. S., Retail Gravity Model, *The Appraisal Journal*, 57, 2, 166-72, 1989.

[McL 87], McLafferty S. L., Ghosh A., Optimal location and allocation with multipurpose shopping in A. Ghosh & G. Rushton (eds), *Spatial Analysis and Location-allocation Models*, Van Nostrand Reinhold, 1987.

[MIN 87], Min H., A Multiobjective Retail Service Location Model for Fastfood Restaurants, *Omega International Journal of Management Science*, 15, 5, 429-41, 1987.

[MON 75], Monroe K. B., Guiltinan J. P., A Path-Analytic Exploration of Retail Patronage Influences, *Journal of Consumer Research*, 2, 19-28, 1975.

[NAE 73], Naert P. A., Bultez A., Logically Consistent Market Share Models, *Journal of Marketing Research*, 10, 334-40, 1973.

[NAK 72], Nakanishi M., Measurement of Sales Promotion Effect at the Retail Level. A New Approach, *Proceedings Fall Conference AMA*, 338-43, 1972.

[NAK 74a], Nakanishi M., Cooper L. G., Parameter Estimation for a Multiplicative Competitive Interaction Model, Least Square Approach, *Journal of Marketing Research*, 11, 303-11, 1974.

[NAK 74b], Nakanishi M., Cooper L. G., Kassarjian H. H., Voting for a Political Candidate under Conditions of Minimal Information, *Journal of Consumer Research*, 1, 36-43, 1974.

[NAK 82], Nakanishi M., Cooper L. G., Simplified Estimation Procedures for MCI Models, *Marketing Science*, 1, 3, 314-22, 1982.

[NEV 80], Nevin J. R., Houston M. J., Image as a Component of Intra-urban Shopping Areas, *Journal of Retailing*, 56, 1, 77-93, 1980.

[NOI 89], Noin D., *L'espace français*, 5th ed., Armand Colin, Paris, 1989.

[O'KE 89], O'Kelly M. E., Miller H. J., A Synthesis of Some Market Area Delimitation Models, *Growth and Change*, 1989.

[OKO 88], Okoruwa A. A., Terva J. V., Nourse H. O., Estimating Patronization Shares for Urban Retail Centers: An Extension of the Poisson Gravity, *Journal of Urban EconoMCI model*, 24, 241-59, 1988.

[OLS 65], Olsson G., *Distance and Human Interaction*, Regional Science Research Institute, Philadelphia, 1965.

[PES 68], Pessemier E., Teach R., Simulation, Scaling, and Predicting Brand Purchasing Behavior, *Proceedings Fall Conference AMA*, 206-12, 1968.

[PIA 69], Piatier A., L'attraction urbaine, *Coopération*, 10, 1969.

[PON 88], Ponsard C., *Analyse économique spatiale*, PUF, Paris, 1988.

[PRA 76], Pras B., Echelles d'intervalles à supports sémantiques, *Revue française de marketing*, 61, 87-95, 1976.

[REI 31], Reilly W. J., *The Law of Retail Gravitation*, New York: Reilly ed., 1931.

[ROB 02], Robert-Demontrond P., Thiel D., Algorithmes génétiques et stratégies spatiales des firmes de distribution, in *Stratégies de localisation des entreprises commerciales et industrielles: de nouvelles perspectives*, G. Cliquet, J-M. Josselin ed., De Boeck Université, Bruxelles, 2002.

[ROG 03], Rogers D., Retail Location Analysis in the United States, *The European Retail Digest*, 37, Spring, 24-25

[SIM 85], Simkin L. P., Doyle P., Saunders J., UK Retail Store Location Assessment, *Journal of the Market Research Society*, 27, 2, 95-108, 1985.

[STA 76], Stanley T. J., Sewal M. A., Image Inputs to a Probabilistic Model: Predicting Retail Potential, *Journal of Marketing*, 40, 48-53, 1976.

[STA 81], Star A. D., Massel M. D., Survival Rates for Retailers, *Journal of Retailing*, 55, 3, 87-99, 1981.

[STE 88], Stern L. W., El-Ansary A. I., *Marketing Channels*, 3rd ed. Prentice Hall, 1988.

[STO 60], Stouffer A., Intervening Opportunities and Competing Migrants, *Journal of Regional Science*, 1, 1-20, 1960.

[STR 48], Strohkarck F., Phelps K., The Mechanics of Constructing a Market Area Map, *Journal of Marketing*, 12, 493-96, 1948.

[TAI 71], Taieb F., Di Meglio P., Un modèle de localisation des surfaces commerciales: PAPRICA, *Urbanisme*, 126, 10-17, 1971.

[TAY 95], Tayman J., Pol L., Retail Site Selection and Geographic Information Systems, *Journal of Applied Business Research*, 11, 2, 46-56, 1995.

[THÜ 95], Thünen (von) J.H., *Der isolierte Staat in Beziehung auf Landwirstscahft und Nationalökonomie*, Berlin, Hempel and Parey, 1895.

[TOM 84], Tompkins J. A., White J. A., *Facilities Planning*. Wiley, NY, 1984.

[URB 69], Urban G. L., Mathematical Modeling Approach to Product Line Decisions, *Journal of Marketing Research*, 6, 40-47, 1969.

[VER 01], Vernette E., Giannelloni J-L., *Etudes de marché*, Vuibert, 2ème ed., Paris, 2001.

[WEB 09], Weber A., *Uber den Standort der Industrien*, Tübingen,, translated into English by Friedrich (1929): *Theory of the Location of Industries*. University of Chicago Press, 1909.

[WEI 84], Weisbrod G. E., Parcells R. J., Kern C., A Disaggregate Model for Prediction Shopping Area Market Attraction, *Journal of Retailing*, 60, 1, 65-83, 1984.

[WIL 69], Wilson A. G. *Metropolitan growth models*, Centre for Environmental Studies, London, 1969.

[WIL 70], Wilson A. G. *Entropy in Urban and Regional Modelling*, Pion, London, 1970.

[WIL 71], Wilson A. G., A Family of Spatial Interaction Models, and Associate Developments, *Environment and Planning*, 3, 1-32, 1971.

[WRI 88], Wrigley, N., *Store Choice, Store Location and Market Analysis*, London: Routledge, 1988.

[ZEL 80], Zeller R. E., Achabal D. D., Brown L. A., Market Penetration and Locational Conflict in Franchise Systems, *Decision Sciences*, 11, 58-80, 1980.

[ZIP 49], Zipf G. K., *Human Behavior and the Principle of Least Effort*, Addison Wesley Press Inc., 1949.

Chapter 7

GIS and Retail Location Models

Introduction

The aim of this chapter is to examine the role of GIS and models within the activity of geomarketing. In a recent paper [CLA 98] it was argued that there have been three key stages in the development of store location methods. First, there was a pre-GIS era in the 1970s and early 1980s, when location analysis was largely based on gut feelings, checklists and analogue techniques. The GIS revolution came much later to the business world than to many other areas of applied geography [LON 95], and hence the second phase can be dated from around the mid-late 1980s when GIS became widespread in many retail organizations. Phase two also saw the resurrection of applied spatial modeling, particularly within companies that saw the limitations of GIS technology. Phase three followed, as Clarke [CLA 98] has written, and was largely about making use of new methodological advances in spatial data analysis, in particular data mining methods (inductive approaches to teasing out the spatial relationships within databases) and optimization methods (building on deductive spatial modeling techniques for locating retail networks).

The aim of this chapter is to build on Clarke's framework by speculating on a fourth stage of development. This is concerned with finding new applications of these advanced methodological approaches, rather than more technological advances in themselves. This has come about as retail growth through organic development (new store openings) has become less common and retailers are looking for more innovative ways in order to expand in the market place. This change in strategy will

Chapter written by Graham P. CLARKE and Stuart HAYES, translated into English by Gérard CLIQUET.

be illustrated by using the case study of the motor industry. In section 7.2 we review briefly the three stages of development [CLA 98] using examples from the international motor industry. Then in section 7.3 we outline new developments in retailing (here largely through the motor industry case study) and offer a new research agenda for store location techniques. Finally, we explore one such new application area – models to help the search for joint venture partners. Some concluding comments are offered in section 7.5.

7.1. Stages in the development of store location methods

7.1.1. *The pre-GIS era*

It seems clear that in the 1960s and 1970s most retailers relied on "gut feeling", "checklist" or "analogue" techniques. Gut feeling is usually thought of as the simplest in terms of spatial analysis. It normally involves the on-site decision of a senior member of staff who obtains a 'gut feeling' for a location through a site visit. As Davies [DAV 77] points out, this should not be under-rated since these individuals usually have the ability to offer very good instinctive judgments. However, it is clear that this type of approach is highly subjective and time consuming. It appears that many boardrooms still witness heated debate as directors offer their personal opinions on the potential of new sites. Similarly, the increasing complexity of the retail scene makes it harder to make such simple predictions. It is difficult even for the most experienced senior executive to stand on a green-field site and predict the drawing power and revenues that might accrue to a new store. A second common methodology in the early years was as the "checklist approach". This is a broad set of procedures aimed at measuring more objectively the size of existing centers (and hence their potential) and at understanding the breakdown of their trade areas in terms of population structure. Consideration of the catchment of a store would include basic population counts based on different drive times around such stores. These population counts could then be broken down and segmented by age, sex or social class. Thus a key question might be: "how many 45–60 year old persons live within 5 minutes drive of a major shopping center?" Comparisons of different sites would then allow the retailer to rank the possible alternatives. The retailer could also compile a checklist of factors that seemed to be associated with stores and performed well, and then look for these conditions elsewhere. Hernandez *et al.* [HER 98] emphasize how important gut feeling and the checklist approach were even in the mid-1990s in the UK amongst a variety of retailers (see Table 7.1).

Technique	Percentage of retailers using technique
Rule of thumb	100
Checklist	63
Analogue	33
Regression	42
Gravity models	37

Table 7.1: *Uses of locational research technique. Source: [HER 98]*

Guy [SIM 85] reaffirms this sentiment:

> Every year millions of pounds are invested in the retail field on the development of new stores, yet the majority of decisions regarding the siting of new stores is still based on a combination of hunch, experience and a few rudimentary calculations.

Analogue techniques were (and still are) also very common procedures for site location in Europe and the USA (see Table 7.1). The basic approach involves attempts to forecast the potential sales of a new (or existing) store by drawing comparisons (or analogies) with other stores in the corporate chain that are alike in physical, locational and trade-area circumstances. This may be done "manually" or through regression modeling. The success of this approach depends on whether or not you can find similar sites across the country and whether you believe you can successfully transfer the trading characteristics across geographical locations. Regression analysis works by defining a dependent variable such as store turnover and attempting to correlate this with a set of independent or explanatory variables. Coefficients are calculated to weight the importance of each independent variable in explaining the variation in the set of dependent variables.

Although more statistically robust than manual methods, there are a number of problems with regression models. The most important limitation is that regression models fail to handle adequately *spatial interactions or customer flows.* That is, they do not model the processes (spatial interactions) that generate the flows of revenue between residential or workplace areas and retail outlets. Although regression models may sometimes demonstrate impressive descriptive powers (through their ability to reproduce the variation in sales across a network), the absence of any process modeling leaves us skeptical as to their ability to undertake *impact analysis* with any confidence.

7.1.2. *Phase II – GIS and more powerful spatial modeling*

Reviews of store location methodologies used in the 1980s and early 1990s begin to show an important shift towards the use of more sophisticated techniques. Clarkson *et al.* [CLA 96] presented the findings of their survey of major grocery retailers in the UK. It is clear that there was a movement towards "models" of various types. However, the checklist approach was still deemed to be fundamental. This is partly because the ease of undertaking such checklists had been increased through the availability of geographical information systems (GIS). Information relating to shopping centers and their trade areas could be *geo-coded* (that is, placed on the computer with a spatial referencing point) and visually *displayed* through maps and graphs. Once the information was stored in the GIS, the user could *buffer* travel times around the new store and then calculate the population within each time band using the standard *overlay* procedure available in most GIS packages. This is illustrated well by several works [BEA 91a, b; HOW 91; ELL 91; IRE 94] and shown graphically in Figure 7.1.

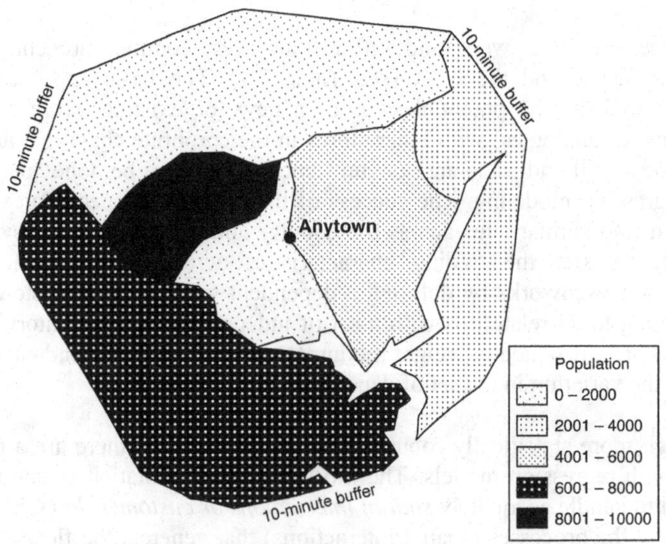

Figure 7.1: *Buffering around a new store and overlaying the population*

Many retailers now use GIS for marketing and site appraisal. Figure 7.2 shows GIS usage by retail sector in the UK in the mid-1990s.

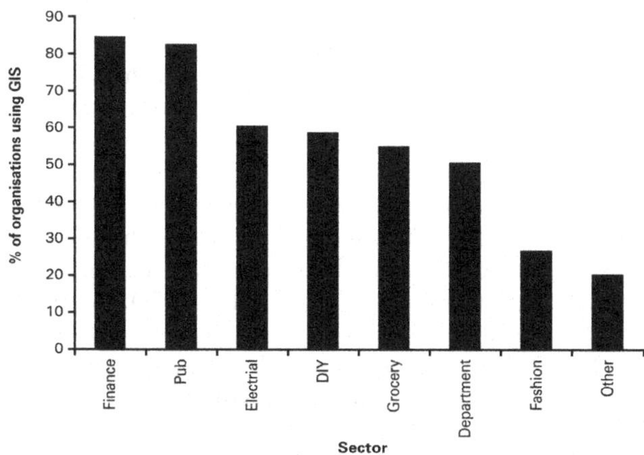

Figure 7.2: *Major UK GIS users (after [HER 98])*

The usefulness of GIS technology has been increased with the arrival of geo-demographic packages, which eventually became coupled with many GIS packages. Geo-demographic systems attempt to profile trade areas into customer segment types. This is especially useful for those retailers whose customers are concentrated in certain geo-demographic segments and who are keen to find localities of the "right type" for their products. The following categories of households are used in the EuroMOSAIC (pan European) geo-demographic system: "elite suburbs", "average areas", "luxury flats", "low income inner city", "high rise social housing", "industrial communities", "dynamic families", "low income families", "rural/agricultural areas" and "vacation/retirement" areas. Although the GIS/geo-demographic approach is popular with retailers, there are two principal drawbacks. First, there is the problem of how to define the trade area and, second, how to adequately treat the competition. As we have shown, the former is normally represented by distance or drive-time bands and it is often assumed that the store will capture trade uniformly in all directions. Even when drive-time bands are drawn in relation to transport networks [REY 91], there is still the assumption of equal drawing power in all directions. These methods also give equal weight of importance to all households within a buffer. If a five-mile buffer is drawn around a new store as the primary trade area, then households close to the site are given the same weight (or probability of patronage) as those 4.9 miles away. In addition, the treatment of the competition is wholly inadequate. The problem is that there is no effective way in most GIS of estimating the new store revenue in light of the level of competition. As Beaumont [BEA 91b] suggests, the method most often used is "fair share" with the potential revenue of the trade area being simply divided between all retailers on some ad-hoc basis (type of retailer, amount of floor space, etc.). Hence, if there are three other competing stores in the buffered trade area of the new store then the new store may be expected to obtain 25% of the revenue generated in that trade area. This simple fair-share allocation could be weighted by store size or by retail brand preferences (market shares) to increase realism. The alternative is to assume that the consumer will travel to the nearest store within the trade area (*dominant store analysis*: see [IRE 94]).

This methodology, whilst offering a useful overview of potential trade area revenue, is fundamentally flawed because of its inadequate treatment of spatial interactions and of competitor impacts. This can normally be shown in all appraisals of existing store trade areas (for more details see [BEN 97]). It should be noted that in more manual trade area analysis some of these problems have been solved quite effectively (see [DAV 84]). However, little of this work has so far appeared in GIS packages to increase the sophistication of the level of analysis.

For these reasons, a number of retailers have looked at the potential of spatial modeling techniques, such as spatial interaction models, which offer the ability to handle customer flows far more effectively.

Let us label any residential zone such as a postal sector or enumeration district (i) and any facility location such as a center or supermarket (j). Then the number of people travelling between i and j can be labeled S_{ij}, and modeled using a spatial interaction approach:

$$S_{ij} = A_i \times O_i \times W_j \times f(c_{ij}) \quad [7.1]$$

where:

S_{ij} is the flow of people or money from residential area *i* to shopping center *j;*

O_i is a measure of demand in area *i*;

W_j is a measure of the attractiveness of center *j*;

c_{ij} is a measure of the cost of travel or distance between *i* and *j*;

A_i is a balancing factor that takes account of the competition and ensures that all demand is allocated to centers in the region. Formally it is written as:

$$A_i = \frac{1}{\sum_j W_j \times f(c_{ij})} \quad [7.2]$$

The model allocates flows of expenditure between origin and destination zones on the basis of two main hypotheses:

1. Flows between an origin and a destination will be proportional to the relative attractiveness of that destination *vis-à-vis* all other competing destinations.

2. Flows between an origin and a destination will be proportional to the relative accessibility of that destination *vis-à-vis* all other competing destinations.

First the model is calibrated to reproduce existing interaction patterns between populations (either at home or at work) and shopping centers. This facilitates the estimation of store turnovers (which may not be available from published sources: few retailers will provide turnover estimates for their competitors for example). Thus, the first use of the models is normally *benchmarking* – comparing model predicted turnovers with actual turnovers in order to get some idea of how well that store is performing – a site potential index (assuming faith in the outputs of the model, of course). That is, given a certain population size and type and the nature of the distribution of all competitor outlets, what would the model predict a certain outlet to be achieving in sales terms? This helps to provide a more objective picture of store potential. Is a store that turns over $3 million per annum doing well or badly in relative rather than absolute terms?

Having allocated expenditures between all retailers in this way, then the most obvious new geographical indicator is that of local market penetration. Such indicators show that market share can vary enormously within regions. Figure 7.3 shows the current market share of a luxury automotive brand in the Netherlands by small geographical area (in this case four-digit postcode or commune). Retailers seldom view market shares at this level of resolution.

Figure 7.3: *Current market share of a car manufacturer in part of the Netherlands. Memo: Mapdata © Geodan IT B.V.*

However, the models are most often used in "what-if? fashion". Having identified the variations in market penetration, the retailer may be keen to improve its performance by opening new outlets in the areas that currently have a low market share. The models can then be used to test the impact of a new store opening. Figure 7.4 shows the impact of opening a new outlet/dealership in the Netherlands.

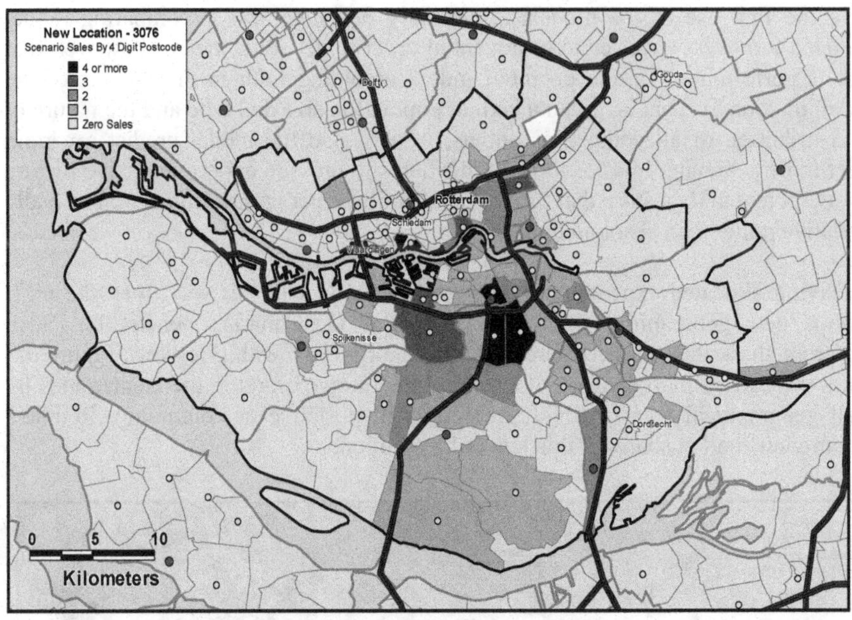

Figure 7.4: *Distribution of sales for a new dealer.*
Memo: Mapdata © Geodan IT B.V.

The use of spatial interaction modeling (still often referred to as gravity modeling in the literature) has increased since the late 1980s. Some organizations now develop these models in-house. Marks & Spencer is a good example of a recent convert to this methodology, especially as they searched for sites outside the UK (see [BON 97]). Others rely on consultancy firms to do the modeling work for them. Examples of firms capable of doing sophisticated modeling include GMAP in the UK (see [CLA 01; BIR 96]), GEODAN in the Netherlands (see [SCH 02]) and the retail modeling team at Ryerson in Canada (see [JON 02]). What are the drawbacks with spatial interaction models? It has been argued that they are more powerful predictors of store turnovers and spatial interactions than any of the other methods so far introduced. They are, however, difficult to calibrate (data intensive), bespoke and esoteric in nature and it is likely that they must be highly disaggregated to fit the case study under investigation. Given the complexities of consumer behavior for different types of goods and services, it is unlikely that a model that fits the car market, for example, can be taken off the shelf to operate in the bingo market (which is one reason why some retail modelers prefer discrete choice models to spatial interaction models; such models, whilst still based on flows, attempt to capture individual shopping behavior much more precisely: see [OPP 01]). Thus the user needs to be a skilful spatial modeler. For these reasons, the availability of off-the-shelf models in some GIS packages may now actually be a rather dangerous development This is because models in packages tend to have to be fairly straightforward and aggregate. As we mentioned above, bespoke models that are used in the real world tend to have to be highly disaggregated! Furthermore, modeling routines so far provided in GIS packages do not come with calibration routines. The advice in one well-known package is simply to use a beta value of 2.0. The beta value depends on many things and such a value may be totally inappropriate (see [BEN 97] for more details). For more details on the use of retail models see [BIR 96, BIR 99] and [CLA 01].

7.1.3. *Phase III – increasing sophistication*

The final stage of Clarke's framework [CLA 98] was based on new methodological developments based on increasing the sophistication of models through optimization. For example, in the long term a company may be interested in knowing what the optimal locations for their local network should be, given the objectives of maximizing either total sales or market share, and how this compares with the existing distribution network. Formally, the type of spatial interaction model outlined above can be rewritten as a mathematical programming formulation, with an objective function (such as maximize revenue) subject to a set of constraints (minimum dealer size, set distance between dealers, etc.). Either the problem can be solved with existing outlets *in situ* or with all outlets free to relocate – referred to as a "green-field" or "clean slate" solution (at least theoretically). A heuristic algorithm has been developed that solves this complex problem on a PC (for a full description of the detail see [BIR 95]). Figure 7.5 shows the outputs of this algorithm applied in the motor industry:

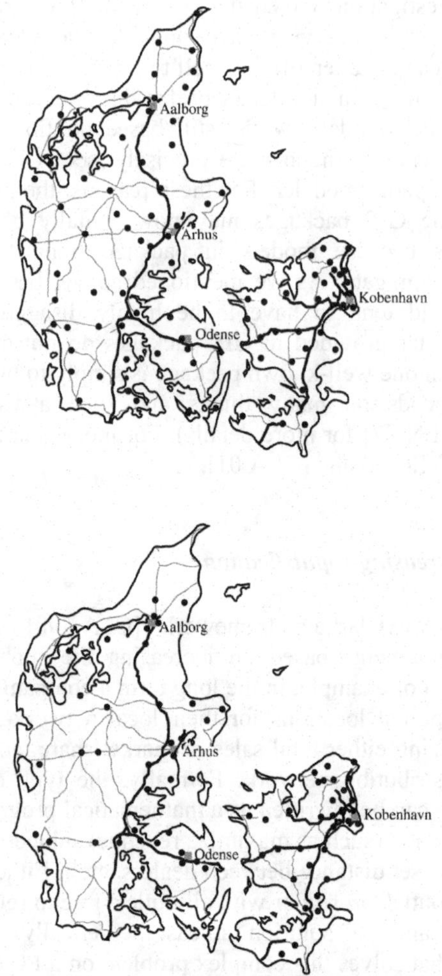

Figure 7.5: *Actual versus "optimal" dealer network for a leading motor company in Denmark*

7.2. Changes in retail distribution: an example from the motor industry

So far we have argued that traditional what-if analyses can be handled well by existing store location methodologies. However, more recently, the requirements of the retail world have changed significantly. Many retailers now believe they have too many stores (the term market saturation is widely banded about) and are looking towards new channels to increase sales. The recent plight of the Rover car group serves as a good illustration of a move towards market saturation within the automotive retail sector, as Gribben [GRI 96] elaborates:

> A SHAKEOUT among Rover dealers could be the prelude to further restructuring of the motor sales network … Rover, the BMW subsidiary, is making deeper than expected cutbacks, with plans to shed up to 160 out of its 511-strong network.

Like the major UK grocery retailers of the late 1980s and early 1990s, the major UK motor vehicle retailers were locked into strategies of accumulation in which capital investment in new dealership expansion programs became the major form of growth. However, as with the major food retailers, major automotive retailers learned from bitter experience the lessons of over-commitment and over-reliance on a strategy of capital accumulation and organic growth. With the concentration of automotive manufacturers brought about as a result of corporate merger and acquisition activity, one has witnessed the tendency of the franchised dealers to decrease the total number of outlets by operating dual-franchise, or even multi-franchise, sites to capitalize on operating efficiencies (for example, the consideration by Ford to dual some of its brands on the same site under the same larger group brand umbrella). Conversely, the reversal by some manufacturers away from dual- or multi-franchising back to solus sales sites has forced dealers to invest in new sites, or to reconfigure existing sites to meet these changing demands [BRI 00]. Car manufacturers have realized the need to create strong brand identity and differentiation. Audi and VW, Toyota and Lexus have all embarked on programs to split the franchises into distinct brand equities located on independent solus sites.

While manufacturers encourage such action, the Government's Trade & Industry department (and more specifically the Competition Commission) and the EU's impending report on Block Exemption seem set to recommend a move towards multi-branded sites as a way to boost competition and lower prices. This could force carmakers to accept multi-franchised outlets, an acceptance of which could have a significant impact on the geography and structure of car retailing within the UK. Increasing involvement by the manufacturers is precipitating a reshaping of the retail landscape, as Briers [BRI 00] suggests: "The family run town center dealership is gradually being phased out. The old owner-occupier dealers … are now practically a thing of the past." The need for huge capital investment in an uncertain macro-economic environment has forced many dealerships to sell up, causing changes to the spatial pattern and spread of dealership location (see Table 7.2).

Number of Franchised Sales Outlets : At 31st December Each Year										
Franchise	1990	1991	1992	1993	1994	1995	1996	1997	1998	1999
Alfa Romeo	71	55	75	78	83	80	79	83	90	89
Audi	-	-	-	-	191	184	164	137	135	130
BMW	162	162	157	156	154	154	156	156	156	155
Chrysler	-	-	71	82	90	94	96	100	106	103
Citroen	231	235	244	246	248	264	255	249	249	244
Daihatsu	98	109	112	124	110	103	96	98	106	97
Fiat	305	250	219	212	216	205	177	186	189	177
Ford	998	968	942	910	872	912	739	793	769	741
FSO	85	-	-	65	65	76	-	-	-	-
Honda	152	151	168	175	171	183	175	177	177	189
Hyundai	160	155	185	165	155	150	150	151	159	165
Isuzu	128	132	135	125	116	114	112	111	116	104
Jaguar	102	99	92	93	94	94	92	92	94	95
Kia	-	121	120	143	143	134	120	100	71	70
Lada	203	202	187	179	169	168	145	-	-	-
Lancia	70	46	50	-	-	-	-	-	-	-
Land Rover	129	127	127	126	125	124	126	124	130	131
Mazda	174	160	137	145	145	142	143	152	149	151
M-B	126	130	132	133	139	140	145	150	155	155
Mitsubishi	110	112	100	100	107	119	115	115	119	116
Nissan	362	150	267	287	295	279	265	256	257	249
Peugeot	400	401	401	398	400	389	370	369	367	364
Porsche	35	32	28	28	28	27	28	31	31	32
Proton	198	203	230	230	211	179	153	140	120	117
Renault	284	265	265	367	358	366	345	340	318	304
Rocsta	-	-	-	123	120	99	78	-	-	-
Rover	**789**	**735**	**676**	**646**	**616**	**541**	**435**	**379**	**325**	**306**
Saab	109	104	106	102	103	101	98	98	97	97
SAO	-	113	115	-	-	-	-	-	-	-
SEAT	148	140	134	143	175	158	125	120	115	126
Skoda	280	264	222	219	228	218	218	208	194	206
Ssangyong	-	-	-	-	-	100	92	88	-	-
Subaru	132	140	145	130	118	116	112	112	112	105
Suzuki	106	122	132	146	149	146	134	130	132	143
Toyota	218	230	257	270	267	253	239	229	228	226
Vauxhall	601	535	534	534	523	503	520	534	523	511
Volkswagen	325	317	318	309	311	303	278	267	268	258
Volvo	264	224	220	220	215	212	179	196	187	183
Yugo	160	161	-	-	-	-	-	-	-	-
TOTAL	**7,715**	**7,350**	**7,303**	**7,409**	**7,510**	**7,430**	**6,754**	**6,471**	**6,244**	**6,139**

Ford's 1995 total includes branches/satellites of Main Dealers counted as sales outlets – previously they were not included as separate sales outlets.
Lancia withdrew from selling RDH cars in the UK in 1993.
During 1993 Renault upgraded most of its second-tier network to Retail Dealer status.
Audi/Volkswagen were counted as one network until 1995 edition.
SAO was incorporated into Kia network and sales ceased in 1994.
Yugo ceased operations during 1992.
Ssangyong acquired by Daewoo during 1998.

SOURCE: Sewell's International: "Franchise Networks 2000".

Table 7.2: *Change in number of dealerships 1990–1999*

So, if the future of the traditional dealer is under threat, how are car manufacturers likely to increase sales? The answer to that question involves the consideration of alternative forms of distribution channel. It can be argued that the future of store location research will change from one of store management to one of channel management. The following strategies will therefore play an increasingly important role in achieving retail growth:

- e-commerce and Internet sales;
- telephone sales;
- TV sales;
- new waves of mergers and acquisitions;
- new strategic joint ventures or partnerships;
- Internationalization.

Each of these is likely to produce a new demand for geomarketing and geobusiness solutions. It is not possible in this chapter to deal with the new research agenda for all these growth channels. To illustrate this, we will examine the use of spatial models to investigate the feasibility of new types of partnerships. The example will be based on the alliance between car manufacturers and major retail grocers. We have already witnessed the foray of supermarket retailers into car sales:

> Sainsbury's has thrown down the latest challenge to the traditional motor retail sector by rolling out a car sales program throughout its 432-strong UK network. The move intensifies competition at a time when prices are coming under increasing pressure, and is likely to lead to other supermarket retailers such as Tesco joining the market. Around 3,500 models will be available, obtained by Sainsbury's from franchised dealers. [AUT 00]

Yet, only one month before Sainsbury's entrance into automotive retailing, Willard [WIL 00] revealed that few automotive dealers anticipated that non-dedicated outlets (such as supermarkets and mail order) would become a feature of the marketplace.

The next section outlines the potential for modeling the impacts of joint ventures in the retail marketplace.

7.3. Modeling ideal partners

The aim of this section is to investigate the potential for new joint ventures using Rover as a case study. The key question is which of the major grocery organizations would make the best partner for Rover in the sense of increasing sales in areas where Rover is currently weakest. It is likely that any supermarket selling cars will not hold much stock, but simply provide an Internet portal, salesperson or catalogue display. Vehicles could be supplied from a central vehicle holding compound, regional distribution centers or from the nearest franchised parent outlet.

Field [FIE 97] provides the example of Daewoo, who chose to install 250 interactive multimedia kiosks in its showrooms and in its substitute Halford's outlets.

In the rest of this section we show the results of modeling the different combinations of Rover and the grocery multiples. The model used is a highly disaggregated spatial interaction model already built by Polk Ltd for the new car market. The methodology involves adding the supermarket networks to the existing car dealer networks and estimating the increase in sales from these new outlets. Since the grocery outlets would not be full car dealers, their attractiveness in the model is much lower than the full car dealers. Figure 7.6 shows the existing market share map for Rover in the UK.

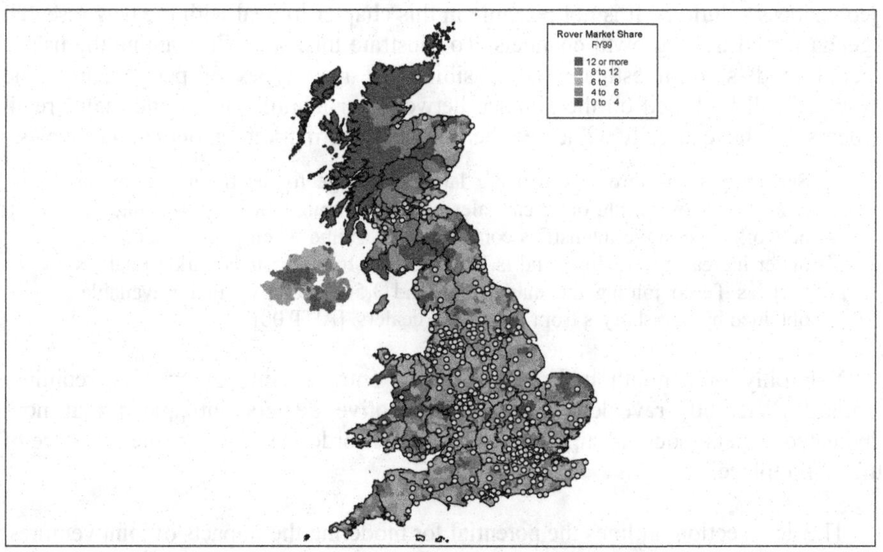

Figure 7.6: *Rover market penetration*

Rover's market penetration shows a distinctive spatial variation. Rover's market share is, unsurprisingly, strongest in those counties where they are well represented, and penetration weakest (less than 4%) in those counties where representation is missing or thin (for example, Rhondda, Merthyr Tydfil and Caerphilly). Market share is weak in those areas having lower rates of provision, notably Wiltshire, Devon and Cornwall, Norfolk, South Wales and those Scottish counties outside of the major urban agglomeration identified previously.

In order to achieve these aims, several model scenarios were run to simulate the impact of incorporating the surrogate grocery supply points into the existing Rover dealer network of 391 outlets. The results presented in Table 7.3 reveal the model results for the nine hybrid grocery–automotive network configurations simulated by the model. We use the results from Table 7.3 to examine four potential partnerships in a little more detail.

Scen ID	Scen Name	Number of Surrogate Outlets	Modelled Volume	Incremental Sales	Additional Sales per surrogate	Perc Diff	Modelled Market Share	Baseline Sales	Cannibal-isation perc	Avg. Surrogate Sales
s0000	**Baseline**	N/A	58827	0	0	N/A	7.48	150	N/A	N/A
s0001	Tesco	428	64507	5680	13	9.65	8.20	142	5.76	21
s0002	Sainsbury	358	63510	4683	13	7.96	8.07	143	5.14	22
s0003	Safeway	329	62502	3675	11	6.25	7.95	145	3.92	18
s0004	Asda	227	63001	4174	18	7.10	8.01	144	4.23	29
s0005	Co-op	190	60712	1885	10	3.20	7.72	147	2.02	16
s0006	Somefield	103	59716	889	9	1.51	7.59	149	1.07	15
s0007	Morrisons	97	60367	1540	16	2.62	7.68	148	1.55	25
s0008	Kwik Save	59	59530	703	12	1.20	7.57	149	0.75	19
s0009	Waitrose	51	59205	378	7	0.64	7.53	150	0.57	14

Table 7.3: *Model scenario summary*

7.3.1. *Tesco and Rover*

It can be seen from Table 7.3 that Tesco has the most supply points in its network. It is not, therefore, surprising to see that Tesco provides the biggest national increment to Rover registrations, with modeled registrations for the Rover–Tesco network forecast to increase by 5,680 units – a 9.65% change in total sales volume. This equates to an additional 13 registrations per each surrogate outlet. This would increase Rover's national market share by almost three-quarters of a percentage point to 8.20%. However, one can also see that the Tesco–Rover network produces the most deflections from the existing network, with 5.76% of all new sales expected to be cannibalized from the existing network. Forecast sales for the substitute dealers are modeled at 21 units. *Model recommendation*: Reject.

7.3.2. *Sainsbury's and Rover*

Sainsbury's is the second most numerous network out of all the grocery retailers modeled. The Rover–Sainsbury's joint network would be forecast to retail an additional 4,683 units, representing a 7.96% increase in national sales. These additional sales represent 13 units per extra supply point, raising Rover's market share by just 0.59 of a percentage point to 8.07%. Like Tesco, over 5% of the new sales are forecast to be deflected from the existing Rover network. Forecast car sales for the Sainsbury's locations are modeled at 22 units. *Model recommendation*: Reject.

7.3.3. *Asda and Rover*

The model predicts an extra 4,174 cars would be sold through Asda outlets if a strategic alliance was formed with Rover. This represents a 7.10% national increase in sales volumes, gained through 227 stores, raising market share to just over 8%. However, 4.23% of these new sales are forecast to be cannibalized from existing Rover dealers, suggesting there is considerable overlap in the partnership network. For each additional Asda outlet grafted onto the existing Rover network, an additional 18 sales would be made. The modeled car sales for each additional Asda outlet are the highest of all the partnership configurations modeled at 29 units. This reflects Asda's 100% large-store content and the highest average floor space of all stores, in excess of 40,000 sq. ft., making them more attractive to potential consumers. *Model recommendation*: Accept.

7.3.4. *Morrisons and Rover*

Despite only having 97 outlets in its store portfolio, the model predicts market share for Rover to increase by a fifth of a percentage point to 7.68% if Morrisons sold Rover cars at their supermarkets. This represents a sales increase of 2.62%. For each Morrison's outlet connected to the Rover network, an additional 16 units would be sold overall – the second highest for all possible network configurations. However, because of the small coverage of the Morrisons store network, Morrisons represents an unviable choice for a *national* retail partner, although may represent the optimal partner in a subset of regions. *Model recommendation*: Reject based on limited geographical impact.

7.3.5. *Ideal partner*

Figure 7.7 suggests that the greatest improvements to national Rover market share with least cost would be attained through an alliance with those supermarkets with the most geographically comprehensive networks. However, the objective of maximizing market penetration at least cost reveals Asda, or to a lesser extent Morrisons, as the optimal partnership configuration. However, the geographical spread of the Morrisons network is spatially contained and, as such, a partnership between Rover and Morrisons would have a comparatively limited national scale effect. Sales are forecast to increase in only 43 counties, compared to 97 for Asda.

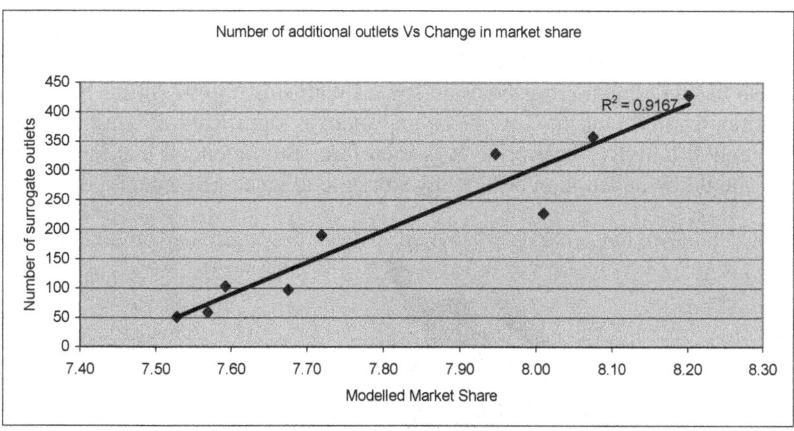

Figure 7.7: *Surrogate network size and modeled market share*

Table 7.4 reveals the national optimal partner when each potential grocery partner is ranked based on the three performance (equally weighted, 1 = low, 9 = high) indicators of:

– average sales made by grocery surrogates;

– average sales made by Rover dealers and surrogates;

– cannibalization (amount of sales cannibalized from parent Rover network dealers by proxy grocery outlets).

Grocery Retailer	Surrogate Sales Rank	Baseline & Surrogates Avg Sales Rank	Cannibalization Rank	Sales per Additional Point Rank	TOTAL	Optimal Partner Rank
Asda	**9**	**4**	**7**	**9**	**29**	**1**
Morrisons	8	7	4	8	27	2
Sainsbury	7	2	8	6	23	3
Tesco	6	1	9	6	22	4
Kwik Save	5	8	2	5	20	5
Safeway	4	3	6	4	17	6
Co-op	3	5	5	3	16	7
Somerfield	2	6	3	2	13	8
Waitrose	1	9	1	1	12	9

Table 7.4: *Results ranking for optimal partner*

The research aim is to identify a national strategic alliance partner for Rover. One can see from Figure 7.8 that Asda represents the optimal partner for joint-venture retailing. Asda has 100% large-store format content in its store portfolio, suggesting that its stores would be more attractive to potential Rover consumers. Asda also has a national representation spread with stores in 97 of the 103 counties. The cannibalization rank of 7 suggests that there is significant overlap between the grocery and automotive networks. It is therefore recommended that an analysis of overlap should be undertaken before any strategic-alliance agreement is formed.

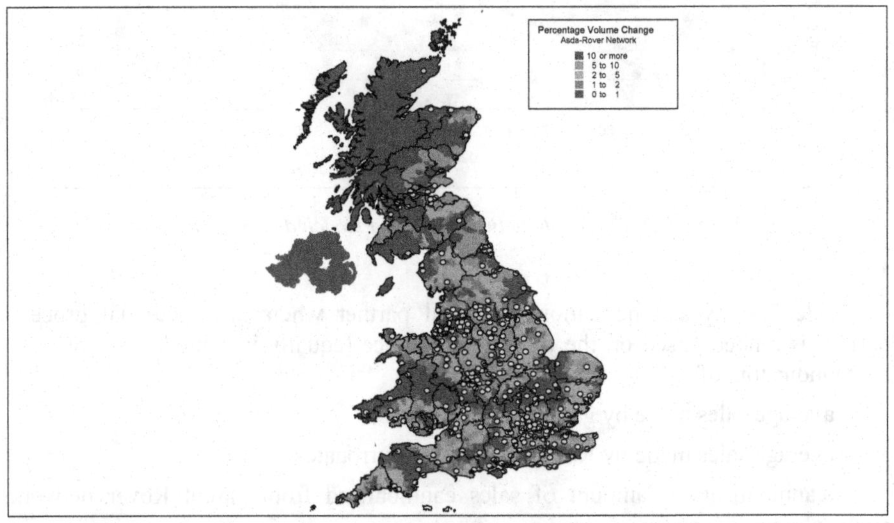

Figure 7.8: *Modeled percentage change in sales for Rover–Asda network. Memo: GEOPLAN©YELLOW: Marketing Ltd*

Figure 7.8 reveals the geographical change in Rover market share provided by the strategic alliance network. There are obvious performance improvements in those counties identified previously as presenting an opportunity for mutual-retailing strategies. Two brief market appraisals will now be undertaken to evaluate the results of the modeling process at the local geographical scale. The first case study is Norfolk in eastern England. The Norfolk market is a large one, both in terms of geographical size (2,069 sq. miles) and the car market at 9,892 units, ranking as the 28th largest volume county market in the UK; Rover sold 462 vehicles in the Norfolk market, equating to a market share of 4.67%, 2.81% lower than the national average of 7.48%. Rover has three outlets in Norfolk. This rate of provision ranks low at 68 out of a total of 77 counties in which Rover has representation, indicating there is a need for greater representation in a high-volume market.

The county therefore clearly represents an area of opportunity for partnership retailing as a means of boosting market performance through additional surrogate representation.

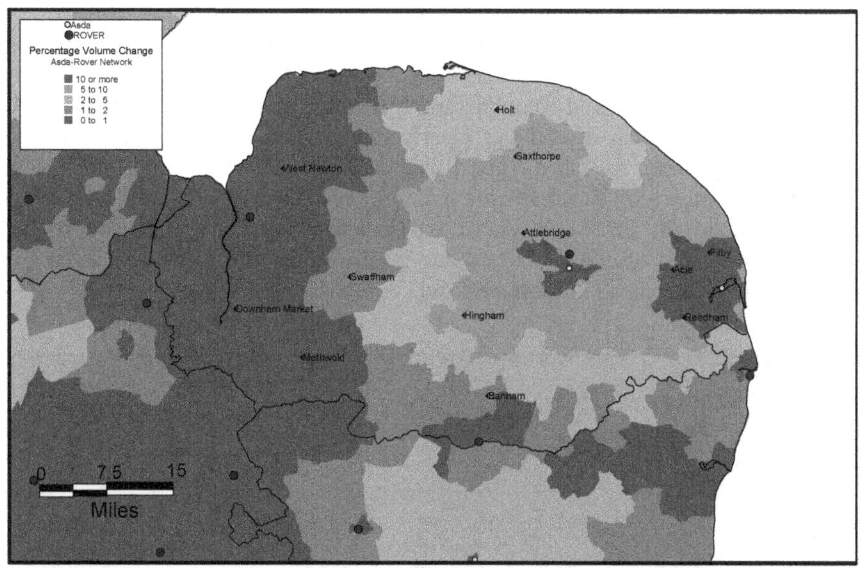

Figure 7.9: *Percentage change in sales for Rover-Asda network in Norfolk. Memo: GEOPLAN©YELLOW: Marketing Ltd*

Figure 7.9 shows the modeled car sales for the two Asda stores in Norfolk. The model predicts that sales would increase from 462 to 487, which represents an increase in market share of 0.25%. The greatest impact can be seen around the Asda store located in Great Yarmouth on the east coast of the county, where sales volumes are modeled to rise by at least 10 percent. Sales volumes are forecast to rise by between 5 and 10% in those postal districts between and in close proximity to the two Asda stores, in places such as Hingham, Attlebridge and Saxthorpe. There is little volume change in those peripheral zones distant from the surrogate supply points, with little change to Rover's sales forecast in places such as Banham to the south of the county and West Newton and Downham Market to the west of the county, where the effect of distance decay can be seen to be having an impact on sales intensities.

The second case study is South Wales. Rover has no current market representation in eight of the counties on the south Wales coast (Gwent, Caerphilly, Merthyr Tydfil, Monmouthshire, Neath Port Talbot, Newport, Rhonda and

Glamorgan) and this is reflected in Figure 7.10 with these counties falling into the lowest provision range. Yet this is a significant area of demand with 10,776 combined vehicle registrations occurring in these counties, where pockets of high demand density and strong registrations counts run along the coast. Rover sold 550 vehicles, providing them with low penetration of the market at 5.10%, low in comparison to the national average market penetration of 7.47% shown in map four. Asda has five supermarkets located in the counties of Monmouthshire, Caerphilly, Newport, Merthyr Tydfil and Rhondda and therefore offers increased access to the market. Thus, this clutch of counties clearly represents an area of opportunity for mutual retailing. Sales for the merged Rover and Asda network would increase to 630 units, an increase of 80 sales. This would increase Rover's market share across the eight counties by three-quarters of a percentage point to 5.85%. Figure 7.10 shows the effect the additional sales made by the Asda surrogates would have on Rover's registration counts in these selected counties.

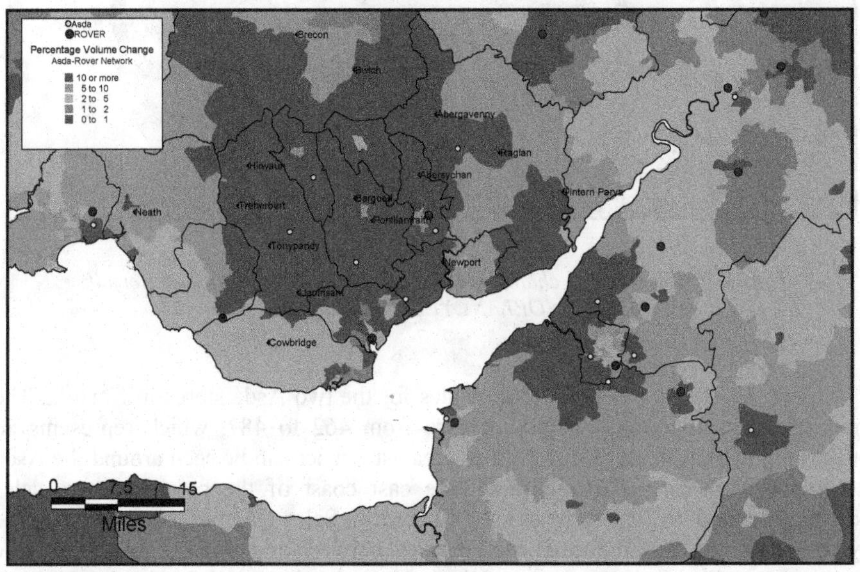

Figure 7.10: *Percentage change in sales for Rover–Asda network in South Wales. Memo: GEOPLAN©YELLOW: Marketing Ltd*

It can be seen from Figure 7.10 that Asda appears as an optimal partner in South Wales, with modeled sales volumes forecast to increase by 10% in those counties without current Rover representation.

7.4. Conclusions

This chapter has attempted a broad review of GIS and models for store location planning and geobusiness. It has been argued that there have been various stages of GIS/model development, culminating in a period of GIS use, which is widespread across retail organizations. However, it is important to stress that GIS and model-based analysis needs to mature and adapt and develop to take account of the changing needs of the retailers themselves as new channels of distribution, and new growth methods such as mergers and joint ventures, become more common. For example, it has been argued here that that it is possible to optimize the efficiency of strategic-alliance retailing by the application of spatial interaction modeling techniques. Through the careful development and application of a spatial modeling framework, we have successfully identified a national level strategic alliance partner for a selected automotive retailer. The research has also revealed that the national optimal network may have a large element of overlap (as illustrated by the Norfolk case study) and further research would be needed to select optimal sites that had a minimal cannibalizing impact on the existing Rover dealers.

7.5. References

[AUT 00] *Automotive Digest* Vol. 29(33), 17 August 2000, p. 1.

[BEA 91], Beaumont J. R., GIS and market analysis, in D. Maguire, M. Goodchild, D. Rhind (eds) *Geographical Information Systems: Principles and Applications,* Longman, London, 139-151, 1991.

[BEA 91a], Beaumont J. R., *An Introduction to Market Analysis*, CATMOG 53, Geo-Abstracts, Norwich, 1991.

[BEN 97], Benoit, D., Clarke G. P., Assessing GIS for Retail Location Planning, *Journal of Retail and Consumer Services,* 4(4), 239-258, 1997.

[BIR 95], Birkin M., Clarke M., George F., The Use of Parallel Computers to Solve Non-Linear Spatial Optimisation Problems: An Application To Network Planning, *Environment and Planning A*, 27, 1049-1068, 1995.

[BIR 96], Birkin M., Clarke G. P., Clarke M., Wilson A. G., *Intelligent GIS: Location Decisions and Strategic Planning*, Geoinformation, Cambridge, 1996.

[BIR 99], Birkin M., Clarke G. P., Clarke M., GIS for business and service Planning, in M. Goodchild, P. Longley, D. Maguire and D. Rhind (eds) *Geographical Information Systems,* Wiley, Chichester, 1999.

[BON 97], Bond S., Gravity modelling and its applicability to the internationalisation of business, Paper presented to 'The Art of Store Location' conference, Henry Stewart Conference Studies, 28/30 Little Russell Street, London, WC1A 2HN, 1997.

[BRI 00], Briers S., Solus Retail Sites Stimulate Massive Dealer Investment *Automotive Management*, 230, March 31, 21-22, 2000.

[CLA 01], Clarke G. P. Clarke M., Applied spatial interaction modelling, in G. P. Clarke and M. Madden (eds) *Regional Science in Business*, Springer, Heidelberg, 137-158, 2001.

[CLA 96], Clarkson R. M., Clarke-Hill C. M., Robinson T., UK Supermarket Location Assessment, *International Journal of Retail and Distribution Management*, 24(6), 22-33, 1996.

[CLA 98], Clarke G. P., Changing Methods of Location Planning for Retail Companies, *Geojournal*, 45(4), 289-298, 1998.

[DAV 77], Davies R. L., Store Location and Store Assessment Research: The Integration of Some New and Traditional Techniques, *Transactions, Institute of British Geographers,* 141-157, 1977.

[DAV 84], Davies R. L., Rogers D. S., *Store Location and Store Assessment Research,* Wiley, Chichester, 1984.

[ELL 91], Elliott C., Store planning with GIS, in J. Cadeau-Hudson and D. I. Heywood (eds) *Geographic Information 1991,* Taylor and Francis, London, 1991.

[FIE 97], Field C., *The Future of the Store: New Formats and Channels for a Changing Retail Environment*, Financial Times Retail & Commercial Publishing, London, 1997.

[GRI 96], Gribben A. Rover ready to cut dealers, *Telegraph*, Issue 356, April 5th, http://www.telegraph.co.uk, 1996.

[HER 98], Hernandez T., Bennison D., Cornelius S., The Organisational Context of Retail Location Planning, *Geojournal*, 45(4), 299-308, 1998.

[HOW 91], Howe A., Assessing potential of branch outlets using GIS, in J. Cadeau-Hudson and D. Heywood (eds) *Geographic Information 1991,* Taylor and Francis, London, 1991.

[IRE 94], Ireland P., GIS: Another Sword for St.Michael, *Mapping Awareness,* April 26-29, 1994.

[JON 02], Jones K., Hernandez T., Applications of retail modeling in the US, in G. P. Clarke and J. C. H. Stillwell (eds), *Applied GIS and Spatial Analysis*, Wiley, London, 2002.

[LON 95], Longley P and Clarke G.P., GIS for Business and Service Planning, *Geoinformation*, Cambridge, 1995.

[OPP 01], Oppewal H., Timmermans H., Discrete choice modelling: basic principles and application to parking policy assessment, in G. P. Clarke and M. Madden (eds) *Regional Science in Business*, Springer, Heidelberg, 97-114, 2001.

[REY 91], Reynolds J. 1991 GIS for Competitive Advantage: The UK Retail Sector, *Mapping Awareness*, 7, 20-25, 1991.

[SCH 02], Scholten H., Meijer E., Spatial retail information – making it more simple! in G. P. Clarke and J. C. H. Stillwell (eds), Applied GIS and Spatial Analysis, Wiley, London, 2002.

[SIM 85], Simkin L P, Doyle P & Saunders J., UK Retail Store Location Assessment, *Journal of the Market Research Society*, 27(2), 96-108, 1985.

[WIL 00], Willard T., Carmakers Survey 'Shot in Arm' as Dealerships Total Stabilises, *Automotive Management*, 235, June 9th, 44-46, 2000.

Chapter 8

Spatial Strategies in Retail and Service Activities

Introduction

To cover a market means, first, to be present physically, thanks either to stores or to a logistical system adapted in the case of mail-order activities to whatever support is appropriate: mail, telephone, Minitel or Internet. Industrial companies are therefore generally represented in markets by their products, which are sold in the stores belonging to retail companies. These are the companies that interest us here, together with companies that provide services. Numerous business owners, bankers, insurers, and others have chosen at times, for the last century and a half, to ensure the growth of their company by identically or almost replicating, their stores in order to create a chain that allows them to expand their clientele geographically. They thus guarantee a superior service to consumers, who can find their favorite products everywhere they go, as well as to industrial companies, which see their products more widely distributed. However, for this to happen, there must be good establishment of stores as a result of implantation in strategic locations on the one hand, while on the other hand good territorial coverage by the chain is necessary in order to obtain a national or even international audience and to be able to serve the entire territory.

Spatial strategies can be broken down into location strategies and chain development strategies. The implementation of location strategies is founded on the techniques already mentioned in the preceding chapters of the second part of this book. The development of store chains in retail, services, hotels, restaurants,

---

Chapter written by Gérard CLIQUET.

banking branches or post offices is not a new phenomenon. One can cite the grocer Félix Potin, whose first store appeared around 1844, followed by a second store around 1860 [CAM 97] before becoming one of the largest food store chains in France, and then disappearing in 1996. Subsequently, department stores, and then variety stores between the two World Wars, supermarkets and hypermarkets, without forgetting specialized superstores, all realized this systematic chain development of their activity. This practice is intended to increase the company's market share and its negotiating power. Yet, market share can only increase if they always cover a superior part of the territory. This also applies to services, especially banks, but also public services like the Post Office, which has been a pioneer in this domain.

Geomarketing cannot ignore the strategic and managerial dimensions of the spatial problems of retail and service companies and the development of which is henceforth involved in the networking of activities. If data and geomarketing techniques create a better understanding of consumer location and characteristics, it is other data possessed by the company that confirm the definition of spatial strategies. Achieving a good-sized territory, and then succeeding in national territory coverage, are soon the fundamental objectives for companies of this type, objectives which are found again in the international development of the chain. Spatial strategies today constitute an element that is inseparable from spatial marketing.

We will therefore attempt to present a typology of spatial strategies, and then deal with the evolution of the phenomenon of the network and of both its spatial and managerial dimensions, before explaining a method of measuring chain territory coverage that is helpful in the definition of spatial strategies.

8.1. Typology of spatial strategies

Two distinct types of location exist: simple and multiple locations (see Chapters 5, 6 and 7). Simple location corresponds to the establishment of a single store. Multiple location deals with the much more complex establishment operation of stores either simultaneously or at different times, either in the same trade area or in several different trade areas.

Once this distinction has been made, it becomes easy to understand that location strategies linked to the search for a trade area and then for a site exist on the one hand, and store chain spatial development strategies, which aim at covering a territory to impose a trade name or a brand, on the other.

These two types of spatial strategies are not totally separable for two reasons. The first reason is based on the fact that a simple location strategy, concerning one store, can later give rise to a multiple strategy by replication of the concept of the store (see section 8.3). The second reason argues even more for the connection of these two types of strategies since, in reality, a simple location strategy always follows a multiple location strategy. In practice, once the choices are made concerning market areas, or trade areas, there is a multi-establishment in the same geographic sector and each store is then the object of a location strategy that can be qualified as individual. We will therefore successively examine store chain location and development strategies.

8.1.1. *Location strategies*

We will examine simple and multiple location strategies dealing with stores belonging to a chain. We spoke above of a two-step decision process concerning the simple location decision: the selection of the trade area and the choice of the site. It must be known that this two-step process becomes a three-step process because the choice of geographic market should be added [GHO 87]. We will revisit this last step, which is at a more macroeconomic level, in section 8.1.2.

Any store location strategy should be conceived within the framework of the marketing strategy of the company. The conception of this strategy requires two important aspects to be mentioned: the type of products or activities studied, the eventual positioning in terms of price and/or quality or in terms of age and thus the chosen segmentation. In connection with product type, the use of geomarketing data is particularly interesting. A business specializing in furniture [CLI 90] or home equipment [GHO 90] should take into account the number of consumers who are homeowners since they are more inclined to invest. However, this characteristic does not apply to supermarkets. A children's clothing store will be concerned with the number and size of families with children [GHO 90]. In connection with positioning, here again geomarketing data can be useful if attention is paid to the revenue of consumers, to their socio-professional category or to their age. In the USA there are supermarkets that target young people and those that target seniors: location strategies resulting from such segmentation are often different. Furthermore, discount stores and luxury stores will not generally be located in the same areas. When these marketing differentiation strategies are applied to stores, they lead to reconsideration of the delineation of trade areas. Applebaum's primary, secondary and tertiary or marginal concentric zones [APP 66] should make way for new methods founded, for example, on the recognition of forms [BAR 00] in order to determine the purchasing zones of consumers. However, unconsciously applying Hotelling's principle of minimal differentiation [HOT 29], certain stores find themselves concentrated in the same locations. This is often the case in furniture (systematically in the Netherlands) or important banking branches but also at times in certain cities for lighting stores (Athens) or jewelry stores (Beirut). In addition, in accordance with the central places theory [CHR 33], certain activities can only be effectively located in urban centers of sufficient size or even in cities sufficiently far from large centers.

The environment, which is increasingly variable, also constitutes a predominant element in the conception of store location strategy. This signifies that one must not content oneself with the current characteristics of the environment. Future changes must also be taken into account. This is possible by implementing scenarios [GHO 82] and developing site choice procedures based, for example, on models like the MCI model (see Chapter 6) [GHO 83]. The MCI (Multiplicative Competitive Interaction) model not only takes into account the geographic situation of consumers *vis-à-vis* each store, but also of all the attraction variables of each store and especially the competition from other stores.

Among the environmental factors directly associated with the marketing problems of the future store, consumer behavior is a determinant element. In particular, the spatial behavior of customers (Chapter 2) appears crucial in the choice of store location. The increase in consumer mobility [MAR 96] encourages companies to rethink their location strategy: the importance of consumer mobility rises as the retail attraction becomes passing [CLI 97], which means temporary consumers not residing in the immediate geographic sector of the store.

Location strategies should respect five principles [LEW 86]:

1. the interception principle or "how to hook the customer?". Measurement of this interception capacity is carried out with the help of road or pedestrian traffic at site accesses, without forgetting the quality and the nature of the traffic.

2. the principle of cumulative attraction or "must businesses of the same type be grouped together?". According to Hotelling's principle [HOT 29], a tendency exists to group together businesses with homogenous activities and, furthermore, a synergy effect can be observed because this regrouping often results in combined attraction superior to the sum of the individual attractions of isolated stores.

3. the principle of compatibility or "what complementarity exists between retail and service activities?". Certain businesses sell very different products more effectively when they are grouped together as opposed to being isolated.

4. the principle of accessibility or "how to make the approach, the traffic and the exit easier for the consumer?". Crucial from the very first visit, all the traffic signal details, the width of lanes and parking spaces, and even sidewalks. In short, all forms of physical access have a major significance.

5. the principle of over-equipment or "how to avoid over-attraction?". This principle can be expounded simply by saying that "too many businesses kills business" as a result of traffic congestion, whether vehicular or pedestrian.

An important point at the strategic level concerns the time period of store openings. Several years can sometimes pass between the moment when the decision to open a new store is made and the moment when this store is actually opened [KAU 00]. Yet, the importance of the effect of surprise can be in the success of a strategy is well known. In this instance, this effect is often zero, for example in the case of hypermarkets in France, since there may be time periods that can last up to 5 to 6 years before it is possible to open the store. Technical and managerial problems are not the only causes. Numerous cases end in failure and lack of permission to open. The Royer law (December 1973), followed by the Raffarin law (July 1996), attempted to slow down the speed of new large store establishments (over 300 m^2) in France. There have been many perverse effects of this, from the corruption of local officials to the creation of a veritable quasi-monopoly situation [CLI 00d; MAR 79].

The conception of a store location strategy thus requires taking into account numerous factors linked to marketing and environmental considerations:

– marketing strategy and environment: positioning, segmentation, product and activity type, consumer behavior;

– competitive environment: characteristics of other stores;

– economic environment: evolution of the population;

– legal environment: regulation of retail establishments.

Store location strategies can be summarized as follows:

– downtown;

– suburb;

– shopping mall;

– away from shopping malls;

– proximity (convenience stores);

– thoroughfare: train stations, airports, roadside stops, in old service stations, etc.;

– high-attraction locations: large resort complexes;

– away from stores: Internet or catalogue business.

These strategies are responses either to the requirements of the hierarchical model of urban retailing (corresponding to the first four strategies of the list above), or to the needs of consumers in terms of type of purchase following a so-called *post-hierarchical* model (corresponding to the last four strategies) [BRO 91].

Some of these strategies can be combined in the overall spatial strategy of a store chain. In practice, chains establish stores as easily on the outskirts as in the downtown area, even if the concept is sometimes adapted, as well as in shopping malls and on thoroughfares.

8.1.2. *Store chain spatial development strategies*

We have just distinguished the location strategies linked to the establishment of a store. For chains, the objectives are different and are situated at a different level in the decision process. The spatial development strategies of store chains are developed with a goal of territorial coverage and sometimes homogeneity of the spatial distribution of activities in a given territory. If the conception process is seen in three steps, it is obviously the first step, the choice of geographic markets, that we should develop here.

Marketing researchers, or more specifically retailing researchers, have worked little in the retail spatial strategies domain. And, even though books and articles exist with the expression "spatial strategies" in their title, most simply describe or explain the methods and models dealt with in Chapters 5 and 6 of this book. However, certain authors have tried to determine the most widely used spatial strategies, especially those that appear to be the most coherent and which are not simply guided by simple circumstantial fantasies. Laulajainen highlighted, based on a historico-geographic study of several American and Scandinavian chains, certain common traits in spatial strategies. He started by affirming that these strategies do not infringe upon the rules associated with the penetration of markets in general. This penetration comes about through development of a store-owned network, through the acquisition of another chain, or through association with other firms (franchise or retailer associations: Leclerc, Intermarché and Système U). Promodès, before the merger with Carrefour, had tried all three strategies to ensure its international expansion: the acquisition of chains in the USA and Germany resulted in a resale several years later; furthermore, the cooperation with SuperValu and Cub Foods in the USA has been stopped. However, the development of store-owned networks in countries where business had remained very traditional (Spain, Portugal, Greece) was crowned with success. Laulajainen [LAU 87] showed that the choice of a spatial strategy depends on several variable criteria from one country to the next:

– establishment legislation;

– the level of modernization of the retail sector;

– market structure;

– the position on the lifecycle curve concerning location;

– the company and the sector;

– the opportunities encountered on location.

Davidson, Sweeny and Stampfl [DAV 88] identified store chain spatial development strategies that aim at several objectives:

– the establishment of new stores;

– the changing of location of existing stores;

– lease renewals;

– the adjustment of the sales area by expansion or reduction;

– the modernization of existing stores.

These same authors look back at a proposal from Management Horizons, a division of PriceWaterhouseCoopers, concerning a three-dimensional matrix showing the impact of spatial strategies on:

– target market segments, in this case localized markets, according to whether dealing with real or potential consumers;

– trade areas, whether or not they are already being served;

– the number of current stores or of stores to be created.

This matrix is much more complex if other elements of the retailing mix are introduced, such as those linked to product strategies. If one only considers the factors linked to location, it can be broken down into two other two-dimensional matrices, each allowing eight strategies to be distinguished, of which six concern spatial aspects since the other two lead logically to the pure and simple absence of the trade area. The six strategies thus defined are therefore:

– market expansion;

– market penetration;

– business performance improvement;

– market diversification;

– market intensification;

– repositioning.

With the *market expansion* strategy, new stores are established in new trade areas, but they are intended for known customer segments: a hypermarket company installs new stores in a city where it was hitherto absent. The *market penetration* strategy consists of establishing new stores in trade areas where stores of the same type, or in other words positioned in the same market, belonging to the same company, already exist. This is the case when a chain of convenience stores increases the number and therefore the density of its store chains in the areas where the chain is already present. *Business performance improvement* encourages the modernization of existing stores to make them more attractive: Carrefour has made its hypermarkets evolve by introducing the concept of “universe of products”. The strategy of *market diversification* aims at establishing new stores in new trade areas aimed towards new customer segments. When a chain of large stores establishes discount superstores in different trade areas from usual, this can be called diversification: this was the case of the Primevère stores developed by Printemps, without much success, in the 1970s. The strategy of *market intensification* signifies that the new stores aimed at new customer segments are established in trade areas where the first trade name is already present. Thus, Auchan establishes superstores specializing in sports products (Décathlon) in the same trade areas as its hypermarkets. Finally, the strategy of *repositioning* is aimed at modifying existing stores in order to attract a new target clientele. The transformation of variety stores into *citymarchés* by Monoprix is an illustration of this.

Each of these strategies can be examined in a more elaborate manner at the spatial level. The *expansion strategy* is probably the "most spatial" insofar as the considerations linked to space are very important. This leads to five so-called *spatial* strategies [DAV 88]:

– contiguous expansion;

– establishing beachheads;

– market clustering;

– skim strategy;

– acquisitions.

Contiguous expansion consists of establishing stores in trade areas close to those where existing stores are situated. All regional chains have proceeded thus. Laulajainen [LAU 87] describes this as a phenomenon of infectiousness applied to the spatial distribution of a product, or in this case a store. Its advantages are logistic in nature, because it affects neither the organization of stock nor the headquarters control facilities, and financial in nature, since it avoids the large advertising investment necessary in regions where the trade name is totally absent. The disadvantages appear at the same time as the inevitable increase in sales and therefore the extension of the chain of stores. Thus, this prevents the seizing of opportunities provided by remarkable sites in other areas, which can then be taken by competitors with little difficulty. The *establishment of beachheads* therefore proves very useful in certain stages of chain development. This strategy can even seem indispensable if the competition is intent on blocking access to the best sites. This is obviously a riskier and more costly strategy, but one that can be profitable in the long term as long as each beachhead is reinforced by a strategy of local expansion. Without such an expansion, it is often preferable to abandon stores that appear to be too isolated. *Market clustering* consists of establishing several stores simultaneously. This strategy is effective from the perspective of an elevated objective in terms of market share. However, it requires, on the one hand, that the establishment restrictions on the sites are not too strong and, on the other hand, that the market is not saturated. It allows advertising and logistics costs to be reduced and the blocking of the competition's access to sites. However, this approach can have, as a consequence, the reduction of the life-cycle of the type of store concerned, since the blocking of the market will lead to the opening of new marketing channels. The danger of cannibalization of sales between markets is also very high. This strategy is more frequent in the USA than in Europe. In the 1970s, chains like J.C. Penny were able to constitute, in the USA, the densest network in the world in terms of department stores by occupying in a systematic manner sites inside shopping centers. This strategy ended with the territorial saturation of these centers. The *skim strategy* aims at taking advantage of the existence of sufficiently profitable target markets regardless of their location. This is not like a beachhead strategy, in which a new distribution knot is created from which a strategy of expansion could develop. The skim strategy will often be that of luxury boutiques, whose paramount goal is buying power. Finally, the strategies of *acquisition* are an effective way of saving time in the conquest of territories. The spatial dimension of such acquisitions has been strongly confirmed [LAU 88]. In practice, if the evaluation of sites proves to be good, with the loyalty of the customer already having been secured, communication effort will be minimal and, most importantly, no effort will be necessary in acquiring the sites, in obtaining authorizations and in constructing the buildings. Only interior adjustments and a change of the trade name will eventually be carried out. The major disadvantage resides of course in the cost of such operations. Wal-Mart has penetrated the German and British markets by buying out local companies (Wertkauf and Spar Handel in Germany, Asda in the UK). Despite considerable financial means, the operation is difficult to render profitable. Promodès was not able to succeed after its buy-out of Plazza hypermarkets in Germany and was forced to resell the chain.

Concerning the *penetration strategy*, five spatial strategies can be distinguished [DAV 88]:

– infilling;

– store enlargement;

– secondary markets;

– recycled locations;

– acquisitions.

The *infilling strategy* consists of checking out all the trade areas likely to welcome one or several supplementary stores in order to create entrance barriers for competitors. The *store enlargement strategy* allows an increase in market share, as well as in profitability; all the models show this as long as regulations are respected. It is thus that the Leclerc supermarkets become hypermarkets over time. *Secondary markets* are the occasion to establish smaller stores, which prove themselves profitable. This is a form of replication of the concept by reducing its size. This strategy corresponds to the spatial strategy of hierarchical distribution developed by Laulajainen [LAU 87], which consists of establishing first in large cities in order to increase brand or trade name visibility, followed by looking towards secondary markets. This chain extension process is inevitable for certain activities such as luxury hotels: this is how the Novotel group, which has since become Accor, was required to rethink and implement this type of strategy when it bought out the Mercure chain in 1974. On the other hand, Wal-Mart constitutes a veritable paradox insofar as this chain, specializing in non-food products, first developed in secondary markets, namely the small and medium towns of the USA. Currently, these stores are being transformed into supercenters, resembling French hypermarkets, by the addition of food products. This firm has therefore used classical strategic methods in reverse and has still become the largest retail company on earth. The *recycling locations strategy* tends to develop with the saturation of sites. These opportunities are supplied by the closing of various stores, without regard to size, whether they are in shopping centers or not and whether through rehabilitation of neighborhoods or of old buildings. In France, the strong development of retail associations like Leclerc, Intermarché or Système U could result in defections in particular of those who retire, given the legal link uniting these merchants. Some are tempted to resell their stores to competitor retail companies. The Leclerc group takes measures to ensure itself a right of preemption. The Raffarin law also imposes restrictions on new hotel establishments: old hotels therefore become prey for the chains, and the owners of these hotels receive an unexpected profit [CLI 00]. The eventual predators are therefore led to organize a geographic information system covering available sites to compare with a geographic information system on potential customers. These types of sites are very much in demand in specialized stores and restaurants, as well as in large stores. *Acquisition* within territories already occupied by the company can lead to the buy-out of competitor stores or to the exchange of sites with other chains in order to create an optimal situation. Numerous merger or acquisition operations have been carried out in France over the past 15 years. Even though they lead to a strong acceleration in territorial coverage, they have the big disadvantage of being very costly. Auchan spent quite some time in "managing" the buy-out of Docks de France, as did Carrefour after the merger with Promodès, periods which competitors turned into profits.

The *business performance improvement strategy* also has an impact on spatial strategies and can be broken down as follows [DAV 88]:

– downsizing;

– reprogramming the merchandize mix;

– making site–specific changes;

– store relocation;

– closing of marginal stores.

A downsizing strategy can have the goal of improving the return on investment by cutting costs. One can take advantage of this by reprogramming the merchandize mix on the most profitable product lines corresponding to the local target, based on a study founded on the geographic data of the trade area: this thus gives rise to geo-merchandizing (see Chapter 12). The site is sometimes rearranged in order to improve its attractiveness. When this is not possible, the store is relocated: this type of operation, which cannot be widespread given its cost, is found in banking and the furniture market, and sometimes even in large stores like supermarkets. If this does not work, marginal stores are closed: variety stores, certain department stores and especially service stations have suffered from such policies.

Diversification, intensification and repositioning strategies lead, as far as location factors are concerned, to the same spatial strategies as those described above. This is the product mix that differentiates them because the targets are no longer the same. Geomarketing data on the trade areas take on great importance.

We have attempted, based on the less than well-developed scientific literature in this domain, which is particularly weak in the marketing researchers' camp, to describe the different spatial strategies that concern individual store or entire store chain location. These strategies, although close to a concept that can be considered aspatial, are specifically concerned with territorial conquest.

8.2. Networking in retail and service activities

Few research studies have been carried out with the goal of better understanding one of the most essential phenomena of the economic development of the end of the 19th and especially of the 20th century. One reason for this lack of interest may come from the fact that the retail trade has hardly sparked the enthusiasm of researchers, at least in France. But this explanation is of little importance when one knows that the *Journal of Retailing* published its first issue in the USA in 1925, a date comparable to that of the publication of the first issue of the *Harvard Business Review* (1923), which can be considered the first important management journal in history (the *Journal of Marketing* appeared in 1936). The reason for this disaffection should therefore be sought elsewhere. The power that has accumulated today in the hands of those customarily known as "distributors" in France, those who desire to be called retailers or merchants once again, is not without consequence on either the economic or the social plane, or even at societal or political levels. Yet, although the retail trade has been studied for quite some time by Anglo-Saxon researchers and in numerous countries currently, this has especially been concerning marketing, strategy or management at the store level. At the level of the retail company, research has mainly sought to develop by analogy the concepts drawn from the marketing of products or services by affirming that, for a retail company, the product is the store [DIC 92]. The major specificity of the retail company remains to be opened up: the importance of space and therefore the fundamentally geographic character of its expansion. Industrial companies have also followed a geographic expansion of their market for quite some time, but the location logic of their production units does not rely on the same principles as that which prevails for retail chains, where the density of presence in territories is generally stronger.

Among the too few research works intended to improve understanding of the approach of these modern conquerors known as retail companies, generally owned by families descended from a particularly enterprising retailer, one finds that carried out by Laulajainen [LAU 87]. His sources were principally American statistical studies, the activity reports of certain chains and even the memoirs or biographies of great entrepreneurs [KRE 83; MAH 66; REI 66] and the histories of several large chains like The Great Atlantic & Pacific Tea Company [BUL 33], J.C. Penney Company [BEA 48], Allied Stores Corporation [MAC 79], and McDonald's [JEN 80]. This is the work of both a geographer and a historian insofar as the author describes himself as restricted in uniting space and time in order to fully understand the expansion of chains. This may actually be the difficulty that puts off a number of researchers. Laulajainen describes and attempts to explain the spatial strategies implemented by large American and Scandinavian chains.

Ghosh and McLafferty [GHO 87] were able to synthesize knowledge in terms of retail and service location, to propose a typology and to develop a rigorous approach dealing with store chain location and development strategies.

In fact, two steps should be distinguished in the retail networking process. The first step corresponds to what can be called the development of a store chain (see section 8.2.1), while the second step concerns the transformation of the chain in the network (see section 8.2.2).

8.2.1. *Store chain development*

The growth of retailing in the form of store chains is an old phenomenon (see the introduction to this chapter), both in France and in the USA, where in 1859 [LEB 63], in the New York region, The Great Atlantic & Pacific Tea Company founded by Georges F. Gilman began [BUL 33], which has since become A&P supermarkets [LAU 87].

Since then, the retail and services trades have continuously grown in the form of chains. And, little by little, structuring elements of the decision concerning the transition to chains appeared. In addition to the will of the business entrepreneur, founded both on the ambition of economic domination and on a certain strategic vision, at least two conditions, linked to the definition of the retail concept to be distributed, seem to prevail in the success of this form of growth: the notoriety of the trade name or of the brand and the maintenance of the uniformity of the concept [BRA 98].

If one admits that the store is the product of the retail company [DIC 92], one can therefore assimilate the trade name to the brand and it appears natural in practice to speak of concept in describing an elaborated version of a product idea expressed in significant terms for the consumer [KOT 00]. This definition of the marketing concept can be perfectly applied to the store, but with the condition that the two essential elements unique to retailing and to service, the *format* on the one hand and the *know-how* on the other, must be distinguished.

The *format* comprises all the permanent attributes of the concept, with some being physical in nature (size) and other being non-physical, either managerial (the sales formula or the type of store) or strategic (positioning).

The size of the store in square meters can be:

– precise, as in the case of Yves Rocher stores with their 50 m^2 (currently the fourth generation of stores should go to 100 m^2), or Ikea with surface areas of 20,000 m^2 (in France, a decrease of this area is envisaged in order to enter smaller cities);

– constrained between 10,000 and 15,000 m^2 like the Auchan hypermarkets;

– differentiated depending on the importance of the trade area that is *a priori* defined, such as, in banking, large branches and neighborhood branches;

– the sales formula: personal sales, self-service, or any combination of formulas;

– the type of store: department store, variety store, hypermarket, supermarket, convenience store, specialized superstore, restaurant, hotel, banking branch, insurance office, travel agency;

– positioning: both in marketing and geography (suburb or downtown), the quality of both products sold and proposed services [BLI 60].

Positioning can either:

– constitute the foundation of the global image of the trade name and of its competitors having the same position: for example, extreme discounters such as Aldi, Lidl or Norma; in this market the true “extreme” discounters can be distinguished from the more moderate discounters (Leader Price); or

– be the basis of the creation of a veritable range of stores following this strict quality/price positioning or more generally by including size or specialization considerations: for example, from as early as the 1930s, department store companies like Au Printemps and Galeries Lafayette began creating their own chain of variety stores in order to respond to the needs of less wealthy consumer during the Depression; hypermarket companies have developed, internally or through acquisition, stores ranging from hypermarkets to convenience stores by way of supermarkets – Auchan preferred to develop specialized superstores, thus implementing a flexible diversification strategy [FIL 89]; finally, hotels are classified according to the number of stars and the Accor group possesses chains that range from four stars (Sofitel) to no star (Formule 1) with three stars (Novotel and Mercure), two stars (Ibis) and one star (Etap Hôtel) in between.

The *know-how* is made up of progressive attributes of the concept. It is considered to be mastery of technical knowledge [REM 98], and therefore non-physical, coming from the development of practices intended to enrich the system of “servuction” (or service production) [EIG 87]. It develops practically every day as a result of the accumulation of experience. It is therefore likely to be substantial and can only be protected by keeping it secret and allowing the originality to be preserved [REM 98]. This know-how is first developed in the exploitation of a store. A sufficient part of this know-how has to be formalized in order to give birth to the concept. However, if the so-called tacit part, in other words the non-conceptualized part, of the know-how is too large, its distribution to the stores may pose problems, either at the moment of the creation of the chain or during its development, since the know-how is increasingly at risk of being imitated and overtaken by competitors. In practice, the more the format is easily observable and therefore imitable, the more the know-how constitutes the heart of the concept and the key element of the day-to-day success of the chain. Know-how is therefore both a major tactical element in daily competition with competitors and a primordial element of the chain's strategy in its geographic development. This day-to-day competition can be intra-type or inter-type [HIR 79]. *Intra-type competition* is competition between identical types of stores: hypermarkets with other hypermarkets. *Inter-type competition* occurs between different types of stores: peripheral supermarkets and variety stores in the downtown areas. This last element becomes more important as the distance between a store and headquarters makes control of concept uniformity more difficult [BRA 98]. This initial know-how, associated with the format, should then be transformed into a replicable concept that can be used in other stores of the same type. Thus, based on the precise definition of these two elements, the geographic diffusion of the concept can, in theory, begin. In fact, however, another very important point in the diffusion must be dealt with before the chain is launched and this concerns the choice of organizational form.

The organizational form of the store chain is a key element in both the speed of store location and the consolidation of the concept. In practice, according to Bradach [BRA 87], store chains find themselves confronted with four challenges:

– adding new units;

– maintaining uniformity across units;

– local responsiveness;

– system-wide adaptation.

The last two challenges apply more to networks that have arrived at the maturity stage and will be mentioned in the next section. However, the first two challenges, adding new units and uniformity, are linked to store chain development.

As far as growth through adding new units is concerned, franchising allows the rhythm of new store establishment to be accelerated [LAF 92]: this organizational form is particularly interesting in the context of a large increase [NEG 00], and even more specifically for goods and services involving short and repetitive purchases [CAV 76]. This system leads to a greater speed of location for a minimal investment on the part of the franchisor, compared to company-owned management, since it is the franchisees who take the financial risks as independent businesspeople under the franchise contract with the franchisor. Figure 8.1 shows how the Campanile hotel chain (Envergure group) developed. With the help of a relative entropy calculation (see section 8.3), it can be seen that franchising (small dashed curve) allowed a more rapid territorial coverage than company-owned management (longer dashed line). The solid line represents the evolution of the total coverage irrespective of the legal status of the hotels.

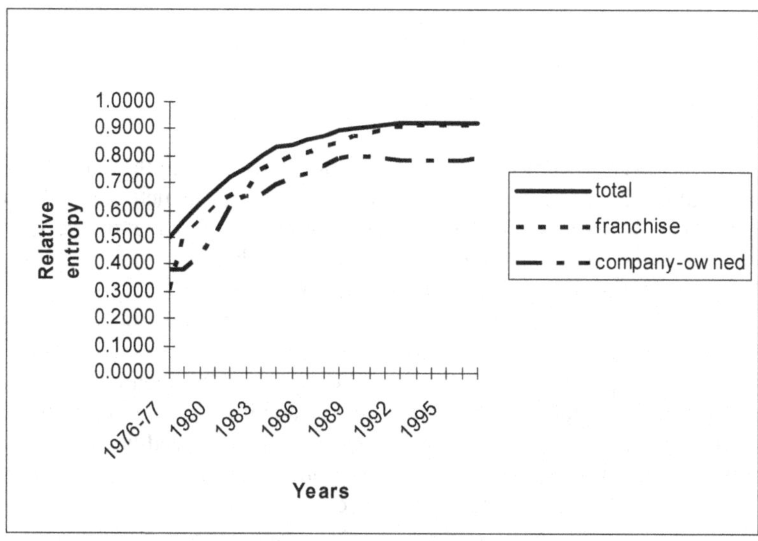

Figure 8.1: *Territory coverage of the Campanile hotel chain [CLI 00c]*

Each store or service location operation requires "geomarketing" socio-demographic data, in other words spatially related data on potential customers in the area in the case of a polar attraction store (Chapter 2) or on passing customers in the case of passing attraction [CLI 97].

However, high speed of location, useful in the face of increased competition, can also be a marketing handicap insofar as the too rapid growth of the chain can lead to some dilution of the brand or trade name image by initiatives on the part of the franchisees, which become increasingly difficult to control as their number increases rapidly. Concept uniformity thus becomes a key element [BRA 98]. This is why a large number of chains are currently organized as multiple forms, which means mixing franchise and company-owned units. The franchised part of the chain allows rapid development, while the company-owned part serves as a mechanism to control concept uniformity as long as company-owned and franchised units are properly distributed throughout a territory. Furthermore, company-owned units that are directly managed by the franchisor can supply data related to local markets, which franchisees are not obliged to provide. In a purely franchised chain, the franchisor cannot possess a true geomarketing information system comparable to that of a company-owned organization.

Once the development stage has been declared as finished, the chain has reached maturity. Strategic and managerial problems are therefore of a different order. They move from a logic of territorial coverage to a logic of spatial densification, or in other words from a chain logic to a network logic.

8.2.2. *From chain to network*

As we have seen, problems encountered vary according to the life-cycle stage of a store chain. The concept is strengthened during the launch stage, before it is replicated on a wider scale during the development stage. The struggle for the best sites is thus often ferocious and the care given to choice of site becomes crucial. This is a preparation for reaching the maturity stage. Chain directors know that the qualities demanded of the manager of these chains are not the same during the launch and development stages as during the maturity stage [CLI 98b]. The first two life-cycle stages predominantly require the qualities of creator and developer: territories must be conquered, not necessarily at all costs, but with discernment. However, the maturity stage sees a decrease in growth leading to the necessary consolidation of knowledge, with viability being the keyword. This stage requires administrative qualities, because the period during which there is a large increase in the number of stores and therefore in sales has been completed; the cost of establishments during that phase, which are at times a little anarchic, for it is necessary to seize opportunities before competitors can act, leave traces that are more or less indelible in the resulting accounts. Restructuring to one degree or another is often necessary; this results in, among other things, location changes or positive or negative evolutions in the size of the sales surface area. When the chain is obligated to turn to external growth, through acquisition or merger with other chains, in order to accelerate its growth, the effects on the overall structure of the chain are even more complex to manage. The question that must be answered is therefore clear: how can degradation of the management and the results of the chain during its passage into the maturity stage be avoided?

Retail or services companies that are looking to expand through a chain will therefore move from a location strategy of placing individual sites next to one another to a strategy of global spatial development. The use of the word global is intentional. One must move from a sequential concept of the establishment of the chain to a reticular (related to network) concept, in other words from an analytical concept to a systemic concept. Fréry [FRE 97] outlines the necessary flexibility of organizations in explaining the advantages of going from chain to network. For multi-establishment businesses or multi-enterprises, like store networks, the dilemma is very specific. However, let us first attempt to differentiate between the concepts of chain and network. Chains evoke the idea of uniformed links connected by the existence of the same trade name, one could say of the same banner, intended to group them together. During the growth phase, as long as shares of local markets are acquired without too much overlapping of the trade areas of adjacent stores, the development of the chain proceeds without major problems. Difficulties arise when there is a growing shortage of available sites and a narrowing geographic gap between the stores of a same chain, especially when the status is different, franchised or company-owned, but also between franchisees.

In a general way, a network can be defined as an "*assembly of small dispersed units, linked together in varying degrees of formality and organized in order to meet common needs*" or even as a "broken-up form [of] system allowing the simultaneous implementation in several locations of a set of actions with a flexible adaptation to the terrain" [BOU 90]. Where the chain reveals the weakness resulting from its weakest link, the network should develop interactions between its members and thus a stronger synergy. Such a concept requires the strength of a pilot and the flexibility of the network.

In a network of stores, this approach involves responding to questions that blend organizational and spatial considerations:

– Where to place franchised stores? Company-owned stores?

– Should a franchisee possessing several stores or several franchisees be preferred?

– Is having a pilot store in the region necessary?

– Should a given region be attacked by using a franchise or a company-owned store?

– Should this policy be systematic or be revisited regularly?

The answer to these questions leads more and more networks to structure themselves with franchised units located around a company-owned pilot store that ensures concept uniformity, stimulation of the local network, the implementation of innovations (*window effect*), the passage of information to headquarters, frequent contact with franchisees, the training of franchisees, and the organization of local promotional campaigns. This organized mix at the local level between company-owned stores and franchises is currently seen in France in the bakery industry [CLI 98b]. Other spatial strategies linked to store status can also be observed. Thus, businesses prefer to have franchised units far from headquarters but to preserve the ownership of closer units [RUB 90]. This is the case for Akéna hotels [CLI 98b].

Concerning organizations, four categories of networks can be distinguished:

– *integrated networks* with top-down power: company-owned management;

– *federated networks* with bottom-up power from elections, associations;

– *contractual networks* with bilateral power: franchise;

– *networks organized like a lattice (or lattice networks)* with multi-centered power, in other words with several poles.

This last form appears predominant in practice and is oriented toward the relationship between the members of the network [CLI 98b]. The objective is to create connections, irrespective of the legal link, in order to circulate better the added value [BOU 90]. This thus explains why new forms of organization exist within store networks: partnership, distributorship, affiliation, appointing a manager, commission-affiliation. Plural forms thus appear more adapted to the maturity stage of the life-cycle of store networks, because they are more flexible [CLI 00a].

The necessary forecasting of the organizational and spatial evolution in the life of a network of stores involves the elaboration of a spatial development plan intended to fix objectives concerning [CLI 98b]:

– territorial coverage;

– the global balance between franchised and company-owned units;

– the local balance between company-owned and franchised units;

– location of pilot sites;

– speed of location.

The plurality of the network cannot be summed up in terms of a simple proportion of franchised and company-owned units, but constitutes a certain managerial state of mind: it is a reticular form, which seeks to unite development and innovation dynamism on the one hand and mastery of the concept and the images of the brand and the organization on the other [CLI 98b], all in a harmonious spatial distribution.

The survival of store chains therefore involves their networking and the development of a review system, both of the marketing plans (related to the evolution of the desires and the lifestyles of consumers) and strategic plans (related to what competitors are doing), without forgetting the technological dimension (trade and services today require investment in equipment that is comparable in price to the investment of industrial businesses). The marketing review can rely on a geomarketing information system and the strategic and technological review on data collected within the actual business and by the different actors in the network.

Among the data possessed by the business, certain data are very easy to collect and are useful in the definition of spatial strategies intended to increase or perfect the territorial coverage of the network.

8.3. Territory coverage and spatial strategies

We have been able to see how important the notion of territorial coverage is in terms of spatial strategies. The conquest of territories goes hand-in-hand with the improvement of market share in retail trade. Industrial firms take advantage of this and therefore see the diffusion of their products increase. The battle for territorial coverage has always existed in commerce, whether at the local, national or international level. One can imagine the stakes at a time when talk of economic globalization and more specifically the opening of European borders dominated discussion [GOG 89].

The objective of this section is to explain a method that enables territorial coverage to be measured. The stakes are high since, for a network of stores, adequately covering a national territory means access to important national media without risking a decline in audience, as well as avoiding ruptures in the logistic chain, which are always prejudicial in terms of both costs and supply times, and putting promotional strategies into place. The historical headquarters of the French hypermarket chain Cora is at Nancy. This chain has naturally established itself in the East of France. Figure 8.2 shows that the territorial coverage of the Cora chain is particularly situated in the north-east quarter of France, with a few stores in the center. The consequences of this situation are both strategic and managerial.

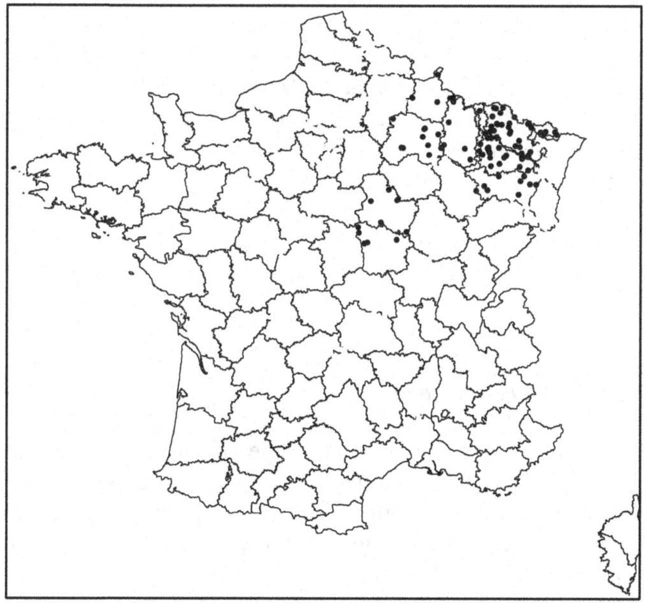

Figure 8.2: *Cora supermarkets in France*

As far as the marketing strategy is concerned, as access to the national media, an indispensable lever for sales, is limited, the Cora chain must be content with the local media, which is efficient for improving the attractiveness of the store but less efficient for the image of the trade name. Large national trade names, although forbidden from advertising on French television channels, shape their image by sponsoring broadcasts and thus avoiding the limitations on television advertising. In addition, the law sometimes favors large distributors. The advertising issue is not the only one to blame. Poor logistics can also lead to a reduction in the profitability of a chain. Sites that are too far from each other lead to rapidly insurmountable cost and management difficulties when there is strong competition. Cora, which does possess several stores in Western France, far from its base, has trouble organizing the supply to these outlying stores and orchestrating promotional campaigns. Measures have been proposed that are based on spatial auto-correlation [RUL 00].

This vision of things providers backing for the idea that in order to survive, in particular in the retail trade, critical size must be attained. At a strategic level, the idea of critical size is the subject of very clear arguments if one considers decisions made by directors of retail companies [FIL 98]. These directors are accustomed to talking about thresholds in terms of sales, with this sales figure increasing by billions of euros per year. Yet, this idea of critical size only takes on its full meaning in spatial terms. In practice, to reach critical size it is necessary to have a sufficient territorial coverage to gain access to the major media. If the law restricts the freedom to open new stores, concentration therefore becomes inevitable. Such a scenario was witnessed after the passing of the French Raffarin law of 5 July 1996 limiting large store locations. The gain in spatial coverage realized by the Auchan hypermarkets when this company bought the Mammouth hypermarkets of the Docks de France group in August 1996 [CLI 98b] can be clearly seen. This increase has been evaluated and the national position of the Auchan hypermarkets has been reinforced compared most of its immediate competitors.

We will first examine a method for measuring the territorial coverage of retail chains, followed by a study of how to analyze spatial strategies based on these measurements.

8.3.1. *Measuring territory coverage*

The measurement of the territorial coverage of a chain can be a supporting element in the definition of spatial strategies. Geomarketing data are not external to the business but actually within its information system. The necessary data are: store location, its opening date in order to understand the evolution of spatial strategies, and its sales surface area.

The evaluation of territorial coverage can be made in at least three ways. In the case of a decision concerning the acquisition of a store chain with the goal of faster expansion of the company's territory, the decision-maker can choose among three solutions. He can refer to simple maps in order to choose which business would bring about the best coverage. This purely visual method has obvious limitations since it is not always possible to make a choice. Another method, complementary to the first, consists of carrying out a simple calculation of store density in relation to the size of the population. However, this global calculation does not allow the coverage to be judged. This same calculation can be carried out for cells of a geographic division: French departments. The work is more detailed but more precise. However, it does not supply a synthetic measure of the coverage. This is why the use of a relative entropy measure has been proposed [CLI 98b]. Relative entropy is used by geographers to measure spatial dispersion and has enabled rural depopulation to be measured [GRO 97].

The same method has been applied to measuring the geographic dispersion of hypermarkets of the principal chains in France [CLI 98c]. This time, given the expansion of this retail format over nearly 40 years, the values follow a positive progression. The advantage of this method hinges more on the comparisons between the chains than in the intrinsic values. The possibility of creating simulations allows precise choices to be established during acquisitions. These operations, which are often decided specifically on the basis of financial criteria or according to objectives in terms of a critical threshold, the limitations of which are known [FIL 98], could thus be based on strategic spatial choices that conform more to the territorial coherence of the new chain that is formed after a merger or absorption.

Taken from information theory, entropy measures are based on the probabilities of events and the degree of uncertainty of these events. The uncertainty is maximum when all the events have the same probability of occurring. The formula for entropy used by geographers relies on the notion of frequency:

$$E = -\sum_{i=1}^{k} f_i \log f$$

where we will give the following significance to the variables:

E = entropy;

k = number of cells of the geographic division;

f_i = frequency of stores in cell i.

The use of relative entropy: $RE = E/\log k$ provides a measure calculated for the interval [0, 1], which allows simpler comparisons between values of spatial coverage of competitor chains. When the value of the relative entropy is close to 1, the geographic concentration is weak [VIG 97] and, therefore, in the case of stores signifies that the territory is well covered.

In practice, a geographic division is chosen first: the departments in France for reasons of simplicity, followed by the addresses of stores, for which the first two digits of the postal code suffice. The calculation of relative entropy is done on the basis of the number of stores in each department [CLI 98a].

Table 8.1 gives the territorial coverage measured by relative entropy for hypermarket chains established in France in 2000. With a smaller number of stores, the Géant hypermarkets have a territorial coverage superior to that of the Auchan hypermarkets despite the 1996 buy-out of the Docks de France Mammouth stores. If associations are taken into account so that common purchasing centers between the Casino and Cora chains (Opéra), and Leclerc and Système U (Lucie) can be considered, the relative entropy values are given in Table 8.2. Comparison of Tables 8.1 and 8.2 also shows the benefit that a Casino–Cora merger would provide in terms of territorial coverage. However, this benefit would have little effect on narrowing the gap between the Leclerc and the Système U hypermarkets.

Trade-names of French hypermarket chains	Number of hypermarkets	Relative entropy value
Auchan	120	0.85
Carrefour	218	0.91
Géant Casino	109	0.86
Cora	57	0.74
Hyper U	32	0.69
Intermarché	94	0.82
Leclerc	406	0.95
Total results for the 7 large chains present on French territory	1,036	0.97

Table 8.1: *Territory coverage of hypermarket chains in France (2000)*

Trade-names of French hypermarket chains	Number of hypermarkets	Relative entropy value
Auchan	120	0.85
Carrefour	218	0.91
Géant Casino + Cora	166	0.91
Intermarché	94	0.82
Leclerc + Hyper U	438	0.96
Total results for the 7 large chains present on French territory	1,036	0.97

Table 8.2: *Territory coverage of hypermarket chains in France given some possible associations between large retailers (2000)*

The advantage of the method hinges on its simplicity of implementation on the one hand and data collection on the other. Without wishing to hide the difficulties that the entropy concept poses in its interpretation [BON 95], its use here with relative values does not seem to pose major problems.

8.3.2. *Analysis of spatial strategies*

Based on measures of store chain territorial coverage, it is possible to analyze spatial strategies, as long as an acceptable dynamic temporal process can be developed; this is an advantage of relative entropy [CHA 95]. This spatial analysis with strategic aims is based on a long developed, but often criticized, concept in marketing: the life-cycle [DEA 50]. Applied to products [RIN 79], this concept no longer convinces researchers and practitioners today, because of its numerous limitations. The difficulty in deciding positioning on the curve during the actual life of the product figures amongst these criticisms: are we at the start of decline or is this a temporary drop in sales? In other words, not knowing where the saturation point is causes the predictive value of the concept to be rather limited [DHA 76]. Furthermore, it is not always easy to obtain sales data on competitor products and the life-cycle curve does not take this into account [TEL 81].

When applied to stores, the level of saturation can be estimated. In reality, the space available for the diffusion of a network of stores is limited. The number of customers necessary to make a store profitable becomes evident rather quickly: it is known for example that a trade area of around a million inhabitants is necessary for an Ikea store of 20,000 m^2. Based on this evaluation, the maximum number of stores is rather easy to identify. This number can vary if, as is currently being done by Ikea, the store format is reduced in order to allow establishment in smaller cities. Furthermore, it is easier to know the number and the location of competitor store sites than to determine the same information for products. These details encourage consideration of the life-cycle curve for stores.

In order to do this, the dates of store openings, internal data which are again easy to collect, are necessary. In practice, two curves can be traced that use the dates. The first is a simple curve showing the combined number of stores. This is how one can see that in France, variety stores like Monoprix entered the decline stage in 1975 and that hypermarkets have reached their saturation point [CLI 00b]. More precisely and better adapted in the case of a given network of stores, the curve can also be drawn with, as the ordinate, the combined values of relative entropy, in other words for the network spatial coverage. The dissociation between the life-cycle curve of franchised units and that of company-owned units, in the case of plural forms, enables either *post facto* understanding of the strategies followed, or helps to balance the two forms of organization *a priori*, particularly during the development stage, in order to better manage the difficult maturity stage of the network. Figure 8.1 showed the development of the Campanile hotel network of the Envergure group. On these curves, it is clear that franchising initially served to cover the territory, followed by store-owned subsidiaries taking over before franchising covered the whole of France. It can also be seen that this coverage was very progressive with a single plateau in the middle of the 1980s, during which the firm reinforced its local presence. If one compares this curve with that of the Ibis hotel network of the Accor group (Figure 8.3), one can see that the Ibis hotels first developed as store-owned subsidiaries before conquering the territory thanks to franchising. An interview with the directors showed [CLI 98b] that, although they had a preference for ownership [LAF 94], the vast number of hotel opening opportunities in the middle of the 1980s led the directors of the network to put their confidence in franchisees.

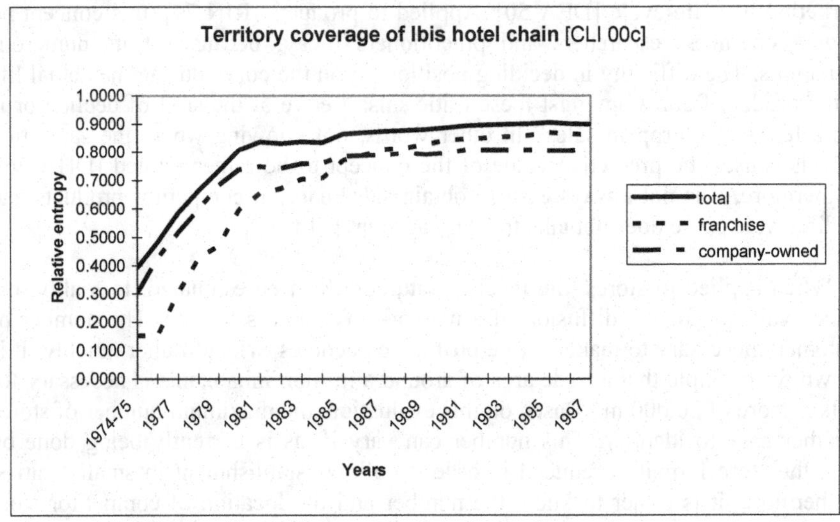

Figure 8.3: *Territorial coverage of the Ibis hotel chain [CLI 00c]*

One can thus analyze the spatial strategies of store networks with the support of life-cycle curves whose ordinates are give in terms of the relative entropy values representing territorial coverage. This analysis can also be done by studying the cumulative curve of the total number of store establishments.

A strong positive gradient of the curve of relative entropy values can be interpreted in different ways:

– stores were established with the goal of territorial conquest: this is the object of a beachhead strategy, which can be clearly identified as it is followed by a period of weaker gradient of the life curve of the network once a strategy of contigous expansion [LAU 87] gets underway locally; this is the *spread effect*;

– the acquisition of a competitor chain, or a merger with another network, well chosen in terms of complementary territorial coverage: the implementation of an acquisition strategy.

A rather weak value of this gradient can have several meanings:

– the new locations have served to reinforce the local establishment of the network as long as the cumulative curve of the number of establishments has a strong positive gradient: this is generally the result of a strategy of contiguous expansion;

– this same phenomenon can be seen when several stores are established simultaneously: this is the application of a *cluster effect* strategy and here again the cumulative curve of the number of establishments retains a strong positive gradient;

– development operations involving the addition of new units have been stopped or slowed if the cumulative curve of the number of establishments has a small or zero gradient; this can be for reasons that are economic or regulatory, as in the case of the application of the Raffarin law in France in 1996;

– the network succeeded in establishing itself throughout the territory and the spatial coverage is almost complete; supplementary establishments will lead to saturation.

The skim strategy is much more difficult to capture with this type of curve since the stores are established more according to the search for buying power than to the aim of systematic territorial expansion.

8.4. Conclusion

We have attempted in this chapter to explain existing knowledge concerning spatial strategies in retail and service firms. The stakes are considerable when one notes the importance that these sectors have attained in the national economy over the past 30 years and in the global economy over the past few years. Economic war has been spoken of in relation to industrial stakes. Today, with the territorial conquests of retail and service firms, one can also speak of global battles that involve firms whose size in sales and personnel terms has overwhelmingly caught up with that of the largest industrial businesses.

A method has been developed that allows territorial coverage to be measured on the basis of data that can also be qualified as geomarketing data but this time of internal origin or from the firm itself. This is a method that has the merit of being simple even if, from a scientific point of view, the concept of entropy always provokes reactions with varying degrees of passion.

Finally, before tackling the final section of this book, which is concerned specifically with marketing dilemmas linked to spatial considerations, it has been worthwhile to provide a managerial dimension to the book. In practice, it was not possible to ignore one of the most important economic phenomena of the last century, the reticulation of the retail trade, a phenomenon eminently spatial with considerable economic and societal consequences.

8.5. References

[APP 66], Applebaum W., Methods for Determining Store Trade Areas, Market Penetration and Potential Sales, *Journal of Marketing Research*, vol. 3, 127-41, 1966.

[BAR 00], Baray J., Cliquet G., Delineating Store Trade Areas Through Morphological Analysis, *The 6th Triennal AMS/ACRA Retailing Conference*, Colombus (Ohio), November 2-5, 2000.

[BEA 48], Beasley N., *Main Street Merchant: The Story of the J. C. Penney Company*, McGraw-Hill, NY 1948.

[BLI 60], Bliss P., Schumpeter, The 'Big' Disturbance and Retailing, *Social Forces*, 72-76, 1960.

[BON 95], Bonsack F., Une interprétation objectiviste de la théorie de l'information, *Revue Internationale de Systémique*, 9, 1, 67-98 1995.

[BOU 90], Boulanger P., Perelman G. *Le réseau et l'infini*, Nathan, Paris, 1990.

[BRA 98], Bradach J. L., *Franchise Organizations*, Harvard Business School Press, Cambridge, Mass., 1998.

[BRO 91], Brown S., Retail Location: The Post Hierarchical Challenge, *The International Review of Retail, Distribution and Consumer Research*, 1, 3, 367-381, 1991.

[BUL 33], Bullock R. J., A History of The Great Atlantic & Pacific Tea Company since 1878, *Harvard Business Review*, 11, 4, 59-69, 1933.

[CAM 97], Camborde P., L'installation de Félix Potin à Paris: le choix d'un métier, in *La révolution commerciale en France: du Bon Marché à l'hypermarché*, J. Marseille ed., Mémoire d'entreprises, Le Monde Editions, 1997.

[CAV 76], Caves R. E., Murphy II W. F., Franchising: Firms, Markets, and Intangible Assets, *Southern Economic Journal*, 42, 572-86, 1976.

[CHA 95], Charre J., *Statistique et territoire*, GIP Reclus, Montpellier, 1995.

[CHR 33], Christaller W., *Die Zentral Orte in Süd Deutschland*, Iena, translated into English in 1966: *Central Places in Southern Germany*, Prentice Hall Inc., Englewood Cliffs, New Jersey, 1933.

[CLI 90], Cliquet G., La mise en œuvre du modèle interactif de concurrence spatiale (MICS) subjectif, *Recherche et Applications en Marketing*, 5, 1, 3-18, 1990.

[CLI 97], Cliquet G., L'attraction commerciale: fondement de la localisation différentielle, *Revue Belge de Géographie*, 121, 57-70, 1997.

[CLI 98a], Cliquet G., Integration and Territory Coverage of the Hypermarket Industry in France: A Relative Entropy Measure, *International Review of Retail, Distribution and Consumer Research*, 8, 2, 205-224, 1998.

[CLI 98b], Cliquet G., *Les réseaux mixtes franchise/succursalisme: complémentarité ou antagonisme*, Report of Centre Rennais de Recherche en Economie et Gestion (CREREG) Rennes 1 University, under a research contract with the Fédération Française de la Franchise (FFF), 1998.

[CLI 98c] Cliquet G., Rulence D., Les opérations d'acquisition des distributeurs en France: mesure de la couverture spatiale des réseaux de points de vente, *Décisions Marketing*, 15, 17-27, 1998.

[CLI 00a], Cliquet G., Plural Forms In Store Networks: A New State Of Mind, *International Review of Retail, Distribution and Consumer Research*, 10, 4, 369-87, 2000.

[CLI 00b], Cliquet G., Large Format Retailers: A French Tradition Despite Reactions, *Journal of Retailing and Consumer Services*, 7, 183-195, 2000.

[CLI 00c], Cliquet G., Plural Form Chains and Retail Life-cycle: An Exploratory Investigation of Hotel Franchised/Company-Owned Systems in France, *Journal of Business and Entrepreneurship*, 12, 2, 75-98, 2000.

[CLI 00d], Cliquet G., Des Garets V., Réglementation des implantations commerciales et stratégies des distributeurs, *15èmes journées des IAE, Biarritz*, 6-8 September, 2000.

[DAV 88], Davidson W. R., Sweeney D. J., Stampfl R. W., *Retailing Management*, 8th ed., John Wiley, NY, 1988.

[DEA 50], Dean J., Pricing Policies for New Products, *Harvard Business Review*, 28, 4, 45-53, 1950.

[DHA 76], Dhalla N., Yuspeh S., Forget the Product Life-cycle Concept!, *Harvard Business Review*, 54, 102-112, 1976.

[DIC 92], Dicke T. S., *Franchising in America: The Development of a Business Method 1840-1980*, University of North Carolina Press, Chapel Hill, 1992.

[EIG 87], Eiglier P., Langeard E., *Servuction: le marketing des services*, McGraw-Hill, Paris, 1987.

[FIL 89], Filser M., *Canaux de distribution: description, analyse, gestion*, Vuibert, Paris, 1989.

[FIL 98], Filser M., Taille critique et stratégie du distributeur: analyse théorique et implications managériales, *Décisions Marketing*, 15, 7-16, 1998.

[FRE 97], Fréry F., La chaîne et le réseau, in *Dedans, dehors*, edited by P. Besson, Vuibert, Paris, 1997.

[GHO 82], Ghosh A., McLafferty S. L., Locating Stores in Uncertain Environments: A Scenario Planning Approach, *Journal of Retailing*, 58, 4, 5-22, 1982.

[GHO 83], Ghosh A., Craig C. S., Formulating Retail Location Strategy in a Changing Environment, *Journal of Marketing*, 47, 3, 56-68, 1983.

[GHO 87], Ghosh A., McLafferty S. L., *Location Strategies for Retail and Service Firms*, Lexington Books, Lexington, Mass., 1987.

[GHO 90], Ghosh A., *Retail Management*, The Dryden Press, Hinsdale, Ill., 1990.

[GOG 89], Gogel R., Larréché J.-C., The Battlefield for 1992: Product Strength and Geographic Coverage, *European Management Journal*, 7, 2, 132-140, 1989.

[GRO 97], Groupe Chadule, *Initiation aux pratiques statistiques en géographie*, 4th ed., Armand Colin, Paris, 1997.

[HIR 79], Hirschman E. C., Intratype Competition Among Department Stores, *Journal of Retailing*, 55, 4, 20-34, 1979.

[HOT 29], Hotelling H., Stability in Competition, *The Economic Journal*, 39, 41-57, 1929.

[JEN 80], Jennings J. J., The Burger Kingdom: Growth and Diffusion of McDonald's in the U.U. 1965-1978, *Abstract of the 35th Annual Meeting, Southeastern Division, Association of American Geographers*, Blacksburg, VA, November 23-25, 1980.

[KAU 00], Kaufmann P. J., Donthu N., Brooks C. M., Multi-Unit Retail Site Selection Processes: Incorporating Opening Delays and Unidentified Competition, *Journal of Retailing*, 76, 1, 113-127, 2000.

[KOT 00], Kotler P., *Marketing Management: Analysis, Planning, Implementation, & Control*, 10th ed., Prentice Hall, Englewood Cliffs, NJ, 2000.

[KRE 83], Kresge S. S., Spilos S., *The S.S. Kresge Story*, Western Publishing Company, Racine, WI, 1983.

[LAF 92], Lafontaine F., How and Why Do Franchisors Do What They Do: A Survey Report, in *Franchising Passport for Growth and World Opportunity*, Kaufmann P. J. ed., Proceedings of the Society of Franchising, Lincoln, NE: International Center for Franchise Studies, University of Nebraska, 1992.

[LAF 94], Lafontaine F., Kaufmann P. J., The Evolution of Ownership Patterns in Franchise Systems, *Journal of Retailing*, 70, 2, 97-113, 1994.

[LAU 87], Laulajainen R., *Spatial Strategies in Retailing*, D. Reidel Publishing Company, Dordrecht, 1987.

[LAU 88], Laulajainen R., The Spatial Dimension of an Acquisition, *Economic Geography*, 64, 171-188, 1988.

[LEB 63], Lebhar G. M., *Chain Stores in America 1859-1962*, 3rd ed., Chain Store Publishing Corp., NY, 1963.

[LEW 86], Lewison D. M., Delozier M. W., *Retailing*, 2nd ed., Merrill Publishing C°, Colombus (Ohio), 1986.

[MAC 79], Macioce T. M., *Allied Stores Corporation: 50 Years of Retail Growth*, The Newcomen Society in North America, NY, 1979.

[MAH 66], Mahoney T., Sloane L., *The Great Merchants*, Harper and Row, NY, 1966.

[MAR 79], Marchand M., Les effets pervers de la loi Royer, *Revue Française de Gestion* 23, 27-39, 1979.

[MAR 96], Marzloff B., Bellanger F., *Les nouveaux territoires du marketing*, Editions Liaisons, Paris, 1996.

[NAK 74], Nakanishi M., Cooper L. G., Parameter Estimation for a Multiplicative Competitive Interaction Model – Least Square Approach, *Journal of Marketing Research*, 11, 303-11, 1974.

[NEG 00], Nègre C., *La franchise*, Vuibert, Paris, 2000.

[REI 66], Reilly P. J., *Old Masters of Retailing*, Fairchild Publications, NY, 1966.

[REM 98], Remoriquet J., *Le savoir-faire dans la franchise*, Report of Laboratoire d'Intelligence des Organisations (LIO) from Haute-Alsace University under a research contract with the Fédération Française de la Franchise (FFF), 1998.

[RIN 79], Rink D.R., Swan J. E., Product Life-Cycle Research: A Literature Review, *Journal of Business Research*, 78, 219-42, 1979.

[RUB 90], Rubin P. H., *Managing Business Transactions*, Free Press, NY, 1990.

[RUL 00], Rulence D., Les stratégies spatiales des firmes de distribution: mesure et comparaisons, in *Etudes et Recherches sur la Distribution*, Economica, Paris, 2000.

[TEL 81], Tellis G. J., Crawford C. M., An Evolutionary Approach to Product Growth Theory, *Journal of Marketing*, 45, 4, 125-132, 1981.

[VIG 97], Vigneron E., *Géographie et statistique*, PUF, Paris, 1997.

PART III

Marketing Management and Geographic Information

Chapter 9

Price and Geographic Information

Introduction

The development of e-commerce has drawn attention to the role of marketing variables, the importance of which is often underestimated: price, availability of products, etc., the set being marked by a new openness in the supply conditions for all the actors: customers, competitors, and distributors, all the way to the producer himself. In fact, these important transformations in the form of trade can be analyzed as a new concept involving the geographic dimension of trade, which has a determining impact on price fixing. After a presentation of the impact of the geographic dimension on each of the components of price, an analysis of geographic price policies will be given.

9.1. The impact of the geographic dimension on the components of price

The integration of the geographic dimension into pricing policy requires first a definition, in more or less restrictive terms, of the notion of price, its components and its determinants.

The components of price

Traditionally, price is considered as the quantity of currency that must be sacrificed in order to obtain the desired product. However, an author like Simon [SIM 00] suggests a more restrictive definition: "by the price of a product of service, one designates the monetary quantity that a buyer must spend to acquire this product

---

Chapter written by Pierre DESMET and Monique ZOLLINGER.

or service." The geographic dimension has little place in this very restrictive vision of price.

A broader vision of price includes taking the consumer's point of view into account: "Price is what is abandoned or sacrificed in order to obtain a product" [ZEI 88]. From this perspective, Zeithaml identifies the main elements of price, which are the objective price, the price itself and the perceived non-monetary sacrifice. The restrictive definition is therefore spread out in two directions essentially by recognizing the pertinence of taking non-monetary components into account and by underlining the possible difference between objective price and perceived price.

The monetary effort is not limited to the sum of the cash payment and should take into account the monetary cost of additional activities preceding or following the purchase (travel in the search for information, for example). In this category, the form of payment also influences the monetary cost: different modes of payment (cash, check, credit card, money order) can thus be joined by different means of receivable payment such as credit or barter.

From the perspective of an enlarged concept, the dimensions of time, integrated into the effort, and of the risk were first proposed. According to Murphy and Enis [MUR 86], the effort is defined as the objective sum of the monetary units and of the time needed to carry out the different phases of a purchase: transportation, purchase, wait time and product implementation (see Table 9.1). Research and transaction costs, which constitute the predominant part of this component, are strongly determined by the geographic dimension. The risk is defined as the subjective evaluation of the consequences of an error during the purchase. The notion of risk encompasses not only the financial risk but also social, psychological, physical and functional consequences of an error of choice during the purchase.

	Dimensions	
	Effort	**Risk**
Monetary	**Financial** Cash Credit Barter	**Financial** Personal Organizational
Non-monetary	**Time** Transport Purchase Expectations Implementation	**Consequences** Social Psychological Physical Functional

Table 9.1: *Dimensions and components of pricing; from [MUR 86], p. 31*

The exploration of non-monetary components remains incomplete because a transaction also includes the exchange of resources other than money or time, such as service, information, image or risk. The cost and the value associated with these resources into account are reflected in the price, for example by a higher price for a product of a prestigious brand or for products of a specific geographic origin.

Geography, for example, has an important impact on the non-monetary dimension of the risk linked to uncertainty. The distance between two exchange partners results in uncertainty linked to the existence and the importance of the demand, which involves a speculative position from the producer and from the distributor, and to the constitution of supplies, the cost of which is passed on in the price. Similarly, the risk connected with the execution of the transaction and with the delivery of merchandise that meets standards or the risk of exchange variations if the contractual currency is different from the local currency and the requirement for exchange implies a delay between the signing of the contract and its execution.

This concept of price, the dimensions of which are both monetary and non-monetary, constitutes an important advance for marketing practitioners because it accentuates the role, both complex and multiple, of price in the purchase decision. Beyond budgetary restriction and the importance of the monetary resource sacrificed, price is also a form of information used as a qualitative guide in monetary and temporal choice [DES 97]. The quality of a product, or the value of a supply, will be evaluated based on objective indicators characterizing the product, the packaging and the information that it carries, as well as the asking price.

The determinants of price

Price is determined according to variable terms that define the functioning of the market. The most important term is the existence and the functioning of a marketplace that allows consideration of the conditions proposed by the suppliers and by the customers concerning comparable supplies of products or services. Markets thus coexist in which price is determined exclusively by the market and is imposed on suppliers and in which the supplier himself fixes a price. The temporal functioning of markets allows continuous markets, with instantaneous prices, to be distinguished from markets with iterative fixing of price (auctions).

The most frequent situation, however, is that in which a freedom in the fixing of prices and some competition between suppliers and customers coexist. In order to fix his or her price, the decision-maker should thus simultaneously take three determinants into account: his or her costs, the reaction of the demand to the prices and the probable action/reaction of the competition. Nevertheless, each of these price determinants can be greatly affected by the geographic dimension.

9.1.1. *The geography of costs*

Certain costs are directly influenced by the geographic dimension: costs of adaptation to the local market and costs linked to distribution and distance.

Effects due to geographic entities

Taking into account actors other than the buyer can modify the equilibrium in the exchange both at the expenses level and at that of the receipts. Political entities, through their regulatory and fiscal powers, transform a continuous space into a discrete space. Local regulations, legal notes in the local language, authorization to enter the market and technical restrictions lead to the adaptation of the product and therefore to a cost supplement. However, this adaptation, as we will see below, can also be considered as an opportunity to make borders more impermeable and to facilitate segmentation.

In the vision of an enlarged monetary cost, taxes will obviously be added to the asking price of the supplier. The diversity in the rate of value added tax in the European Union clearly shows the importance of the geographic dimension. The effect on receipts can once again be related to the consequences of public decisions, such as subsidies, but also to the intervention of third parties who can make payment directly (like an insurer) or indirectly (loss of advertising during a telephone communication). Here again, the diversity of social security and reimbursement arrangements clearly shows the complexity of a medicine price policy at the European level for a pharmaceutical firm.

Finally, the action of a state can be limited to indirect intervention by means of price restrictions (the price of books in France), by price augmentation, as during periods of high inflation, by a negotiated fixing of a price (pharmacy), or by a constraint of overall revenue by the fixing of overall income levels.

Effects due to distribution and distance

The principal restriction on the price of a product corresponds to its cost. This includes several components, which include the fabrication cost of the product and the cost of its distribution. The first category is the variable cost covering the direct production and distribution expenses. In addition to this variable unitary cost, the distribution of fixed costs and general expenses leads to the calculation of a cost price influenced by the choice of distribution keys for the fixed costs. The choice of these keys, which is arbitrary and contestable, underline that the notion of an objective price does not exist as such.

The location of production units can lead to a difference in production cost according to the geographic location of factories. However, local factors have an even greater impact on the distribution costs, as much for services as for products. These costs correspond to two functions:

– a commercialization function that is related to familiarizing potential customers with the supply, prescription, negotiation and management of the exchange;

– a logistical function in the spatial management of the physical flows associated with the stocking/storing, the delivery and the return of merchandise.

Because a large number of products is often managed by a distributor, the distributor frequently opts for a price policy where the remuneration of his or her service is a direct function of the purchase cost of a product, to which he or she applies a multiplying factor in order to obtain his or her sale price. When specific expenses, such as that for delivery, can be identified, their integration into the price can be made at three levels: they can be included directly in the sale price, included in the monetary and billed costs by a specialized intermediary, or even ignored and transferred to the final customer, who accepts them as part of his or her monetary and non-monetary costs.

The interaction with distribution decisions

Price is freely fixed by the actors of the transaction. This signifies that it is the actor in direct contact with the customer, often the distributor, who fixes his sale price in an autonomous manner. Yet, at the economic level, the interaction between the decisions of the producer and the distributor lead to less than optimal decisions when they are taken independently of each other. A unique multiplying coefficient applied by a distributor can thus lead to the fixing of too high a price and thus to a decrease in sales that is detrimental both to the distributor and the producer. In order to optimize the profitability of the chain, a systemic approach and a coordination of price policies between the localized actors at different points must be achieved.

It is often the producer who implements this approach and integrates the response of an independent distributor into his final sale-price fixing decision, so that the distributor receives a discount corresponding to his service. The geographic dimension is directly concerned in this decision so that the distribution can either be integrated by national chains, with the transfer price fixed, or be carried out by independent distributors, with the problem of parallel deliveries.

The impact of the Internet

The existence of a physical resource, with varying transport costs, characterizes the supplies of goods and services. However, the global networking of the actors through the Internet on the one hand fundamentally changes the economy for the management of flows of information and the organization of certain markets, while, on the other hand, it accelerates the dematerialization of the monetary resource [DES 00].

The Internet modifies distribution costs by reducing part of the cost linked to geography. It pushes a producer or supplier of services to completely review his or her distribution policy both in the strategic plan (choice of direct or indirect distribution) and in the tactical plan (missions assigned to distribution). An Internet site can appear as a supplementary distribution channel or, even going beyond that, it can give rise to new supplies or inverted mechanisms in the mode of price fixing, but openness seems guaranteed in all cases. As a general rule, when innovations affect distribution channels, the impact can materialize either as a threat of substitution or as a complementarity effect (see Table 9.2).

Factors	Dominant effect of complementarity	Dominant effect of substitution
Access to Internet by the customer	*Weak*	*High*
Value of Internet offer and traditional channel	*Different*	*Similar*
Product delivery mode, cost and time	*Costly and immediate physical delivery*	*On Internet*
Product standardization and/or variety search	*No: standardized or standardized product with variety-seeking customers*	*Standardized product with non-variety-seeking customers*

Table 9.2: *Determinants of complementarity or substitution effects [ZOL 00]*

This effect of complementarity or substitution between the channels [KUM 99] depends on the activity sector and notably on customer Internet access, on the supplementary value of the supply proposed by the new channel, on the delivery conditions and on the characteristics of the product. However, online trade has the same faults as any distance selling, the products cannot be touched and clothing cannot be tried on. This argument could be one of the major obstacles to the development of autonomous Internet commerce and could lead to the establishment of mixed distribution circuits in which traditional channels, more influenced by the spatial dimension, will retain an important place.

9.1.2. *The geography of the demand*

In relation to the demand, geography plays a role in the definition of the development of the product/service asked for and is an effective segmentation variable.

Prices: the monetary element and the information element

For the consumer, price plays a double role: on the one hand, it forms a monetary resource, subject to a restriction (respecting a budget) or corresponding to a minimization objective (searching for the lowest price); on the other hand, it is a piece of information allowing a level of quality to be inferred when knowledge of the quality is scarce.

Price is a signal of quality when the quality of the product is not easy for the buyer to evaluate. Assuming a positive relationship between price and fabrication cost, the customer supposes that a high price corresponds to a high-quality product (theory of inference). This effect plays principally to the two extremities of the demand curve, where the elasticity takes on positive values. The lowest prices are rejected since the products are considered to be of low quality. For the highest prices, the budgetary restriction is greatest, and therefore the demand is lower, which encourages endowment of the product with a supplementary attribute: its social distinction capacity. For this attribute, certain customers are ready to accept a higher price (snobbery effect). Other than the price, the other information carried by the product, such as the country of origin, can constitute convergent or opposed signals [FAU 94].

The geographic perception of the supply by the buyers or the role of the country of origin

The country of origin has often been identified [PET 95] as a valorization instrument of a brand. Through cultural attributions, information on the country transforms itself into an indication (favorable or unfavorable) of the perceived level of quality of the product or into a symbolic attribute, an element of differentiation. If a customer infers a higher quality and bases his or her choice process on a search for value, the business can ask a higher price. Research shows that the effect of consumer perceptions, his or her attitude and his or her purchase intentions are well established but it appears that this does not necessarily lead to competitive advantage in terms of a premium that the client is willing to pay [AGR 99].

A differentiated demand in behaviors and in expectations

On the basis of the image of cartography, one can consider that local geographic data is added, as one layer on top of the other, to the spatial location, which is a fundamental piece of information usable as a demand segmentation criterion.

Spatial location (x,y) is the principal key that allows the variable costs mentioned above, such as the transport cost associated with home delivery, to be determined. This location is an important determinant of behaviors and it is particularly well-known that the spatial and temporal distance to be covered to reach a store is a structuring variable for its trade area.

Location also allows a customer to be connected with statistical, administrative or commercial entities. These entities, which have the immense advantage of being used mainly in other contexts, allow, on the one hand, a better statistical understanding of the behavior of targets and on the other hand, a way to carry out generalizations by way of other known variables. Thus, it is possible to aggregate and to compare the behaviors at the level of a block, a street, a town, an arrondissement, or a county, just as this can all be done at the mail-delivery route level.

In addition to the permanent location, indicated by home address, new perspectives are opened up by the instantaneous location associated with the possession of a mobile phone or a GPS system in a vehicle. The immediately delivered information can thus take into account the geographic environment: for example, communication of a promotional offer from a nearby store.

Geographic information reveals itself as a valuable key for the segmentation of purchase behaviors. That the consumption of cooking oil and margarine is very different between the north and the south of France or that urban consumption differs from that of rural communities will not surprise the reader. Upstream of behavior, the preferences or the weight accorded to certain characteristics are also localized, either because of the implantation of ethnic groups or as a result of the concentration of certain population sectors in terms of age group, level of salary or education. If taste is one of the variables that comes immediately to mind, it can also be mentioned that, for example, the price elasticity of high-consumption products is higher in low-income areas.

The segmentation criteria of the demand

The different geographic levels can serve as customer segmentation criteria since they are directly operational criteria which allow the direct implementation of actions by the selective distribution of leaflets (see Chapter 11).

Geographic information can also characterize the influence of culture in the valorization of products. In reality, a part of the value can be linked to the image of a product, itself influenced by temporary factors (an advertising campaign) or permanent factors (brand, country of origin, etc.). The cultural interpretation of the country or of the region of origin can have a positive valorization effect on the image or, on the contrary, lead to devaluation or even rejection of the product, as in the case of a boycott.

The geographic dimension therefore influences, in a predominant manner, the pricing policy through a differentiated demand, differently valorizing the physical and informational characteristics. The spatial dimension is, in addition, a very good segmentation variable since it unites strategic advantages, such as different behaviors and expectations, with tactical advantages concerning implementation.

The third determinant of the pricing policy, the actions/reactions of the competition, is also directly influenced by the geographic dimension.

Box 9.1

According to a 1995 TMO (INRA network of survey institutes) study of 36,756 people carried out in 40 countries on five continents, the country that produces the best product is perceived very differently according to the type of product and depending on the responding population:

Products	France, best manufacturer country...		
	According to the French (%)	According to the Europeans (%)	According to the world population (%)
Very up-market cars	11.3	2.2	1.6
Mid-market cars	67.8	14.3	3.9
Public electronics	16.1	2.5	0.6
Beer	14	2.5	1.2
Cigarettes	25.6	4.3	1.3
Chocolates	21.7	4.1	2.7
Fragrance	93.4	72	57.9
PCs	11.9	1.7	0.5
Films	50.6	9.5	3.3
Wines	98.7	43.7	30.9
TV programs	54.1	8.7	2.3
Cameras	11	1.7	0.5
Jeans	10.3	1.8	1.1

The national sentiment, which appears throughout the evaluation of French products by the French, is analogous to that which was revealed by the study for the other countries. However, in addition to the subjective character, certain anomalies must be pointed out: according to 12% of French responders, France makes the best personal computers, with 11% seeing France as the best producer of cameras, while no national brands could be identified.

9.1.3. *The geography of the competition*

Geography touches the competitive dimension through the composition of the competitive universe. The increasing globalization of markets has led a large number of sectors to become "internationally competitive" industries. This evolution has been accompanied by important debates about what has seemed to impose itself as a new doctrine, "universal standardization", which would lead to a reduction of the importance of the geographic dimension [WIN 86].

Numerous factors combine in bringing about the standardization of products: the integration of markets and the globalization of transportation systems have both been welcomed favorably by the different actors; the augmentation of international competition, both in the domestic market and abroad, encourages research into economies of scale. However, one must be wary of concluding that standardization is inevitable, as it only constitutes one of many possible options. Three major hypotheses, which have not been validated in all sectors, seemed in the 1980s to be necessary to the success of a standardization strategy (see Table 9.3).

Conditions According to [LEV 83]	**Limits** According to [WIN 86]
Homogenization of worldwide needs	No evidence of homogenization Increased market segmentation in each country
Universal consumer preference for products of low price and acceptable quality	No evidence of universal sensitiveness to price Low price positioning presents questionable advantages A standardized low price can be impractical for some countries; too low for some, too high for others
Economies of scale in production and marketing costs	Some production techniques enable decreases in production cost for non-standardized products Production cost is often just a minor component of the total cost

Table 9.3: *Conditions and limits of a standardization strategy*

International low-price strategies

Several years later, the place of a one-price strategy, based on low prices, appears to be well-established in an international dimension [COL 97]. This option seems to be especially supported by more stimulated competition, upstream of the strategies of the distributor, as well as the globalization of the distribution trade names. In fact, it appears that the analyses of the earlier authors [LEV 83, WIN 86] deal especially with the perspective of the producer and supplier, while that of the second author [COL 97] provides an analysis of distribution. The evolution of the relationships between manufacturers and retailers, in favor of the latter, for consumer goods but also more generally, has been a determinant in the evolution of the analysis of the competition in each market and in the pricing policy choice that results from it.

Whether they are a function of expenses, of the demand or of the competition, price determinants are affected by the geographic dimension. However, this dimension maintains an even stricter relationship with the pricing policy in the sense that the spatial dimension is an integral part of the pricing policy in its international expression.

9.2. Geographic pricing policies

Price fixing adheres to principles previously established by taking into account the following three principal components: costs, demand and the competitive situation. The international dimension balances this choice in relation to the chosen distribution or location policies abroad.

Following the example of other components of international strategy, price can thus be conceived either in the standardization option linked to the search for globalization or with the worry of adaptation in the multi-domestic approach. Multi-domestic strategies are, for many businesses, founded on expenses and, for one out of two businesses in this situation, the margins are higher in the domestic market than in the international market. The principal reason reported by firms that favor taking demand into account in price fixing is, in two out of three cases, the prestige of their brand [SAM 94].

Three points will be developed: the specificity of export pricing, international pricing policy decisions and the management of effects due to the existence of borders, such as parallel imports.

9.2.1. *The specificity of export pricing policies*

The broad options of international pricing policy concern the integration of transport costs. With exports, prices are specific in the underlying contracts and therefore in the sharing of monetary costs (transportation) and non-monetary costs (customs passage) associated with the transaction. The crossing of a border, together with the uncertainties and disputes that can possibly arise, has thus imposed a contractual normalization of the expression of prices.

Export tariff options

In a simpler approach, in which only the production price of a product and its delivery cost are considered, three policies are possible:

– a factory price (excluding works), in which the producer does include the logistics (transport and insurance). This practice allows the declaration of a one very low price, including or not including taxes according to whether private individuals or businesses are being addressed. Non-discriminatory in its principle, authorizing a complete transparency of tariff conditions, according to economists, this practice should prove itself to be the one that contributes to better social well-being [BEC 76];

– an all-inclusive delivery price for which the seller takes on all handling costs towards the delivery point. This is also a single price irrespective of customer location and it relies on a cross subsidy of delivery costs between the different markets. As easy and simple to communicate as the first option, the delivery price has the disadvantage of imposing on the supplier the management of functions for which he or she may be poorly positioned. Furthermore, the absence of flexibility allows the adaptation of price to take into account neither local competition conditions nor exchange rate variations;

– an adjusted price taking care of and invoicing delivery expenses, which is sometimes carried out in an *ad hoc* manner, depending on each destination, but more often with a fixed price in several areas.

The decision to take delivery costs into account in the tariff is directly linked to the management of a store's trade area. In particular, it allows this area to be enlarged by the implementation of a cost compensation policy related to the remoteness of the store. Thus, the higher monetary costs accepted by the customers living far from the store are often proportionally lower than those of customers living nearby. This practice can be justified, on the one hand, by the fact that this tertiary area, located very far from the store, is large and includes many potential buyers and, on the other hand, by the already high cost of travel towards the store that these customers must accept.

Theoretical research shows that the choice is not exclusive and that it is a combination of these pricing policies that is preferable [FUR 83]. The rate is worked out based on a delivery price with the possibility for the customer to take possession of the merchandise in the store and obtain a discount. For a demand that is linearly dependent on prices, a study has shown that the base price corresponds to that of a delivery to a point situated in the middle of the trade area and that the subsidy on the deliveries carried out beyond this area should be 50% of the cost of the delivery. In contrast, if the elasticity of the demand to the price is constant [BAS 95], the recommendation is to add a margin to the transport cost, which allows a lower price to be set.

Incoterms

When the distribution of a product/service is international, the firm is faced with a more complex choice that concerns the provisions to be included, delegated or left to the customer (transport, insurance, customs, etc.). This tariff is found in the standardized Incoterms of international trade (see Table 9.4).

Ex works	+ transportation, insurance and handling costs
Free carrier	+ shipping costs
Free on board	+ transportation costs
Delivered at frontier	+ harbor duties and taxes
Delivered duty paid	

Table 9.4: *Example of export price calculation*

Being a member of diverse political and administrative communities is a variable that allows the effects of borders to be identified and the costs associated with their passage to be evaluated. Marketing decisions are thus influenced in terms of cost:

– directly, by taxation, or by the reconditioning and the differentiation imposed on products concerning product packaging or the elements of information on the product (label and instructions);

– indirectly by the regulation, either of establishment (authorization, obligation of a joint venture with a local partner, etc.) or of the flows of merchandise (import authorization, etc.) and of capital.

Box 9.2. *Disparity of value added tax rates and "fraude au carrousel"*

According to a recent report of the Department of Internal Trade at Brussels, the disparity of value added tax rates (from 12 to 25% according to the country), which necessitates a declaration of intra-community exchanges in the selling country, the value added tax being paid in the customer country, generates around 100 million declarations coming from 24 million businesses. It is estimated that 5% of the merchandise exchanged is not the object of a withholding tax; a system of organized fraud, called "*fraude au carrousel*", has allegedly developed, consisting of causing the same merchandise to cross over borders several times to avoid fiscal services and to get it back to the initial supplier. The total amount of this fraud could be €10 billion annually. The harmonization of the value added tax rates would limit this organized fraud and would make withholding possible in each country of production, and would furthermore facilitate the taxation of commercialized non-material goods on the Internet. At the current time, as a result of the absence of harmonized rates, a value added tax on the Internet would pose multiple collection problems: in which country did the download take place, which rate should be applied, how should it be monitored?

These elements influence pricing policy (general supplementary expenses, taxes) and the distribution policy with, for example, local establishment and the exportation decisions.

9.2.2. *International pricing policy*

Pricing policy has several issues that are unique to the international level. First there is the question of the dynamic management of the price in the framework of the international life cycle of a new product. There is also the question of the transfer price of merchandise circulating between the subsidiaries of an international firm. Finally, there is the question of the management of price differences among the different countries in order to avoid the uncontrolled flow of merchandise.

The theory of international diffusion

When there are availability restrictions, the diffusion of a product can be spaced out in time and space. The availability restriction can be physical, as with the number of copies of a film, or be concerned with the risk management of the information demand, with the level of demand for a product not being well-known; certain markets therefore play the role of test markets.

In the theory of the international diffusion of products [DAH 91], it is the principal market that is first served. This market benefits from the weakest elasticity of prices and from a strong sensitivity to innovation. Covering the fixed costs with the revenue from this initial market allows a more aggressive penetration price, which no longer takes the variable cost into account, to be adopted. It is on the basis of this mechanism that the principle of cultural exception and of the support for creation in the movies sector was established.

International diffusion can also deal with a product, such as a book, for which the demand is difficult to predict, while the costs are sensitive to the economies of scale. Centralization of the production leads to there being a low variable cost for a high production volume and the residual stock left after sale in the first country is then offered in other markets.

When the firm possesses a subsidiary in the country being considered, it controls both the transfer price to the subsidiary and any later transfer price. The firm no longer controls the latter when it exports in an indirect manner, going through local intermediaries (import–export companies, brokers). The firm should adjust the means of fixing the base price to the characteristics of its choices of internationalization and therefore take into account the type of contract proposed for the export.

Transfer price policy

For a multinational firm with establishments in the form of local subsidiaries, the transfer price policy consists of fixing a transfer price between the subsidiaries situated in the two states. With these being subject to different taxation regimes, the transfer price can either make the profit margin appear in the country where the taxation is more favorable or repatriate the profit to the head office. This fiscal optimization is obtained by the increase/decrease of the prices of goods exchanged between the subsidiaries and by fixing the amount of the royalties linked to the know-how or to a brand.

However, the risk incurred with this practice should not be underestimated [MCA 92]:

– legal risk: the fixing of transfer prices should be based on elements that are not concerned with the administration (market price, cost elements, etc.) for the accounting results can be questioned, which poses the risk of double taxation;

– risk of demotivation of the local subsidiaries, whose loss of control of the return on results will be globally reduced and less directly linked to their actions.

9.2.3. *Parallel imports and pricing policy control*

If a business distributes its product brand in different countries, through the intermediary of accredited distributors, following a logic of differentiation, or even of discrimination by price, it is always possible for these same products to appear, in a so-called *gray* market, at lower prices to the end-customer.

Gray markets and parallel imports

The gray market corresponds to the marketing, not controlled by the supplier, of its merchandise through an uncontrolled distribution channel that brings together three actors:

– the dishonest distributor, officially accredited by the supplier, who supplies the merchandise to the gray channel. This is possible because the purchase price can be reduced because of the volume increase;

– the gray distributor, who sells the merchandise in the destination market at a lower price than that proposed by the local accredited distributor;

– the intermediary, who may be one of the two distributors; he or she cannot but profit from the possibility of profit arising from a gap between supply and demand.

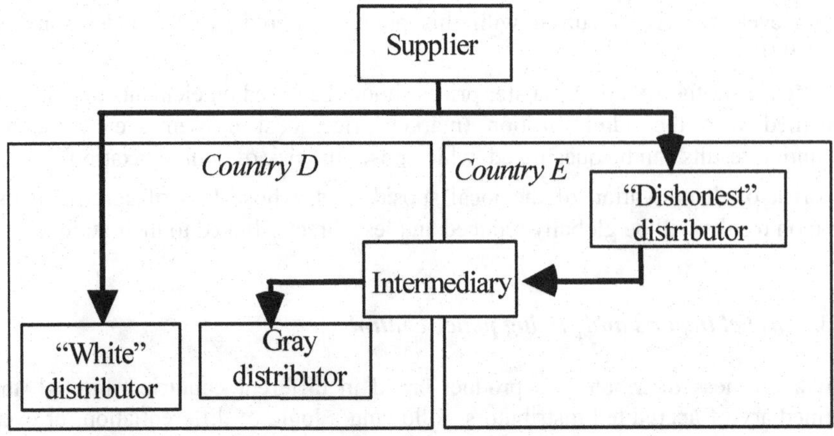

Figure 9.1: *Organization of a gray distribution channel*

The causes of gray markets

The development of a gray market can affect volume or, more frequently, prices. The price difference between the accredited and non-accredited distributors is due either to specific purchase conditions, to increased productivity or even to a different offer of service. The main reasons are:

– *product unavailability*: in this case an intermediary will take on the responsibility of satisfying a demand frustrated by the supplier's decision not to market a particular item in a particular geographic area;

– *an exchange rate gap*: when tariff changes do not reflect the changes in the currency exchange rates between countries, an intermediary with low overhead costs will take advantage of this difference;

– *a temporary price reduction* or a *differential pricing policy* based on the market that is decided by the supplier in order either to increase his or her penetration into a specific market or to reduce the stocks accumulated during distribution;

– *a quantitative reduction policy* on the part of the supplier, who hopes to benefit from economies of scale and who will therefore encourage the build-up of orders;

– *a productivity gap* in the supply channel or a *gap of service* to the sale or in the after-sales service.

The development of a gray market poses important dangers for the distributor and for the supplier: a short-term decrease of profitability for the supplier [BUC 93], erosion of the capital of the brand, a decrease of profitability for the distributor, erosion of the influence of the distribution concept.

Policies to implement to counter gray markets

For the producer, who is the owner of the brand, it is a question of both understanding the gray market better and preventing or reducing its development. This objective can be achieved by the suppression of tariff imbalances, by direct action on the market or by indirect action on the environment of the actors.

The first type of action concerns the marketing mix itself. Tariff imbalances can be suppressed, especially when they come from quantitative reductions. One can, for example, reduce the importance of the discount associated with the size of orders. If there is a temporary imbalance (exchange rate variation) and not a deliberate geographic discrimination policy, prices can be adjusted. In the opposite case, the differentiation of the product or of the packaging must be reinforced, a strong factor in market compartmentalization. However, this differentiation is costly and restricted to the search for economies of scale. Communication policies can be used to boost the image of the service provided by its distributors and can devalue the product that is available in the gray market (absence of warranty for example).

Direct action on the gray market is often an inappropriate policy in the medium term. If the channel is well-identified, the producer can take direct action on volume (repurchase of the merchandise, interruption of delivery to *dishonest* distributors), on prices (increase the mark-up at the intermediary level in order to reduce the final profit of the distributor) or even on the distributors themselves by buying them out. Judicial prosecutions are also part of a signaling strategy to the networks, by which the possessor of the brand announces his or her intention to defend his or her territory and to protect his or her distributors.

Action on the distributors is also possible. The first stage of this consists of putting an information system in place that allows the participants and the importance of the flows to be updated. Control of "*white*" distributors can be intensified, depending on the regulations, through specific clauses in the conditions of sale. The flows can be reduced by the improvement of the profitability of the accredited distributors, by providing cost reduction support (personnel training, for example) or by the valorization of the distributor's service through exclusive offers.

Because of the existence of this parallel market, called the gray market, it appears that the geographic dimension in the approach to prices requires vigilance of the highest order. When costs are taken into account, to the specificity of the demand and the competition should be added this uncontrolled competition from the products of the firm themselves.

The price corridor

The existence of regional economic entities, such as the European Union, and the creation of large regional markets, such as l'ALENA or Mercosur for North and South America, should lead to a better functioning of the markets. Factors such as the increase of transparency and competition and the disappearance of border-crossing costs should lead to lower prices because the existence of any price gap over and above the transport cost of the merchandise will be exploited by intermediaries [SIM 93].

If the price gap between the countries is too large, there is the risk of merchandise flows developing that are outside the firm's control. Commercial and financial damage can be significant if products and brands are not identical between markets, for example if the quality of a brand of detergent is different from one country to the next. International pricing policy is therefore subject to the restriction of a maximum gap between the prices applied within a same free-trade zone. Without a voluntary policy from the producer, if the price gap is greater than 10%, then arbitrage becomes profitable and parallel imports will cause prices to tend towards a single price level with the lowest price as the level of reference.

Box 9.3. *Gray markets and competitive stimulation*

In the absence of European harmonization relative to the fixing of prices for medication, the problem of parallel imports has found itself at the heart of a specific interaction between state politics, business strategies and consumer preferences.

The parallel importation in question can be defined as the organization of a transborder flow of medicines organized by the operators who can be considered as wholesalers, in parallel with intra-European sales, organized by the manufacturing laboratories. More generally, the parallel importer causes a medicine bought or made in the exporting Member State (where its price is generally low) to made available in an importing Member State, where the price has been fixed by the national authorities at a price that is high enough to allow the parallel importer to operate with a margin only for this operation.

Over past few years, European institutions have progressively questioned the principle by which parallel imports favor competition in the pharmaceutical sector. Parallel imports, following the "catch and compete" practice, do not modify the structure of the supply to the pharmaceutical market and have no appreciable effect on the price of medications to the consumer. Thus, these parallel imports are not carried out in the founding spirit of the Common Market, according to which free trade, which is indispensable for competition, should first and foremost benefit European consumers.

The fixing of prices in specific markets should therefore take into account the risks of causing lower prices in related markets, in relation to the importance of the volumes concerned: parallel imports from Spain into Portugal are, for example, less worrisome than those from Belgium into France or Germany. In certain cases, when perfect permeability of borders exists, it may be profitable to no longer be present in a small market.

To avoid this catastrophic scenario, this author recommends first establishing a corridor of European prices, the amplitude of which would correspond to the arbitrage threshold determined by the costs of transport and of adaptation and by the margin necessary to attract an intermediary. The author recommends setting up this corridor in such a way as to maximize the overall profit of the area.

The use of this approach means, however, depriving subsidiaries of all autonomy in price fixing, which goes against a policy of decentralization. Nevertheless, the principal limitation of this approach is that price variations beyond the producer's control, such as those resulting from exchange rate variations, cannot be taken into account.

Box 9.4. *Example: determination of a price corridor; source: [DES 97] from [SIM 93]*

A producer with a marginal cost of 5 is present in two countries A and B, of which the demand functions are:

$Q_A = 100 - 10.0P_A$ with an elasticity evaluated at $e_{q/p} = -3$
$Q_B = 100 - 6.67P_B$ with an elasticity evaluated at $e_{q/p} = -2$

The optimal price fixed independently for each country leads to $P_A = 7.5$ and $P_B = 10.0$ and a overall profit of 229.

A fixed single price for the entire market would be $P = 8.5$ with a benefit of 204, or a reduction of 10.9% in comparison to the preceding solution.

By considering an arbitrage cost of 15% in relation to the highest price, a price corridor of 15% leads to $P_A = 7.98$ and $P_B = 9.39$ and an overall profit of 224.2 or a sacrifice of 2.07% in comparison with the first solution.

9.3. Conclusion

The geographic dimension should play an important part in the pricing policy of a firm. It affects each of the determinants of the pricing policy, costs, demand and competition. Distance is an important determinant of the distribution cost, itself constituting a significant part of the overall cost of the product. Demand is fundamentally spatial and this aspect affects its importance as well its behavior and its preferences. Different geographic data serve as structuring variables for marketing. Finally, the local character of the competition, even if it seems to be reduced as a result of globalization, remains an important factor.

However, geography is also one of the dimensions of pricing policy. The concept of an increased price, integrating the monetary and non-monetary dimensions, allows a policy of either taking or not taking financial responsibility for transport costs in Incoterms. Geography is also an interesting segmentation variable because it is both pertinent from the point of view of the difference in behavior and operational for the implementation of a specific market policy on geographic segments. Geography manifests itself through the putting in place of a dynamic approach to the diffusion of new products or through the utilization of a differentiated pricing policy in relation to the demand and the intensity of local competition.

However, several factors can limit the efficiency of price discrimination between markets:

– the actions of public authorities, which may strongly restrict transfer price policy within a multinational firm;

– the action of the markets themselves, which put in place unofficial distribution channels for merchandise when price gaps between countries are too large.

In the medium term, the setting up of free-trade zones also leads to a reduction in the freedom of maneuver of firms, which must learn to manage international price corridors.

9.4. References

[AGR 99], Agrawal Jagdish and Wagner A. Kamakura, Country of Origin: A Competitive Advantage?, *International Journal of Research in Marketing*, vol. 16, p. 255-267, 1999.

[BAS, 95] Basu A. and Mazumdar T., Using a Menu of Geographic Pricing Plan, *Journal of Retailing*, vol. 71, 2, pp. 173-202, 1995.

[BEC, 76], Beckmann M., Spatial Price Policies Revisited, *Bell Journal of Economics*, vol.7, 2, pp. 619-629, 1976.

[BUC 93], Bucklin L., Modeling the International Gray Market for Public Policy Decisions, *International Journal of Research in Marketing*, vol. 10, pp. 387-405.

[COL 97], Colla E. and Dupuis M., *Le défi mondial du bas prix*, Publi-Union, 1997.

[DAH 91], Dahringer D. and Mühlbacher H., *International Marketing*, Addison-Wesley, 1991.

[DES 00], Desmet P., Politiques de prix sur Internet, *Revue Française du Marketing*, vol. 177-78, 2-3, pp. 49-68, 2000.

[DES 97], Desmet P. and Zollinger M., *Le Prix: de l'analyse conceptuelle aux méthodes de fixation*, Economica, Gestion, 1997.

[FAU 94], Faulds D., Grunewald O. and Johnson D., A Cross-National Investigation of Relationship Between the Price and Quality of Consumer Products 1970-1990, *Journal of Global Marketing*, vol. 8, 1, pp. 7-25, 1994.

[FUR 83], Furlong W. and Slotsve G., Will That Be Pickup or Delivery?: An Alternative Spatial Pricing Strategies , *Bell Journal of Economics*, vol. 14, 1, pp. 271-274, 1983.

[KUM 99], Kumar N., Les politiques de distribution, *Dossier Le Commerce électronique, Les Echos*, 12-13 November, pp. 8-9, 1999.

[LEV 83], Levitt T. Un seul univers, le marché?, *Harvard L'expansion*, autumn, pp. 6-17, 1983.

[McA 92] McAulay L. and Tomkins C., A Review of the Contemporary Transfer Pricing Litterature with Recommandations for Future Research, *British Journal of Management*, vol. 3, 1, pp. 101-122, 1992.

[MUR 86], Murphy P.E. and Enis B.M., Classifying products Strategically, *Journal of Marketing*, vol. 50, July, pp. 24-42, 1986.

[PET 95], Peterson R.A. and Jolibert A. J. P., A meta-analysis of country-of-origin effects, *Journal of International Business Studies*, vol. 26, 4, pp. 883-899, 1995.

[SAM 94], Samli A.C. and Jacobs L., Pricing Practices of American Multinational Firms; Standardization vs. Localization Dichotomy, *Journal of Global Marketing*, vol. 8, 2, pp. 51-73, 1994.

[SIM 93], Simon H. and Kucher E., The European Pricing Time Bomb and How to Cope with it, *Marketing and Research Today*, February, pp. 25-36, 1993.

[SIM 00], Simon H., Jacquet F. and Brault F., *La stratégie prix*, Dunod, 2000.

[WIN 86], Wind Y. and Douglas S., Le mythe de la globalisation, *Recherche et Applications en Marketing*, no 3, pp. 5-26, 1986.

[ZEI 88], Zeithaml V., Consumer Perceptions of Price, Quality and Value: A Means-end Model and Synthesis of Evidence, *Journal of Marketing*, vol. 52, July, pp. 2-22, 1988.

[ZOL 00], Zollinger M., Les effets de la réglementation sur la relation duale prix-information dans le choix du consommateur, *Gestion et Droit*, B. Amann ed., Actes des Journées Nationales des IAE, Bayonne-Biarritz, Dalloz, pp. 155-175, 2000.

Chapter 10

Advertising Policy and Geographic Information

Introduction

The objective of this chapter is to show the increasing importance of geographic information in advertising, described as a "mass communication made for the account of interests which are identified: that of an advertiser who pays a media to diffuse a message which is generally created by an advertising agency" [AAK 75]. The principal objectives of a commercial campaign are to increase the awareness of the brand, to create a preference for a product, to lead consumers to buy, etc. For the last few years in France, the sectors that have invested most in the communication domain are: distribution, food stuffs, mobile telephony, automobiles, services and beauty/hygiene products. The commercial strategies of firms, in the majority of cases, have been developed by advertising agencies specialized in creation, direct marketing, promotion, etc. These agencies assume several roles including strategic thought, conception, realization and production of commercial announcements, negotiation and transactions with the different suppliers, as well as the choice of means to diffuse the message [VER 00].

The sums invested in advertising campaigns are very large. Thus one campaign can cost many thousands of Euros between the creation and the purchase of space in the mass media. In the light of such expenses, firms go all out and ensure that the message conceived will be effective in affecting the intended advertising target. It is to respond to this expectation, legitimate on the part of the advertisers, that geomarketing was introduced into the advertising world. This tool allows the impact

---

Chapter written by Karine GALLOPEL.

of a commercial to be improved as a result of a better understanding of the individuals that it addresses in terms of socio-demographics (age, sex, socio-professional category, etc.). This information is increasingly associated with the territories of occupation and with the zones of mobility of the prospects, leading to a geo-coded information system called *geomarketing of zones* (or *of stocks*) or *of flows*. The geomarketing of stocks links the socio-demographic and behavioral characteristics of the population to spatial data (region, city, etc.). The geomarketing of flows follows the travel of individuals in a given geographic area associated with the information that qualifies them. All of these data are stored in *data warehouses* [MIC 97, SCH 99] and give rise to the concept of a digital cartography system. Increasingly, numerous service providers promote software that links map backgrounds to databases. The development and visualization of these computerized tools represent the most highly specialized uses of geomarketing. However, throughout subsequent discussion, this last term will be employed when dealing with associating with a geographic territory the quality of its inhabitants and of its passers-by.

Three dimensions will be discussed in this chapter. In section 10.1, we will describe how a spatialized computer system can become an important support in optimizing the expected results of a communications campaign and thus reassuring the advertisers. In section 10.2, aspects of a more operational nature will be tackled through the presentation of the principal users and uses of geomarketing in the advertising domain. Finally, we will finish, in section 10.3, by describing the potential of this tool for pioneering actors in this domain. With very few research studies having been published on the topic of the spatial dimension of communications, we have deliberately chosen to describe the practice in this area and to subject it to critical analysis. These developments are based on interviews carried out with professionals, together with a documentary study of the professional marketing press.

10.1. The use of geographic information in advertising strategy

In this section, the constituent elements of an advertising strategy will first be described, followed by a description of the advantages of geomarketing in optimizing the efficiency of campaigns at the level of creation and of choice of media. Following this first section, we will present the different users of geomarketing in advertising.

10.1.1. *The constituent elements of advertising strategy*

Advertising strategy can be broken down into two elements: copy strategy and the media plan. The first constituent, or the creation strategy, concerns the content and form that the message will take, which are essential factors in the performance of a commercial advertisement in terms of memorization and adhesion. More closely linked to the spatial dimension because of the geographic distribution of the media, the second constituent, or media strategy, concerns the choice of media. The objective of media planning is defined as the "selection and definition of the means of use of the media and of the supports" [DEC 99]. A media is a collection of supports of the same nature (television, radio, etc.), and a support is a physical vehicle that transports the information to the audience (CBS News, *The Financial Times*, etc.). Depending on the budget of its client, its objectives, the specificity of the product, etc., the advertising agency first asks itself where the broadcasting location of the message will be (mass media or communications channel of outside that media?) [LEN 01, VAR 94]. The mass media is the collection of the vehicles of information carrying a large broadcast potential (radio, television, press, display ads, cinema, Internet). Below-the-line advertising encompasses all forms of support that do not go through the mass media (corporate patronage, sponsorship, on-site advertising, public relations, etc.). The next step is selecting the media and the support or supports to choose in order to develop the communications campaign. These are chosen according to their capacity to transmit the message to the intended target while minimizing cost, in other words by addressing the individuals who are "useful" for the advertiser (potential consumers, leaders of opinion, etc.), and this at a cost that corresponds to the budget of the client [DEC 99].

In summary, the advertising agency's mission is to conceive a message that will meet the objectives assigned to the campaign. To verify a campaign's success, effectiveness tests are sometimes carried out before or after the launch of a commercial message. These tests measure indicators such as the degree of the message's visibility, its memorization potential, its attention value, its comprehension, the membership that it sparks, its credibility, the modifications of intention and of behavior that it generates, etc. [CAU 88, CAU 00, GRE 87, IRE 88]. The specific effectiveness criteria of the media plans are also evaluated in order to ensure that the advertising message has been diffused to a large number of individuals belonging to the target audience intended by the advertiser, as many times as possible, all while promoting the brand [CHA 00]. All of these indicators together offer the advertiser more guarantees concerning the impact of the conceived message and the pertinence of the media plan chosen. They reassure, and this is why advertising agencies, firms that sell media space, are on the lookout for such criteria, which become sales arguments in attracting advertisers. Geomarketing is used in this context of research into the effectiveness of mass communications campaigns.

10.1.2. *Geomarketing, commercial objectives and copy strategy*

Increasing the effectiveness of an advertisement can be achieved through knowing the target of communication better in terms of socio-demographic characteristics, purchase behaviors, location, travel zone, etc. Geomarketing, which collects such data, aims at improving the effectiveness of campaigns, because first it allows more precise and more pertinent communication objectives to be fixed with regard to the situation of an advertiser in a considered market. For example, the national French newspaper *Le Monde* visualizes, thanks to a geomarketing system, its market shares on a map of France. Rather than launching an identical campaign throughout the national territory, territories that are under-penetrated compared to the potential sales are identified and promotions are carried out in these particular regions (more forward placing of the newspaper on display stands, more intense point-of-sale advertising, etc.).

Second, geomarketing allows the content of an advertising message (copy strategy: promise, tone, benefit) to be targeted on the basis of local, regional or national specificities of the intended target so as to create a stronger impact. In practice, the more that individuals are implicated in and concerned by the objective of the advertisement, the higher the chance that it will be effective. For example, an advertisement for banking products will have more impact if it presents student credit in a majority student neighborhood, and real estate credit in an area where the majority of families rent their homes. In summary, having a geographic representation associated with the characteristics of the intended target is important in guiding advertisers in the objectives of their campaign and in the creation of their message. This is even more true today, now that local actions are carried out by a growing number of firms which feel that national campaigns addressing everyone but no-one in particular are not effective enough [MAR 96]. Such territorial strategies, known as micro-marketing, result in taking a geographic criterion into account for a better adaptation of the objectives and the content of the commercial advertisement. Advertising agencies confronted with communication dilemmas segmented in territorial terms therefore have a particular interest in having a geomarketing tool to meet their expectations.

When the target of the advertiser is international, taking the culture of a given geographic area into account is equally essential to the optimization of an advertisement's creative content (see Chapter 2). The adaptation of messages is actually strongly advised in order to make gains in effectiveness [CRO 94, DEC 91, USU 92, AGR 95, LEV 83]. Thus, it is preferable to adopt an honest and informative tone in Germany, an entertaining and clever tone in France, a serious tone of good taste in Denmark, etc. [BON 90]. The problem is that for obvious reasons of cost and homogeneity of the brand's image, the implementation of a strategy of adaptation is sometimes tricky. An alternative solution between total adaptation (which optimizes the impact of the campaign) and the standardization of the message (which allows substantial savings to be realized) consists of opting for a standardized positioning or *glocalization* (a neologism constructed from the expression "think global, act local"). The advertising theme and positioning are therefore identical in all countries, but marginal local modifications are carried out from the point of view of the creation of the advertisement (change in tone, colors, actors, etc.). International firms often adopt such a strategy, following the example of Coca Cola or McDonald's, which do not diffuse exactly the same message throughout the world and integrate the language and the symbols of the country in which the brand is displayed. The modification of advertisements in relation to the geographic zone of diffusion is, however, less necessary when the advertisements show basic products or high-tech products that respond to the same objectives of use from one country to the next (razors, baby diapers, VCRs, CD burners, etc.). Furthermore, advertisements for products that are "symbols" of a country (Levi's jeans, hamburgers for the USA) or products that represent the *savoir-faire* of a region (luxury products for France, pasta for Italy) do not require an adaptation because they are desired because of their geographic origin, which is a synonym for image and for quality, and a commercial advertisement should, in contrast, insist on the origins of the brand by using evocative visual or verbal elements [DEC 91, DEC 99, USU 92]. The modification of advertisements in relation to the geographic zone of diffusion is also not necessary when the advertiser's target is transnational, or relatively homogeneous, even if the target occupies distinct geographic territories. It has been noted that young Parisians, New Yorkers and Muscovites have similar sensibilities in terms of values, hobbies, musical tastes, etc.

In conclusion, when the use of geomarketing in optimizing the creation objectives and strategy of an advertising campaign is considered, it must be underlined that the precision of the information used by firms varies according to their means and their communication territory: the information is often cursory and intuitive in the case of an international communication strategy because of the cost and the difficulty of collecting reliable data that are not out of date. However, in the case of a national advertisement, the level of cartographic analysis is sometimes rather sophisticated: the decision-maker relies on administrative maps (regions, blocks) or urban maps (streets of a city) in order to adapt the objectives and the content of a commercial campaign.

10.1.3. *Geomarketing and media strategies*

The fundamental thing that geomarketing brings to improving the performance of a communications policy is concerned with the media strategy. The goal of this is the selection of media and support(s) for transmission of the advertising message that will limit the expenditure by the advertisers in the purchase of advertising space. In other words, it is a question of reaching a large number of "useful" individuals, or those who belong to the client's communication target. In order to choose one media or support over another with regard to this limitation, media planners rely on, among other factors, criteria of power, repetition and affinity. The *power* of a support represents the support's ability to cover the intended target and is calculated based on the useful audience represented by the readers, listeners, movie goers or television viewers of a press, radio, cinema or television support who also belong to the advertiser's target [DEC 99, LEN 01]. The *repetition* of a support is calculated based on the support's ability to deliver the message many times during a short period of time. Radio and display ads offer a higher repetition potential than does the cinema. Finally, the *affinity* of the support is the relationship between the share of the target in the audience of a support (the useful audience) and the share of the target in the total population.

The knowledge of all of these indexes for the available supports informs the media planner and helps him or her construct an optimal plan. A synthetic indicator is often used in orienting his or her decision, the GRP or Gross Rating Point, which reflects the average number of contacts between a support and 100 individuals belonging to the advertiser's target audience. This is the key indicator on which agencies rely in order to select a support with the right CPM (cost per 1,000 people), which represents the cost of an advertising insertion divided by the number of people belonging to the target multiplied by 1,000. A support associated with a high GRP and a reasonable CPM limits the cost of purchasing of space and will therefore be attractive for an advertiser. These ratios are measured based on information on the audience of relative supports; these are, first, the socio-demographic characteristics of the individuals (age, sex, activities, etc.), then their behaviors (press publications bought, television shows watched, nature and frequency of purchases realized, etc.). In recent years, in the advertising domain, these data have been linked to geographic areas (cities, regions or neighborhoods, etc.), to population travel flows, and even to the commercial offer of a given territory (number of stores and those present). One thus, finally, has a system of geo-coded information that can be used to choose the supports which will maximize the number of contacts between the message and the public it addresses. The "food" of geomarketing data warehouses is taken from the French National Institute of Statistics (INSEE) files for individuals and for businesses, from data sold by private and specialized companies, from studies that measure the audience of advertising supports, from data collected by the sellers of advertising space, and from the data collected by advertisers about their consumers.

To illustrate what geomarketing brings to the development of a media plan, let us take the example of a firm that addresses Internet users. Based on a system of spatialized information, the advertiser knows that the target is localized for the most part in French cities of more than 100,000 people and in the Parisian agglomeration, that it is more mobile than the average French population, travels for longer times and uses public transportation more often. As a result, and in order to increase the opportunities for Internet users to see and hear the commercial message, a pertinent media plan should integrate exterior advertising supports (signs, bus-stop shelters, etc.) situated in large cities and in trains, subways, bus stations, etc. This means a smaller expenditure on the purchase of space insofar as the support will have been selected according to the appropriateness of its audience to the location and the mobility of the campaign's communications target.

In response to the needs and expectations of the advertisers who wish for more targeted communication actions, an increasing number of firms that sell advertising space are integrating geomarketing systems into their product offering.

10.1.4. *Users of geomarketing for advertising means*

The technology advance that has occurred makes the establishment of databases possible and the French economic crisis of the 1990s have resulted in a reduction of communications budgets dedicated to the mass media in favor of 'below-the-line' activities outside the media: corporate patronage, sponsoring, public relations, direct marketing (see Chapter 11). This reduction of budgets is explained by the difficulty of measuring the effectiveness of mass communication actions, by the sometimes prohibitive costs of space in the media, on the radio, in the cinema, in the press, in display ads, and by the weak impact of messages diffused in an environment overloaded with information. Because of this, advertisers are neglecting mass communication and lean more toward more individualized and relational marketing [BOY 00, PEP 98]. Such a situation has obviously not left the advertising world unaffected, and more particularly the sellers of commercial space in the mass media. Most of the time, the purchase of space goes through specific firms that manage a particular support. The clients of these firms (buyers of commercial space) are the media agencies, the advertising agencies and the advertisers. The media agencies are very important clients who negotiate with advertising space sellers the purchase of large quantities of advertising space in various types of media (television channels, radio stations, display/billboard networks, movie theaters, press inserts, websites, etc.), which are then resold to the advertising agencies or the advertisers. These products are often accompanied by related advice on the optimization of the media strategy.

The growing concern of advertisers about better productivity from their investment and an increasingly competitive context have led sellers of space and media agencies to equip themselves with increasingly high-performance tools for research and optimization of media plans. It is in this context that geomarketing (or the more or less precise hybridization of a geographic territory in terms of the socio-demographic and behavioral data of the population that occupies it or moves through it) appeared on the French scene at the beginning of the 1990s. In practice, it has been proved that this tool allows an advertiser to optimize his or her advertising strategy at three levels. This will first be at the level of objectives and of the copy strategy, since this tool allows the content of a commercial message to be refined and made more effective. It is also a valuable aid in the media strategy creation framework as it allows more targeted communications actions to be developed. It offers the double advantage of optimizing the communications expenses of the advertisers while addressing a large number of prospects. Thanks to geomarketing, among other things, communications costs in certain types of mass media have regained certain dynamism and it has been possible to increase the selling price of the supports. These advantages explain why an increased number of sellers of advertising space have turned to this method. Throughout the second and third sections of this chapter, the manner in which these actors in the advertising world use geomarketing will be related in detail.

10.2. The principal users of geomarketing in the advertising domain

The sellers of advertising space in the mass media have a great interest in geomarketing. We will describe the usage by firms that are most advanced in geomarketing in order of their expertise: display, the cinema, the press.

10.2.1. *The use of geomarketing in the display domain*

Display is outside advertising that is mainly visible in urban areas. Its principal formats are signs of four by three meters in size positioned in high-traffic areas (in front of traffic lights, at an intersection, in the parking lot of a hypermarket, etc.) and on urban furniture (signs, displays in or on public transportation, etc.) [DEC 99, GAV 00, LEN 01]. An advertiser wishing to diffuse a commercial message on signs situated in France buys several signs that are described as a *network*. He or she can also rent them individual units, but this is rare. Renting of such units is generally carried out for a period of seven days. For the past few years, display has ranked third in the media investment of French advertisers behind the press and television. The cost of this system is relatively high but it has several advantages such as a large audience, possible geographic selectivity (for example the catchment area of a store), and an inevitable support for mobile individuals; they attract attention if the creation is carried out well. The major disadvantages are a difficulty in measuring the power and affinity of displays and therefore a weakness in terms of targeting.

For about the last 10 years, geomarketing has been used by display firms to compensate for this last disadvantage. This domain has always been a leader here, since it is concerned with territories of communication and has therefore always needed a geographic representation of the signs to visualize the proposed offer. N practice, the display domain considers itself to be a micro-local media that addresses a specific group of individuals who constitute its audience. In order to attract advertisers to the proposed signs, it is vital to quantify and to qualify this audience. The quantification is measured by the number of people who pass by one of the signs of the network, studied at least once on the eve of the survey [CHA 00]. The qualification of the audience relies on the integration, into a system of geo-coded information, of data related to the socio-demographic and behavioral characteristics of individuals who live around the signs or who regularly pass by.

Geomarketing is used by display firms for many reasons. First, it is a support tool for positioning advertising signs in strategic locations and for creating new products. Positioning signs is a question of identifying on a map the most populous geographic areas, the "best" populated geographic areas (or those occupied by the targets of the advertisers) and the geographic areas that are least saturated with competitor displays. This increases the strength and the affinity of the network as well as improving the quality. In addition to this geomarketing of stock, the mobility of the prospects is also taken into account through the geomarketing of flows. This consists of integrating data related to the mobility of French people, such as the communities of residence linked to workplaces, the average daily time of travel, the share of transport costs in the overall household costs, etc. [MER 01], into an information system. In transportation display in particular, having precise information on the traffic is crucial in constructing high-performance communications networks and thus in attracting advertising clients. To this end, studies are regularly carried out by transportation companies in order to quantify and qualify the travel characteristics of the population. This information, associated with the modes of transportation and the routes taken by travelers, is taken into account by bus and rail stations and airports to optimize the locations of their display signs. Using knowledge of travel in a given territory and of the characteristics of the travelers ideas for new products and communications supports to reach the "nomadic" target of certain advertisers can be created. For example, some sellers of commercial space propose using a train or bus for commercial advertisements, as was done in advertising Play Station, which covered an entire train with its name. Special factual operations are also organized. They are carried out through the presence, in train stations and airports, of hostesses who distribute leaflets or samples, or even give advice at exhibition stands. The transit locations of travelers also sometimes become an advertiser's presentation theater: for example, chair lifts have been installed in a Paris train station for Motorola, a Milky Way was constructed for Danone's Evian, and some passengers even witnessed windows being cleaned by mountaineers using the product Ajax. Finally, it is common sense, validated by data from a geomarketing system that orients the choice of location of a network or the creation of new support offers so that they reach with the highest certitude the targets aimed at by the advertising clients.

Second, geomarketing has allowed a considerable amount of time to be saved by the sales force of display firms. Before meeting a client with whom he or she is in contact (advertiser, media agency or advertising agency), the salesperson of a display network can now very easily, based on a geomarketing software program, position the signs that he or she proposes in a communications territory. Furthermore, he or she can accompany them with pertinent information for the potential buyer of the product, such as the density of consumers, the specificity of the population of the area, the position of a category of stores in relation to the display network, etc. (see Box 10.1). Simulations can be carried out; the salesperson selects for example several sign offers that interest the client and makes them appear on a computer screen. A printed copy then allows the different proposals of the display firm to be visualized and the positions of the signs to be compared with the catchment area of the advertiser. Finally this copy helps the client make a choice that is compatible with his or her stores, target and budget. Before the existence of geo-coded and digitalized data, this basic task of visualization of the offer took much more time because spots representing the signs proposed by the display firm had to be glued by hand onto a map. This tedious operation was repeated for each new demand and for each new client. In summary, the arrival of geomarketing reduced the preparation time for commercial visits for the firms that sell display networks.

Third, geomarketing provides a “preview” for display firms, highlighting the performance of their support in terms of targeting. Geomarketing is useful for positioning of signs in order to determine their audience with more precision. To attract advertisers to a network, it is necessary “to prove” to them that a large number of people belonging to their communications target are going to pass by the sign and therefore see the advertisement. This means quantifying and qualifying the audience of a network in order to calculate a GRP. This ratio represents a sales argument since it reflects the proximity of the media to the target of the advertiser. The higher the ratio is, the more the support is seen to be effective and the more the signs can be sold at higher prices. The current tendency of display firms is to rely on the geomarketing of stock. More precisely, they integrate into their databases information related to the socio-demographic and behavioral characteristics of the individuals who live in the territory of occupation of their supports in order to make them more attractive to the eyes of the advertisers (see Box 10.1). The geomarketing of flows is also used to identify the reasons for and the origins of travel, the duration of trips and the profiles of prospects who pass by a sign. These geographic information systems (GIS) thus become optimization support tools for a communications campaign and the display firms respond using these, with figures and maps in support, to the advertiser’s expectations in terms of targeting and of proximity of the network to potential customers such as executives, young people, Internet users, etc.

Lastly, geomarketing helps display firms segment their product offer. Rather than proposing non-specialized networks that put off clients today, the marketing offer has been rethought and the display firms have created, by relying on their system of spatialized information, ranges of signs that are more adapted to the problems of advertisers, in order to achieve new market shares. These results in the creation of specific product ranges intended to reach the targets that interest the majority of customers (executives, urban, young people, Internet users, etc.). For example, special display networks in train stations that had been conceived to attract advertisers of luxury products were abandoned because of the bad image that they carried. Thanks to the geographic information system that highlights the routes taken, consumption behaviors and the number and the profile of executives who take the train, the firm that sells display in those places developed a product for its “luxury” clients. The signs of this network, sold at a higher price that a non-“geomarketed” product, are situated on the train station platforms close to the first class exits. Luxury brands that rarely advertised in train station display ads have already begun taking advantage of this space (Chanel, Dior, Jaguar, etc.).

Box 10.1: *Geomarketing; a sales and research tool for the Avenir network; taken from an interview with the director of the Avenir studies, March 2001 and a presentation brochure on the Geo-logic geomarketing tool from Avenir*

When a salesperson for *Avenir*, a media selling firm, goes to visit a client (a media agency in 80% of the cases), he or she takes a "geo-logic" demonstration CD-ROM with him or her, a marketing tool that the company has used since 1995.

"Geo-logic" is a set of processing processes and of geographic representations that constitute a readable pattern of the territories. It allows the "geo-logic" profile of the positioning of the signs that make up the network to be visualized. For example, for a sign located at 104 rue de Courcelle in Paris, the following can be determined:

– the consumption indexes of the area in which it is positioned (an index of 237 for fresh-cooked dishes);

– the frequentation of businesses by inhabitants (in this neighborhood, less than 20% of households frequent the closest Leclerc hypermarket);

– the number of inhabitants;

– their socio-professional category (an index of 126 on the superior socio-professional categories), etc.

This tool allows the media selling firm to propose a network of signs and surfaces to its clients, which ensures the maximum GRP. For example, in the network known as "Empir", the advertiser buys 5,000 signs throughout France for a GRP guaranteed to be higher than 1,100. Thus, in the end, the advertiser uses fewer signs but with a better efficiency/price ratio.

Alongside these formatted offers, display firms also propose renting signs by the unit, personalized products which respond more precisely to the communications objectives of each advertiser. Let us imagine, for example, a firm that sells its brand only at stores Z and wishes to maintain its market share in a given geographic area. The ideal would be to select only the signs in cities where the stores Z are found and in which the potential for consumption is high. Certain display firms propose to the advertisers that they assemble the useful sign(s) by using a geomarketing tool to select the pertinent surfaces. By the same token, it will certainly be possible to sell, eventually, advertisement signs that only appear at certain hours or on certain dates, chosen according to the travel habits of the client's target. This type of offer is difficult, however, to implement today, because signs do not allow a large number of displays to be unrolled. In future, new display technologies, such as diode or plasma screens, will offer the same flexibility as television since the advertisements will no longer be on paper posters. Commercials will remotely animate and can be frequently and instantaneously changed, every hour for example.

In conclusion, the use of geomarketing by display firms gives them an undeniable competitive advantage. In practice, the audience for their signs is henceforth qualified and their proximity to the target of the advertiser can be evaluated more precisely. "Geomarketed" networks are therefore more attractive and their selling price can be, for good reasons, raised. Behind these advantages, however, lie limitations on the use of a system of geo-coded information. The first limitation resides in the fact that display companies are not free in how they position their advertising signs in France. Thus, it is not certain that the best location found with the help of digital maps will be negotiable with the locally elected officials of the urban area considered. The second limitation relates to the reliability of the data collected for feeding into the data warehouses. They are "fed" by the results of declarative surveys, which have the disadvantage that they lack reliability and precision in interviewee responses. The third limitation is concerned with the rigidity of the display media, which reduces the possibilities of hyper-segmentation of the product offer, as it is not yet possible to rapidly change the advertisement shown on a poster display. A final difficulty that confronts display firms is the proper understanding by the clients of what geo-coded information systems contribute. Some think at times that geomarketing is a purely marketing view that allows supports to increase their rates without significantly improving the performance of advertising campaigns.

10.2.2. *The use of geomarketing in the cinema domain*

The cinema is the smallest of the five principal mass media in terms of advertising investment. This is explained by its very strong selectivity, which confers upon it a limited power at the national level. The audience, which is constituted of all the individuals who have been to a movie during the seven days preceding the survey [MAR 98], is composed mainly of young people aged 15–24, of highly educated individuals and of superior socio-professional categories (Médiamétrie). Because of the particular profile of the public of this media and of the motive of being at the cinema (to enjoy oneself), the advertisements that are shown are often suggestive, spectacular and high in emotional content. The cinema medium is therefore of very little interest of advertisers with a large target audience, a demonstrative tone of communication and a need of repetition of their message. The principal advantage of the cinema is that it generates very high rates of advertising message memorization because the prospect who receives the message is captivated and available. Furthermore, this support performs well at the level of the socio-demographic and geographic selectivity [LEN 01]. The proposed prices of this medium are relatively onerous because of the targeting possibility that the cinema offers. The investments realized here have seen a strong progression in recent years as a result of the projection of mass market films (blockbuster films) and of the development of multiplexes, the goal of which is to reach a larger clientele [DEC 99]. These multiplexes, constructed on the outskirts of urban areas, show diversified films that can please the whole family.

Geomarketing is used by companies that sell commercial space in the cinema for several reasons. First, it helps to position cinematographic complexes in a territory.

The same logic as that used by display firms or distributors in determining the area of location of their support or their store (see the second part of the book) is adopted by cinema construction companies. It is a question of identifying the right spot for the cinema in order to attract a large number of potential cinemagoers. The catchments areas of cinemas were formerly evaluated based on the number of inhabitants of urban agglomerations; companies invested in places on the basis of the number of individuals residing less than half an hour's drive from the cinemas analyzed.

As with display, a system of geo-coded digitized information offers the possibility of visualizing the commercial networks proposed by the cinema to their client. Thus, maps with points allow the identification of theater supports associated with their audience profile and the power of these. By putting into place a geomarketing tool, the cinema also has at its disposal more specific information on the individuals who frequent it. This makes it possible to attract new advertisers by comparing the catchment area of an old cinema with that of the multiplex. Distributors are among the clients that have recently broadcast advertising messages on the big screen. Hypermarkets interested in communication of brand and proximity are thus investing more and more in cinematographic support. This success can be explained, among other things, by the fact that moviegoers are now described in terms of profile, where they come from and their consumption behaviors. By relying on such indicators, distributors interested in campaigns that aim at establishing an affection relationship in a fulfilling framework thus use the cinema to address customers from the catchment area of a store.

As with display firms, certain companies that sell commercial space rely on stock geomarketing in order to segment their advertising supply. Based on qualified cartographic representations that follow, specific products are developed to reach targets valued by the advertisers (see Box 10.2).

Box 10.2: *Geomarketing and the development of new products at Médiavision taken from an interview with Eric Merklen, Médiavision marketing director, May 2001, and a Médiavision presentation brochure*

The media selling firm Médiavision has used geomarketing since 1998. The principle consists of establishing *Bassins d'Attraction Cinématographique* (*BAC* or movie theater trade areas) around multiplexes that have been constructed since 1993. The BACs correspond to the potential clientele of each cinema complex evaluated based on the access time between home and the cinema. The goal is thus to qualify this audience in order to meet the expectations of the advertisers in terms of targeting. This has been done with the help of the construction of a geomarketing information system. The data fed into this system are taken from the INSEE and the consumption panel Sécodip. They are modeled on real data furnished by research companies. Geomarketing enables the media selling firm to determine the profiles of "*cinéphiles*" (film enthusiasts) and to distinguish the differences of the volumes of consumption of certain products according to geographic areas. Based on these values, special offers are elaborated: "Vision Premium", for example, brings together the 23 *BACs* mainly frequented by executives; "*Vision Céréales*" is related to the 40% of French households that account for 40% of total spending on cereals. Still based on geo-coded data, the media selling firm proposes a choice to its clients, in addition to these fixed offers, of a variable number of screens related to the advertiser's target audience. Since putting this geomarketing into place, Médiavision has attracted new advertisers, notably amongst food stores and large distributors. For the future, the media selling firm is considering the conception of a European offer, based on the geomarketing tools of the subsidiaries in Spain, Switzerland and the Netherlands.

Finally, more precise knowledge of the characteristics of moviegoers who frequent a certain cinema (or *stock geomarketing)* has allowed an expansion of its range of commercial products. This has resulted in the establishment of factual systems that are proposed to advertisers who target a population category in the geographic area corresponding to the trade area of the cinema. In physical terms, it is possible, in a cinema, to carry out commercial operations such as the distribution of samples, seat personalization, taste-testing, and even the dissemination of an advertisement in magazines offered by cinemas.

Throughout these different uses, geomarketing represents an opportunity for a medium, such as the cinema, that has been neglected by certain advertisers. It has caused, among other things, hypermarket companies, a client that has previously rarely used the cinema, to become more present in big-screen advertising. As a result, this has led to a rise in the sales of the support. Despite this potential, the fact remains that there are a certain number of limitations, similar to those mentioned in the developments relative to the use of geomarketing by the display media.

10.2.3. *The use of geomarketing in the press*

The press, first among French media in terms of advertising space sales, is a heterogeneous ensemble composed of several supports [DEC 99, GAV 00, MAR

98] including the non-specialized national daily press (*Le Monde, Libération, Le Figaro*, etc.), the specialized national daily press (*L'Equipe, Les Echos, La Tribune,* etc.), the regional daily press, which wields extensive power in France since it is read by more than 50% of the population and is present throughout the entire territory (*Ouest France, Les Dernières Nouvelles d'Alsace, Le Dauphiné Libéré,* etc.), the regional weekly press, the periodical or general public magazine press (*Géo, l'Express, Biba, Télé 7 jours, Femme Actuelle,* etc.), the specialized or professional press and finally the papers locally distributed at no cost with classified and real estate advertisements. Consumer magazines developed by certain companies are also included in this no-cost category. The principal advantages of these different press media supports are a good selectivity of the communications target on basis of the socio-professional and geographic criteria and acceptable rates, while the disadvantages are related to the quality of printing, which is at times mediocre, poor knowledge of the audience for certain titles (the cost-free and dailies in particular) and an advertising charge that is high at times. The difficulty of measuring the number of times that a copy has been taken and read through by the reader must also be added to this list.

Specific firms handle the sale of advertising space of the different titles on the French market. They also manage the inserts sold in the press titles. The proposed rates depend on the location chosen (front page, political section, etc.), on the size (half or whole page) and on the color of the message (black and white, color). The advertising receipts of the different press categories vary. For certain titles, their survival depends upon these receipts and it is thus crucial for these titles to do everything possible to maintain or increase them. Since the beginning of the 1990s, purchase of advertising space in the press has been in decline [DEC 99], which indicates the need to have solid arguments to attract advertisers. This is done by highlighting two essential qualities that a press title must possess in order to attract a client: not only a large audience[1] but also a qualification of this audience in socio-demographic and geographic terms in order to carry out more targeted communications actions.

1. The audience of a title is made up of all the individuals who have read or flicked through a newspaper or magazine during the reference period (the month for a monthly, the day for a daily), whether it was bought by that individual or not [MAR 98].

Box 10.3: *How Ouest-France, a local daily newspaper, uses geomarketing, taken from an interview with Stéphane Baranger, assistant director of research and development for Ouest-France*

Conserving the readership of a daily like *Ouest-France*, which includes 42 local editions, signifies that it is necessary to remain close to the preoccupations of the people living in the territories served by the paper. To help with this, geographic data furnished by INSEE are associated with a background map of the entire West of France.

The volume of data related to a commune that is contained in an issue of the newspaper is measured by the number of lines. These data are related to the number of households in these same communes. From these associations come maps onto which is transcribed the "daily average number of lines per 1,000 households" belonging to the area studied. A study of this representation thus allows "anomalies" to be seen more easily. If the number of lines of the newspaper dedicated to a commune or to a collection of communes during the period analyzed is weak in comparison to its population, a particular color alerts the newspaper's editors. Based on this constant, the diagnosis can lead to two levels of decision: strategic in terms of reinforcing the leading article offer (by adding pages for example) or corrective in terms of resolving a local dysfunction (absence of a correspondent for example).

Geomarketing has been used by a majority of these firms for more than five years. It is especially useful in the editorial domain, where it is used as an editorial management guide to securing the loyalty of clients and thus maintaining a certain audience level. The number of readers, which reflects the power of the medium, is the result of the program, the content and the editorial of a title. The idea is to produce geographic maps that cover the dissemination zones of a newspaper and to refine, with the help of a computerized visualization, its content so that it responds in the best way possible to the wishes of the buyers. As buyers will be more loyal to a daily if it deals with local issues, it is thus important to regularly include articles that mention the town or region inhabited by the readership of a title (see Box 10.3). The geomarketing tool allows the frequency of the article subjects that appear in the dissemination zone of the newspaper to be evaluated simply. If a disparity is noticed between the market share of a particular geographic sector and the proportion of articles dedicated to this zone, the editor in chief carries out an adjustment. For example, if a town that attracts a large number of subscribers has been "forgotten" in the preceding days, these neglected areas are identified using a spatialized information system and the "error" is repaired. Thus, geomarketing allows the themes to be tackled in a newspaper to be ranked according to their sales potential and helps maintain or increase its audience [MAR 00; CBN 01]. As a result, it is the size and the profile of the readership on which the sellers of press commercial support rely to attract advertisers and to fix the price of advertising inserts.

Taking into account the geographic dimension in the press domain means that the editorial content and advertising inserts vary according to the dissemination zone of the title. One thus talks of the territorial division of an edition, which consists of proposing different articles that depend on the town or country in which the newspaper is distributed. This procedure responds to two objectives: maintaining and increasing the number of readers and satisfying the needs of advertisers who are searching for ways to communicate at the local level. In practice, companies have a heightened need for supports that allow them to carry out local communications actions [MAR 96]. For this reason, they welcome the offer from the commercial press to disseminate message in a restricted geographic area that nonetheless covers the client's target population. This also allows national papers to attract a larger category of advertiser, for which access was previously impossible because of the high advertising space costs. This geographic segmentation is currently very widespread at both national level and international level. Thus, magazines such as *Elle, Marie-Claire, Newsweek, National Geographic, Time,* etc. are translated into the local language and modify their editorial and advertising content according to continent, country or region, embodying more localized and more targeted actions. The limit to the extension of such a process is the difficulty in managing too sophisticated a division at the fabrication and dissemination level of the newspaper. Furthermore, the advertisers have a division of customers that does not necessarily correspond to the newspaper's division, which is often administrative in nature [BEN 98]. To compensate for these disadvantages and at the same time respond to the local demands of the advertisers, certain newspapers price the commercial inserts based on the "useful" geographic area of the advertiser [MAR 96]. A final difficulty is related to the heterogeneity of the population residing in certain territories. In practice, how should the type of information and the advertising inserts to be distributed be determined for a metropolis like Lille, where families exist in which the husband works in Paris, the wife at Tourcoing and the children study at Villeneuve d'Ascq [BEN 98]?

With a degree of improvement less than that described for display and the cinema, geomarketing is also used in the press domain to develop new commercial product offers. Highly sought after by the press, socio-demographic criteria are pertinent data in attracting advertisers interested by a particular consumer profile. By associating these criteria with geographic and behavioral data, specific joint deals or assortments of several newspapers have seen the light of day. Their purpose is to reach prospects of whom companies are particularly fond. Among the principal ones, one finds the "PQR 66", which includes the vast majority of the regional dailies distributed in the French territory within a single commercial offer. Studies on the audience of the press indicate that more than 50% of executives living outside the Parisian agglomeration read a regional daily press title. This shows the interest an advertiser whose potential clients have such a profile will have in this joint deal, depending on his strength and his proximity. These new offers give rise to marketing offers that reflect the affinity, power and cost-saving measures of the supports that they integrate [LEN 01]. Currently there are around 70, but those which rely on both socio-demographic and geographic data are still few in number. This can be explained by the fact that the data related to the audience's territory of occupation are not well-known and/or are little exploited by the newspapers. Knowledge of the location where the prospects reside (or the geomarketing of stock) is sometimes supplemented by information related to their mobility (geomarketing of flows). These data are useful in the editorial domain for several reasons. On the one hand, they allow the distribution area of the newspaper to be fixed with more accuracy. Thus, the daily *Le Parisien* is sold today more than 100 kilometers outside Paris, given the extension to the residents of the Ile-de-France and as a result to its readers [MAR 96]. On the other hand, this gives ideas for new products in order to reach the target of the superior socio-professional categories. Studies have shown that executives travel a great deal and that they spend more time than the average on planes and on trains [DEV 97]. On these transport networks, the traveling executives are generally male and young; they have high purchasing power and generally travel a lot in their personal life as well. Based on this information, a specific advertising system (consumer magazines) was launched to reach this target audience. It responds to the expectations of certain advertisers, notably optimizing the media coverage of executives in France who travel, who number in the millions. Thanks to their editorial content, which relates closely to the preoccupations of traveling executives, these consumer magazines have been successful with businessmen [BEN 99] and, as a result, with the advertisers who wish to target them.

To complete the discussion of the use of geomarketing by the press, we will say that the geo-coded information systems used by this medium are less widespread than those developed by display firms and the cinema. There are still a limited number of firms in the press domain that have geomarketing software and thus precise information on the characteristics of their readership, its location and its mobility behaviors at their disposal. These gaps could be bridged, on the one hand by systematically integrating into the tools of measurement of the audience questions related to the location and the mobility of readers and, on the other hand, by exploiting information on file about subscribers or about classified ads for free newspapers.

We will finish this chapter dedicated to the spatial dimension in the communications policy of firms with a section on the potential users of geomarketing, notably the radio and television media.

10.3. The potential users of geomarketing in the advertising domain

Radio and television remain very discrete and evasive when it comes to using geomarketing tools, mainly because they are at the beginnings of its development.

10.3.1. *The use of geomarketing in the radio sector*

Radio is ranked third in media investments [LEN 01]. Numerous stations make up the French radio offer. The Superior Audiovisual Council classes them in several categories, to which corresponds a list of precise and strict rules in terms of advertising receipts:

– Category A stations or association radios (TSF, etc.) have access to local advertisements.

– Category B stations group together local commercial services or regional independents (Alouette, Voltage, Ado FM, Vitamine, etc.) and have access to local and national advertisements.

– Categories C and D bring together local commercial services or regional franchisees or members and the FM radios affiliated with a thematic network (NRJ, Fun, RTL2, Nostalgie, RFM, Europe 2, Radio Classique, BFM, etc.). The service of these stations is national but it is possible, for category C, to realize local switch-overs at the programming or advertisement level.

– Category E concerns national non-specialized radio (Europe 1, RMC, RTL, etc.). They do not have access to local advertisements, because the broadcast duration of their regional programs is less than three hours.

– The stations of Radio France where only collective interest campaigns or those realized by collectives are authorized.

The cost of insertion of a commercial message in a radio program varies according to its length and its location and then depending on the strength and affinity to the target of the radio station on which it will be broadcast [GAV 00]. The principal advantages of radio are the possible repetition of an advertisement, the loyalty of listeners and the selectivity in terms of calendar, target and geographic territory. The major disadvantages are a deficit at the creativity level, the commercial congestion of certain channels and the lack of precise and reliable studies to measure the radio audience[2] [DEC 99, GAV 00]. This audience is actually difficult to evaluate, because, on the one hand, it relies on the declarative and, on the other hand, that listening locations are extremely varied: at home, in the car, at work, moving about (portable radios) and even on the Internet [CHA 00]. The results of audience studies, which are most of the time carried out by specialized firms, are very important to radio channels because they show its commercial effectiveness (the GRP). It is in this context of performance measure research that geomarketing is little by little making its appearance in the radio stations that are authorized to broadcast local advertisements and have ample financial means (mainly categories C and D).

The socio-demographic criteria were, until recently, the principal sales arguments of the radio support in attracting advertisers. Each station knows the average profile of its listeners, for example, executives for France Inter and France Info, 15–25 year olds for Fun Radio, etc. Since local switch-overs have been increasing, this information is associated with useful geographic data for clients who wish to carry out local communications actions. The principle is to get to know the advertiser's communications target, then identify where it is situated in space in

2. The audience of a radio station includes anyone who says they have listened to the station in the 24 hours prior to questioning.

order to propose the stations of the network that broadcast in the corresponding geographic territory. However, this practice has limitations, since the stations offered do not necessarily broadcast in all the areas that are useful for the advertiser. Furthermore, this fragmentation of the offer at the national level complicates buying space for a client who wishes to act locally. In practice, radio companies propose few or no products that gather together an ensemble of stations in two, three or several geographic areas selected by the advertiser, which restricts the advertiser in broadcasting his or her message throughout the entire national territory [MAR 96]. Moreover, another limitation, already mentioned, concerns the length of regional programming, which must be more than three hours in order to authorize broadcast of local advertisements [BEN 98].

Next to this geomarketing of stock, the geomarketing of flows is equally interesting for a medium like radio that is listened to outside the home. Knowing where the listener is coming from and where he or she is going, knowing the origin of his or her journey and destination, etc. are significant data for advertisers like distributors [MOA 01], restaurateurs and hotel operators. In reality, more than one out of every four French people listens to the radio in his or her car for an average of more than an hour and 15 minutes daily. This is a godsend for attracting hypermarkets and supermarkets to the radio between the hours of 5 and 8 pm, when listeners return home from work. This is the ideal moment to encourage them to make a detour towards a store situated close to the route they take and thus to create traffic in the store. With radio investments being marked by a strong seasonality (the peak being at the end of the year), geomarketing of flows is also a promising way of limiting this congestion and spreading out the broadcast of commercial messages. To do this, sellers of radio commercial space analyze the mobility behaviors of the French during the months of July and August, which supplies them with sales arguments for promotional inserts intended for restaurant and hotel chains, when holidaymakers migrate towards their vacation destinations. Furthermore, at these now opportune times, commercial offers can follow the consumers into the regions of their travel. Special commercial products are thus launched during the summer season. They gather together advertising messages broadcast on different stations in the most frequented departments during the July/August period. Such seasonal offers are also proposed by certain press, display and cinema companies.

10.3.2. *The use of geomarketing in the television domain*

Television is second only to the press in terms of advertising expenditure in the mass media. Its principal advantage is its influence (the French watch an average of 3 hours and 52 minutes of television a day). The television channels have very precise data at their disposal concerning this audience, the data coming from panels. The number of viewers, as well as their socio-demographic profile, is linked to a given broadcast, which allows a better targeting of the advertising campaigns launched in this medium. Its principal disadvantages are the high cost of advertising space and the congestion of advertisements on the screen, which without a doubt hinders the effectiveness of campaigns [LEN 01].

Geomarketing is used very little by the TV channels because the geographic selectivity of the broadcast area of an advertisement is rarely possible, but evolutions of the French audiovisual scene will most likely modify this. If the non-specialized national channels are currently predominant, the progress of satellite, cable and digital equipment will soon allow a more sophisticated fragmentation of this medium [LEN 01]. The emergence of thematic, local and foreign channels should therefore lead more and more sellers of TV commercial space to equip themselves with a geo-coded information system.

Today, the beginnings of geomarketing are seen in national programs that are de-localizing. The M6 channel is part of this, but the channel, which initiated local switch-over at 8:30 pm in 1990, is forbidden from carrying local advertisements (decision of the Superior Audiovisual Council). This is not the case for France 3, which obtains very satisfying audience scores for its 21 regional news programs. Thus, thanks to the socio-demographic and behavioral data on the television viewers in a geographic broadcast area of regional programs, it is possible to refine the advertising strategies of the channel's advertiser clients concerning the objectives of commercial campaigns (image objective in order to maintain a market share or awareness objective when the brand is not widely bought in a given geographic area). This information on the audience is furnished by the consumer and distributor panels to which most national advertisers subscribe. Next to national channels that carry out local switch-over, there are also local channels that broadcast their programs over a limited geographic area (Télé Toulouse, Paris Première, etc.). The data on the audience of their programs is now available (since August 2001), but only twice a year. Another obstacle to the development of a geomarketing tool is the limited financial resources of most local audiovisual structures.

This currently restricted usage of territorial segmentation in the television domain is therefore explained by an unfavorable technological and regulatory context. Between a market of still underdeveloped local channels, the quasi-inexistence of audience measurement instruments on the local channels and a regulation that bans advertisers interested in local actions (distributors) from advertising screens, it is currently not very relevant for the firms that sell TV commercial space to invest in a spatialized information system.

10.4. Conclusion

Geomarketing, in terms of taking into account geographic information about a territory in order to refine an advertising strategy, has been used for quite some time in an intuitive manner in the communications sector. This chapter endeavored to show that its utilization relies increasingly on precise and reliable analysis tools. Progress in computer technology has allowed such advances.

Stages of the communication policy	Content	Geomarketing contributions
Objectives	To increase awareness, sales, image, etc.	Adaptation of the communication objectives according to consumption behaviors of the population of a targeted geographic area
Creation strategy	Promise, consumer benefit, proof, tone	Adaptation of the content and the form of the message according to socio-demographic characteristics (behavioral and cultural) of the local population
Media strategy	Choice of the media, media planning, etc.	Selection of a medium according to the geographic proximity of its audience to the advertiser's target

Table 10.1: *Summary of geomarketing contributions to advertising strategy*

A summary of the main points of what geomarketing offers to advertisers' communications policies shows that it is a pertinent instrument for carrying out more targeted and therefore certainly more effective advertising actions (Table 10.1).

In summary, geomarketing helps in optimizing of advertising campaigns, whether at the level of objectives, of the message content level or the diffusion support choice. The media agencies have understood this and that is why more and more are investing in geographic information systems in order to market their supports better. They are responding in this way to the targeting and proximity needs that advertisers express and are attempting to "tailor" actions to a mass medium. The geomarketing of flows and of stocks is used by the supports visible from the outside, such as display, radio and the press, while only area geomarketing is of interest to those who "consume" in a fixed and closed location such as the cinema and television.

Table 10.2 offers a summary of the main undeniable advantages, as well as the disadvantages, of the use of geomarketing in advertising for the sellers of space for the principal mass media, who use this tool extensively.

Introduced at a time when socio-demographic criteria revealed themselves to be insufficient for determining the complexity of consumer behavior, geomarketing is certainly of interest in launching more effective communications campaigns. However, obstacles to its use still exist. The main ones are the high cost of digitized maps, databases and their processing [BOY 00], along with the lack of reliability of certain data. The difficulty of having a qualified workforce to carry out this pertinent statistical processing, which affects the decision-making, must also be added to this list.

Media	Advantages of geomarketing	Limitations of geomarketing
Display	Optimization of the placement of posters in advance The best visualization of the network proposed by the company Sales argument (a higher GRP, a better targeted campaign) Segmentation of the product offering available	Advertisers are not free to determine the position of posters Poor understanding of the contribution of geomarketing on the part of certain clients Unreliable and inadequate data The rigidity of the medium
Cinema	Optimization of the placement of cinemas in advance The best visualization of the offer proposed by the company on a national basis Attraction to advertisers interested in the same catchment area as the cinema Segmentation of the product offering available	Cinemas cannot be situated just anywhere Unreliable and inadequate data
Press	Optimization of editorial content in advance Territorial segmentation that corresponds to the local requirements of advertisers New titles proposed Segmentation of the product offering available (coupled with titles)	Risk: Themes are organized to match the interests of the readers, not in order of importance Management of the fabrication and distribution processes limits territorial divisions Too many titles present in the market The advertiser's catchment zone may be different from the distribution zone of the title Lack of knowledge, reliability and exploitation of geographical information
Radio	Territorial segmentation that corresponds to the local requirements of advertisers New products proposed	The advertiser's catchment zone will not necessarily be the same as the coverage of the station The zone covered is difficult to evaluate The regulatory context is restrictive Unreliable and inadequate data
Television	Territorial segmentation that corresponds to the proximity requirements of advertisers	Nonexistent data for local channels The technological and regulatory contexts are not favorable

Table 10.2: *Advantages and disadvantages of geomarketing for the mass media*

10.5. References

[AAK 75], Aaker D.A. and Myers J.C., *Advertising Management*, Prentice Hall, 1975.

[AGR 95], Agrawal M., Review of a 40 Years Debate in International Advertising, Practitioner and Academician Perspectives to the Standardization/Adaptation Issue, *International Marketing Review*, vol.12, 1, 1995.

[BEN 98], Benoit J-M., Benoit P., Pucci D., *La France redécoupée: enquête sur la quadrature de l'hexagone*, Belin, Paris, 1998.

[BEN 99], Benouaich Y., *Les consumer magazines*, Les presses du management, 1999.

[BON 90], Bonnal F., Les goûts publicitaires des Européens, in *Six manières d'être Européen*, D. Schnapper and H. Mendras, ed. Gallimard, 1990.

[BOY 00], Boyer L. and Burgaud D., *Le marketing avancé, du one to one au E-Business*, Editions d'Organisation, 2000.

[CAU 88], Caumont D., Les niveaux de contrôle en publicité, essai de clarification, *Recherche et Applications en Marketing*, vol. 3, 4, pp. 1-22, 1988.

[CAU 00], Caumont D., Budget et contrôle de l'efficacité publicitaire, in Vernette E., *La publicité. Théories, acteurs et méthodes*, La documentation française, pp. 169-195, 2000.

[CBN 01], CB News, Quand le géomarketing redécoupe la PQR, 648, 26/02 to 04/03 2001, pp. 24.

[CHA 00], Chandon J.-L., Elaboration du plan média, in Vernette E., *La publicité. Théories, acteurs et méthodes*, La documentation française, pp. 133-167, 2000.

[CRO 94], Croué C., *Marketing International*, 1994, De Boeck Université, 1994.

[DEC 91], Decaudin J.-M., *Stratégies de publicité internationale*, Ed. Liaisons, 1991.

[DEC 99], Decaudin J.-M., *La communication marketing*, Economica, 1999.

[GAV 00], Gavard-Perret M.-L., Les acteurs du marché publicitaire, in Vernette E., *La publicité. Théories, acteurs et méthodes*, La documentation française, pp. 43-78, 2000.

[GRE 87], Grégory P., Le contrôle de l'efficacité publicitaire, *Recherche et Applications en Marketing*, vol.2, 4, pp. 71-83, 1987.

[HEL 00], Helfer J.-P. and Orsini J., *Marketing*, Vuibert, 2000.

[IRE 88], IREP, *Mesurer l'efficacité de la publicité*, Les éditions d'organisation, 1988.

[LEN 01], Lendrevie J. and Brochand B., *Le nouveau Publicitor*, 5th edition, Dalloz, 2001.

[LEV 83], Levitt Th., Un seul univers: le marché, *Harvard-l'Expansion*, automne, 1983.

[MAR 96], Marzloff B. abd Bellanger F., *Les nouveaux territoires du marketing. Enquêtes sur le géomarketing et le marketing relationnel*, Editions Liaisons, 1996.

[MAR 98], Marcenac L., Milon A. and Saint-Michel S.-H., *Stratégies publicitaires, de l'étude mercatique au choix des médias*, 4th edition, Bréal Editions, 1998.

[MER 01], Mermet G., *Francoscopie*, Larousse, 2001.

[MIC 97], Micheaux A., *Marketing de bases de données*, Editions d'organisation, 1997.

[MOA 01], Moati P., *L'avenir de la grande distribution*, Odile Jacob (ed), 2001.

[PEP 98], Peppers D. and Rogers M., *Le one to one*, Editions d'Organisation, 1998.

[SCH 99], Schmittlein D., La force d'une base de données bien gérée, in *l'Art du Marketing*, Village Mondial, pp. 136-140, 1999.

[USU 92], Usunier J.-C., *Commerce entre cultures: une approche culturelle du marketing international*, PU, 1992F.

[VAR 94], Vartanian J.-C., *Le média planning*, Economica, 1994.

[VER 00], Vernette E., *La publicité. Théories, acteurs et méthodes*, La documentation française, 2000.

10.6. Bibliography

Marketing Direct

- "Géomarketing, quand cartographie et BDD se marient", 19, April 1997, p.35-48
- "Géomarketing, l'âge de la maturité", 28, May 1998
- "La révolution du géomarketing ordinaire", 35, March 1999
- "Géomarketing: encore jeune mais déjà mature", 37, May 1999
- "Géomarketing, l'Internet établit la norme", 45, April 2000
- "Géomarketing" 45, April 2000

Marketing Magazine

- "France Cadres: un concept, deux titres", 27, January-February 1998, p. 65
- "L'affichage mesure son efficacité sur les ventes", 29, April 1998, pp. 61-62
- "La mobilité, nouvelle donne de la consommation médias", 30, May 1998, p.67-71
- "La PQN récolte le fruit de son marketing", 31, June-August 1998, pp. 67-73
- "Mobilier urbain: vers un marché concurrentiel", 34, November 1998, pp. 85-88
- "L'affichage est intégré dans le parcours du voyageur", 39, April 1999, pp. 69
- "A la recherche de l'annonceur perdu", 39, April 1999, pp. 77-81
- "Mediapolis développe le 'géo média marketing', 40, May 1999, pp. 53-54
- "Le marketing du temps ou la chronomobilité", 40, May 1999, p. 16
- "Agences médias. Vers une expertise multifacettes", 41, June-August 1999, pp. 44-47
- "Affichage grand format, la reconnaissance des annonceurs", 42, September 1999, pp. 81-87
- "Consoplan'R: de la BDD comportementale au médiaplanning", 44, November 1999, pp. 55
- "France Bus met Lyon en modèle", 45, December 1999, pp. 90
- "Géomarketing: un outil de construction et de ciblage pour les médias", 48, March 2000, pp. 89-93

– "Les médias nationaux à la recherche de proximité", 49, April 2000, pp. 105-107
– "L'affichage mesure son efficacité et son image", 50, May 2000, pp. 71-72
– "France Bus Publicité revoit son mix marketing", 50, May 2000, p. 75
– "La gare, l'espace multiservices de demain", 51, June-August 2000 pp. 6-7
– "Quand le monde virtuel influe sur le nomadisme physique", 51, June-August 2000, pp. 97-101
– "Géopolis élargit son expertise", 53, October 2000, p. 111
– "Ecrans Plasma: JCDecaux double la cadence", 53, October 2000, p. 89
– "Affichage, le marché affiche ses ambitions", 53, October 2000, pp. 97-102
– "Pilotage rédactionnel: le géomarketing s'attaque à la PQR", 53, October 2000, p. 60
– "les cadres, une cible à recadrer", 54, November 2000, pp. 111-113
– "Voyageurs franciliens, des consommateurs de rêve", 54, November 2000, p. 105
– "Avenir revoit son offre marketing", 54, November 2000, p.103
– "Nouveaux supports: la mobilité à l'honneur", 55, December 2000, p. 97
– "Avec Vision'Air, Médiavision fait du sur mesure", 58, March 2001, pp. 65-66

Websites

www.aacc.fr (association des agences conseil en communication)
www.carat.fr
www.circuita.com
www.dauphin-affichage.com
www.insee.fr
www.mediametrie.fr
www.pqr.org (presse quotidienne régionale)
www.snptv.org (syndicat national de la publicité télévisée)
www.uda.fr (union des annonceurs)

Chapter 11

Direct Marketing and Geographic Information

Introduction

Direct marketing brings together some very diverse practices, the economic importance of which is far from negligible (31.2% of the advertising expenditure of French firms corresponds to investments in specific media or direct marketing: source France Pub, 1998). In parallel to this quantitative increase, an improvement in quality can be observed, with the opening up of all activity sectors and of the media.

Reinforced by this double extension of practice, direct marketing is no longer only an alternative to the traditional channels of distribution or a channel of original communication; it is a mode of application of marketing. More precisely, Desmet defines it as "a marketing method/approach which consists in systematically collecting and exploiting in a database individual information on a target and managing a personalized transaction" [DES 01].

As a marketing approach, direct marketing presents the standard market analysis steps. It offers, however, several traits of specificity both at the analysis and choice or target level and at the transaction management level.

The first specificity concerns the nature of the data used, which are individual and longitudinal. The data collected on the targets are individual data and not a detailed description of market segments. A direct marketing operation therefore deals with a list of individuals who are contacted personally after having been selected according to the probability of a favorable response to the offer (scoring techniques). And, rather than contenting itself with a single knowledge criterion, the

---

Chapter written by Christine PETR.

direct marketing approach involves constantly incrementing this knowledge of prospects by enriching it with information related to the operation underway (response and nature of the response, no response) and to the collection of dialogue opportunities with the client.

The second specificity concerns the priority given to direct contact between the firm and the consumer. That this is not through distribution intermediaries/middlemen presents advantages (no incoherence of positioning between the firm's products and the retail trade name, no dependence on distribution networks, etc.), but it also imposes strong restrictions linked to the management of the entirety of the transaction [DES 01].

With these transactions being carried out in a geographic area that is neither homogeneous nor geometric, but is on the contrary characterized by specificity according to the terrain, the climate, and the manner in which human beings are appropriated to it [GRE 00], it is not possible to conceal the criteria used. Because there is much to gain from systematically integrating the geographic and spatial components into the operational strategy and practices of firms [CLI 99], this chapter explores the possible contributions of the introduction of geographic information into the direct marketing approach.

Section 11.1 details the modalities of direct geomarketing, depending on whether the firm adopts an approach centered on the commercial potential of the territories or an approach concentrated on the location of its customers and prospects. Section 11.2 deals more particularly with the dilemma of defining the territory and with the choice of the geographic scale that seems the most pertinent in direct marketing.

11.1. Taking space into account in direct marketing

In direct marketing, two approaches are possible when dealing with the introduction of space and geography into the analysis and the targeting of the individuals with whom to communicate. The first approach, described in section 11.1.1, is a marketing analysis of target territories. It deals with qualifying the territories in order to define those in which direct marketing actions should be carried out or reinforced, with the over-representation of individuals potentially interested in the firm's offers taken into account. The alternative approach aims at centering the analysis on the individuals whose address coordinates are already available (section 11.2). More adapted to the logic of relational marketing, this approach deals with locating consumers (customers, prospects, individuals referenced in behavioral databases) in the geographic area in order to then define a direct marketing policy adjusted to these individuals and to their closest neighbors. For reasons of clarity, these two ways of introducing geography are distinguished here, but a firm would be well advised to combine these two direct marketing approaches.

11.1.1. *The analysis of target territories*

When a firm chooses to adopt an approach centered on the territory rather than on individuals, the techniques and the media of direct marketing allow it to improve its performance. An operational tool among others, it does not represent a priority and systematic mode of intervention concerning the consumers. Consequently, if an organization refines its segmentation by introducing geographic data, it continues to manage a portfolio of products according to the usual priorities. If these products are conceived in order to respond to the demands of the market segments identified by socio-demographic and behavioral criteria, the definition of commercial offers is not based on individual information.

Consequently, despite being centered on the territory, the analysis method remains rather trivial since it consists of qualifying the territories in terms of relative under- or over-representation of individuals having certain predefined characteristics. After details have been given of the two approaches of this method of analysis and the qualification of target territories, the principal direct marketing actions that a firm can put into place in selected territories will be discussed.

Direct marketing applied to a territory

The analysis of target territories is differentiated according to the level of dependence of the firm on its commercial space. One can thus distinguish the case of locally implanted businesses that must adapt to their finite commercial space from the case of businesses that, although they have high-performance logistics, have a national or international range.

For locally based firms such as stores and service locations, the territory is a restricted space. Their commercial space corresponds to a finite geographic space (the trade area), the dimensions of which are relatively fixed. It represents for the firm a source of restrictions and of opportunities to which adaptation is beneficial. The adaptation of the offer to the local specifics is not new. It makes reference to the precept "Think Global, Act Local", which is the answer to interrogations on the globalization of markets [LEW 83]. Knowing that truly universal supranational segments are rare and that they only exist for several cross-cultural products [LEH 96], the rule says that one should attempt to adapt the unique strategy of the firm through local operational actions. How much the marketing offer needs to be adapted depends, however, on the sensitivity of the product to consumer values (see Chapter 3) and to the cultural environment in a more general manner [USU 90]. Thus, with eating and cooking habits, which are very sensitive to local uses and conventions, it is preferable to transform the consumption goods in terms of these behaviors rather than attempting to change the behaviors (Campbell, cited in [KEE 94]). Conversely, for computer and software products, commercial standardization is more easily imaginable independently of local characteristics.

In order to adapt the offer and to define "domestic" commercial proposals, the principal task of the analyst is to identify the particular identities of the geographic area considered. This analysis includes two constituents. The first aims at understanding the specificity of the local residents by listing their restraints and their motivations as consumers. One must have a good understanding of their opinions, their attitudes, their consumption practices and their spatial practices, their ways and customs, etc. This point is essential because omitting the characteristics linked to the commercial location of consumers can have important commercial consequences [CHA 97]. As a supplement to the analysis of the behavioral and individual specifics of the residents of a territory, the second analysis constituent consists of listing the more structural identities of the environment. Restrictive legal requirements, climatic qualities, infrastructure development, exclusivity of certain distribution networks, advertising bans on certain products, etc. are all characteristics that represent sources of restriction and of opportunity. Table 11.1 lists certain questions that should precede the definition of the commercial offers in "geo-domestic" direct marketing.

Study topics	Examples of questions
Access infrastructures and internal infrastructures	What is the coverage of highway networks? What is the importance of rail traffic? Which distribution system should be favored: direct distribution or point-of-sale outlets?
Distribution channels and points of sale	What are the most developed distribution channels? What is the available floorspace area in the stores? Is POP advertising usually implemented?
Possible partnerships	To whom should consumers be sent in case of problems? Who can manage after-sales service?
Media and household equipment	What is the media coverage of highway networks? What is the audience for each type of media? What is the equipment rate for reception appliances (TV sets, radio, telephones, and computers)?
Regulation	What are the legal obligations before any direct marketing action? Are games, contests and coupons legal? What kind of data must not be stored in a database? Is the official language compulsory in written communications? Is it allowed to refer to ethnic aspects? ...

Table 11.1: *"Geo-domestic" offers in direct marketing*

Based on this knowledge of the consumers of each geographic area, the firm is going to be able to adjust its offer to the local characteristics. This adjustment can deal simultaneously or separately with the choice of product or service proposed, the method of sale, the means of payment, and the promotional elements, as well as selection of the means of communication (the supports chosen, the degree of personalization, etc.).

With the success of a direct marketing offer being rather closely dependent on the pertinence of the behavioral catalyst, the promotional offer is often one of the first elements to be adjusted to the local context. In order to determine the attributes of a locally successful promotion, diverse characteristics of the selected area must be taken into consideration, including economic and legislative factors, the commercial and media infrastructure and cultural data. By adapting and adding to the remarks of Foxman [FOX 88] and of Desmet [DES 92], Table 11.2 presents several examples of local characteristics that need to be studied in order to judge the appropriateness of a promotional technique in a geographic distribution area.

Personalization of the communication represents a second adaptation modality of direct marketing offers to the specificity of territories. In addition to choosing the right medium (see Chapter 10), it is also a question of increasing the personalization of the message sent to each selected individual in the target territory. It is interesting to show to the prospect or the client that he or she is not a stranger and that one knows the environment in which he or she lives and his or her local customs. By thus anchoring the direct marketing message in the local environment, a meaning and a reality are given to it which results in its being taken seriously and the reader feeling involved. This personalization of the creative content can be expressed in many ways. The most obvious personalization is choosing the language used at the regional level. For example, in the USA, if the target belongs to the Spanish-speaking community, writing the message in Spanish will contribute to raising the rate of response. By the same token, in India or in Russia, countries where ethnicity and local languages are numerous, using the regional language is a personalization factor that is of interest.

Promotional tools	**Local characteristics**
Contests, lotteries and games	Favorable legal context Religious culture not impregnated with fatalism
Price cut-off	Avoid areas with a negotiation culture and those where price-posting is rare Be careful about legal limits (in France, the notion of the privileged offer can impinges on consumption rights and competition principles [MIS 2000]) The particular case of coupons: a high rate of literacy and the absence of social depreciation of coupon-redeeming behavior
Postponed premiums and gifts	Temporal orientation in the long run Steady economic conditions (weak inflation rate) Symbolic association with gifts
Trials and samples	The most easily generalizable offer, but also the most expensive

Table 11.2: *Characteristics of geographic areas and choice of promotional tool*

Beyond the choice of language, personalization can be more sophisticated. By relying on knowledge of the territory where the target is located, the text can make reference to the local setting on numerous occasions. In order to give an idea of its possibilities, Figure 11.1 presents an example of direct mail advertising having optimized knowledge of the environment of each prospect [ALL 92].

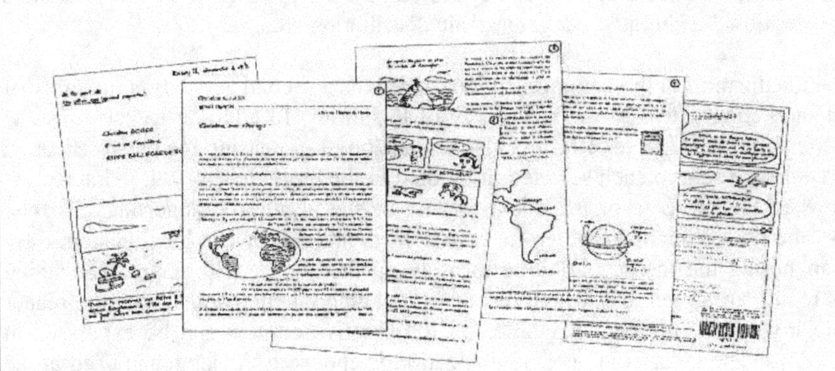

Topics and mechanisms:
A long letter posted in Roissy from a grand reporter addresses the addressee with familiarity, and refers to a common past (a pretext for multiple citations of his geographic environment).
Supports:
An envelope with an accompanying postmark of Roissy.
A bundle of 6 A5 sheets of paper (label holder – letter of 4 pages – subscription bulletin).
A mini-journal of routing mail with: the mini-journal written by the editorial staff, the insert with a subscription offer, the reply on envelope (to return to Roissy), the post-script of the editor in chief of the news-magazine.
Documentation on local territory:
Application to each area of the name of the former French provinces (from a post-revolutionary dictionary) and of the names of the inhabitants of a commune (directory of "*gentiles*").
Personalization based on geographic information:
✓ Enrichment by geographic coordinates and clear translation of these data:
calculation of the jet lag;
calculation of the distances between cities;
choice of tourist sites shown and represented with figures according to their proximity;
choice of the local recipe and of the local newspaper of the geographic area;
Adaptation of the text according to the distance between the monuments and the addressee's home location: "we could go … one night" (>100 kms), "we could go cycling" (<30 kms), or "I expect you tell me what has really changed in …" (km = 0).
✓ Enrichment by census data (number of inhabitants).

Figure 11.1: *The mailing "Alter Ego" of Chronaxies pour Grands Reportages*

In addition to these optimization approaches in the promotional offer and the personalization of the message, the knowledge of local information means that small blunders, which would prove the absence of a real understanding of the firm concerning the needs of the consumers that it contacts, can be avoided. For example, in order to sell a work-out set, it would be ill-advised, in the body of the communication, to make reference to work practices that do not correspond to those of the area considered. Similarly one should avoid making reference to the end of a professional activity at the beginning of the evening when one communicates with individuals living a geographic area where the custom is that office activities end in the middle of the afternoon.

Having looked at firms that introduce geographic information in order to adapt to a limited commercial area, let us now consider the second modality of direct marketing applied to a territory. This concerns firms that are independent of the geographic area and consider the commercial environment. This type of approach is mainly convenient for businesses with a national or international range since their strategy implies the taking into account of a widespread commercial horizon. However, it can also be of interest to other businesses, such as those whose products deal with markets in a geographic niche (physical or climatic restrictions). For example, a hunting and fishing supplies business whose products only appeal to those who frequent certain geographic spaces (island, coastal, swamp, etc.) will identify all of the territories with these physical characteristics in order to communicate and send proposals only to the individuals living in these areas [HAE 00]. Furthermore, if there are new innovations, this approach can help firms located in markets in which the demand has a tendency to become saturated.

This process of identifying target areas resembles supply marketing. It is not a question of adapting the offer to the local demand but rather identifying the territories geographically spread-out in which the inhabitants are the heart of the target of an already defined offer. The firm must change the geographic scale in order to identify potentially fruitful sub-territories. By targeting the areas in which the inhabitants are the closest to the heart of the target, the firm can direct its efforts towards geographic areas where the rate of increase in relation to its commercial offers should be higher. With the core of the offer being predefined based on internal factors, the task is no longer to analyze the local market in order to propose a personalized offer but to find the markets corresponding to a given offer. This clientele is described according to socio-demographic, economic and behavioral criteria. Knowing the profile of the typical customer, one must look for individuals who resemble this customer since they should be the most favorable to the attributes of the product and the most receptive to the method of sale. The introduction of geography therefore corresponds to the stage of identifying the geographic areas in which this typical customer is most represented.

This stage requires the geographic territories to be qualified according to the probability of a positive response from their inhabitants to specific and direct commercial offers. It consists of calculating the rate of penetration of the target market within the local population and comparing it with a normative average. This average can make reference to three types of information. First, the score obtained at the next higher level (national for regions, regional for departments/counties, communal for neighborhoods, average set of blocks). It is thus a question of evaluating the potential of a territory in relation to the larger space that encompasses it. Second, this average can correspond to that of the firm. In addition to the assessment of the coverage incoherence that often leads to rationalizations of the geographic framework, the goal is thus to assess the performance of local outlets with the potential of the territory taken into account. Third, the firm can clarify its decisions with information on the competition. Are competitors located in the same territory? What is their market share and rate of penetration of the trade area? Is it really pertinent to engage in a competitive struggle? The final choice will be made taking into account the strategic orientations of the firm.

If these decisions relating to the spatial coverage of the firm are taken at a more global level (see Chapter 8), direct marketing actions will come increasingly from local outlets. The following point introduces these diverse actions by distinguishing them according to the character of the communication, whether it is addressed or not addressed.

Direct marketing actions in target territories

Whether the territory of action is reduced to a trade area or spread over a much larger commercial space, the actions presented here concern the firms which center their analysis approach on the geographic space. By making statistical inferences based on market studies, or by projecting the significant correlation observed on the current clientele, these firms will have knowledge that they can use in order to select the areas of the actions of their direct marketing operations.

In the operations framework of non-addressed direct marketing, the firm aims at constructing a file of individuals who are sensitive to the firm's offers. The detail of these recruitment operations is listed in Table 11.3.

In the absence of data concerning the target market other than its geographic location, the simplest recruitment operation consists of communicating in an extensive manner throughout the entire area considered. In order to initiate making contact with the firm (written, telephone or electronic reactions), one can either use the five mass media or mailbox distribution (*all mailboxes* distribution). However, these operations, carried out in a uniform manner on a large scale, only yield good rates of response on rare occasions. In order to optimize them, it is preferable to analyze more closely the operation's target and to specify the locations and the media to be favored.

Information on the target	Choice of media and place of delivery
Territorial benchmarking (zip code)	Advertising in local mass media Mailshot in every mailbox
Information on housing demographic and socio-economic data	Selective mailshots Local "animations" in qualified areas
Behavioral information Products and brands purchased Points of sale and places frequented (leisure and work places) Most preferred traditional media Electronic media	Sampling and couponing on products Direct advertising and promotional animations frequented places Direct advertising in local media (press, radio, television) Direct advertising on local most frequented websites

Table 11.3: *Non-addressed operations on target territories*

For this, the firm can qualify the target according to its habitat. This then enables a selection of distribution areas that more strongly match the habitat considered. Thus, to sell lawn and garden equipment, it is pointless to distribute a catalog in neighborhoods with apartment complexes having no garden or yard. A better strategy would be to concentrate direct communications efforts on areas affected by the offer, such as residential areas or urban districts. When the product responds to a need that is not defined by the habitat, the firm can qualify the target according to demographic and socio-economic criteria. These criteria allow individuals to be described according to age, sex, family situation and socio-professional category. An example would be for an information offer on funeral contracts. Priority should be placed on advertising in neighborhoods where the senior target market is over-represented. By the same token, a bus/coach company's catalog offering organized tourist travel packages that do not fall within school holidays should avoid areas where the number of families with school-age children is high. Finally, when these distinctions are not sufficiently differentiating, one must rely on behavioral data. As there are often significant correlations between certain behavioral acts and the expected behavior, the objective is thus to describe the probable behaviors close to the target individual. The behavioral acts that serve to better characterize the heart of the target can be concerned with purchase habits (products or brands purchased, location and frequency of purchase) as well as leisure practices (type of activity and location), professional activity (sector, type of business, career), the preferred media (daily newspapers read, radio stations listened to, television channels and programs watched, electronic media practices), etc.

Once the target market is precisely characterized, the problem is then to select the priority territories and neighborhoods with which to communicate. This results in excluding the spaces where the product proposed in the direct message does not correspond to a need and in selecting the areas where the over-representation of individuals having certain characteristics leads one to think that the offer will be well received. By adopting such an approach, the firm realizes distribution savings (fewer messages distributed) and observes better response rates in the remaining areas. The advantage of these approaches to targeting recruitment areas is, in the short term, to substantially improve the profitability of the operation and, in the long term, to acquire credibility with consumers by showing the firm's ability to communicate intelligently.

By limiting itself to the territories in which the target consumer is more likely to be present, these recruitment operations can thus take the form of either a non-addressed communication distributed in a selective manner or commercial partnership operations with the owners of locations frequented or brands preferred by the target customer.

In the first case, by adopting a communications logic that allows the prospect to make direct contact with the firm, the media used are the *mailbox* and the mass media. It is pertinent to choose the correct medium for sub-communal operations (neighborhoods of a town) while the mass media, even in their local editions, remains more adapted to a larger geographic targeting scale (canton, district, department, region). And, in selecting the most interesting neighborhoods of a town, it is helpful to rely on the Insee data relative to a block and *Iris* sub-communal divisions. If the data available at these scales is sufficient, the firm can carry out a selective distribution in the mail boxes of these areas. If, on the other hand, different or more detailed information is required, the firm will either have to solicit diffusion organizations that have already identified rounds or carry out projections of identified typologies available in the market on communal territories that interest it.

In the second case, by relying on its knowledge of behaviors and activities at the heart of the target, the firm will be able to identify the locations (businesses, sports centers, offices, etc.) where it has strong chances of finding this target. With the knowledge of these "target locations" within selected territories, the firm therefore must consider partnerships with the owners of these locations. These commercial cooperative efforts can lead to putting promotional animations (games, promotional coupons, etc) and on-site advertising into place. These two types of operation should adopt a logic of direct communication with direct contact between the prospects and the firm or the collection of the individual coordinates of consumers with a view to subsequent operations. Finally, when the behavioral information refers to products purchased or preferred brands, the modalities of making contact are different, but the principle remains the same. With the firm expecting to find a high rate of penetration of its target market among the buyers of these products and brands, localized operations of samples or free trial offers of the firm's products should be put into place.

Once the consumer has made contact with the firm, he becomes an individualized target. Having recorded his personal or professional information (phone, address), the firm will from that point on be able to communicate with this *hot prospect* (individual having been active after receiving an offer) by personalizing its messages and its offers. This second constituent of direct marketing actions corresponds to addressed operations. Whether via mail shot or telemarketing, the principal advantage is allowing, from the very first contact, a strong individualization of the communication. In order to carry out this type of action properly, the initial step consists of acquiring a file of individuals residing in the considered area. In the same way as for non-addressed, good knowledge of the characteristics of the target is the key to optimizing direct marketing operations. However, in this case, the optimization no longer resides in the choice of the locations and the media to favor but in the selection and cross-referencing of qualified files.

In the case where there is limited knowledge of the target, the files that a firm will rent for its operation can simply be compilation files. In general, these files only include a list of names and addresses with no other geographic qualification than the road and the postal code. If certain firms carry out analyses based on the first name which allow projections on the age and the probable social level of each individual, this remains approximate. Consequently, because there is a lack of knowledge that would allow true personalization and often a reduced fraction of people belonging to the heart of the target, the rates of response stagnate at very disappointing levels. Distributing a mailing to all the individuals of a compilation file for a given geographic area means operating in an extensive manner. Also, in order to optimize the operation and to increase its profitability, the profile of the target must once more be refined.

If the same three sources of qualification of consumers are used as those in the framework of non-addressed operations, the files to be selected will be different (see Table 11.4). Thus, when the information useful in qualifying and selecting the prospects comes from the habitat, the firm rents files of professionals in the habitat. The firm can also acquire compilation files with a codification of sub-communal zoning (block or *Iris* coding) that it will qualify with the information on the structure of the habitat. It is this last approach that will also be used when the target is not defined by its socio-economic or demographic components. Actually, these data are available at the block level.

Finally, when the data useful for the qualification is behavioral, the firm rents the files corresponding to the sought-after behaviors. In order to obtain the names and the coordinates of the buyers of a specific brand, one rents the file of the customers of that brand. In order to know the consumers who regularly frequent certain stores, one acquires the files taken from operations to secure the customer loyalty or the files superstore membership cards. In order to identify the regulars of certain leisure locations or sports centers, one relies again on the customer files. In order to collect lists of individuals making up the regular audience of certain media, one solicits the files of newspaper and magazine subscribers as well as the customer files of cable networks and Internet service providers.

Information on target	**Selection of prospect files**
Territorial benchmarking	Compilation files with selection of zip codes
Information on housing	Files of housing businesses Compilation files with codification of sub-communal areas
Demographic and socio-economic data	Compilation files with codification of sub-communal areas
Behavioral information Products and brands purchased Points of sale and places frequented (leisure and work places) Most preferred traditional media Electronic media	Brand and product files Private card member files of points of sale and leisure and work places Subscriber files of written media E-mail files (geographic qualification by the access supplier or service provider)

Table 11.4: *Addressed operations in target territories*

Regardless of the original file, the geographic selection of the individuals corresponds most often to the choice of individuals whose postal code coincides with the geographic areas aimed at by the operation. If one wants to carry out a geographic targeting at the French sub-communal level, the block code corresponding to each address must be identified in order to conserve, in the final list, only the names of the individuals residing in the chosen areas. In order to do this, tables of correspondence between postal addresses and the block codification exist. However, these correspondences are not systematically available, as will be mentioned later. The sub-communal targeting approach is currently limited to towns of more than 10,000 inhabitants and to agglomerations of more than 50,000 inhabitants. The efforts related to the codification of the entirety of the French territory will soon allow, however, a more generalized application of this procedure.

11.1.2. *The geographic location of consumers*

From now on, it is no longer a question of qualifying territories in order to take a census of individuals but to locate individuals whose postal coordinates are already possessed by the firm. These addresses are grouped in a file of customers or prospects whose unifying element is not territorial location but more often a behavioral characteristic (subscriber to a magazine, regular buyer of a product or a brand, etc.). Knowing that within the set of data in the fil, there are always the coordinates of each individual, when can the firm use this essential geographic information? After having briefly explained the approach for locating postal addresses, the two means of analysis of this location will be described.

Location of addresses

In order to use the geographic information available through the postal address (as shown in Figure 11.2), the firm first goes through a location of individuals phase.

By using geo-coding software, the firm positions each individual address on a map or gives each address a geographic identifier. After determining the limits of the territories under consideration (choice of the configuration and of the required scale level), it introduces complementary data describing them.

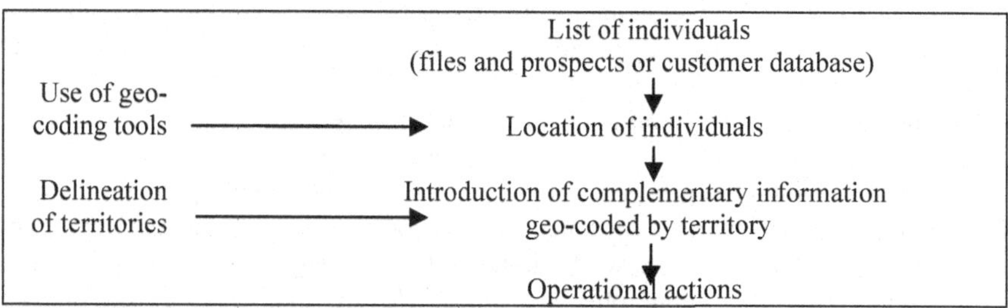

Figure 11.2: *From consumer location to direct marketing actions*

The analysis of located consumers

Once the geographic location of the prospect or of the customer is known, the firm can then adopt two approaches. The first relies essentially on the geographic anchoring of the individual (uni-localized analysis). The second takes into account the location of the consumer in relation to the firm (bi-localized analysis).

When the firm adopts a uni-localized approach, it sets out to identify the territories where current or potential consumers are situated. In addition to adapting the offer and personalizing the communication (approach previously presented for the case of direct marketing; see also Chapter 10), it deals with orienting the canvassing actions.

At the sub-communal level, the idea of prioritized canvassing in the neighborhoods where the prospects and the customers are already numerically numerous relies on the following principle: individuals choose to live in a neighborhood that corresponds to their socio-economic class or that just above it [BAI 84]. Knowing that the individuals choose to live in a neighborhood according to their social class or avoid living close to different people (Berry, 1965, cited in [CHA 98]), the living area expresses a voluntary grouping. There is, therefore, within the neighborhoods of the same town a homogeneity that can constitute an interesting segmentation criterion. With this initial homogeneity being reinforced by a process of cultural homogenization [COS 84], a firm should identify the sub-communal zonings where the number of their prospects as customers is already sizable. Thus, in addition to an action addressed to this already individualized target, it is preferable to carry out recruitment operations on these areas where there is a strong possibility of encountering consumers who resemble this target.

When the firm adopts a bi-localized approach, it proposes analyzing the professional or personal location of the consumer in relation to its own physical locations or to those of its partners. This signifies that the geographic anchorage of the individual is analyzed in terms of metric distance by road and of temporal distance. This type of contact is offered on firms' websites (Darty, Go Sport, etc.) or through the customer service phone reception (assistance service, etc.) in such a way as to direct the prospect toward the closest and most rapidly available correspondent.

Within the framework of an addressed direct marketing operation, this consists of personalizing the communication by indicating the coordinates of the outlet/branch to which the prospect should address himself (geographic appointment of the clientele according to variables of time of access and accessibility). This approach thus matches a downtown trade-name to a strategy of differentiation which aims at valorizing the geographic proximity [MOA 01]. Taking the physical consumer–firm relationship into account is also useful in dealing with and anticipating certain logistic aspects. For example, in mail-order sales, integrating the spatial dimension is fundamental in order to predict the conditions under which the e-offer is made available. If the target territory is characterized by access difficulties (lack of infrastructure, quality of access dependent upon climatic conditions, etc.), these difficulties must be anticipated either by looking for a local partner capable of stocking the supply and redistributing it within the expected time or by readjusting the guarantees made to the consumer (longer delivery periods, service after sale only where available, etc.).

At a time when the Internet is showing its incredible potential in de-localizing and opening up of companies, mentioning the physical relationship between the prospect and the firm may seem surprising. In practice, with connection modalities to the World Wide Web being easy and the infrastructures of transmission of high-bandwidth data, selling and distributing (by downloading) digitized products (software) is a task freed from metric distances and transport limitations. In similar fashion, services such as sale of transport or insurance benefits, translation, advice or even psychotherapy no longer necessarily require a location as long as the confidence of the consumer is ensured. On the other hand, in order to distribute physical and material products, the physical relationship remains undeniable. If a virtual geography of supply and demand exists that has important consequences for commercial strategies [REY 97], physical space retains its influence on the business universe. The Internet represents a tool of deconstruction of the physical commercial space by the creation of a virtual commercial space, but it does not offer the possibility of being definitively freed from physical space. If the arrival of the virtual network has led to a wave of proclamations of the imminent end of physical commercial spaces, reality tells another story. The Internet has had an undeniable impact on the physical commercial space of stores and service provider locations, but it is more an extension of their principal mission. In practice, they have ceased to be simply places for stocking up; they have also become places of social interaction [AUB 99].

Regardless of the use of geomarketing information, the problems of demarcating territory and of the level of precision remain essential. The following section deals with these in order to shed light on actions that are critical to a pertinent introduction of geography into direct marketing.

11.2. The definition of the territory and the level of geographic indirect marketing

Geographic analysis can be anterior (analysis of territories) or posterior (location of individuals) to the research and the identification of target customers. Since geographic analysis is based on the research into representation gaps between consumers and the overall population, the size and the configuration of the geographic area of study strongly influences the results. This dilemma of defining the territory will be developed before tackling the question of spatial scale to be used.

11.2.1. *Definition of territories*

The goal of spatial analysis is to observe recurring and significant phenomena. In the context of marketing, this is a question of identifying the characteristics of the inhabitants of a geographic area. This homogeneity of the socio-spatial class ("social group living in a geographic space", Reynaud [REY 81]) has two explanations. The first, determinist in nature, assumes that location influences the individual. The second, inspired by theories on the constitution of social groups, can be summarized by the familiar expression, "birds of a feather flock together". Irrespective of the cause, this correlation between presence in a territory and the specificity of the consumers has been confirmed several times, which justifies the application of geographic segmentations [FIL 90]. Thus, for the inhabitants of economically underprivileged regions [DER 90, TRI 90] or those of rural areas [CHA 88, MOR 89, PEL 89, PIN 89], the geographic adjustment strategies in the plan of the marketing mix cover all their characteristics.

However, in order to have the chance to identify significant characteristics of socio-spatial classes and in order for them to be usable during operations, the principal problem that has to be solved is the division of space into commercially coherent territories, or territories in which the commercial and marketing approach of the firm is able to be adjusted and standardized at the same time. In creating these divisions, the criteria used can either make reference to stable characteristics of the space considered or be based on the practices of the individuals residing in this space. Once again, we distinguish these two options, while in commercial practice territorial demarcations are always the result of a combination of criteria.

The choice of territorial division that relies on criteria linked to space corresponds to the need to have relatively stable demarcations. Among the criteria used, one can particularly distinguish administrative criteria, geophysical and climatic criteria and criteria based on human activity. Concern about obtaining a stable definition of the territories particularly relates to the dilemma of institutional organizations that have a duty to propose a spatial division conceived for all and for a long time. In order to do this, these organizations rely most often on existing administrative borders. The Insee proposes increasingly refined divisions of urban areas and zones of employment so that the spatial unity of the diffusion of economic or socio-demographic information is able to suit all the applications (local government, public businesses, developers, commercial businesses, etc.). However, the borders used remain those of geo-administrative divisions that date back to the French Revolution. If these administrative limits often use coherent natural borders in order to carry out the spatial division of French territory, they do not always make sense at the more refined levels. They are undeniable because the functioning of the administrative infrastructure and of postal distribution firms is intrinsically linked to these divisions, but they are not sufficient. Among other criteria that can be used, geophysical and climatic aspects provide an interesting approach to dividing up the territory. By taking into account natural barriers and distances, geophysical criteria allow duration (access times, delivery times, response times, etc.) to be calculated and especially to delineate borders. Among these borders, some do not correspond to natural elements (rivers, mountains, etc.). On an urban scale, a wide boulevard can represent a border that consumers will avoid or will not think of crossing. Whether it is the need to look for a pedestrian crossing that is too far away, the necessity of waiting for traffic to stop at a light or, more simply, the absence of a visual perspective on the other side of the street due to the incessant passing of vehicles, at the urban level, "borders" exist that should be taken into account in order to optimize direct marketing campaigns. What good is communicating with residents of a neighborhood or even an opposing sidewalk if the store or agency is situated on the other side of a border that is perceived to be difficult to cross? Finally, climatic criteria allow meteorological particularities of geographic space to be identified. These divisions are especially pertinent when the offer is a function of local climatic conditions (outdoor sporting activities or even indoor sports facilities, types of clothing, food of varying calorific levels, etc.).

In order to have an ever-increasingly coherent and qualifying network of a territory, the description of the territory must be supplemented with other criteria, including those that describe human activity and those related to infrastructures. Among the most traditionally used criteria in describing the importance of human activities, the rate of urbanization is a key variable. This urban/rural distinction has strong differential potential concerning diverse individual consumer practices. The importance of leisure and travel for urbanites, the values and division of more traditional roles amongst rural couples, over-representation of single-parent homes and divorce in large agglomerations, etc., the list of distinctions between urban and rural inhabitants is far from being complete. The more the logistics and the distribution modalities of the offer align with the criteria describing the quality and the level of adjoining infrastructures (distribution network, media coverage, road accessibility, and academic establishments), the more likely it is that the commercial proposal of the firm can be made the object of diverse scenarios. Even if these criteria have already been proved to be useful, the maps that they allow to be drawn covering the French national territory tend to be less stable than in the past as a result of a sharp increase in the mobility of the residents [BEN 98]. In other countries where the level of mobility remains low, they are still particularly relevant since they discriminate between individuals in their reaction to direct marketing media [MER 99]. On the other hand, industrialized countries, including France, must adapt themselves to a new territorial dynamic. In this context, division according to a network of characteristics can present an interesting complementary perspective.

Without questioning the preceding distinctions, which make sense since they cover effective restrictions and express real issues, the second option proposes defining the territory as a superposition of networks of characteristics (residence, profession, purchase, leisure), of representations, of values and of identifications [BEN 98]. This option, centered on the consumer, aims at moving away from sometimes inadequate administrative and normative calibrations of the territory in order to carry out appropriate market segmentations. Thus, calibrating a market at the national or community level presents the advantage of assimilating it in a homogeneous space from the administrative and regulatory point of view, but does not allow a truly homogeneous overview of consumers to be obtained. In practice, can a firm appropriately associate the needs and practices of Alsatians with those of their Breton compatriots or of those overseas? Can one lump together a Spaniard from Andalusia and a Dutch Walloon? Because the disparities are too great, it is often preferable to ignore administrative limits in order to identify behavioral similarities. This explains why, instead of looking to meet the needs of a standard European consumer who does not exist, proximity in regional consumption should be sought in order to identify targets that are identical even though they may be far apart geographically. By relying on the practices of consumers, firms can identify areas that make more sense from a marketing point of view because they represent the geographic anchoring of a market segment.

However, as the analysis must be adapted to each commercial situation, the configuration of the territory is different every time. This therefore poses the problem of which geographic unit to favor. In reality, what level of geographic precision allows adaptation to all the analytical and operational needs of the firm?

11.2.2. *The level of geographic precision*

Faced with the elasticity of the territory according depending on how it is defined and with the need to aggregate the data according to ever-changing conditions, there is a tendency towards defining micro-territories [MAR 96]. In the specific domain of direct marketing, since extensive work has been done with the postal code, the address has now become the favored unit for the geo-referencing of information. After we have discussed the advantages and disadvantages of this choice of postal address, analysis at the sub-communal scale from the view of *direct micro-geomarketing* will be considered.

The postal address as a unit of geographic analysis

In an addressed communications leaflet, the postal address has two qualities. First, it is data that is systematically available. Even the most succinct compilation file possible includes this data, the utilization of which was initially limited to the function of making contact. The second quality is that it is geographic data that is both precise and refined. Knowing that each postal address corresponds to an exclusive location, it is normally impossible to mix up individuals. Moreover, a correctly defined postal address (which includes not only the street number but also the number of the residence) is the highest possible quality unitary geographic scale. It is therefore easy to aggregate the geo-referenced data to the postal address in all its possible configurations, which makes it possible to respond to the diversity of the commercial dilemmas.

Along with these qualities, the geographic unit of the postal address has three deficiencies. The first is linked to the normalization and standardization problems of storing addresses in the files of businesses. For quite some time, an entire technology aimed at normalizing addresses has been developed in order to attempt the integration, in the same database, of coordinates taken from different sources. The ultimate operational objective is to eliminate duplications and, if desired, to benefit from preferential rates offered by postal distribution organizations. Even if software capable of standardizing coordinates and "de-duplicating" automatically a file of postal addresses now exists, there will always remain a part of the data that is unmanageable, which will be a function of the type and rate of error that the firm accepts. Is it better to eliminate false duplications by deleting individual coordinates that appear to be similar (overkill strategy) and thus lose potential targets or is it preferable to retain true duplications ("under-kill" strategy), thus risking communicating several times with the same person but with spelling differences and small errors in the address? In order to avoid this, in the stage preceding the management of duplications, the postal address variable should be verified and corrected. In fact, during the computerized collection of this data, it is always possible for an error to sneak through. However, in order to carry out corrections automatically, one must have a reliable frame of reference for the set of French postal codes, the index of the street numbers, etc. However, currently only French towns of more than 5,000 inhabitants have roads coded (the annual "Rivoli" file, which contained 20,090 "rivolized" towns in 2001), despite a tendency towards the systematic recording of street codes for all towns.

The second deficiency of geographic analysis calibrated to the address is concerned with legislative restrictions dealing with the protection of individual privacy. During the census of the French population (which hitherto has taken place once every nine years but which is gradually moving to a reduced periodicity), following the recommendations of the CNIL, the Insee has set out to preserve the anonymity of people (order of 05/22/1998 relating to the treatment of data following the 1999 census) and to limit the diffusion of sensitive data (nationality and migrations). Thus, the data available at the most refined levels is limited (see Table 11.5). It is possible to obtain tables of correspondence between the addresses of "rivolized" towns and the codification of the block. This therefore authorizes the use of data available at the block level to carry out qualifications of sub-communal zonings. However, with the data incorporating all of the census items only being available at the Iris scale (grouped into blocks), the diffusion of information is unable to access a hidden statistic (results concern about 2,000 inhabitants). So, even if it is possible to qualify urban areas in order to attempt to communicate individually with consumers, a certain statistical vagueness about these individuals still remains. Even though he resides in a given neighborhood, the consumer may be very far from the typical profile of his or her neighborhood. Consequently, the commercial proposal will not catch his or her attention and will not bring about the behavior hoped for by the firm. To deal with such situations, firms wishing to engage in direct marketing operations at the sub-communal level should look elsewhere for the information that will allow them to continue to increase the success rate of their operations.

Sub-communal areas	Related urban areas	Type of information available*
Ilot 15 (equivalent to a block) ≈ 175 inhabitants	Communes of more than 10,000 inhabitants Most communes between 5,000 and 10,000 inhabitants	Division of the population by sex and age categories (0–19, 20–39, 40–59, 60–74, 75+ years) Division of housing into four categories (main home, occasional home, second home, vacant home) Number of persons in main homes
Iris 2000 (small district or set of blocks) ≈ 600 households	Communes of more than 10,000 inhabitants Communes that are agglomerations over 50,000 inhabitants	Every key figure from the census Excluded topics: employment, immigration and nationality

* Only local authorities and other state organizations concerned with urban development can use this other information in their own territory.

Table 11.5: *Census data available at the sub-communal level*

The third deficiency of the postal address is the consequence of this data protection legislation. Because few variables are available at this scale, firms cannot easily acquire qualifying information. If public organizations limit the diffusion of information, the possibility of hiring specialized businesses to carry out studies remains. Thus, the typologies of sub-communal neighborhoods and zonings carried out by private organizations often respond to a firm's need for information. When these typologies are insufficient, it is possible to rely on behavioral data available in the restricted mega-bases for the target territories. Other data on firms is also available at these levels. However, because of the level of precision required, the analysis must be adapted every time. Yet, "the more refined the level of detail of the analysis becomes, the fewer automated analysis formats exist" (Yves Allard, CEO of Chronaxie, from a January 2000 interview). In order to obtain useful information at the sub-communal level, the firm should therefore create its own analysis tool.

In the absence of automatically available data, these custom-made sub-communal analyses represent a high cost, which can constitute an obstacle to territorial qualification at the most sophisticated scales. This consequently means that there are problems concerning the optimal level of analysis, the pertinence and the profitability of analyses on a scale more detailed than the Iris or the town.

The sub-communal analysis level

According to Yves Allard, if the use of the location of prospects targeted at the communal level or higher allows an improvement in the performance of an addressed direct marketing operation from 15 to 20%, this improvement can be doubled if one works at the levels more specific than the Iris.

In addition to the profitability optimization potential (as shown in Figure 11.3), the sub-communal analysis also allows businesses to introduce, in their trade area, the identification of territories that potentially present opportunities rather than relying systematically on a policy of adaptation. For example, a banking agency can work toward locating its best clients by calculating a rate of penetration by sector and by combining these data with socio-demographic, economic and behavioral data taken from mega-bases or from panels of consumers, in order to evaluate an area of high potential situated in the edge of the zone covered by the agency. By being aware of these areas, the agency will then be able to send a selectively distributed recruitment message (non-addressed in mail boxes or addressed by mail shot) to the priority areas.

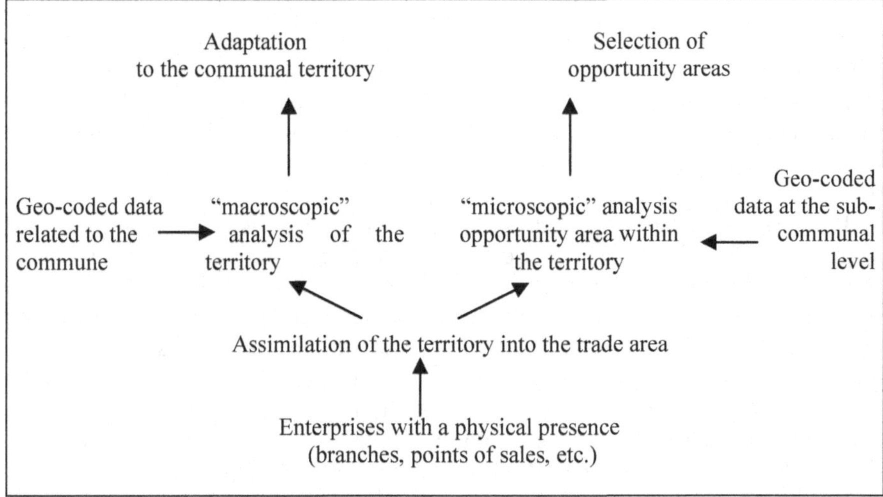

Figure 11.3: *Introduction of a selection logic for target territories at the sub-communal level*

Through this example, the potential of analyses carried out at very specific levels in urban space can be seen. However, the scales currently favored remain the neighborhood or the town. In practice, these two levels of geographic precision represent half of all professional geomarketing operations (45.8% of businesses favor these two levels of precision in their operations according to a 2001 GeoXpand study [EGW 01]). This choice can be explained in part by difficulties that businesses encounter in the acquisition of useful information at more precise levels. Thus, professionals who work at the block or the street level (20.8%), with information not being automatically available, must rely on diverse information sources, which must be identified and researched. Then an attempt has to be made to harmonize them because they will rarely have been conceived according to the same standards. Because of these technical difficulties, the overall cost of obtaining these data, which requires the provisions of a custom service or the implementation of an internal analysis (purchase of data, analysis of time, software purchase, personnel training, etc.), represents a formidable obstacle to the realization of geographic analyses at very precise levels.

Even though the arbitrage between the access cost to sub-Iris information and the expected benefits of operations thus optimized still leads businesses to favor scales larger than the block, an increase in the amount of automatically available geo-referenced data offered at lower levels should lead to a change in the panorama of direct geomarketing practices.

11.3. Conclusion

The use of geography in bringing an analytical approach to commercial activity is not new. Many firms and regional branches have always mapped their sales results in order to reflect ways in which their actions can be optimized (re-dimensioning of trade sectors, transfer of client portfolios, increasing the number of sellers, etc.).

If today is seeing a "geomarketing revolution", this is due to the technical progress of the availability of these tools. Although the cost of the software programs allowing this instant access to the data for a mapped area continues to be an important obstacle to the systematic introduction of geography into the trade approach (30% of firms cite the cost as one of the current disadvantages of geomarketing [EGW 01]), the situation is evolving. Thus, thanks to recent technological innovations and to the Internet, these geographic geo-referenced information management software programs (GIS) are becoming more accessible [BRU 00]. Supplied in the form of services from specialized operators or carried out by non-local personnel thanks to the use of a business intranet, trade analyses of territories and spatial analyses of consumers have become increasingly easy within firms.

At the same time, the principal geographic organizations have become involved in standardization procedures and the search for compatibility and this also contributes to the development of the use of geography by direct marketing firms. The National Geographic Institute, as a specialized French organization concerned with cartography, has thus placed on the market an increasing number of vectorized maps as they have been introduced into the Institute's geographic information systems. Recently, the Insee has supplied correspondence tables between the fine zonings (towns, *Iris*, block) and the frames of reference for the roads in towns and has proposed services aimed at defining information at the block level (to relate the block coding to the postal address). Finally, various private organizations have commercialized typologies that qualify territories at the sub- or super-communal level that can be projected into the Insee divisions (typical profiles are Médiapost, Zad5000 of Claritas, etc.).

In the French framework, businesses now have at their disposal all the tools necessary in order to qualify, down to the level of the address, the prospects and the clients in a territory. However, the use of geographic or geo-referenced data exposes the firm to new difficulties. In particular, even though obtaining localized information currently costs 10 times less than in the early days of geomarketing, the analyses have also become much more complex. By going down to very precise levels, the firm now finds itself confronted with overabundant data that it is not always able to manage. The problem of the relevance of these direct micro-marketing analyses arises. The current preference for the level of precision to be the town or to the neighborhood seems to render unnecessary the potential sub-communal direct marketing approaches, but also shows that the professional approaches are still rather poorly adjusted to the available complexity.

Finally, since these conclusions characterize a static account of space, what can one think about the recent professional and institutional efforts aimed at more effectively understanding and using the dynamics of the spatial travel of consumers?

In 1999, the Insee completed a study on the residential mobility of the French in terms of Iris data on professional and academic mobility. The results of the comparative analysis between 1990 and 1999 showed a multiplication and a lengthening of home-to-work travel (see Chapter 3). If we look at several professional experiments aiming at profiting from this new data, we can expect to see a more generalized development rapidly appearing in the approaches to and the practices of direct communications. Thus, in Strasbourg, the Original.com company suggested using the windshields of the inhabitants' vehicles as a new vector of communication. The content would be adapted to the types of trips made by the owner of the vehicle; this increase in consumer mobility reintroduces complexity and randomness at a time when the efforts of companies are tending towards the establishment of predictive rules.

This increase in consumer mobility should also be studied in the long term. For example, with the increasing number of divorces, a new class is developing. What will geographic anchoring be worth in relation to this class? If the location of individuals loses its potential to qualify individuals and to predict behavior, must the value of geographic information be questioned or should it be integrated by adopting a more dynamic approach? The future application of geographic information in direct marketing will no doubt be less concerned with a set of localized points than with a network of traits defined by the spatial coverage of consumer practices.

11.4. References

[ALL 92], Allard Y., Document de présentation du mailing 'Alter Ego' pour Grands Reportage, Entreprise Chronaxie, Paris, 1992.

[AUB 99], Aubert-Gamet V. and Cova B., Servicescapes: From Modern Non-places to Postmodern Common Places, *Journal of Business Research*, vol. 44, no. 1, pp. 37-45, 1999.

[BAI 84], Bailly A. *et al.*, *Les concepts de la géographie humaine*, Masson, Paris, 1984.

[BEN 98], Benoit J-M., Benoit P and Pucci D., *La France re-découpée*, ed. Belin, Paris, 1998.

[BRU 00], Brusset O., L'Internet établit la norme, *Marketing Direct*, no. 45, April, pp. 61-77, 2000.

[BYR 91], Byrd D., *Le marketing direct: une affaire de bon sens*, Top Editions, Paris, 1991.

[CHA 88], Charrier J-B., *Villes et campagnes*, Collection géographie, Masson, Paris, Milan, 1988.

[CHA 97], Charrière V. and Gallo G., La carte du personnel, note Interne Monoprix, 1997.

[CHA 98], Charrière-Grillon V., L'influence des espaces géographiques sur les valeurs et sur le comportement du consommateur, PhD, January, University of Paris Dauphine, 1998.

[CLI 99], Cliquet G., Marketing et géographie: il est temps de réagir!, *Tribune Libre*, Association Française de Marketing, no. 4, July, http://www.dmsp.dauphine.fr/Afm/AFMFr/tribuneLibre/tL4.html, 1999.

[COS 84], Cosinschi M. and Racine J-B., Géographie et écologie urbaine, in *Les concepts de la géographie humaine*, Masson, Paris, 1984.

[DER 90], Derbaix C., Décisions économiques, famille et chômage, *Recherche et Applications en Marketing*, vol 5, 3, pp. 53-68, 1990.

[DES 92], Desmet P., *Promotion des ventes: du 13 à la douzaine au marketing direct*, Nathan, Paris, 1992.

[DES 01], Desmet P., *Marketing direct: concepts et méthodes*, 2nd edition, Dunod, Paris, 2001.

[DUB 90], Dubois B., *Comprendre le consommateur*, Dalloz, Paris, 1990.

[EGW 01], Etude de GeoXpand Worldwide, in "Géomarketing: mature mais pas assez démocratisé", *Marketing Direct*, no. 55, May, pp. 105-107, 2001.

[FIL 90], Filser M., Méthodologie d'élaboration d'une typologie de clientèle en marketing direct, *Revue Française du Marketing*, no. 126(1), pp. 57-67, 1990.

[FOX 88], Foxman E., Tansuhaj P. and Wong J., Evaluating Cross-National Sales Promotion Strategy: An Audit Approach, *International Marketing Review*, vol. 5, 4, pp. 7-15, 1988.

[GRE 00], Gréneau de Larmalière I. and Staszak J-F., *Principes de géographie économique*, Bréal, Paris, 2000.

[HAE 00], Haegele K., Hunting and Fishing, *Target Marketing*, vol 23, 4, pp.107-109, 2000.

[KEE 94], Keegan W.J. and Leersnyder J.M., *Marketing sans frontières*, InterEditions, Paris, 1994.

[LEH 96], Lehu J-M., *Le marketing intéractif*, Les Editions d'Organisation, Paris, 1996.

[LEW 83], Lewitt T., The Globalization of Markets, *Harvard Business Review*, 1983.

[MAR 96], Marzloff B., Bellanger F., Les nouveaux territoires du marketing, enquête sur le géomarketing relationnel, Collection Points de Ventes, ed. Liaisons, Rueil-Malmaison.

[MER 99], Merchant A., Direct marketing in India, *Direct Marketing*, vol 61, 11, pp. 49-51, 1999.

[MOA 01], Moati P., *L'avenir de la grande distribution*, Odile Jacob, Paris, 2001.

[MOR 89], Mormont M., Vers une redéfinition du rural, *Recherches Sociologiques*, vol 20, 3, pp. 31-349, 1989.

[PEL 89], Pellegrino P., Société rurale?, *Recherches Sociologiques*, vol 20, 3, pp. 423-431, 1989.

[PIN 89], Pinson C. and Jolibert A., Comportement du consommateur, *Encyclopédie de Gestion*, vol. 1, Economica, pp. 345-389, 1989.

[REY 81], Reynaud A., *Société, espace et justice: inégalités et justice socio-spatiale*, collection Espace et Liberté, Presse Universitaire de France, Paris, 1981.

[REY 97], Reynolds J., Retailing in computer-mediated environments: electronic commerce across Europe, *International Journal of Retail & Distribution Management*, vol. 25, 1, pp. 29-37, 1997.

[TRI 90], Trinquecoste J-F., Un cadre d'analyse du comportement du consommateur chômeur, *Recherche et Applications en Marketing*, vol 5, 2, pp. 65-87, 1990.

[USU 90], Usunier J-C., *Management International*, Presse Universitaire de France, Paris, 1990.

Chapter 12

Products and Geographic Information: Geo-Merchandizing

Introduction

Beginning in the 1920s, the first research studies on trade activities placed geography at the heart of the investigations [SHE 88]. Today, as in many other economic sectors, distribution companies use geographic information in order to improve their decisions [SEG 99], dealing mainly with the location of stores and the commercial management of networks. Concerning location, a decision that determines in large part the success of a company [CHA 00, TED 97], geography intervenes when choosing the countries and the regions where to locate, a type of location (shopping mall, downtown or periphery), or even this or that neighborhood or specific site. Numerous normative location models (see Chapter 6) have been proposed for companies in networks, such as banks or retailers [GHO 87, LIL 92]. In addition, the conceptual analysis of spatial strategies is in the development [CLI 98, RUL 00] (see Chapter 8). As far as management of trade is concerned, geography is involved when dealing with the adaptation of price to the characteristics of a trade area [MON 97]. It will also be concerned with the distribution of messages (catalogues, prospectus, display materials, etc.) in some geographic areas more than others, according to the expected efficacy of the communication. However, in this chapter, we will not be discussing location strategy, pricing (see Chapter 9) or communications policies (see Chapters 10 and 11), but policy concerning the supply/offer, knowing that it is on decisions on this that the geographic dimension also reveals itself to be fundamental. Thus, in the hypothesis on which the retailer bases his or her assortment without taking into

---

Chapter written by Pierre VOLLE.

account climatic, economic, demographic and psycho-sociological differences linked to geography, the offer will probably be out of step with customer expectations. Consequently, the effective productivity of the store will be inferior to its potential productivity.

Let us take the example of the window dressings market, consisting of net curtains, curtains, blinds and associated accessories like rods. Studies show that the more modest classes buy considerably more net curtains while better-off classes buy more curtains. Moreover, the discriminating criterion for window blinds is not the socioeconomic category, but age: younger households buy more blinds than older households. For a company specializing in home furnishings, consideration of these consumption data allows the assortment to be adjusted at the individual store level (especially the share of each product type) according to the proportion of wealthy households and young households in the trade area[1]. However, it is important to note that the decision does not consist only of adjusting the assortment to the characteristics of the consumers in the trade area; it is also a matter of taking the competition into account. Following the same example, it is therefore a question, for a given company, of adjusting the offer in window dressings according to the offering proposed by competitors. With all other things being equal, if a competitor proposes a highly discounted offer in a given area, such a store will be automatically perceived as providing less of a choice; the situation will be extremely different if the store is the only one in the area that offers this type of products. Consequently, if a company wants to appear as the main supplier for this category, it should increase the number of products offered in the areas where competition is strong.

The practice of adapting the assortment to a geographic base is sometimes called *geo-merchandizing*. At this stage of the discussion, it is important to define more precisely the term "merchandizing" (see [FAD 00] for a general understanding of the domain). Some people give a very broad definition of this activity. Merchandizing is "everything that takes place at a place of sale in order to improve trade performance" or "all of the ways which help to move the product in the store" [WEL 01]. However, for this last expert, and in a more precise manner, merchandizing covers four concrete functions: the definition of the assortment (products offered, etc.), the presentation of the products in the store (movables, alignment, etc.), the promotional activities (promotions, information about the store) and the management of the section (maintenance, stocking, etc.). Knowing that the profitability of the store depends both on the products sold and on their prices,

1. It will, however, be necessary to consider carefully the data available for the trade area. In practice, the target of the company will not necessarily be representative of the population. For example, the proportion of young households is important if, and only if, these young households fit the target profile of the company (actual target or target aimed at). If this is the case, this information becomes fundamental in adapting the assortment, while, if it is not, it is not relevant. This point seems obvious, but professionals do not always appear to correct this bias systematically when they use geographic data.

certain people even include the fixing of prices as part of the function of merchandizing [MCI 99]. Furthermore, merchandizing can deal with very different units of decision: a group of stores, of course, but also a mail order/distance retailer (the conception of a catalog or of a selling site, etc.), or even a shopping mall or a given neighborhood of a city (the choice of retailers to include, surfaces to allot, locations, etc.).

In the sections that follow, the analysis is limited to dealing either with the functions of merchandizing or with the units of decision studied. Thus, we will limit ourselves to the definition of the assortment, a function that is more important than all others and which is strongly linked to the marketing strategy of the company. As far as units of decision are concerned, we will focus on grocery retailers and specialized companies. The other functions (presentation, promotional activities and management) and the other decision units (catalog retailers, shopping malls, etc.) will therefore not be mentioned.

In this chapter, we systematically tackle geo-merchandizing from both a managerial and a theoretical perspective. We will attempt, first of all, to explain why this practice is developing, by invoking both sectoral arguments and wider theoretical arguments. We will then propose a typology of practices, from the total absence of taking geographic information into account all the way to tactical or even strategic geo-merchandizing. We will conclude the chapter with an examination of the difficulties posed by the implementation of a geo-merchandizing policy and by several research proposals for this emerging domain.

In the guise of a disclaimer to the reader, it is important to specify that even if the practice of geo-merchandizing is becoming more generalized, research on the subject is recent and the number of publications is not great. Because this, what is written here should be considered as an attempt to put the practice into perspective on the basis of theoretical frameworks (opening research perspectives is the primary goal of this chapter) rather than as a synthesis of an abundant existing literature. At this stage of development, several of the theoretical arguments formulated below are therefore of a speculative nature.

12.1. The factors explaining the development of geo-merchandizing

Geo-merchandizing is an increasingly common practice, especially among grocery retailers. If this practice is difficult to quantify (how many companies or categories of products are concerned, for example), it is clear that the specialized press and professional meetings use it quite a bit.

There are many examples. The British company Tesco has announced that its data warehouse serves "to refine the assortment according to the needs of the trade areas", among other functionalities (segmentation of customers, stock management, and adjustment of promotional policies, etc.). In addition, Saresco, which manages stores at airports, has adjusted the 18,000 references proposed for the characteristics of each of its 100 boutiques. For example, the area reserved for cognac is larger in shops where Japanese customers are more numerous. Independent companies seem particularly advanced in terms of geo-merchandizing, in light of their decentralized culture. For example, Système U organizes its assortment at three levels (the joint section (i.e. the selection common to all stores), the regional and local supplements); the constructing of the offer therefore clearly integrates the geographic dimension. Monoprix also uses geographic information in order to modify its assortments [CHA 00]. Thus, one of the stores in the chain has a perfume section of 114 m² compared with 175 m² in comparable stores, while the consumption indexes for the trade area showed a strong potential (index 172). Based on these data, a decision was made to increase the area of the section by 86%, to 212 m². As a result of this enlargement, sales increased by 54%[2].

Geo-merchandizing has developed at the same time as the growth of geographic information systems and as more sophisticated data has become available [LAT 01]. With this being said, several strategic mechanisms can be used to explain why these methods have spread in the distribution sector. In reality, an information system, however sophisticated it is, will never be utilized unless it responds to a strategic requirement. In this chapter, we suggest that geo-merchandizing responds to three such demands: organizational differentiation, the attractiveness of the trade name and negotiating power with suppliers. At the same time, several theoretical approaches can be put forward to explain these demands, notably the spatial differentiation of products, the consumer decision process, attraction models, competitive analysis and even the political economy of channels.

12.1.1. *From consumer spatial heterogeneity to organizational differentiation*

Consumer spatial heterogeneity and store frequentation behaviors argue for a strong organizational differentiation. In other words, it seems necessary to integrate the diversity of the milieux within the organization (structure, decision process, modes of management, etc.).

Spatial heterogeneity of behaviors

We will not consider the diversity of values and of consumption behaviors at the international level, a subject that has already been the object of much research [VAL 93]. However, this diversity also is found at regional and local levels, a phenomenon that is somewhat less well documented [CHA 98] (see Chapter 3).

---

2. It should be noted that the sales figure per square meter decreased 17% (which says nothing, however, about the evolution of the profit margin).

In France, studies carried out by institutes based on mega-bases or panels show large disparities from one region to the next. Three examples are: ice cream consumption varies from an index of 91 (Parisian region) to one of 116 (South-East region); milk consumption varies from an index of 88 ("Centre" region) to an index of 111 (Parisian region); and the consumption of beer varies from an index of 80 (South-West region) to an index of 152 (North region)[3]. The disparity of consumption indexes is probably even stronger at the local level, even within the same region.

This phenomenon of spatial heterogeneity of consumption is explained both by the action of the milieu on the individuals – an "environmentalist" perspective – and especially by a mechanism of geographic self-selection. Individuals have a tendency to live in neighborhoods comprised of people who resemble them. These phenomena of grouping together have been studied for quite some time, notably by sociologists from Chicago [FIS 97].

However, irrespective of the processes that explain these spatial configurations of consumption – a subject that goes far beyond the framework of this chapter – the retailer finds himself faced with a heterogeneous market for each product category[4]. The quantities consumed vary greatly from one area to the next, as do preferred brands, the sensitivity to retailers' brands, price elasticity, etc. In one way, each trade area therefore constitutes a specific market.

The geographic diversity of price elasticity has been largely brought to the fore in scientific literature[5]. Thus, following the work of Bolton [BOL 89], Hoch and his colleagues [HOC 95] have shown that two thirds of the price-elasticity variation from one store to the next is explained by demographic and competitive variables indigenous to the trade area studied (level of education and salary, real estate values, geographic proximity to discounters, etc.). If Kalyanam and Putler [KAL 97] are less clear concerning ketchup, this does not diminish the fact that price elasticity variations from one postal code to the next can be explained by certain socio-demographic differences. This result is also confirmed by Mulhern and his colleagues [MUL 98] in a study which deals with the liquor sections within 35 stores of the same company. These results on the variations of elasticity to the promotions from one area to the next have been studied for France by Macé [MAC 00].

---

3. One could guess that a number of underlying factors may explain these disparities: for example climate (ice cream), demography (milk), and consumption culture (beer).
4. Furthermore, even if local consumption is homogeneous, the demand for a product or a store could vary in a sensitive manner – by a factor of two according to the studies proposed by Géopotentiel (http://www.lsa.fr). This is explained both by the location of the store in its trade area and by the quality of the traffic generated, which is itself a function of the marketing strategy of the company (target aimed at, dimensions of positioning, etc.).
5. Here, we will not distinguish between price elasticity and promotional price elasticity.

If the consumption behaviors vary greatly from one zone to the next, they will obviously also affect the store-choice criteria, notably the role of the assortment in the decision of frequentation[6] [ARN 83, FOT 93]. Other facets of the frequentation of stores – such as the frequency of visits – can also vary from one trade area to the next, in parallel with socio-demographic differences [KIM 99].

These numerous studies show therefore that the spatial heterogeneity of consumption behaviors and frequentation of stores make the adaptation of trade policies to the specifics of each trade area necessary.

Adaptation and differentiation of the organization

The integral acceptance of a distribution concept can present a certain number of strategic advantages [GOL 01]. Standardization makes it possible to communicate a clear positioning, leads to scale economies and gives the ability to implement decisions rapidly since the network is homogeneous.

However, an entire wave of the literature in strategic management has shown that the adaptation of the company to its environment is a condition of performance, or even of survival in the middle to long term [VAN 85]. If the components of the business are confronted by different milieux, it is important that each component adapt itself to its environment and that the business internalize the diversity of the milieu, thus leading to a differentiated organization [LAW 67].

If one takes the parallel between the case that interests us here, a distribution business that aims to reinforce its chances of reaching high performance levels will therefore need to differentiate itself (at the strategic and organizational level), because each store finds itself in a very specific trade area. Studies show precisely that the highest-performing distribution companies have learned to adjust their assortments to the characteristics of the trade areas in which they operate [GRE 99]. Geo-merchandizing therefore plays a fundamental role by allowing the retailer to adapt to the diversity of the environment, to the particular requirements and demands of each market[7] (quantities purchased, brands preferred, choice criteria, etc.). Among the different means of action, merchandizing is without a doubt one of the most fundamental and most flexible in allowing an organization to differentiate itself.

6. These criteria are not stable in an area, or even exogenous, because they depend on the competitors present. Thus, the arrival of a competitor like Wal-Mart in a trade area obviously modifies the hierarchy of the choice criteria [ARN 98].

7. At the international level, the adaptation of assortments to targeted countries is also a condition of success [AZI 00].

12.1.2. *From the usefulness of an assortment for the consumer to the attraction capacity of the store*

For decades, customers have become accustomed to buying a large number of products under the same roof, during a single visit (the one-stop shopping phenomenon), in order to decrease their costs for transport and the search for information. In order to respond to this, the role of distribution therefore consists of constructing a coherent and attractive assortment composed of a large number of references, within the restriction of a fixed space.

However, even if multiple purchases constitute the general case in reality, most of the economic spatial models consider the purchase of a single product or, in the more complex models, the purchase of two products simultaneously [EAT 97a]. With the gravitation models, the attraction capacity of a large number of stores is measured with a simple indicator: the size or the number of references offered. Having said that, this approach does not allow a valorization of the coherence of the assortment[8]. In reality, in order to meet the demands of potential customers, the references should not only be numerous, but should also be chosen to be complementary or substitutable and to form, in the end, a coherent lot.

The geo-economic models currently available therefore only have a very remote connection with reality: either one considers a retailer who sells only one product (or two products at the most), or one considers that the number of references *itself* constitutes a factor of attraction, no matter what the references are (whether preferred or not, unique or not, etc.). Although the gravitation model constituted a methodological and conceptual advance, the complementarity and substitution links between the products are still ignored[9].

One-stop shopping: the search for variety and flexibility

The consumption of a particular product generally produces a marginally decreasing usefulness, irrespective of the degree of satisfaction that it produces at the outset. With the consumer drawing an intrinsic pleasure in not always consuming the same products, he or she therefore searches for variety [AUR 91]. However, variety has a high information cost (identifying the alternatives, informing oneself and comparing them, etc.). Because of this, the client strongly valorizes one of the functions of the retailer, that which consists in aggregating the offer, after

8. For the same universe of products, this approach also does not allow recognition of the differences between the narrow and deep assortments (the strategy of the specialist) and the wide and somewhat deep assortments (the strategy of the generalist). In other words, with equal surface areas (or an identical number of references), the generalist and the specialist will automatically have the same attraction capacity.

9. This question seems to be fundamental and cannot be shrugged off under the pretext that the formalization is extremely complex [BEG 88]; in these conditions, the formalized approach should be put in parentheses (at least initially).

selecting the best choice possibilities, which in part involves his reputation [SCH 00][10]. This "informational" efficiency of the retailer – which allows consumers to compare easily the offers within an acceptable time and place range – is particularly important in a society where information is dispersed and where innovations are frequent (hence an elevated risk). As a result, if the consumer valorizes variety for an innovative product category, if he or she suffers a high information cost and if he or she fears risks, the retailer will therefore be advised to enlarge the assortment in order to bring a informational value to the customer. However, this strategy of constructing an attractive assortment is not necessarily valid for all types of customers, which makes an area by area assessment necessary[11].

Several authors have also shown that the consumer particularly valorizes "flexible" assortments [KAH 91]. In practice, the customer is generally in a situation of uncertainty concerning his or her preferences and future choices. As a result, he or she valorizes both the assortments that include his preferred products (see section 12.1.1) and the assortments that include dissimilar products.

As an illustration, if one considers an assortment that includes n products, product $n + 1$ will be strongly valorized if it is part of the entire set of consumer considerations (its probability of being purchased is not zero) and if the product is different from the n products already proposed. It is clear that product $n + 1$ being perfectly substitutable for product i, which is part of the assortment, does not increase the total attraction capacity of this assortment[12].

One knows that these links of complementarity and of substitution depend little on the objective characteristics of the product [AUR 93]; products that are not very similar can finally fulfill the same functions in a given situation, such as a glass of Coca Cola and a glass of Evian water to quench one's thirst, even if the two products do not really resemble one another (substitution without similarity). It is therefore difficult to understand the relationships without studying the cross-

---

10. In other words, the retailer should not settle for presenting an exhaustive offer in order to pretend to fulfill his or her function efficiently. He or she should also select and give a hierarchy to the offer, or stratify it. Let us note that the first conceptions of electronic trade did not take this function into account, favoring instead "hyper-choice" [VOL 00]. However, hyper-choice presents a large number of disadvantages for the potential customer.

11. The negative side effects of too large an assortment should also not be neglected, notably on the time spent in the store. In other words, if the number of references rises, the organization of the section should be perfect, lest the customers fall into great confusion. Construction of the assortment and presentation therefore go hand-in-hand.

12. However, let us note that this result can be modified if the consumer wishes to engage himself in comparison shopping (he visits the store to compare the products before choosing), because the store is used as a source of information. Being able to verify that two products are equivalent and therefore to facilitate a choice is in itself a function of the retailer. This can particularly be the case in certain product categories (telephones, for example).

elasticity between products[13]. If the retailer wishes to optimize his or her assortment, he or she should respond to the demands of variety and flexibility. To do this, he or she should more specifically know the cross elasticity between the products that constitute his or her assortment (between large categories and between references for a given category), so that he or she can construct a coherent and therefore attractive assortment. Yet, this cross-elasticity varies significantly from one area to the next. For example, product P_1 can be substitutable for product P_2 in area Z_1, but not in area Z_2. As a result, it will be more appropriate to propose conjointly P_1 and P_2 in area Z_2 rather than in area Z_1.

Spatial differentiation and the advance of goods

In classic economic theory, exchanges are realized without any reference to space [EAT 97a]. To get around this deficiency, economists, notably Debreu, have proposed defining all merchandise on the basis of a set of differential properties, including the date and the location at which this merchandise is available. Ponsard [PON 88] writes, "[the] same product accessible in two different locations therefore defines two distinct merchandises." However, for the same author, if an actualization is possible on a temporal scale (meaning that the value of merchandise available in the future can be determined from that of merchandise immediately available by applying a discount factor), this actualization is not possible on a spatial scale. In other words, "it is impossible to express the local value of distant merchandise using an exchange rate that would be to space what the discount rate is to time." In fact, one cannot say that an individual systematically depreciates far-away products. Faced with this impossibility of handling time and space in a similar way, the objective of geographer–economists consists of proposing an analysis framework specific to the spatial economy, like the one developed by Eaton and Lipsey [EAT 97b]. Here, consumer preferences are distributed in a continuous space of parameters that describe the nature of each product. Consumers attach a preference of varying degrees to certain locations and can therefore be described by their coordinates in this space[14] (or their "address"). Once the original framework is specified, the authors revisit the conceptual tools of the geographic economy, such as the central places theory [EAT 97c].

In particular, according to this central places theory [CHR 33], goods can be characterized by their range, meaning "the maximum distance that a consumer [is willing] to travel in order to acquire this good." An assortment capable of attracting a large number of visitors is therefore composed of goods having a high range.

13. For more precision, it must be pointed out that these links of complementarity and of substitution concern either the moment of purchase or the moment of consumption.

14. A fundamental question is to determine the number of parameters necessary in order to restore the richness and the affinity of the preferences.

The construction of an attractive assortment

In order to construct an assortment that is attractive to the eyes of the targeted consumers, the retailer should identify the products with a strong range, coherent with the mission of the company and with the territory of the brand[15], and support these products by proposing complementary products that respond to the variety and flexibility demands of the consumers. Within the framework of this chapter, our conclusion consists of saying that these analyses will be carried at the local level, because the notions of variety, flexibility and range vary from one trade area to another. This is notably the case because the judgments of consumers are subjective and related to the competitive commercial offer, which varies precisely from one area to the next[16].

12.1.3. *From the capacity to propose a reorganization of the trade area to the negotiating power of the supplier*

At this stage, we have postulated that geo-merchandizing is developing because it allows the retailer to reinforce his or her position in the market, as much *vis-à-vis* his or her clients as his competitors (degree of adaptation to the environment and attraction capacity). However, geo-merchandizing is also developing in response to the demand of the suppliers. Thus, beginning in the mid-1990s, the Kronenbourg brewery suggested the use of Pluton +, an analysis application of geographic data that allows merchandizing recommendations to be formulated concerning 1,200 trade areas; each French store of more than 1,000 m² can obtain a merchandizing recommendation for its beer section that is adapted to its specific case. In 1997, the Marne and Champagne Diffusion company (Lanson, Alfred de Rothschild, etc.) proposed a system for calculating the theoretical potential of each of the 1,100 French hypermarkets, with merchandizing advice as support. Based on the examples mentioned above (and numerous others), one can say that geo-merchandizing constitutes a stake in the rather tense relationships between manufacturers and retailers. In fact, it can be seen that the geographic approaches of merchandizing have largely been pushed by manufacturers, generally ones who are leaders in their category. Each manufacturer wishes to demonstrate to the retailer his or her expertise in the market, so as to reinforce his or her position in negotiations and his or her role in the political economy of the channel [DHA 01, FIL 89].

---

15. This does not mean that the distribution company should introduce any product into its assortment under the pretext that the range is high. The reference to the mission of the company should allow a filtering of the products that are "compatible" with the company, in the same way as extensions of the brand are judged more or less compatible with the parent-brand if they enter in the territory-product of the brand [CHA 96].

16. The subjective character of judgments formulated by consumers can be explicitly introduced into attraction models, as shown by Cliquet [CLI 90].

To conclude this first section, one can say that geo-merchandizing is becoming more widespread under the *joint* pressure from retailers (search for a better adjustment with the environment and a stronger attraction capacity) and from manufacturers (search for stronger negotiating power). However, if geo-merchandizing is henceforth to be a common technique, the variety of practices in this domain is important. Certain retailers will content themselves with adapting the total surface area of the store to the size of the trade area, while others will calculate the potential sales per category and allocate space accordingly. This is why proposing a typology of practices is necessary.

12.2. A typology of geo-merchandizing approaches

In terms of distribution, irrespective of the theme studied, it is essential to clarify the level of analysis. Because of this, the following sections will deal with the geo-merchandizing of a given company in its national territory.

12.2.1. *The premises of geo-merchandizing*

Certain companies implement their distribution concept across the company, irrespective of the characteristics of the trade area. This is the case for several *hard discounter* networks, especially German ones, for whom the search for the lowest cost is so imperative that the slightest shift in relation to the base concept is sought. Professionals also consider that Intermarché does not play the geo-merchandizing card very much, at least much less than other networks of independent stores such as Système U and Leclerc, for whom local adaptation is the keyword [CHA 00]. However, company-wide implementation is rare. For example, even if products are rigorously identical from one location to the next, the architecture of McDonald's restaurants is adjustable (surface area, decoration, etc.) according to the city or the neighborhood in which the unit is located, which is in counterpoint to the extreme standardization of the products. Furthermore, for very diverse reasons (variability of real estate cost, availability of areas, attitudes of equipment suppliers, etc.), stores are often very heterogeneous in terms of surface area. For example, the 360 Monoprix stores vary from less than 1,000 m^2 to more than 3,000 m^2.

The surface area of the store is very often determined by the size of the trade area, as shown in Figure 12.1, which is for a company specializing in home equipment[17] (89 units). A coefficient of correlation of 0.82 was found between the two series, significant at $p < 0.001$. The first stage of geo-merchandizing consists of adapting the sales surface area to the trade area[18]. The assortment therefore has to be

17. This analysis was carried out by the author and was not published.

18. Note, however, that this simple approach, which consists of adjusting the surface area of the store to the size of the local market is not systematically followed. A recent study [LOR

modified. However, in this configuration, which we will call *the premises of geo-merchandizing*, the adaptation of the assortment to the trade area is not programmed directly. It is the result of another decision; that of adjusting the sales surface area. The adaptation of the assortment is only a consequence, generally considered as a restriction linked to the sales space and not as a strategic opportunity to keep closer to the expectations of the target.

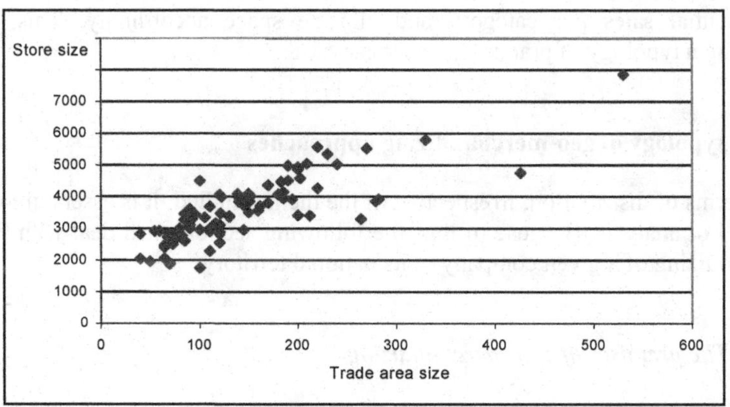

Figure 12.1: *Relation between store size (in m²) and trade area size (in thousands of inhabitants)*

However, geo-merchandizing is used with much more complex decisions, whether tactical or strategic geo-merchandizing is concerned.

12.2.2. *Tactical geo-merchandizing*

Putting a geo-merchandizing policy into place initially means fixing three parameters: the geographic unit, the product unit and the type of adaptation.

For the geographic unit, the company can adapt its assortment decisions at the regional level or at the level of each store. With most companies being organized around a regional base, deciding not to adapt the assortment at this level appears to be a first step in using and refining a geographic information system, determining

---

99] carried out on a non-specialized American company (81 stores studied) showed that the correlation between the size of the stores and the size of the sales area is only 0.31 (this correlation is only 0.27 when one considers the potential market in terms of value rather than of number of inhabitants). In this study, more than half the stores had a surface area that differs appreciably from the optimal surface area (that which would allow maximizing sales per m²).

the most pertinent performance indicators, learning the managerial aspects linked to geo-merchandizing, training the personnel to use the tools, etc. before carrying out a more refined adaptation, store by store.

For the product unit, the company can adapt the assortment at the universal level, at category level, for product segments or for specific items. Two types of products, which can take on a truly strategic dimension, require careful consideration: the brands of the retailer (and the initial prices) and the regional products. It goes without saying that, depending on the level of precision retained, the necessary items of information for making decisions that relate to the circumstances will be increasingly numerous. It is therefore necessary to adapt the aims to the available means. Depending on their degree of maturity in terms of geo-merchandizing, certain traders will content themselves with making decisions that deal with *meta-categories* and others will be able to make decisions dealing with precise items.

To conclude the discussion of the type of adaptation, the company can simply content itself with reviewing each product unit, asking if each product will be included or not in a given geographic unit. However, the company can go further in the implementation of geo-merchandizing and tackle more complex questions, such as how much space should be allocated to each product unit. For example [CHA 00], a Monoprix store had an index of 37 for consumption in the baby-wear department in its trade area (defined by a radius of 15 minutes on foot from the store). As a result, the surface area allocated to the department was decreased from 61 m² to 24 m². The department was reorganized, which led to an increase in sales of 8% and an increase in sales per m² of 164%.

Determining whether a given product unit should occupy more or less space in a given store is an important question. If this question has been the subject of much research at the level of specific categories (meaning how space should be shared between the items of the same category), the allocation of space *between* categories, which is a very strategic decision, has only been the subject of a few research studies. As Desmet and Renaudin [DES 98] show, the elasticity of sales to the space varies strongly from one category to another. The average elasticity is 0.21 with a large variance: this elasticity is high for fruits and vegetables and underwear (around 0.5), but not significantly different from zero for tools or baby-wear. If the results of this study on a French chain of variety stores cannot be directly generalized, taking these differences of elasticity into account still constitutes a measure of profitability, with the possibility of being able to adjust this elasticity to local conditions (store type, socio-demographic profile of the area, etc.) and to put in place a more refined geo-merchandizing policy.

In summary, certain traders will content themselves with making decisions concerning the presence or the absence of certain categories at the regional level (case 1 of Table 12.1), while others will allocate a different space to specific items, store by store (case 2 in Table 12.1). Case 3 is discussed below (see section 12.2.4).

	Region			Store		
	Category	Segment	Item	Category	Segment	Item
Absence or presence	1					
Allocated space				3		2

Table 12.1: *A typology of geo-merchandizing approaches*

However, it goes without saying that a company can adapt the sophistication of its approach according to the type of product considered. Thus, for certain products the decision will be rather basic (presence or absence of the category), while for others the approach can be much more sophisticated, determining the space to allocate, item by item. The decision whether or not to handle all the categories in the same manner can be justified fully, at least initially, when the company is at the learning stage. This having been said, the retailer can also decide that the sophistication that has been agreed is not necessary for all categories, only for the most strategic ones. In this manner, the company concentrates more of its means of analysis and its coordination efforts on the most important categories, those which play a determining role on the consumer traffic and/or on the consumer basket, or even on the image of the store (price, choice, freshness, etc.).

12.2.3. *Strategic geo-merchandizing*

Beyond the tactical decisions that deal with the presence or the absence of certain products and on the space that is allocated to them according to the trade areas, geo-merchandizing can sometimes take on a truly strategic dimension. From our point of view, geo-merchandizing becomes strategic when a company puts into place an organization that does not solely rely on the size of the stores or on the regional geography, but on differentiated formats.

Certain companies structure themselves around large regions and others introduce a segmentation of stores according to their size. For these two configurations, geo-merchandizing is not really strategic because it does not change profoundly the ways of working.

However, certain companies go further. They group their stores according to different formats and give a different commercial status to each one them[19]. By

19. In the long run, one could even envision different managerial responsibility for each of these formats (although, to our knowledge, no company has done this so far).

acting in this manner, the company pursues a truly strategic approach, because it becomes *structurally* an aggregation of differentiated formats, each format constituting a different strategic domain of activity. The strategic segmentation of a group of stores is determined on the basis of the potential of the area for the whole range of products in a type of supply (grocery and hardware for example), the size of the store (a variable that remains fundamental) and the competitive environment (the presence or absence of discounters, for example).

An approach that was put in place by Monoprix in 1998 will serve as an example [CHA 00]. Although the company does attempt to impose the general Citymarché concept through its institutional communications, the whole group of 360 stores (after the buy-out of Prisunic in 1997) is still divided into two large families, which form a total of seven groups of stores. The first family includes 174 stores (the Citymarchés, *stricto sensu*), while the second family includes the stores that do not offer grocery items. The family of the Citymarchés is organized around four groups of stores: the City Stars, the Citys, the Ali Plus and the Classiques[20]. Each format possesses its own characteristics (surface area, type of neighborhood or town, proportion of sales in food, potential). Once the stores have been segmented, a different assortment and tariff policy is assigned to each format. Thus, the dermo-cosmetics section is strongly developed in the City Stars; an assortment of men's and children's clothing is differed; and cultural products and homeware are also represented. The pricing policy is much less aggressive than in the Ali Plus stores, because these stores generally face formidable competition from a variety stores (Intermarché, hard discounters, etc.).

To conclude this section on geo-merchandizing practices applied to the strategic perspective, before going on to consider the tactical approach, we will give an example of implementation.

12.2.4. *A geo-merchandizing application: a model for space allocation between product families*

To our knowledge, only one scientific research study directly linked to this subject has been published [CAM 00]. The objective of this article was to determine whether the adjustment of the space allocated to each category, store by store, causes the total profit of the retailer to increase. The researchers proposed two models that will allow *in fine* the retailer's profit to be modeled as an aggregation of profit per category, taking the interactions between these categories (complementarity and substitution relationships) into account.

20. A supplementary segmentation allows the isolation of the City Stars and the Ali Plus, which represent a particularly high potential in grocery retailing.

The first model allows the sales of a particular category to be explained on the basis of three sets of factors: variables specific to the category (notably the space that is allocated to it and the space allocated to the other categories), variables specific to the store (notably its size) and variables specific to the trade area (notably the degree of competition in the area and the socio-demographic and economic profile of its inhabitants). The second model allows the total sales of each store to be explained on the basis of the characteristics of that store, the characteristics of the area and the attraction capacity of the proposed categories. The two models are linked together by this last variable called the *intrinsic attraction of proposed categories*. The effect of each category on the consumer basket is captured in the first model, together with the cross-elasticity (i.e. the way in which the increase of sales of a category can affect the sales of complementary or substitutable categories).

Finally, based on these two models, the authors have formulated a total profit optimization model, which leads to recommendations in terms of allocation of space between categories. This profit optimization at the company level takes into account the total sales of each store, the share of each category within each store, the unitary profit per category and the management cost of each category (a linear function of the number times it is restocked).

This research leads to practical recommendations that can be implemented rather easily. In practice, these models allow two effects of each category to be captured: an effect on the attraction capacity of the store (*traffic* effect) and an effect on the sales of complementary and substitutable categories (*consumer basket* effect). Furthermore, these two effects depend on numerous contextual variables linked to the store and to the trade area in which it operates[21]. One can therefore determine whether or not geographical differences taking into account in the rules for allocating space between categories has an effect on the company's profit.

It is not necessary to give the specification of each model here and interested readers are naturally invited to read the original article. On the other hand, after having explained the main aspects of the conceptual model, it is probably appropriate to underline the principal outcomes of the research. We should point out

21. It should be noted that the direct effect of the characteristics of the store and the characteristics of the trade area on the stores does not necessitate adapting the space allocated to each category (for example, total store sales are a function of the purchasing power of the inhabitants of the area, no matter what the category). On the other hand, the indirect effect of the store characteristics and the area on the attractiveness of each category (and their effect on the traffic and/or the consumer basket) is the subject of the research. In other words, an advantage of this model is that it distinguishes between the direct effect and the indirect effect of geographic variables on performance. In this way, it is possible to determine precisely what can be gained by a better allocation of space between categories (according to the extent of the indirect effect, via the differential attractiveness of categories from one area to another).

that this was a study carried out on a non-specialized company (of the *hypermarket* type) composed of 55 stores. Based on the recommendations formulated by the directors of the company, the researchers broke down the stores into 17 large categories, organized into four sets: *basic* products (grocery, self-service dairy products, etc.); the *loyalty* products (fruit and vegetables, fish, bakery, sliced deli products, etc.); *textile* products (shoes, women's clothing, etc.); and the *luxury* products (brown goods, home equipment products, cultural products, sports articles, etc.). The data covered 2 years, which gave 1,870 (55 × 17 × 2) options from which the models could be constructed. The socio-demographic and economic variables available for each area (30 variables initially) were synthesized, by factor analysis, into four non-correlated factors: young families; modest families (multiracial areas including single-parent households and households with a low income); middle-class families; and families with only children (notably older households). Two variables complete the description of each area: the number of "nomads" (individuals who work in the area, without living there) and the nature of the milieu (urban or not).

The model that allows the total sales of each store to be estimated has a good fit ($R^2 = 0.63$). It highlights the direct effect of the socio-economic and demographic characteristics of the area on sales. However, only two variables are shown as significant for sales: the urban nature of the area (a dummy variable) and the presence of families from the middle class. Even if the competitive variable is (positively) related to total sales, the *direct* effect of the characteristics of the area is modest in the end. However, total sales are definitely linked to the attractiveness of the proposed categories, which shows a strong *indirect* effect[22].

The results show that the local variables have a significant impact on the sales of each category, but that this influence varies strongly from one category to the next. Thus, the sales of *basic* categories are little influenced by local variables, while sales in the *textiles* or *luxury* categories are strongly linked to local conditions. The results for the category of products that influence loyalty are mixed. Thus, the sales for delicatessen and fish sections are significantly linked to local conditions, which is not the case for fruit and vegetables and the bakery.

The study also shows that the sales of each category are linked to competitive conditions (the presence of other non-specialized stores as well as presence of specialized stores in the area), to the space that is allocated to them, as well as to the space that is allocated to other categories[23]. However, this cross-elasticity is not all significant; far from it. In certain cases, the space allocated to a category influences the sales of other categories in a positive fashion (complementary products) or in a negative fashion (substitutable products). Some other results are surprising. Thus,

22. Total sales are also linked to a most important control variable: the size of the store.

23. The elasticity of the sales to the space allocated is globally similar, category by category, to results already published [DES 98].

for example, the space allocated to the delicatessen section is positively linked to the sales of shoes. These results can be explained by the layout of the departments and the time passed in these departments by customers (notably standing in line to for sliced products).

The share of sales explained by the variables retained in the study varies strongly from one category to the next. Thus, the determination coefficients for the fish section, the bakery and the self-service dairy products fall in a range between 0.65 and 0.70, because a large number of variables are significant (size of store, space allocated, intensity of the competition, local socioeconomic conditions). On the other hand, the sales of some other categories remain unexplained, with R^2 close to 0.2 (women's clothing, children's clothing, meat) or even 0.05 (interior hobbies). No matter which aspects are considered, taking local conditions into account (especially the socioeconomic and demographic profile of the area) leads to significant and clear improvements, with increases of the determination coefficient between 0.08 and 0.26 according to the category.

In conclusion, how does the adaptation of the space allocated to each category manifest itself in terms of profit for the retailer? The profit model used by the researchers gives an answer to this complex question, taking into account the margin rate for each category and, admittedly considerably simplified, but realistic cost function. The conclusions are as follows: by adapting the space allocated to each category based on local information, for an unchanged assortment, the net result increases by 12.8%, which, in the context of hyper-competition between retailers in markets that are often mature, should not leave companies indifferent[24]. The authors also show that their methodology leads to concrete recommendations. Thus, they divide the whole group of stores into four types and for each type present recommendations on the space that should be allocated to the categories. Each type should finally adjust the allocation of between two and six categories, which implies a partial, rather than a total, reorganization of the sales space (the proposed solution is therefore flexible).

This research shows therefore that the adaptation of the space allocated to each category is a realistic approach, with data that are obviously sophisticated, but still macroscopic (the total assortment is "only" divided into 17 categories). Of course, this is only an isolated empirical application, which needs to be confirmed with other data, but following the particular results presented here, the methodology followed can be duplicated in other retail companies with a rather weak analytical constraints (widely available data, relative complexity of models, reasonable calculation time).

24. The increase in the net estimated result given by Montgomery [MON 97], following the putting in place of a *micro-marketing* pricing policy, is between 33% and 83%.

However, despite the stimulant that it is, this study does not mask the real difficulties of implementing a geo-merchandizing policy and does not exhaust the potential research even.

12.3. The implementation of geo-merchandizing

The application of geo-merchandizing runs into difficulties that concern appropriate information and knowledge about the effects of complementarity and of substitution and about control systems. We will thus try to discern new research avenues.

12.3.1. *The difficulties of implementation*

The implementation of a geo-merchandizing policy involves as many marketing difficulties as organizational ones, linked notably to the increased autonomy of managers in the field. Finally, these two difficulties converge and make inevitable the establishment of a monitoring system for marketing performance, taking geographic specificities into account.

Identifying pertinent geographic information

The company that sets out on a geo-merchandizing policy should bring together a large number of data. More importantly, the company should identify the pertinent information, since all available geographic information is not useful. This will be a question of precisely defining which variables to collect in each trade area: socioeconomic and demographic indicators, forms and intensity of competition, etc. It will also be a question of identifying the most significant variables in order to explain the performance of each category (knowing that these variables can vary from one category to the next) under the restriction of availability of data, with reasonable deadlines and costs [LAT 01].

As we have seen above [CAM 00], local factors act directly and indirectly on the performance of a store. A geo-merchandizing policy should distinguish these two types of influence. In practice, the local factors that have a direct influence on performance do not require assortment adaptation, apart from an adjustment of the size of the store (during establishment or afterwards). On the other hand, the local factors that have an influence on the relative attractiveness of a given product should be examined closely. The company can function on the basis of typologies (trade areas, stores) or optimize the assortment for each store. Even if the second path is naturally more complex, the elaboration of typologies is also a complex task.

Identifying the role of each category in store performance

It will also be necessary to determine the role of each category in the performance of the store (effect on the traffic and effect on the consumer basket), which mainly assumes knowledge of the effects of complementarity or substitution. Without knowledge of this inter-dependence between categories or between references, decisions can result in a decrease in performance.

More generally, the mass of data necessary to estimate the effects of complementarity and substitution can quickly reveal themselves to be unmanageable. For example, Montgomery [MON 97] has shown that for a chain of 100 stores and a category including 10 products, the number of parameters to be estimated goes up to 100,000. Even if sophisticated econometric procedures allow the lack of data at the store level to be skirted, the estimation of micro-marketing models supposes a high degree of expertise.

Evolving the control system

The implementation of a micro-marketing policy generally leads to giving more autonomy to store managers. However, as Blattberg has pointed out (cited in [MON 97]), "variations of price and assortment can destroy the image and the positioning of the trade-name[25]." The principal cost of this policy consists, therefore, of putting into place adequate systems of coordination so that the autonomy and the responsiveness of the field can be implemented with some homogeneity in the assortment. This homogeneity allows power of the media to be used (notably advertising) and allows a company to benefit from economies of scales (at the purchase level, logistical level, etc.). In other words, if the store chain can (or should) differentiate itself in order to take advantage of the differences observed in the field, the forms of coordination should become more sophisticated at the same time.

This supposes taking the geographic specificities into account in the construction of norms (return per m²). From this point of view, comparing the performance of a store with the standard of its group (if the company functions with a typology of stores) can reveal itself to be misleading. These typologies – which are entirely pertinent at a strategic or organizational level – are too broad for this type of use. More sophisticated benchmarking procedures should be put into place [GRE 99],

25. Montgomery's study [MON 97] on setting up a differentiated pricing policy per store includes the restriction that the same average price is kept after the new tariff policy is put into place, *for the category studied*. This allows, according to the authors, an unchanged image-price to be maintained. Let us note that the perception of the average price depends on the products considered or purchased, these products varying from one customer to the next. This notion of average price therefore has little meaning at the store level (it should however be noted that professionals use this notion rather widely for reasons of practicality, reinforced by price follow-up tools).

which correct the performances of each store according to the local potential and the competition.

In summary, putting a geo-merchandizing policy into place has a major effect on the marketing information systems, whether it is a question of identifying pertinent information – in an ever-increasing mass of geo-marketing data – of understanding the store as an aggregation of interdependent categories and not as a whole, or even of evolving control systems in order to integrate local specificity.

12.3.2. *Research avenues*

Research avenues on geo-merchandizing are very open, with only one academic research study having been published up to the present [CAM 00]. Furthermore, geo-merchandizing is part of a larger reflection on micro-marketing of the point of sale (the term mainly used by researchers) or *site marketing* (the term used by professionals). The dilemmas are therefore interconnected, notably those of the assortment and of price, or even those of the assortment and promotional communications, with media advertising being understood as a reduced assortment [VOL 99].

We will retain two particular issues: understanding of the link between product categories and the adaptation of services to local specificities. However, other themes appear equally interesting.

Understanding the relationship between categories

Chen and his colleagues [CHE 99] have shown that certain categories generate rather weak direct sales (the notion of accounting profit or AP), but that their effect on the performance of the point of sale is considerable (the notion of marketing profit or MP). These categories allow traffic to be created and complementary products to be sold, without losing sales of other categories. If the retailer removes such categories from the store (or if he or she decreases the space allocated to them), performance will decrease more than just in the sales of that category (decrease in visits and in sales of complementary products). The empirical application carried out by these researchers shows that cosmetics generate a MP index six times higher than the AP index. In other words, this category earns six times more for the store than the sales of the department itself. Conversely, certain categories have a MP index inferior to their AP index (notably meat and bakery). The authors suggest that if marketing investments are realized in relation to sales – and not to marketing profit – decisions are less than optimal.

Knowledge of the marketing profit generated by a category (which is therefore not linked to sales) is a very precious piece of information in decision-making (space in the store, place in a leaflet, etc.). However, estimation of the marketing profit demands considerable competence. Furthermore, this profit can vary appreciably from store to store, because the same category can play a very different role according to the type of customers or the nature of the competition. The same category will justify a visit to a given store – or will generate complementary purchases in that given store – but not necessarily in another such store (a point that is not always discussed by the authors, but which adds complexity to an already complex analysis).

At this stage, it appears essential to highlight the operational methods that allow links between categories to be identified, in order to update the phenomena of complementarity and substitution. To do this, it is necessary to call on numerous research studies on competitive phenomena between brands/references, before applying to these analyses the necessary pragmatism of the retailer who wishes to take full advantage of the data available to him or her.

Adaptation of services

The arguments given concerning the adaptation of assortments are equally pertinent for services, in a competitive context where these services constitute both a source of additional profit (ticket agency, travel agency, etc.) and an eventual area of differentiation (daycare, bagging, etc.). Knowing the cost of implementation (for example, bagging) and/or the risk of delivering a poor quality service (daycare), it is clear that these services cannot be proposed everywhere. A decision has to be made which services should be generalized in order to be able to justify positioning and which services should be adapted.

So far, to our knowledge, no research has been published on this subject. However, an exploratory study carried out by the author shows that customer interest *vis-à-vis* services of the same chain varies significantly from one area to the next, but only for certain services. The degree of customer interest *vis-à-vis* 12 services (180 households) was measured in two trade areas with different socioeconomic and demographic profiles (a rather rural area in Normandy and an urban area near Paris). Overall, the most called-for services are: technical support, a fast check-out aisle and a customer service/information area in the store (more than 90% of customers manifest a strong degree of interest). A store loyalty card with means of payment, a children's nursery, home delivery, bagging or carrying products to the car interested fewer than 20% of customers. Furthermore the rank of services according to their degree of interest is identical in the two areas studied. On the other hand, for the most interesting services (advice and information), the Parisian area showed significantly less interest than the Normandy area. The demand for service is therefore weaker in the Parisian area, probably due to a larger number of alternatives: the hypermarket does not play the same role for these customers. Even though care has to be taken in generalizing the results, this study shows that the adaptation of services at the local level is a differentiation opportunity, all while the increase in inferred costs must be controlled.

Other themes

Other research avenues can be identified, notably the transposition of geo-merchandizing to distance selling companies. Thinking is already advanced in terms of international merchandizing (most retail companies adapt their offer to the different countries in which they are located), but remains at an early stage for commercial websites. Technically, sites can construct tailored assortments. However, examination of recent practices shows that the sites are sometimes behind traditional companies (*E-commerce,* September 2001). In addition to the technical possibilities, the rules for adapting assortments naturally remain to be defined according to individual criteria [VOL 00]. This is a question of a totally new domain for which, to our knowledge, no large-scale academic research has been carried out.

The transposition of geo-merchandizing approaches to transit trade (major highways, train stations, airports, etc.) may also represent an interesting research avenue, because this type of trade is strongly increasing, mirroring increased consumer mobility. In this context, geo-merchandizing faces a supplementary difficulty, linked to the volatile nature of the target: the nature of the target varies both on the spatial level (different locations) and on the temporal level (the same location at different times).

Finally, the question of the performance of the retail company is found at the heart of debates on the generalization of geo-merchandizing practices. Partial studies, although already extremely complex, have estimated the gain linked to implementing these practices at the categories level [CAM 00]. This having been said, while it has been necessary to wait more than 60 years before it has been shown that market orientation causes the performance of a business to increase – in a complex network of interactions with innovation and driven strategy [HAN 98] – it is important to be able to show the reality of the gains in the efficacy and efficiency brought by these new practices.

12.4. Conclusion

The development of geo-merchandizing is linked, on the one hand, to the new capacities taken from the GIS and, on the other hand, to the traditional dilemma: globalization or adaptation. It turns out that currently retailers are looking to adapt their assortments. In this, the geo-marketing studies help them insofar as the geographic segmentation of customer expectations allows the development of an offer that corresponds to these expectations. This is a question of a more tactical implications. Note all chains have adopted the same policy and (with exceptions) it has been the independent networks that have implemented geo-marketing. On the other hand, certain trade businesses have adopted a more strategic approach by developing a strategic segmentation of their group of stores and by differentiating the store formats.

However, the implementation of geo-merchandizing meets obstacles insofar as the pertinence of geographic information is sometimes difficult to define, along with the role of certain product categories compared to others. In addition, control systems should look to keep abreast of the image and the positioning of the company. The development of real site marketing, the study of the relationship between the product categories and associated services are all new fields of research.

12.5. References

[ARN 83], Arnold S. J., Oum T.H., Tigert D.J., Determinant Attributes in Retail Patronage: Seasonal, Temporal, Regional and International Comparisons, *Journal of Marketing Research*, May, 20, 14-157, 1983.

[ARN 98], Arnold S.J., Hendelman J., Tigert, D.J., The Impact of a Market Spoiler on Consumer Preference Structures, *Journal of Retailing and Consumer Services*, 5, 1, 1-13, 1998.

[AUR 91], Aurier P., Recherche de variété: un concept majeur de la théorie en marketing, *Recherche et Applications en Marketing*, 6, 1, 85-106, 1991

[AUR 93], Aurier P., Analyse de la structure des marchés: réflexions et propositions théoriques sur la relation entre deux alternatives de choix, *Recherche et Applications en Marketing*, 8, 1, 77-95, 1993.

[AZI 00], Azimont F., Le merchandizing comme illustration de la dialectique 'global-local', *Market Management*, 1, 41-48, 2000.

[BEG 88], Béguin H., La région et les lieux centraux, in *Analyse économique spatiale*, Claude Ponsard, ed. Presses Universitaires de France, Paris, 1988.

[BOL 89], Bolton R., The Relationship Between Market Characteristics and Promotional Price Elasticities, *Marketing Science*, 8, 2, 153-169, 1989.

[CAM 00], Campo K., Gijsbrechts E., Goosens T., Verhetsel, The Impact of Location Factors on the Attractiveness and Optimal Space Shares of Product Categories, *International Journal of Research in Marketing*, 17, 255-279, 2000.

[CHA 96], Changeur S., Chandon J.-L., Le territoire-produit: étude des frontières cognitives de la marque, *Recherche et Applications en Marketing*, 10, 2, 31-52, 1996.

[CHA 98], Charrière-Grillon V., *L'influence des espaces géographiques sur les valeurs et sur le comportement des consommateurs*, PhD Managing, Université de Paris-Dauphine, 1998.

[CHA 00], Charrier A., Ghanem-Domont C., Le marketing de site, *Libre-Service Actualités*, no. 1660, 20 January, 2000.

[CHA 00], Charrière-Grillon V., Gallo G., La mutation des magasins populaires: le cas Monoprix, in *Encyclopédie de la vente et de la distribution*, edited by A. Bloch and A. Macquin, Economica, Paris, 2000.

[CHE 99], Chen Y., Hess J.D., Wilcox R.T., Zhang Z.J., Accounting Profits Versus Marketing Profits: A Relevant Metric for Category Management, *Marketing Science*, 18, 3, 208-229, 1999.

[CHR 33], Christaller W., *Die Zentral Orte in Süd Deutschland*, Iena, translated in English under the title (1966): *Central Places in Southern Germany*, Prentice Hall Inc., Englewood Cliffs, New Jersey, 1933.

[CLI 90], Cliquet G., La mise en œuvre du modèle interactif de concurrence spatiale subjectif, *Recherche et Applications en Marketing*, 5, 1, 3-18, 1990.

[CLI 98], Cliquet G., Integration and Territory Coverage of the Hypermarket Industry in France: A Relative Entropy Measure, *International Review of Retail, Distribution and Consumer Research*, 8, 2, 205-224, 1998.

[DAH 01], Dhar S.K., Hoch S.J., Kumar N., Effective Category Management Depends on the Role of the Category, *Journal of Retailing*, 77, 2, 165-184, 2001.

[DES 98], Desmet P., Renaudin V., Estimation of Product Category Sales Responsiveness to Allocated Shelf Space, *International Journal of Research in Marketing*, 15, 443-457, 1998.

[EAT 97a], Eaton B.C., Lipsey R.G., *On the Foundations of Monopolistic Competition and Economic Geography*, Edward Elgar, London, 1997.

[EAT 97b], Eaton B.C., Lipsey R.G., Product Differenciation, in *On the Foundations of Monopolistic Competition and Economic Geography*, Edward Elgar, London, 228-271, 1997.

[EAT 97c], Eaton B.C., Lipsey R.G., An Economic Theory of Central Places, in *On the Foundations of Monopolistic Competition and Economic Geography*, Edward Elgar, London, 166-182, 1997.

[FAD 00], Fady A., Seret M., *Le merchandizing: techniques modernes du commerce de détail*, Vuibert, 4th edition, Paris, 2000.

[FIL 89], Filser M., *Canaux de distribution*, Vuibert, Paris, 1989.

[FIS 97], Fischer G.-N., *Psychologie de l'environnement social*, Dunod, 2nd edition, Paris, 1997.

[FOT 93], Fotheringham A.S., Chain Image and Store-Choice Modeling: The Effects of Income and Race, *Environment and Planning A*, 25, 179-196, 1993.

[GHO 87], Ghosh A., McLafferty S.L., *Location Strategies for Retail Service Firms*, Lexington, MA: D.C. Heath, 1987.

[GOL 01], Goldman A., The Transfer of Retail Formats into Developing Economies: The Example of China, *Journal of Retailing*, 77, 2, 221-242, 2001.

[GRE 99], Grewal D., Levy M., Mehrotra A., Sharma A., Planning Merchandizing Decisions to Account for Regional and Product Assortment Differences, *Journal of Retailing*, 75, 3, 405-424 1999.

[HAN 98], Han J.K., Kim N. and Srivastava R.K., Market Orientation and Organizational Performance: Is Innovation a Missing Link?, *Journal of Marketing*, 62, 4, 30-45, 1998.

[HOC 95], Hoch S., Kim B.-D., Montgomery A.L., Rossi P.E., Determinants of Store-Level Price Elasticity, *Journal of Marketing Research*, February, 32, 17-29, 1995.

[KAH 91], Kahn B.E., Lehmann D.R., Modeling Choice Among Assortments, *Journal of Retailing*, 67, 3, 274-299, 1991.

[KAL 97], Kalyanam K., Putler D.S. Incorporating Demographic Variables in Brand Choice Models, *Marketing Science*, 16, 2, 166-181, 1997.

[KIM 99], Kim B.D., Srinivasan K., Wilcox R.T., Identifying Price Sensitive Consumers: The Relative Merits of Demographic vs. Purchase Pattern Information, *Journal of Retailing*, 75, 2, 173-193, 1999.

[LAT 01], Latour P., Le Floch J., *Géomarketing: principes, méthodes et applications*, Editions d'Organisation, Paris, 2001.

[LAW 67], Lawrence P.R., Lorsch J.W., Differenciation and Integration in Complex Organizations, *Administrative Science Quarterly*, 12, 1-47, 1967.

[LIL 92], Lilien G.L., Kotler P., Moorthy K.S., *Marketing Models*, Englewood Cliffs, NJ: Prentice Hall, 1992.

[MAC 00], Macé S., Le micro-marketing du point de vente et l'efficacité des promotions, in *Etudes et recherches sur la distribution*, coordinated by Pierre Volle, *Economica*, 247-267, 2000.

[McI 99], McIntyre S.H., Miller C.M., The Selection and Pricing of Retail Assortments: An Empirical Approach, *Journal of Retailing*, 75, 3, 295-318, 1999.

[MON 97], Montgomery A.L., Creating Micro-Marketing Pricing Strategies Using Supermarket Scanner Data, *Marketing Science*, 16, 4, 315-337, 1997.

[MUL 98], Mulhern F.J., Williams J.D. and Leone R.P., Variability of Brand Price Elasticities across Retail Stores: Ethnic, Income, and Brand Determinants, *Journal of Retailing*, 74, 3, 427-446, 1998.

[PON 88], Ponsard C., *Analyse économique spatiale*, Presses Universitaires de France, Paris, 1988.

[RUL 00], Rulence D., Les stratégies spatiales des firmes de distribution: mesure et comparaisons, in *Etudes et recherches sur la distribution*, coordonné par Pierre Volle, Economica, Paris, 13-27, 2000.

[SCH 00], Schmitz S.W., The Effects of Electronic Commerce on the Structure on Intermediation, *Journal of Computer-Mediated Communications*, 5, 3, 1-24, 2000.

[SEG 99], Segal D.B., Retail Trade Area Analysis: Concepts and New Approaches, *Journal of Database Marketing*, 6, 3, 267-277, 1999.

[SHE 88], Sheth J.N., Gardner D.M., Garrett D.E., *Marketing Theory: Evolution and Evaluation*, John Wiley & Sons, NY, 1988.

[TED 97], Tedlow R.S., *L'audace et le marché: l'invention du marketing aux Etats-Unis*, Editions Odile Jacob, Paris, 1997.

[VAL 93], Valette-Florence P., Valeurs et consommateurs européens, *Recherche et Applications en Marketing*, 7, 4, 1-2, 1993.

[VAN 85], Van de Ven A.H., Drazin R., The Concept of Fit in Contingency Theory, *Research in Organizational Behavior*, 7, 333-365, 1985.

[VOL 00], Volle P., Du marketing des points de vente à celui des sites marchands: spécificités, opportunités et questions de recherche, *Revue Française du Marketing*, 177/178, p. 83-101, 2000.

[VOL 99], Volle P., *Promotion et choix des points de vente*, Vuibert, Paris, 1999.

[WEL 01], Wellhoff A., *Le merchandizing: bases, nouvelles techniques, category management*, Dunod, 5th edition, Paris, 2001.

List of Contributors

Valérie CHARRIERE
CNAM, Paris, France

Graham P. CLARKE
University of Leeds, UK

Ian CLARKE
University of Lancaster, UK

Gérard CLIQUET
University of Rennes 1, France

Pierre DESMET
Paris-Dauphine University, France

Delphine DION
CNAM, Paris, France

Jean-Pierre DOUARD
University of Nancy II, France

Karine GALLOPEL
University of Rennes 1, France

Stuart HAYES
University of Leeds, UK

Christine PETR
University of Rennes 1, France

Pierre VOLLE
Paris-Dauphine University, France

Monique ZOLLINGER
University of Tours, France

Index

P

Q, R

S

T, U, V

W, X, Y, Z.